Tennyson's Characters

Tennyson's Characters

"Strange Faces, Other Minds"

BY DAVID GOSLEE

University of Iowa Press · Iowa City

University of Iowa Press, Iowa City 52242
Copyright © 1989 by the University of Iowa
All rights reserved
Printed in the United States of America
First edition, 1989

Design by Richard Hendel

Library of Congress Cataloging-in-Publication Data
Goslee, David.
   Tennyson's characters: "strange faces, other minds" / by David Goslee.—1st ed.
     p.   cm.
     Includes index.
     ISBN 0-87745-246-6
     1. Tennyson, Alfred Tennyson, Baron, 1809–1892—Characters.   2. Characters and
characteristics in literature.   I. Title.
PR5589.G6   1989   89-33468
821'.8—dc20   ·   CIP

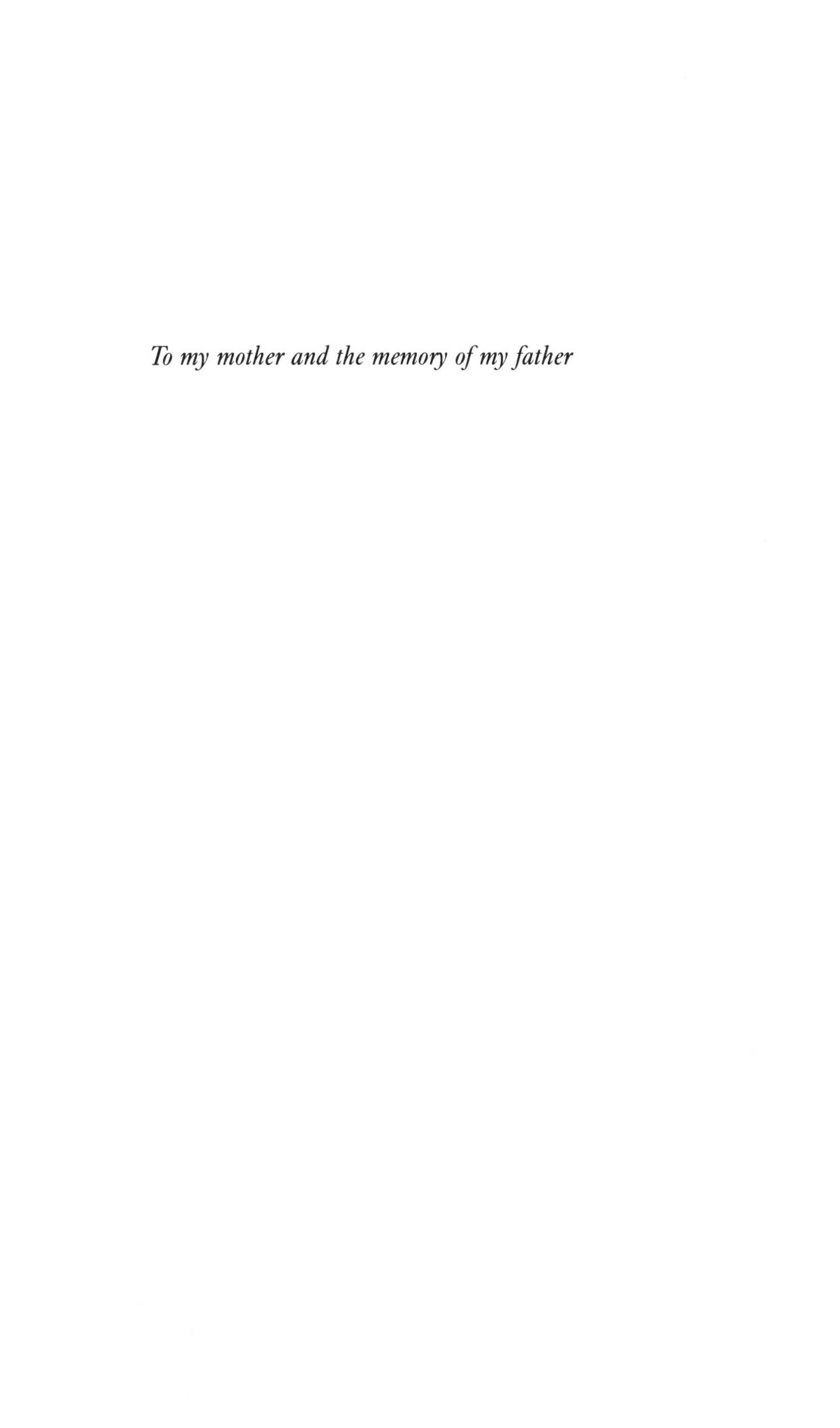

To my mother and the memory of my father

CONTENTS

Acknowledgments / ix

Introduction / xi

1 The Adolescent Poems / 1

2 The 1830 Volume and *The Lover's Tale* / 19

3 The 1832 Volume / 39

4 The 1842 Volume / 60

5 *In Memoriam* / 93

6 *The Princess* / 115

7 *Maud* / 135

8 The 1859 *Idylls of the King* / 157

9 Longer Poems of the 1860s / 189

10 The 1869 Idylls / 203

11 The Last Idylls / 223

12 Some Late Poems and "Merlin" / 240

Notes / 257

Index / 297

And I, the last, go forth companionless,

And the days darken round me, and the years,

Among new men, strange faces, other minds.

"Morte d'Arthur," ll. 236–38

That story which the bold Sir Bedivere,

First made and latest left of all the knights,

Told, when the man was no more than a voice

In the white winter of his age, to those

With whom he dwelt, new faces, other minds.

"The Passing of Arthur," ll. 1–5

ACKNOWLEDGMENTS

For permission to examine and quote from numerous Tennyson manuscripts, I would like to acknowledge Lord Tennyson on behalf of the Tennyson trustees; the Master and Fellows of Trinity College, Cambridge; the Houghton Library, Harvard University; the Huntington Library, San Marino, California; the Henry W. and Albert A. Berg Collection, New York Public Library; the Harry Ransom Humanities Research Center, University of Texas at Austin; and the Edgar Shannon–Alfred Tennyson Collection, University of Virginia Library.

For allowing me to reprint portions of already published articles in chapters 1, 4, 6, 7, 8, and 11, I would like to thank the editors of *Victorian Poetry*, *JEGP*, *SEL*, *The Huntington Library Quarterly*, and the Edwin Mellen Press. A grant from the Hodges Fund of the University of Tennessee Department of English provided me with released time to work on the manuscript during the spring of 1982. One of my colleagues, Richard Kelly, read and made valuable suggestions on an earlier stage of this study; another, Allen Dunn, helped me work through some of the critical ramifications of the Introduction. Linda Hughes combed through a late version of the complete manuscript and sent me eight sheets of yellow legal pad, both sides crammed with astute queries and suggestions.

Numberless times in the course of my research and composition I have felt deeply indebted to Kirk H. Beetz, whose thorough and eminently usable bibliography helped me locate many valuable articles, and to the manuscript work of Christopher Ricks, John Pfordresher, Susan Shatto, Marion Shaw, and Joseph Sendry. The more I consulted the manuscripts themselves, the more I marveled at the precision and perceptiveness of these scholars. Finally, two successive heads of the Tennessee English department, John Fisher and Joseph Trahern, offered unfailing support of this project and unbounded confidence in its eventual completion.

A t a special session on Tennyson during the 1983 meeting of the Midwest MLA, an open discussion on Princess Ida kept circling around this unresolved question, How could Tennyson put a fine woman like this into a poem like that? James Kincaid betrays a similar frustration with this incongruous gap between character and context; as he describes the other characters ganging up on the victorious Ida, he protests, "They are out to kill her."[1] These frank admissions of critical empathy encouraged me to explore a paradox that had long troubled me: fictional contexts throughout Tennyson seemed to place constraints upon the characters who inhabited them, while characters throughout Tennyson seemed self-consciously restive within these or any other constraints upon their fictional autonomy. If they represented fully assimilated aspects of Tennyson's personality, why did he so often attack them or hedge them about? If, on the other hand, he had weighed and rejected the values they embodied, why did he give them such vitality, such potential, such grudging license to state their own case? For their part, why did these characters seem to decenter their own texts for no motive beyond declaring their independence from them?[2]

When I sought to interpret this conflict between author and character, I expected it would follow some conventional split between self and society, child and parent, desire and repression, id and superego. Instead I found throughout Tennyson's poetry an elaborate and remarkably consistent psychomachia, a structural model which not only dramatized the original conflict but shaped it into an elaborate yet flexible pattern of meanings. In each poem a centered, cloistered, but still vulnerable authorial presence is threatened by some Other—a personification of divine, sexual, or natural power—which encroaches upon it from the fringes of the poem's imaginative universe. Almost invariably, however, a vatic speaker or a preternatural agent mediates between the authorial presence and the Other—interpreting, humanizing, or conciliating an otherwise alien cosmos.

The Component Figures

One figure, which I call the authorial presence, carries a number of Tennyson's biographical traits; yet this figure, initially at least, is neither deprived nor decentered. In fact it bears little resemblance to the dark, disturbed, fragmented young Tennyson we find in the more modern biographical works of Rader, Ricks, and Martin, the Tennyson whose sense of loss is so pervasive that Auden identifies it with the loss of the womb at birth.[3] Instead, established at the center of a concentric universe, it possesses the vatic, mystical powers and perceptions more freely ascribed to the poet in the biographies by his son and grandson.

Perhaps afraid to acknowledge the threatened authorial presence as either a presence or authorial, Tennyson sets it alternately too near and too remote from him to stand as a clear surrogate. In so doing, however, he neither fragments the self into a tidy allegory nor projects it into some interpersonal context. Instead he multiplies the self, allowing it to act and react on different levels simultaneously. It sometimes appears as a human figure, sometimes is only heard as a barely identifiable voice, sometimes must be inferred through our own vague sense of something lost. When mediators appear as third-person characters, like the high-born maidens of 1832, the authorial presence can often be equated with the poem's narrative voice. When mediators appear as speakers, as in the dramatic monologues and *Maud*, this presence may be reduced to a tone that renders them both persuasive and somehow unreliable. When the mediators fail, either by surrendering their sanctuary like Arthur or by actively joining forces with the Other like Enoch Arden, the authorial presence can itself dwindle into a kind of Lacanian absence, an almost nihilistic hole in the center of what remains a stubbornly egocentric cosmos. Because of this constant telescoping of levels, the concept of some independent authorial presence grows almost meaningless whenever Tennyson claims to speak in his own voice within his confessional poems. Our deepest understanding of the entity "Tennyson," after all, still comes from these very poems.

Since the authorial presence also frequently assumes the role of a psyche, it virtually presupposes the incursion of *some* kind of outer reality. To quote Barbara Johnson: "Even if truth is but a fantasy of the will to power, something still marks the point from which the imperatives of the not-self make themselves felt."[4] As Priscilla Johnston puts it, "Tennyson's visionaries . . . are generally accosted unsuspecting (often unwilling and unworthy) by an outside force."[5] Indeed its very fullness of possession renders the authorial presence vulnerable to the incursion of a figure so vaguely defined that I could give it no name besides the Other. Lurking just offstage, these embodiments of divine, sexual, or natural power are described by Johnston as "Tennysonian unwelcome outsiders: Heracles, slouching toward the Hesperides to steal the apples that will destroy civilization; Modred, leering into the precarious bliss of Guinevere's bower; and the outlaws and infidels who impinge upon the bright order of King Arthur's realm" (pp. 72–73).

The Other also includes other categories defined by earlier critics: Paden's God figures, Tucker's measure of Doom, Ryals' fatal woman, Joseph's fatal goddess, Albright's sublime, Tennyson's own portrayals of natural flux.[6] These categories can be merged because the function they share, that of some incursion from outside the poetic context, here outweighs their obvious differences; for Tennyson the existence of such figures may indeed have preceded their essence. While this pattern may suggest that all these figures are only aspects of some larger entity, each one makes such exclusive demands that Others are never even compared anywhere in Tennyson's canon. While the Other always appears individually, individually it never succeeds in encompassing whatever powers it possesses. While it may be "Other," it cannot be *the* Other but only an agent, manifestation, or representative of something which cannot even be imagined from within the poem's fictive world.

In all these poems, however, some figure mediates between the authorial presence and this threatening power.[7] Confronted with a variety of presences and Others, these mediators adopt a variety of responses. Some, like the Fair Women in Tennyson's dream, venture actively into the domain of the Other, declaring the space neutral and the opponent a finite figure upon it. Others, like the Sisters in "Hesperides," fortify some sanctuary of the authorial presence, virtually telescoping their own imaginative powers into those of their creator. Still others, like Ida, create secondary mediators of their own, so attenuating the links between poem and poet that the authorial presence itself fades into apparent irrelevance. As such, they too include several previously defined categories: Stevenson's high-born maidens, poets and other artists, virtually all of Tennyson's protagonists, and many of his least likely speakers. In every case, however, the mediators work to personify or otherwise delimit the Other, to reduce it to its agent and to reduce the agent to just another character.

Tennyson's Process of Revision

Because this psychomachia seemed too structured to capture the anarchic confrontation between author and character that I had hoped to account for, I began examining individual poems for changes made between manuscript draft and final version. Yet the pattern of composition I found reappearing throughout Tennyson's career seemed only to foster this structure. The poems which I and others saw as the most interesting often retained at least one draft substantial enough to be coherent but preliminary enough to differ significantly from the printed text.[8] In revising this draft, Tennyson usually strengthened its fictive integrity as a means of taking the model public.

Throughout these revisions, however, he stubbornly refused to renounce what remained an intensely subjective world-view. Instead, by transferring much of this subjectivity to the authorial presence, he rendered this presence a more vulnerable, more limited part of what could then become a more alien but ultimately more comprehensive poetic universe. This revision in turn demanded still greater autonomy in the mediators and hence still greater indeterminacy in the outcome. Even when these mediators remained faithful to the authorial presence, even when they succeeded in delimiting and domesticating the encroaching Other, the integrity of the model again reasserted itself: the revised versions of many poems confronted new incursions of outside forces very different from those in the original draft.

Here, finally, appeared the link between the fictional autonomy I had gone looking for and the apparently rigid, spatially defined model I had found. As mediators grew more creative with each revision, they often grew away from the values they were to protect and toward others of their own devising. If they had first appeared as projections of the authorial presence, they now worked to achieve some fictive reality outside it. If they had already appeared within the manuscript draft as characters, they now worked to escape from dramatic context or author or both. They demanded to be judged, moreover, not by the moral implications of their actions, but by the same aesthetic criteria used to evaluate their poetic vehicle.

Tennyson worked hard in these revisions to control this autonomy, often differentiating his voice from his characters' through what John D. Boyd and Anne Williams refer to as *erlebte Rede*.[9] Yet despite his addition of a more judgmental tone, a more "realistic" social framework, and more rigid structural boundaries, such limitations actually limited his control. As the revised drafts "made space," as they asserted the fictive integrity of their own world, they also demanded dramatic autonomy in their actors as a sine qua non of their own existence. In so doing they stripped a measure of both artistic and imaginative control from Tennyson as a conscious artist and bestowed it upon the process by which the poem virtually wrote itself.

In this process, conflicts implicit within a given poem worked themselves out dramatically within the analogous drama of the poem's composition. Instead of going in search of negative capability like Browning, Tennyson wrote himself into it.[10] In fact we can identify his creations only as they assume a rich and varied fictional life outside the authorial self. While some critics have argued that they reappear with compulsive regularity throughout the poet's career, I hope to show that each of them is contesting a different relationship with the author and that each is in quest of a different fulfillment.

The Model's Mode of Being

As Jonathan Culler points out, even within a closed linguistic system like Saussure's "to identify differences responsible for meanings one needs to treat some meanings as if they were given."[11] Hence any evidence for causal sequence within Tennyson's poetry must be made *in terms of* and *by means of* the spatial structure I would be trying to explain. My first chapter, in fact, will bear out the Derridean claim that the effect exists implicitly within every cause, the supplement within every origin: the model and the roles which constitute it subvert causal claims of temporal priority by remaining always, already implicit within any origin I might propose for it. If such causes exist, as I shall argue later, they operate not only before Tennyson's earliest poetry but before his earliest memories.

In thus privileging spatial relations, I am actually following Tennyson's own example. Since he consistently translated growth and change into spatial opposition, he could return to the same model despite his shifting attitudes toward the conflicts mapped within it. Just as a twenty-year-old road map will probably get us to our destination even though the actual landscape may have changed beyond recognition, so the model allows us to find our way within poems from different periods much as it enabled Tennyson to give a local habitation and a name to the changing drives and voices within him.

Because it remains more a conventional map than a map of misreading, this model does not follow the deconstructive strategy of subverting system by turning it against itself.[12] Instead of exploiting this reflexivity, the model offers a referential projection of self-reference. But just as a given pattern can map the circuits on a microchip or the stars within a galaxy, so this pattern makes no a priori claims about the scale of its referent. It approximates configurations both of Tennyson's psyche and of his world, approximates, in fact, a similarly triangular structure which René Girard finds underlying most Romantic fiction:

> The triangle has no *Gestalt*. The real structures are intersubjective. . . . Changes in size and shape do not destroy the identity of this figure. . . . The purpose and limitations of this structural geometry may become clearer through a reference to "structural models." The triangle is a model of a sort, or rather a whole family of models. But these models are not "mechanical" like those of Claude Lévi-Strauss. They always allude to the mystery, transparent yet opaque, of human relations.[13]

Because Girard's structure maps "human relations," it also presupposes what has become one of the least fashionable yet least dispensable elements of literature, character. Critics committed to some extraliterary agenda typically decenter a text by superimposing an impersonal ideology upon it; yet even they often expose the ideology already implicit within it by measuring its power to control, reshape, or repress the potential for autonomy of the figures subject to it.[14] As Culler (p. 29) points out, moreover, not all poststructuralists accept this divorce of structure and personality: "Bloom strives mightily to set his work against [that of Derrida and de Man], insisting that the human subject is a ground or source rather than an effect of textuality: 'the human writes, the human thinks, and always following after and defending against another human' [*A Map of Misreading*, p. 60]."

As Morton Kaplan and Robert Kloss freely admit, psychological criticism is particularly dependent upon human figures: "Fictional characters are representations of life and, as such, can only be understood if we assume they are real. . . . A theoretical consideration of how literary characters have their counterparts in life is in itself hardly extraneous to an understanding of the text."[15] Pushed to its limits, of course, this approach would drive us not only to wonder how many children had Lady Macbeth, but to worry about the effects two such homicidal parents would have on their psychological development. Meredith Anne Skura avoids such literalism by positing an interaction between fictive and psychological reality: "The play between character and world within the text is really one aspect of the more general tension between characters as characters, and characters as part of a state of mind which pervades the work."[16] In his analysis of character in narrative and drama, however, Baruch Hochman suggests the mechanism by which Tennyson's model asserts itself against such interpenetration: "The organization of the whole text creates a space—an area where converging perspectives meet—within which the character subsists."[17]

Because the model remains more a spatial *mise en scene* than a plot, it leaves its participants room to develop: The authorial presence can create new mediators, or it can be stripped of the one it has. The mediator can create secondary mediators of its own, or it can collapse into the authorial presence. It can qualify the Other into near harmlessness, or it can be corrupted into becoming its agent. The Other can reduce the two remaining roles into insignificance, or it can metamorphose into a sympathetic mediator. Because the mediating figures in particular must establish themselves as different by definition from the opposing entities on either side of them, with every revision their roles grow more paradoxical, their motives more overdetermined, and their responses more unpredictable.[18] In short they grow more like the complex, fully developed characters in fiction or drama.

Relation to the Biographical Tennyson

In the last decades, authorial intention has grown just as problematic as character: "capitalist ideology . . . has attached the greatest importance to the 'person' of the author. . . . The image of literature to be found in ordinary culture is tyrannically centered on the author."[19] Exposed here by Marxism as the slave of bourgeois ideology, the author has been dismissed as part of the intentional fallacy by new criticism, fragmented by structuralism into cultural codes, psychoanalyzed by Bloom as part of an oedipal conflict with earlier mentors, finally subverted by poststructuralism as the mouthpiece of logocentrism.[20] We can, however, make at least a provisional case for the amalgam of traits, values, and obsessions which all critics implicitly validate when they write that "Tennyson is here trying . . . , seeing . . . , claiming . . . , arguing . . . ," etc. Such a Tennyson is well represented by his own statements and by numerous biographies. As we move from Hallam's *Memoir* to Nicolson, to Charles Tennyson, to Buckley, to Ricks, to Martin, we encounter Tennyson presented with greater evidence and deepening psychological insight. Yet we encounter less a series of different individuals than different attitudes toward a figure who remains more stubbornly himself than do any of his literary contemporaries. This figure, moreover, remains consistent with the first-person persona in *In Memoriam* and other confessional poems—consistent largely because Tennyson's fear of disclosure and his laconic inarticulateness in prose render these poems still our best clues to his inner life.

If the evidence of intention is as strong for Tennyson as for any poet, the complexity of its operation is implicit in the claims of Nicolson, Paden, and E. D. H. Johnson that Tennyson's inspiration often lay beneath his conscious control, that his compositional process is at least as significant as his stated purpose, that he often wrote better—or at least differently—than he knew how. While I would agree that we are now better judges of Tennyson's best work than was either Tennyson or his age, I would *not* agree that we need to jettison those portions of it which were written late, or confront contemporary social issues, or are lacking in dreams and visions, or revel in high seriousness. The model I am proposing does *not* present the darker, more antisocial, more modern, more "interesting" aspects of Tennyson as forces sporadically disrupting a coherent world-view, a polished formal surface, and a decorous moral tone. Instead the model presents the struggle between autonomous figures and forces as the basis and defining characteristic of Tennyson's poetry.[21]

In this sense the model is in control of Tennyson. For one thing, his increasing skill in controlling his characters seems only to have called forth their increasing skill in asserting their own autonomy. Thus, while his struggle with them only intensified throughout his life, the outcome of this struggle changed from volume to volume, even from poem to poem.[22] From the adolescent poems to those of 1832, the mediator dwindled from prophet to jilted lover to besieged artist. From the early 1830s through 1850 Hallam transformed himself from the pledge for all of Tennyson's mediators to a thrall of that ultimate Other, death, to a witness to Tennyson's own power of controlling this very transformation. From the late 1850s through the 1870s, sexual love degenerated from the mediator of last resort in *Maud* to the most insidious manifestation of the Other in the *Idylls*. Yet apart from Hallam's death, the circumstances of Tennyson's life remained strangely distant from either his choice of subjects or his treatment of them. As an imaginative opportunist, he could respond to external suggestions for the same reason that he had to rely upon them: he did not know—and ultimately did not want to know—exactly how and exactly what he was creating.

In a different sense, however, both Tennyson's efforts to take control and his willful ignorance of how to do so betoken an implicit acknowledgment that the model was somehow his own.[23] This unconscious commitment to its integrity may suggest that he needed it to protect him against an otherwise threatening imaginative reality. This need, in turn, may explain why he confronted life, even a life sheltered by his family and friends, primarily in poetry. It may also explain his famous phobia about criticism. Criticisms of his poetry, I think, became an attack on the validity of the model and hence a threat to his only means of facing whatever reality lay beyond it. By the same token, praise meant very little to him, principally because he knew intuitively that he was being praised for the wrong reasons, that no one else could perceive either the source of his imaginative power or his need to invoke it.

The model was also his ticket to continued creativity. It allowed him to achieve dramatic variety and movement within a static, egocentric perspective. While he admittedly wasted many of his own later years trying to write dramas, in 1879 he passed on to Matthew Arnold some revealingly tactless advice: "Tell Mat not to write any more of those prose things, like *Literature and Dogma* but to give us something like his 'Thyrsis,' 'Scholar Gypsy,' or 'Forsaken Merman.'"[24] At that point Arnold, even more than the "three parts iced over" that he admitted to being in 1853,[25] had for years been deserted by the lyric muse. That Tennyson never was, at least for long, may be attributed in part to the resolutely lyric model through which he continued to confront experience.[26]

Psychological Parallels

While Tennyson's self-multiplication within this model makes it difficult to fit him into one neat psychological category, he has already been interpreted in terms of several. In the early 1940s, for example, W. D. Paden argued in Freudian terms that the sequence of violence, discovery, and the doom of a paternalistic God dominated the adolescent *Poems by Two Brothers* while the "mask of age" transformed present desire into past guilt within a surprising number of later poems. My model does maintain what Freud calls a topography encompassing three conflicting roles;[27] it even assigns to the mediator the belated genesis of the ego and a similar role in playing off the contradictory demands of two opposing forces. But this mediation is consistently more creative and more liberating than the defense mechanisms of the Freudian ego. More important, the mediator cannot serve as a reality principle, simply because the only reality within the universe of the Tennyson poem is that created by the three roles themselves. For Freud, moreover, the id preexists the others, inhabits the unconscious center of the human psyche, and controls the flow of its energy. The superego does not even appear until the child's effort to identify with the father brings on the period of latency. Freud's model is thus so dominated by desire and its repression that Ernest Jones can claim that "only what is repressed can be symbolized"[28] and Leo Bersani that "the disguised repetitions of inhibited desires constitute the coherent self."[29] In Tennyson's poetic universe, however, the violent, amoral, anarchic Other initially appears on the fringes while the centered authorial presence initially enjoys a repletion which Tennyson can claim as once or as potentially his own.[30] Hence his poems typically speak less of a desire for what is absent than of a fear of losing what is already possessed.

This image of the central self with a psychological landscape spread concentrically around it may suggest a model more Jungian than Freudian. From Lionel Stevenson on, of course, Tennyson's deserted women have been seen as anima figures.[31] More recently Gerhard Joseph has found in Tennyson's concentric structure the ever more inclusive Jungian circles through which the soul must pass on its way to psychological maturity.[32] Usually, however, Tennyson's soul does not *want* to go anywhere. Jung's model, like Freud's, is based on desire, here the desire for an identity which Tennyson seems to claim as his origin, not his goal.

This equation of desire with return may in turn suggest Lacan's linguistically determined psychology. There the subject becomes subjected both to the Father's phallic denial of any return to the Mother ("le non du Père") and to subjection within a linguistic system ("le nom du Père") where the shifting referent of the grammatical subject "I" betokens the impossibility of any psychic autonomy.[33] Tennyson's authorial presence first has to "say" itself, and so define itself against the Other; then it must submit to further fragmentation in the increasingly autonomous responses of a mediating figure. In both systems, moreover, the Other appears as a fragmenting force from without. For Rose, Lacan's "le grand Autre," the unattainable object of desire, can be seen as either male by association with the father or female as the ultimate projection of the lost mother (pp. 32–33, 50–52). Because Tennyson presents such fragmentation as only threatened, however, he presents the same male or female sexuality as the threat itself.[34]

Lacan claims that the original bond with the mother cannot survive language and hence expression. But through his authorial presence Tennyson can indeed express this oceanic diffusion of the self, described as primary narcissism within ego psychology and its offshoot, object-relations theory. Wright notes that for the followers of Melanie Klein, "the medium of the artist becomes the mother's body" (p. 84). For D. W. Winnicott, form becomes a transitional object, which can be alternately the mother, the self, both, and neither (pp. 92–96). For Skura, "the true building blocks of the imagination are . . . primitive fantasies . . . , holistic experiences out of which all sense of self as opposed to the world, and all distinction between fiction and reality will only later be precipitated" (p. 78).

Tennyson's poetry is likewise blatantly, triumphantly, unapologetically regressive. Even when physically besieged or endangered, the domain of the authorial presence often opens inward into its own universe. It can encompass both male and female fulfillment, and because the beloved object is often kin and still more often grows up within the same household, it can transform even sexual desire from an absence to a return to plenitude. The best description of primary narcissism in Tennyson is Tennyson's own, the Prince's explanation that he owes his sympathy with Ida's cause to the influence of his mother,

> breathing Paradise,
> Interpreter between the Gods and men,
> Who looked all native to her place, and yet
> On tiptoe seemed to touch upon a sphere
> Too gross to tread, and all male minds perforce
> Swayed to her from their orbits as they moved,
> And girdled her with music.
>
> (VII, 301–7)[35]

The Prince's astronomical confusion, however, suggests that in trying to describe everything, both he and these psychologists risk describing nothing. Both in fact beg the question of how a poet can use all the linguistic and conceptual powers of maturity to recreate an inclusiveness which can exist only in default of these powers.

Ultimately, Tennyson's answer to this question approximates that offered by Wright: "The creative act repeats the experience of separating from the mother" (p. 84).[36] Skura broadens this focus to include successive, ever more delimiting encounters with reality: "Old concerns and images take on new and more mature forms as [the child] grows. . . . Any one fantasy is really a series of fantasies from different stages of life" (pp. 88–89). Tennyson's strategy combines these two: he goes back consistently to the primal confrontation with some reality outside the self, yet he neither rejects nor submits to this intrusion, either within a given poem or in some progression from one poem to another. Instead he achieves the impression of temporal progression by superimposing potential responses within a spatial overlay. The narcissistic authorial presence, the Other as either paternal threat or feminine temptation, the mediator as a measure of childhood autonomy—within almost every psychological model these represent successive stages. By continually juxtaposing them within the same physical setting, Tennyson can continually reevaluate what there might be of gain or loss within what would otherwise remain an irreversible process of maturation.

The Tennyson Canon

Tennyson continued to manipulate, subvert, and reinterpret temporal process throughout his seventy years of productive life. The majority of his most important poems were conceived early and then underwent an indefinite period of incubation every bit as important as the composition of the final text. Since the incubation period for most of these began with Hallam's death, the death might itself seem a watershed. Within the context of our model, however, it seems less a unique, inexplicable, external cause than one of several internally generated challenges, a challenge in whose light any authorial affirmation had to be modified before it could be reaffirmed. Within early drafts of his adolescent poems, for example, fictional characters and inspired speakers discovered that they were powerful mediators; in the revised versions they discovered that their powers had been severely limited. Tennyson's next-written long narrative, *The Lover's Tale*, tried to reestablish personal autonomy by naturalizing the model, transforming its roles into people. The roughly contemporaneous lyrics of the 1830 volume, on the other hand, tried to dissect the model, to isolate each of its roles within apparently disparate poems. The 1832 volume then demonstrated that one particular role, that of the besieged artist, could convert the sanctuary of the authorial presence into a base for inroads into the domain of an apparently invincible Other. While it might be tempting to posit Hallam's death as the destroyer of this sanctuary, previous manifestations of the Other had already destroyed both the fanatical smugness of St. Simeon and the visionary idealism of the speaker in "The Two Voices."

In reality, Hallam's death transformed him from the model and pledge for all Tennyson's mediators into an Other both undeniably real and stubbornly resistant to metaphorical manipulation. As such it forced Tennyson to begin lavishing upon the role of Other the same attention he had previously reserved for his mediators. Within the great monologues and narratives from 1833–34, the mediators themselves seem powerless and almost paralyzed, but they do establish Tennyson's power to create fictional extensions of his own bereaved self. During the course of their poems, they also gradually win an image of the Other clear enough to contemplate some escape from it. When Tennyson tried to effect similar escapes within the "public" poems of the 1842 volume, however, he transformed confrontations with aristocratic stasis and lower-class anarchy into covert confrontations with monstrous Others from his own imaginative past.

Tennyson was well into the agonizing seventeen-year composition of *In Memoriam* before he could replace Hallam with even provisional mediators. Worse still, their limited success in appropriating the Other only brought it back in new, more impersonal parodies of Hallam's loss. Yet these same incursions brought Tennyson to realize that the Other derived its power from the personified form which earlier mediators had tried to foist upon it. This realization permitted his late-written sections to transform Hallam into a mediator who needed Tennyson to speak for and through him. In *The Princess*, by contrast, Tennyson encountered the creative power of individual characters. Many of these, in trying to reshape the entire poem in their own artistic likeness, appear as embodiments of the Other to those around them. To mediate this formal anarchy, however, both Prince and Princess must also reshape a fairy-tale setting which they discover to be the domain of an Other couched within the poem's claustrophobic structure.

The equally tortured composition of *Maud* achieved an uneasy, bizarre, but ultimately impressive collaboration. Here the poet, powerless to celebrate romantic love in the modern world, must turn to a mediator who sees this world as so completely the domain of a personified Other that he can cling to nothing except love personified. While this mediator's uncontrolled imaginative power destroys both him and his love, the poem reaffirms the validity of his original vision. This same commitment to love turned the manuscripts of the 1859 *Idylls* into a battleground. Each succeeding idyll included agents of the Other whose sexual freedom grew increasingly threatening to the increasingly conservative poet. In the process of delimiting them, however, Tennyson's revisions granted them a humanity which blurs the distinction between mediator and Other and threatens the integrity of the model itself.

In the poems of the 1860s, the opposite progression produced a similar threat. When Tennyson sought to escape the world of sexual license for a more conventional one, the dehumanizing social forms within *Enoch Arden* and *Aylmer's Field* threatened to transform his mediators into agents of a thinly disguised nihilism. A few years later the Other, again manifested as natural flux and sexual license, refused to be personified as Venus and drove

Lucretius to submit to it in suicide. The failure of Tennyson's escape turned him back to the *Idylls*, now with a clearer image of the specific Other threatening Camelot and a clearer conviction that Arthur alone could oppose it. Arthur's court, however, had already dismissed him as irrelevant to his realm and their poem. Thus when Tennyson tried to shore up the king's authority within revisions of the "Coming" and the "Passing," he only left him suspended in the psychic space between creator and creation, less a mediator than an elegiac authorial voice calling attention to the gaps left in the story by his own absence.

In his late poems, Tennyson's compulsion to reappropriate the fictional autonomy of his characters drove him to stand the model on its head. He spoke in his own voice; he compelled several mediators to proclaim his own past intimations of immortality; he even called up past mediators and forced them to retract their original visions. In their place he set up the Other of death as the ultimate measure of all more proximate values. Within "Merlin and the Gleam," in particular, he marshaled all these strategies in one last brilliant attempt to redefine his entire career and the characters he had created within it.

This intensely personal relationship between author and character may seem more fitting for a playwright or novelist. Critics revel in stories of Balzac's deathbed call for the doctor out of his own *Comedie Humaine*[37] or Pirandello's "interviews" with characters asking him to bring them to life. Lyric poets may not be supposed to think of their characters as "real" people, but Hallam Tennyson described his father as "lov[ing] his own great imaginative knight, the Lancelot of the *Idylls*" (*Poems*, III, 462n). Parodying Blake's description of Milton, Steven C. Dillon concludes, "Tennyson is yet . . . of the party of Lancelot, and he knows it."[38] Lancelot lived for him, as he does for us, less through those qualities Tennyson admired than through those he feared. Throughout his poetry we encounter a stubborn integrity in characters we are obviously meant to reject and a troubling duplicity in characters we are obviously supposed to admire. I began my study of Tennyson by trying to account for such anomalies; I can best continue it by taking them up in chronological order.

Tennyson's Characters

CHAPTER ONE

The Adolescent Poems

The perceptive recent studies of early Tennyson and the Romantics share what seems to me a dangerous assumption, the assumption that Tennyson's imagination differs from theirs because his imagination looks inward. Carol Christ's contrast of Romantic perception and Victorian perception provides us with an influential example: "The rich depiction of detail in Keats's lyrics suggests the ability of the self to expand into the world; Keatsian detail in the poems of Tennyson or the Pre-Raphaelites more often signals obsessive contemplation by a character fixated in some morbid emotion."[1] Margaret Lourie (p. 11) draws a similar contrast between Tennyson and Shelley: Shelley "most often concerns himself with intellectual processes and their relation to an ideal. But . . . the later poet took as his regular haunt the earlier, more primitive, less intellectual layer of the psyche. . . . Where Shelley was philosophical, Tennyson is psychological, and it is this buried psychological space that Tennyson's best early poetry explores." For Herbert Tucker (p. 20), "in Tennyson's poetry . . . the object world is whelmed in a tide of . . . voices that merge—as in the long view Tennyson's precariously achieved personae merge—into the roar or pulse of an inevitable, unutterable power."[2]

For me, both Tennyson and the Romantics begin by looking into themselves; both end by positing some reality beyond the self. They differ primarily in what they see at the beginning and what they posit at the end. Implicit within much of Romanticism rests the claim epitomized by Keats: "What the imagination seizes as Beauty must be truth—whether it existed before or not. . . . The Imagination may be compared to Adam's dream—he awoke and found it truth."[3] The Romantics could not at first grasp the implications of this claim; they could not consistently exploit it; they could not, most of them, maintain their faith in it; and yet their single greatest legacy to literature remains this image of the human mind actively shaping its own reality, an image "of eye, and ear,—both what they half create, / And what perceive."

It was this same claim that Tennyson could not make, could never conceive of making. To be sure, his earliest extant poems—the translation of Claudian's "Rape of Proserpine," "Armageddon," and *The Devil and the Lady*—appear remarkably assured for a fourteen-year-old. Though dependent on Pope in the first instance, Milton in the second, and Elizabethan drama in the third, they remain far less derivative and far more daring in their imaginative speculations than corresponding efforts by the young Romantics. Yet all his freedom and daring manifests itself within a universe already inhabited by other presences. Instead of creating, therefore, Tennyson's imagination discovers; instead of acting, it reacts.

One of these preexistent presences appears often as a male divinity, either the Judeo-Christian God or a less clearly identified devil; another appears as aggressively female and often connected with natural flux. Yet from the poems we can learn remarkably little about the origins of these presences or their relation to the self. In this absence of evidence, most recent studies of Tennyson the Romantic rest upon an earlier critical assumption that these presences were specters of Tennyson's psyche. While these specters have been interpreted variously as surrogates for the poet's father and mother or as projections of his sexual fears and desires, most such interpretations go back to W. D. Paden's *Tennyson in Egypt*, a psychological study so voluminous in its research and so sensitive in its interpretations that it has never been superseded.

After painstakingly duplicating the reading of the adolescent Tennyson, Paden finds that otherwise trivial or incomprehensible poems can be explained as cryptic encounters with adolescent sexuality. Dreams of the naked Egyptian girls encountered in Savary's steamy *Letters from Egypt* are grotesquely transmuted into the longings of a thirst-racked serpent for a herd of "lordly headed buffaloes." Even such repressed expressions of desire, however, are invariably punished by "violence and the Doom of God." In fact the punishments themselves are commonly distanced within a mask of age, wherein youth becomes age, temptation becomes guilt, and anxiety becomes grief. Poems like "I Wander in Darkness and Sorrow" and "I Dare Not Seek My Father's Halls" implicitly equate distance with paternal judgment. Finally, when Tennyson celebrates priestly cults ministering to some divine presence, he is hoping to lose his guilt-ridden identity in acceptable service to an otherwise implacable father figure.

Paden, I think, offers convincing interpretations for these two selections from the 1827 *Poems by Two Brothers*, both mechanical efforts to hide behind an impersonal, derivative form.[4] The set of early poems we will focus on, however, Paden relegates to bibliographical articles and virtually ignores within his book. In these poems, Tennyson refuses to avoid those outside presences I refer to as agents or manifestations of the Other. Instead he confronts them honestly, openly, but still not directly.[5] Since he cannot survive without establishing some kind of mediation between himself and this Other, Tennyson bodies forth his imaginative powers, often in a telescoping series of emanations projecting still further emanations.[6]

Because of the changing number of mediators and their changing distance from the authorial presence, we can find the pattern repeating itself in poems from different genres. Both the exalted personal voices of the "Armageddon" monologues and the deeply subjective male leads of *The Devil and the Lady* betray very similar origins and roles. Even though one group confronts a Christian god figure and the other a female embodiment of cosmic flux, all these voices, apparitions, and intermediary characters work to establish, measure, and protect some personal sanctuary.

While Byron might "want a hero" for his *Don Juan*, Tennyson needs such heroes constantly—yet paradoxically the need itself creates an imaginative autonomy which rivals Romantic claims for the autonomy of imaginative truth. In one sense Tennyson's own psyche must contain the Other, the mediators, the authorial presence, and the imaginative space which these three roles together define. In another sense, however, the unexpected integrity won through this interaction can transcend the tangled thoughts, desires, and fears which spawned it. Preserved from the psychological reduction to which Paden subjects the *Poems by Two Brothers*, the model on which these poems structure themselves asks to be taken as Tennyson offers it to us—simply as a given.

Tennyson's first significant poem extant, his fragmentary translation of Claudian's "Rape of Proserpine," presents clear examples of Other, authorial presence, and mediator. As Johnston points out ("Demeter," p. 72), the Other here is Dis himself, mobilizing his legions to attack Jupiter for failing to provide him with a mate:

> Now Hell's misshapen monsters rush to arms
> And fill the wide abyss with loud alarms;
> The haggard train of midnight Furies meet
> To shake the Thunderer from his starry seat, . . .

> Now had all Nature gone to wrack again
> And Earth's fell offspring burst their brazen chain,
> And from the deep recesses where they lay
> Uprisen in wrath to view the beam of day.
>
> (ll. 53–56, 63–66)

This threat of an aggressively sexual incursion makes the eventual abduction of Proserpine seem no more than a necessary compromise. A. Dwight Culler, however, interprets the threat itself as a pretext for a parallel incursion within "a ritual in which the [poet-]priest enacts the process of his own inspiration":[7]

> Seraphic transports through my bosom roll,
> All Phoebus fills my heart and fires my soul.
> Lo! the shrines tremble and a heavenly light
> Streams from their vaulted roofs serenely bright,
> The God—the God appears! the yawning ground
> Moans at the view, the temples quake around.
>
> (ll. 7–12)

The very similarity between the poet's divine afflatus and Dis's infernal uprising carries its own dangers. Yet the passage from Claudian does, I think, offer a middle distance, does in fact mediate between creative self and outer threat. Powers no less formidable than "the dire Parcae" fall "before the throne of gloomy Pluto," and Lachesis' plea that he refrain from raising his "standard in the gulph of hell" succeeds so well that "the God was struck with sudden shame / And his wild fury lost its former flame" (ll. 97–98).

Tennyson's apparent loss of interest soon after this point suggests that he undertook the translation itself to establish several different kinds of control: the domestication of Latin epic into Augustan couplets, the assumption of Claudian's infernal muse, and finally the placation of his awesome antihero. Even here, however, the mediation may have succeeded too well: an exultantly chthonic, phallic force erupting into his world and his "soul" may have seemed terrifying; Dis working out a negotiated settlement with the powers-that-be must have seemed, by contrast, disappointingly tame.[8]

Apocalyptic Lyrics

Translation allowed Tennyson only two alternatives: giving up or submitting to the fictional world of his original. In his own poetry he had a third option, and while he published neither "Armageddon" nor *The Devil and the Lady*, he brought both back for repeated, radical revision. In fact many of his early poems can be interpreted as progressively more successful efforts to mediate the blatantly infernal, aggressively sexual Other which first appeared in "Proserpine." Because Tennyson could not yet admit that this psychomachia needed some Other, he had not yet learned to protect it within his revisions. Instead the figure of Dis, appeased within the fragment itself, dwindles further within the radical transformations from one draft and one poem to another: from the destination of "The Coach of Death" to a camp opposing that of Christ in the earliest "Armageddon," to a monumental pavilion in the Trinity revision, to a whimsical mediator within the first (Harvard) version of *The Devil and the Lady*, and finally to a comic stereotype who must surrender all mediation to the Magus within the Trinity revision. Simultaneously, however, a series of new, equally alien Others suddenly arises from the void left by this progressive abdication.

"The Coach of Death," apparently Tennyson's least personal account of divine judgment, may have grown most immediately from his own boyhood experience. A morbidly sensitive fifteen-year-old with an aunt who gleefully predicted his damnation, Tennyson needed the ballad form to hide his involvement in the grim subject of this poem, the journey of the damned toward hell.[9] He can use this mediating mask, however, to exorcise the threat by trying on attitudes which his Aunt Mary could hardly have sanctioned. As his narrative voice joins the recently damned, he admits that

> Whoever walks that bitter ground
>   His limbs beneath him fail;
> His heart throbs thick, his brain reels sick;
>   His brow is clammy and pale.
>
> But some have hearts that in them burn
>   With power and promise high,
> To draw strange comfort from the earth,
>   Strange beauties from the sky.

(ll. 25–32)

Ricks compares the lines (*Poems*, I, 86n) to the Ancient Mariner's compulsion to tell his tale; yet if Tennyson's compulsion arose originally from guilt, he has transformed it into a fascination with the infernal. The profusion of supernatural machinery—"burning slime," "windows of shaven bone," lights of "simmering fat"—actually reduces the poem to a mockery of the romantic ballad.

A more orthodox attitude seems to prevail when the damned see first the beauties of the vanished earth and then the Coach of the Blessed carrying their counterparts toward heaven. Here the Harvard manuscript ends. The revised manuscript used by Ricks, however, continues with a passage reinforcing Tennyson's ambivalence toward the whole theocentric cosmos. Changing from a parody of Coleridge to a more serious borrowing from Milton, the poem follows the Coach of Death across a replica of the bridge of Sin and Death and finally into hell itself. Hell, however, turns out to be a splendid pavilion with statues of the same mythical beings about whom Tennyson was reading at the time—Dionysus, Chus, Chaman, On, Oph, Esta, and even a thinly veiled representation of Noah:

> Beneath the span of Heaven's bow
> A wondrous keel there sailed
> Behind him on a carved field
> With peaky waves engrailed.
> (ll. 185–88)

If his Aunt Mary claimed these literary interests led to damnation, Tennyson seems to have replied implicitly that he would have interesting company and not-unpleasant surroundings.

While he is allowing the ballad form of this poem to mediate for him, Tennyson must literally circumvent the divine Other. To mediate between his guilty, vulnerable self and the more imminent judgment of "Armageddon," he must employ a more vatic voice and a more exalted station. Since Tennyson has here expanded his imitation of Milton to include the verse form and biblical subject, this persona can enter his poem just as freely as the narrator of *Paradise Lost*. Unlike Milton, however, he need not follow the shifting scene of action. As he plants himself atop "the mountain which o'erlooks / The valley of destruction" (I, 14–15), his visionary powers now let him assume an impartial stance only implicit within "The Coach of Death." Even before his mediating angel arrives, this vatic speaker can see not only "ranges of silver tents beside the moon" (I, 128) but "full opposite within the livid West . . . dark pavilions" and "a standard, round whose staff a mighty snake / Twined his black folds" (I, 133, 136, 140–41). From this spot, midway between the camps of Christ and of Satan, he can hold both powers in static, impotent tension; yet he needs both, particularly the phallic serpent, to define his visionary world.[10] In fact this whole "picturesque" description depends on a balance of good and evil, beautiful and terrible, within the landscape itself. Consequently when the angel finally clears the battlefield of the "obscuring" influence of Satan, he leaves not the Fields of the Lord but a wasteland:

> An icy veil
> Of pale, weak, lifeless, thin, unnatural blue
> Wrapt up the rich varieties of things
> In grim and ghastly sameness.
>
> (IV, 21–24)

This angel appears as the first of many secondary mediators in Tennyson, receiving his imaginative power from the original mediator just as that figure received it from the authorial presence. While the angel adds one more buffer between this presence and the supernatural conflict, his primary mission is to initiate the speaker into the mystical experience which, to paraphrase Culler (p. 19), turns "an apocalyptic vision" into an "experience of apocalypse." This vision of "objects . . . as from the inside out" (Tucker, p. 45), rivals Blake's Milton entering the world of his own creation through his Shadow (plate 14) and seems like it a thoroughly Romantic internalization of religious cosmography. Aidan Day suggests that the poem's "transcendental reference . . . is subverted by . . . [this] celebration of his own prophetic spirit," and Albright finds throughout the poem an "insistence that visionary poetry is nothing but an elaboration of the minute processes of vision itself" (p. 16).[11]

Yet we should recognize throughout how closely the world now drawn within Tennyson mirrors the one he has just projected and held at imaginative arm's length. As the speaker first "stood upon the mountain which o'erlooks / The valley of destruction" (I, 14–15), so now he seems "to stand / Upon the outward verge and bound alone / Of God's omniscience" (II, 25–27). He witnesses a similarly visionary cosmos, only intensified, as Tucker points out (pp. 44–47), by the almost synesthetic piling up of sense perceptions. Even his apparently blasphemous inclination to "have fallen down / Before my own strong soul and worshipped it" (II, 49–50) echoes his effort to veil his eyes before the dazzling angel. Here as elsewhere, Tennyson's famous visionary experiences do not transcend the imaginative model we have been describing; they merely transport it to another level.[12]

The 1828 Trinity revision of "Armageddon," roughly contemporaneous with the revised *Devil and the Lady*, reinterprets the opposing camps as citadels for opposing states of being. Satan's standard entwined with a living snake becomes a row of serpentine columns interspersed with sculpture-filled niches. This Pavilion of Idolatry, closely resembling that at the end of "The Coach of Death," includes among its pagan sculptures those of the ark, the rainbow, and the dove from the story of Noah. Tennyson's source meant to prove the pagan figures merely fabled perversions of the biblical ones,[13] but the mythic eclecticism of his mediating speaker undermines the apocalyptic framework for the whole vision. The "silver tents" of the other camp, for example, he replaces with a Heavenly Pavilion in the east. Here, behind a series of ever-receding, ever-more-splendid structures, "two doors of blinding brilliance" disclose only the base of a throne and the snowy skirting of a garment. He hopes to turn his remoteness from the vision into evidence for its grandeur: if only this much can be seen by the privileged speaker, then the enthroned figure himself must be truly unimaginable. Yet because mere columns and mere skirting can no longer threaten the authorial presence, they can no longer support his visionary world. Gone is the angel's clearing away the field of battle for "the Day of the Lord God"; gone too is the speaker's intuition of "tumultuous throbbings on the vast / Suspense of some grand issue" (IV, 33–34).[14] The focus here shifts from a future event to a past vision of that event, now clearly related to a definite present:

> for but dimly now,
> Less vivid than a half-forgotten dream,
> The memory of that mental excellence
> Comes o'er my Spirit and I may entwine
> The indecision of my present mind
> With its past clearness.[15]

In the earlier "Armageddon" (as in the later "Mystic") the visionary experience was a point of stasis from which to observe cosmic conflict; here the stasis becomes that of the speaker's rational mind reviewing the conflicting impressions produced by his earlier vision.

By the time Tennyson returns to these powers in his Cambridge prize poem, "Timbuctoo," Dis has disappeared and the enthroned figure has taken up residence within a legendary city. Instead of distancing this city from the authorial presence as a threatening manifestation of the Other, the mediating speaker now seems to be distancing it from the real world as a vulnerable sanctuary for vulnerable authorial values. In so doing, however, he only makes it more vulnerable to nineteenth-century criteria of reality. The visiting angel, himself now reduced to the Spirit of Fable, predicts that Timbuctoo, when reached by "keen *Discovery*," will "darken, and shrink and

shiver into huts, / Black specks amid a waste of dreary sand" (ll. 242–43).[16]
The angel then "part[s] Heaven-ward" and leaves the speaker in the dark of
the oncoming night.

Culler describes this change (p. 21) as "part of the series of alterations
that take us from the priest of Claudian to the prophet of Armageddon to the
more inward and humane conception of Romantic poet." For W. David
Shaw, the poem portrays "a moment of cultural change, in which the youthful visionary is asked to channel his Romantic and Miltonic heritage, the
whole burden of the past, through the narrow passage of his mind."[17] Using
both Hallam's comments and the parallels between his "Timbuctoo" and
Tennyson's, Day argues convincingly (pp. 59–63) that Tennyson borrowed
his friend's self-consciously Romantic thesis but reached his own more pessimistic conclusion: "a sense that the new heart and pulses recently given to
the world may in fact signify nothing more than a deeply ambiguous vitality"
(p. 70).

At this, the point of Tennyson's first clear debt to the Romantics, we might
profitably examine more closely the nature and extent of that debt. Bloom
has interpreted Hallam as the embodiment of a high Romanticism which
Tennyson could neither recapture nor surpass.[18] From here it is but a step to
Tucker's claim ("Strange Comfort," pp. 16–17) that in the first "Armageddon," "Tennyson did not know just how belated he was, but by the time he
produced 'Timbuctoo' . . . the burden of his revision was to accommodate
a chastening awareness that the poetic hour was even later than he had
thought." Against this burden of belatedness, however, we might set Tennyson's brazenly acquisitive response to Shelley: "Alastor was the first poem
of his I read. I said 'This is what I want!'"[19] Margaret Lourie indeed shows
him plundering Shelley, just as Ricks has shown him plundering Keats; yet
he takes not so much the phrases which Day finds Hallam borrowing (pp.
60–63) but rather turns of phrase, tricks of syntax, rhythms of speech. These
he assimilates almost automatically and then reapplies to contexts which differ from their originals as much as *The Ancient Mariner* differs from the travel
books "used" by Coleridge.[20]

Thus when we look at "Timbuctoo" as fictional space, a poem bemoaning
its own impotent belatedness reveals a strategy foreshadowing that which
Tennyson will describe in *In Memoriam*, section 5: "In words, like weeds, I'll
wrap me o'er / Like coarsest clothes against the cold" (ll. 9–10). In fact the
integrity of the central vision seems "wrapped o'er," protected by the more
derivatively Romantic fabric surrounding it. We need to remember that the
very subject of Timbuctoo stood at three removes from Tennyson: chosen by

the university, urged on him by his father, and interpreted by both Hallam and Hallam's poem. Day feels (p. 66) that Tennyson here avoids his earlier problem "of how best to define the place of a cosmically expanded human mind in relation to a [traditional] God"; yet the framing visions—the murky Western Isles, "filled with Divine effulgence," and the Spirit's rococo image of Timbuctoo, "her Pagods hung with music of sweet bells"—simply cannot carry the conviction of even the pavilions in the revised "Armageddon." The proud irrelevance of these central visions seems evident in the speaker's question, "Wide Afric . . . is the rumor of thy Timbuctoo / A dream as frail as those of ancient Time?" (ll. 57, 60–61). Tennyson seems here to be asking himself whether he can salvage his subject from the conflicting demands made upon it and him. Never again would he fix his peripatetic vision within a spot so vulnerable to imaginative erosion.

While Tennyson may have dissociated himself from this Romantic frame, however, he was already exploring ways to compensate for its insufficiency. Timbuctoo may not be able to stand against "keen *Discovery*," but Discovery itself, because of its very alienation from Tennyson's inner world, is already being transformed into a replacement for the diabolic figure which has been revised out of existence. As "the waving of her wand" shrivels the gorgeous visions of the human imagination to "black specks," Discovery stands as an antipersonification;[21] yet as Day has pointed out (p. 68), her arrival is anticipated in an earlier metaphor. There legends which only exist, Tennyson admits, "in the heart of Man" still inspire a "yearning Hope which would not die" (l. 27):

> As when in some great City where the walls
> Shake, and the streets with ghastly faces thronged
> Do utter forth a subterranean voice,
> At midnight, in the lone Acropolis,
> Before the awful Genius of the place
> Kneels the pale Priestess in deep faith, the while
> Above her head the weak lamp dips and winks
> Unto the fearful summoning without:
> Nathless she ever clasps the marble knees,
> Bathes the cold hand with tears, and gazeth on
> Those eyes which wear no light but that wherewith
> Her phantasy informs them.
>
> (ll. 28–40)

This description does reveal the fear that, as Day puts it (p. 68), "all poetic dreams may be groundless fantasies containing no element of higher truth"; but it does considerably more. Here a metaphorical vehicle for the mediating speaker appeals to a second mediator of her own devising in the face of some hostile power. And as the apparently impotent idol, its cold hand warmed by the Priestess' tears and its dead eyes lit by her own, becomes "the awful Genius" of "the lone Acropolis," so the apparently impersonal earthquake becomes a "summoning," yet another Dis-like infernal power manifested by "ghastly faces" and a "subterranean voice." Here the vatic voice of the poem is not just anticipating his combat with Discovery, he is already beginning his mediation by retreating into an imaginative world where the combat can be physically lost yet metaphorically won. Thus while the objects of these individual visions may be threatened, the model from which they grow reasserts itself, with other players but with a vitality which subsumes any reality exterior to it.

The Devil and the Lady

While not central to "Timbuctoo," Tennyson's personification of Discovery as a depersonalizing woman marks an important transition between the "Armageddon" poems and the equally complex revisions of *The Devil and the Lady*. In fact even the Harvard manuscript of the play, though apparently contemporaneous with the first draft of "Armageddon," undercuts each of the roles within that poem. Here we find the angelic mediator transformed into a shrew whose curses frustrate her husband's voyage, Satan's infernal powers shrunken into the obliging servant left to guard her, and the poet figure faceted into the host of ineffectual suitors who immediately besiege her.

This last group of stock characters, though the least interesting of the play, represent perhaps our best introduction to it. For one thing, they alone remain nearly constant from the early Harvard manuscript (written, according to Tennyson's grandson, Charles, when the poet was fourteen) to the Trinity manuscript extensively revised and enlarged about two years later.[22] For another thing they dramatize the crudest, most direct, and least successful mediation between the subject and object of desire. Where the vatic speaker of "Armageddon" held opposing cosmic forces at a distance, here the suitors' desires,

> though, like telescopes,
> They bring far things awhile beneath the view,
> They cannot 'minish the long interval
> And space between the object and the wish.
>   (III, i, 225–28)

Tennyson clothed the mediating speakers of the "Armageddon" poems in classical, Miltonic, and Romantic rhetoric; here, clothing the suitors in professional jargon, he mirrors and mocks their shared compulsion to encompass the world in words. Specifically he shows each suitor trying, not just to possess Amoret sexually, but to seize verbal and hence imaginative control of her, of his rivals, of the entire action:[23]

> *Campano* . . .
> How shall the airy ardent kiss make way
> Through the thick folds of that dark veil, which bars
> All access to the fortress of thy soul.
> *Antonio.* Ay! Ay! unveil.
> *Angulo.*   Disperse thy '*nebulae.*'
>   (III, i, 57–60)

Yet their desires, like those of the "Armageddon" speaker, remain veiled in ironies: each wants to reduce his object to his own narrow linguistic universe, and each convinces himself of ultimate success; yet as Tucker puts it (p. 35), "Language itself . . . holds character hostage and keeps action in perpetual abeyance." Where the earlier speaker's success in banishing God and Satan won him a new opponent in "Timbuctoo," here the suitors' pleas to see the "real" Amoret win them a similar reward at play's end:

> A pretty flower of Sulphur shall ye find me.
> My thoughts begin to burn: a Devil's heat
> Glows through me to the core: have at ye, Sirs!
>   (III, iii, 61–63)

Here, as throughout the entire play, the Devil's selfless devotion to the Magus seems an implicit renunciation of his birthright. Though heir to Claudian's rebellious Dis, he seems to have accepted the impassivity of the serpentine columns in the Trinity "Armageddon." Yet especially within the Harvard manuscript of the play, he can mediate successfully precisely because vestiges of the Other still cling to him. Within this draft the original stage directions describe him upon his initial appearance as "a blue devil" and among the dramatis personae as "a certain comical blade."[24] As daringly successful as his counterparts in Marlowe or Goethe, Tennyson's Devil takes control of this manuscript draft by imbuing it with an imaginative reach which remains thoroughly and convincingly Shakespearean:

> I'd dive i' the sea,
> I'd ride the chariot of the rocking winds
> Alarumed by the thunder's awful knell
> Or from the horned corners of the moon
> I'd pluck the charmed flowers that flourish there.
>
> (I, i, 84–88)

Yet even the Shakespeare is far from derivative: from a bizarre amalgam of the preternatural characters in *The Tempest*, Tennyson has created a chthonic force just as comfortable in the heavens as Ariel, a Caliban who seeks not to ravish the master's daughter but to safeguard the honor of his wife.

Ultimately, of course, the Devil may fare no better than the suitors. In the folk tale outlined in Francis Palgrave's article, the wife so thoroughly outmaneuvers him that he confesses he would rather "tend all the swine in the woods of Westphalia, than undertake to keep one woman constant against her will."[25] And the planned ending, as Paden argues, may have borne out his foreboding that his task will prove futile. Even within the Harvard manuscript he must acknowledge to Amoret that she baffles him:

> Thou art the painted vision of a dream,
> Whose colours fade to nothing—a fair rainbow
> Mocking the tantalized sight—an airy bubble,
> O'er whose bright surface fly the hues of light,
> As if to hide the nothingness within.
>
> (I, v, 170–74)

As Other she remains a prismatic image which reflects all efforts to describe her as empty projections of the male imagination. Yet of all the male characters he alone does not desire her:

> if my fates had bid me
> To tread the thorny path of life with thee, . . .
> Would I be hurried like the dust of the earth
> With every gale of passion to and fro.
>
> (I, v, 39–40, 50–51)

Hence he alone can see her for what she is not; he alone can play her part with enough conviction to fool not only her suitors but the Magus himself.

From his perspective, after all, she remains no less insubstantial than all other human claims to cosmic importance: "What have the worlds / Of yon o'er-arching Heaven—the ample spheres / Of never-ending space, to do with Man?" (II, i, 18–20).

Paden (p. 27) holds up this youthful play of mind as the very quality Tennyson himself may have lost with the advent of puberty between this production at fourteen and the composition of the derivative *Poems by Two Brothers* two years later. And indeed the Trinity version of this drama, roughly contemporaneous with that volume, fragments even the Devil's cosmic disinterestedness into philosophical quibbles on the one hand ("O suns and spheres . . . / Are ye realities or semblances . . . ?" [II, i, 40, 42]) and into slapstick humor on the other ("I lit / I' the grey o' the morning on a blue-nosed Monk / And plucked him by the beard" [I, ii, 23–25]). The draft itself seems to lament the passing of such speculative daring. When the Devil, in several inserted speeches, tries to speculate further upon Amoret, he discovers that she has become both more evanescent and more dangerous. Originally he had argued that discipline would effectively "dam up" her fluid nature. Now he fears lest the Magus should

> leave some avenue
> To her insinuating and sapping force . . .
> Whence her ebullient spirit may leap forth . . .
> and enlarging straightly
> May hurry thy frail mound down its rough bed.
>
> (I, v, 103–4, 108, 110–11)

Even his futile effort to exorcise her depicts all her senses as avenues of dissimulation. Her tongue is

> Worse than an adder's fang.
> It prompts the brain to hatch, the hand to execute,
> The heart to shake off conscience, the back
> To throw away the burden of restraint,
> The saucy foot to spurn authority.
>
> (I, v, 34–38)

Finally, when he commands her to lie quiet "without the movement of one naughty muscle," he seems to invest her whole body with the power of sexual invitation.

Does the Trinity manuscript support the Devil's image of Amoret as a man-trap? In the speeches added to her soliloquy after the Magus' departure, she claims rather that she is only a victim of his superhuman longevity: "His years are countless as the dusty race / That people an old Cheese" (I, iv, 136–37). Against the legion of Tennyson heroes who bewail the loss of their beloved to unequal, loveless marriages, Amoret and Guinevere stand as the only extended portraits of women trapped in such a marriage. Culler's frankly sympathetic interpretation of Amoret (p. 11) even links her name to the power of Omnipotent Love which the Magus invokes at the opening of the Trinity manuscript. The repulse he suffers in his intended voyage thus becomes Love's judgment upon him for his demeaning suspicions and the even meaner insults of his diabolic servant.

While we might all like to see the much-abused Amoret vindicated, the revenge she plots in this draft hardly seems motivated by Omnipotent Love. The curse she hurls at the retreating Magus seems motivated instead by an equally potent sexual frustration: "The big waves shatter thy frail skiff! the winds / Sing any thing but lullabies unto thee!" (I, iv, 139–40). In fact the power of her curse to call up this storm supports the Devil's admission that the cosmic reach of his imagination is no match for the cosmic reach of her sexuality. Both he and the Magus, in Gerhard Joseph's words, are "contesting the nature of the universe conceived of as a woman" (p. 124).

Amoret's usurpation of the Devil's now-waning power throws the whole burden of mediation upon the stooped shoulders of the Magus. His role as a senex figure within Renaissance comedy may seem to support Paden's conjecture ("Hödeken," p. 47) that at play's end he will discover "a seventh wooer nearing his goal." He has already admitted that he lacks the power to penetrate "a woman's mind." The Trinity revision emphasizes these limitations in his new description of each individual as "a complicated Engine" and in his new invocations to the personified goddess, Distrust. For all these suspicions, however, he persists in seeing Amoret as the embodiment of beauty and purity—gem, flower, spring, garner—and not as the corruption threatening these treasures—taint, canker, mud, "foul consuming worm."[26] When he blandly accepts her feigned promise of fidelity, he seems much blinder to her role as Other than was the Devil.

Because of his almost total passivity, critics have consistently measured the power and normative value of the Magus by his one significant action, the attempt to embark on his "important" but otherwise unspecified journey. For Culler, as we saw, the Magus' failure stands as the revenge of "Omnipotent Love." For Joseph (p. 123), "the combat that the Magus wages against the black shapes clinging about his boat ends in his triumph." For Tucker (pp.

37–39), his failure paradoxically measures his, or at least the poet's success: "Wrapped in an emblem of his power [his magic scarf], the Magus is also rapt by a fate that lies beyond his power but that seems also to collaborate with it, to produce a complex stalemate. . . . The individual exertions of the Magus disclose . . . a higher, not quite personal power that contains them, in a manner that is frustrating and fulfilling at once."

In fact the stalemate Tucker describes, while both important and undeniable, results from a progression associated with the Magus throughout this draft. This progression—visionary projection, followed by engagement, followed by collapse—certainly characterizes his encounter with the sea; the stern resolution with which he braves the storm subsides, like the sea itself, after his third failure: "Some spells of darker Gramarie than mine, / Ruled the dim night and would not grant me passage" (III, ii, 136–37). Yet the same progression characterizes his encounter with Amoret; his bold decision to counter his wife's charm with diabolical power subsides into the concession later resorted to by the browbeaten Merlin: "Well, Amoret, I will believe thee true" (I, iv, 87). Even his opening encomium to Love contains sixteen lines of impressive, if rather bombastic, invocation—but no predicate:

> thou great Despot
> Who bindest in thy golden chains the strong
> And the imbecile—thou immortal Pan-Arch,
> Tyrant o' the earth and sea whose sunless depth
> And desolate Abyss is vivified
> And quickened at thy bidding—thou vast link
> Of the Creation—thou deep sentiment!
>
> (I, i, 16–22)

We are left, not with Glendower's problem of spirits who will not come when called, but rather with the problem of a spirit who is called but not told to come at all.

This spirit may be, as Tucker describes it, a "not quite personal power," but his later descriptions of it as "fixed Fatality" and the poet's "*sense* of doom" both ignore the connections Tennyson draws throughout this draft between images of flux and of woman—Amoret in particular. While Tennyson, as Tucker claims (p. 37), may have "surprised . . . himself" with the intensity of the Magus' soliloquy, the whole draft emphasizes the old man's dogged stasis in the face of sexual transience and corruption. In fact it is in the revision and *as* revision that the Magus attempts the only mediation available to him. The same free play of mind which the Harvard draft attributed to the mediating Devil has now degenerated into the natural change manifested in Amoret. Hence the Magus must stand as both witness and measure of this degeneration:

> When couched in Boyhood's passionless Tranquillity,
> The natural mind of man is warm and yielding,
> Fit to receive the best impressions,
> But raise it to the atmosphere of Manhood
> And the rude breath of Dissipation
> Will harden it to stone.
>
> (III, ii, 176–81)

Such remarks certainly seem to brand the Magus as Tennyson's earliest example of Paden's mask of age (p. 53), an old, often guilty figure used to distance the poet's very immediate fear of sexuality. Even here, however, we should notice the terms of the metaphor: youth and innocence are free and open; maturity and "Earthliness" petrify the mind; earlier and later within the same passage they brand it, drown it, dry it out like a "seaplant" out of water. In the context of the Trinity revision, the mask of age seems itself to become the "immense" two-year distance from which "passionless tranquillity" now appears as the mental and emotional freedom which produced the original draft.

In fact the implications of the play deepen in the very process of darkening: Amoret matures from a frustrated wife to the embodiment of a willful desire which typifies the male condition as well as her own; the Magus in turn matures from a Renaissance senex to a mediator who can function both inside and outside the authorial self. He becomes both a hero locked in unequal struggle with cosmic change and an authorial voice moralizing on the inevitability of his failure. The Devil lives without desire and hence without fear; Amoret, as she announces, lives without hope; the Magus, like the maturing Tennyson, must live torn by the irreconcilable demands of all three.

Both the Magus and the vatic speaker of "Timbuctoo" must confront new or newly defined manifestations of the Other; yet both these mediators move inward as well to assume attributes which Tennyson's poetry privileges as somehow his own. In so doing they appropriate an almost bemused acknowledgment of the gap between desire and fulfillment, a celebration of some more synthetic past, and a faith that as the affirmation of vision has brought threat, so threat will of itself bring new opportunities for affirmation. In both these poems, therefore, we could claim that the mediator has grown indistinguishable from the authorial presence. Yet Dis's protean transformations—from Other to extinction, to mediator, to stock character—force us to recognize that all the roles within our model remain so fluid that the labels we assign to them must remain somewhat arbitrary. Far more constant is the spatially defined tension present between the roles, a tension so strong that it simply creates new characters to fill its vacancies.

CHAPTER TWO

The 1830 Volume
and *The Lover's Tale*

Just as it did within his adolescent poems, Tennyson's model establishes continuities between the lyrics of his 1830 volume and his long, roughly contemporaneous narrative, *The Lover's Tale*.[1] Both confront earlier manifestations of the Other, now partially disguised but ultimately just as frustrating. Both posit a series of mediators, who in turn try on different forms of isolation and imaginative projection. Finally both find their deepest, if not most satisfying, expression through jealously protected emanations of the authorial presence: the despairing projections of the 1830 volume and the Lover who internalizes a hostile reality within a series of flashbacks and visions. Even the most significant differences between the lyrics and the narrative exist apart from genre. The narrative, as I will argue later, tries to naturalize the model, tries to reduce its figures not just into personalities but into people. The lyrics, on the other hand, try to dissect the model, try to isolate each of the roles and to conceptualize it within apparently disparate poems.

Poems of 1830

The weighty, ordered progression we are claiming for both works may seem equally remote from the self-indulgent sentiment of *The Lover's Tale* and from the triviality of the 1830 lyrics. Yet Clyde de L. Ryals, in what remains the fullest treatment of that volume, has already addressed this last charge. At the outset he may seem to grant it: "The collection is a hodgepodge: the serious alternates with the trifling, the original with the conventional; there is no note of certainty, almost no development of a given tone, subject, or theme."[2] Later, however, he claims (p. 39) that "underneath all this prettiness and oscillation, we find Tennyson seeking for a workable construct upon which to base his poetry." And still later he concludes (p. 40) that "Tennyson was making further exploratory incursions into the realm of the mind, measuring his own concepts and emotions against the forces of the hostile world."

Within the adolescent poems we have already met both the "forces of the hostile world" and the "concepts and emotions" (usually embodied in figures) which Tennyson opposes to them. Even what Ryals calls the "hodgepodge" may only disguise the embarrassing fact that he was seeking a "workable construct" more from psychological need than from aesthetic taste. By fragmenting the authorial presence, the mediator, and the Other throughout the fifty-some lyrics in the volume, Tennyson could pretend a dispassionate analysis of the model itself, could explore the possibility that, wrenched from their dramatic context, these figures might collapse into tame abstractions. To this end he reduces the female manifestations of the Other into impersonal flux and the male manifestations into an ambiguous series of enthroned figures. Within another set of 1830 lyrics, he classifies the different mediators within the adolescent poems into four different imaginative strategies for confronting the outside world. As we might expect, the "successful" applications of this strategy make for rather sterile poetry. Yet whenever the model reasserts its integrity within an individual poem, it transforms the poem itself into an intensely troubling drama.

Tennyson's disinterested fascination with the impersonal vastness of interstellar time and space is apparent in his first remembered lines: "The rays of many a rolling central Star / Aye flashing earthward have not reached us yet" (*Memoir*, I, 20). The "Chorus," pointedly ascribed to "an Unpublished Drama, Written Very Early," also celebrates a violent, anarchic universe:

> The lawless comets as they glare,
>   And thunder through the sapphire deeps
>   In wayward strength, are full of strange
>   Astonishment and boundless change.
>   (ll. 27–30)

Within another unpublished drama, we remember, the Devil's fascination with Amoret seemed of a piece with his fascination with the cosmos:

> Oh! ye shine bravely now
> Through the deep purple of the summer sky.
> I know that ye are Earths, as fair, and fairer
> And mightier than this I tread upon.
>
> (II, i, 25–28)

Yet in the revision his reflections on temporal relativity are set off against his recollection of a clock in hell, whose pendulum "sound[s] *'Ever, Never!'* through all the courts of Hell, / Piercing the wrung ears of the damned that writhe / Upon their beds of flame" (I, v, 237–39).

While patently absurd as an effort to measure an everlasting torment, the Devil's division of temporal change into alternating opposites foreshadows a strategy employed by several of this volume's conventionally stylized, formally balanced lyrics. Reinterpreting change not as Amoret's wasting sexuality but as paired oppositions, these lyrics win Tennyson a clearer interpretation of his earlier encounters with natural flux. Understanding, however, is not control. In their very evenhandedness, the 1830 poems discover in this flux an equally destructive kind of psychic entropy. Shaw describes them (p. 74) as "echo[ing] the protesting cry of Heraclitus, heard down the ages: 'All things give way: nothing remains.'"

In fact the very world they portray seems to have settled into a lower, more uniform energy level. A set of elaborately paired lyrics presents their oppositions as mirror images of the speaker's own thwarted desires: "Nothing Will Die" almost as if to thwart his longing for stasis in the hell of natural change; "All Things Will Die" only in the sense that he will soon be prevented by his own death from enjoying them. If the speaker actually probes specific objects in nature for the secret behind their mutual opposition, he receives only a debilitating parody of his own questions. In "The How and the Why," for example, his frustration cuts through the sheer dreadfulness of the poetry:

> The little bird pipeth—"why? why?"
> In the summerwoods when the sun falls low
> And the great bird sits on the opposite bough,
> And stares in his face and shouts, "how? how?"
>
> (ll. 26–29)

He can, in fact, be certain only that such oppositions are leading him inevitably toward dissolution: "We laugh, we cry, we are born, we die, / Who will riddle me the *how* and *why?*" (ll. 8–9).

The earlier male manifestations of the Other, whether divine or diabolical, here maintain an equally frustrating ambivalence. Approaching in anger but shrinking into impotence when invoked in time of need, these figures consistently deny the poet an opportunity either to ignore or to propitiate them. The god figure thus assumes moral force only at the expense of physical force, and physical at the expense of moral. As Amoret diffused into entropy, so this inverse proportion secularizes a religious figure into a series of morally ambiguous but potentially threatening presences: some male, some female, some as impersonal as the cosmic entropy we have just encountered.

This metamorphosis and its effect on Tennyson can best be analyzed through his development of a single image—the throne. He inaugurated this image in the Heavenly Pavilion of the second "Armageddon" and then in "Timbuctoo" set it still farther away from "keen *Discovery*" as the "thrones of the Western wave, fair islands green" of the Hesperides. Ultimately, the image rests on two conspicuous details from his source in Revelation, a central seat of God and a series of radiating objects or veils like the encircling heavenly host.[3] As the god or devil figure becomes secularized, however, these details also change their significance. If the figure appears hostile, the throne still represents a judgment seat, and the objects which mark the boundaries of its domain appear as either a collective veil or the circle of those drawn to their doom. The throne of "The Mermaid," as Hughes has noted (*Glass*, p. 50), enables her erotic power to destroy the immortality of her would-be admirers. Even when married, she imagines herself ringed by amorous sea creatures. Also deep below the surface, in this case buried within the earth, is the female personification of hatred in the curious sonnet, "The Pallid Thunder-Stricken Sigh for Gain." Hatred lures these wretches to their doom with veins of gold radiating from her central cave up to the earth's surface.

Another submerged figure, the Kraken, has commonly been located deep within the psyche. As Joseph puts it (p. 36), "One cannot help suspecting that the deeps from which he rises are more than physical, that they are the uncharted recesses of the mind itself."[4] Within this interior landscape, however, the Kraken appears as another of the enthroned figures, in this case less divine than diabolical. Once we pass "below the thunders of the upper deep," the whole scene groups itself around him:

faintest sunlights flee
About his shadowy sides: above him swell

> Huge sponges of millennial growth and height;
> And far away . . .
>
> > enormous polypi
> Winnow with giant arms the slumbering green.[5]
>
> > > (ll. 4–7, 9–10)

While the Kraken may not be literally throned upon the "huge seaworms" on which he feeds, the spatial deference shown him by his otherwise awesome attendants sets him up as an image of Might half-slumbering on its own right flipper, another of those manifestations of the Other whose threat is tempered only by their somnolent refusal to attack.

When this central power becomes less hostile, the throne itself withdraws in space and time and the surrounding veils begin to repel the suppliant. In some of the earlier poems in the 1830 volume, these barriers merely challenge the speaker's power. For the Mystic the "congregated hours . . . hold aloft the cloud / Which droops lowhung on either gate of life" (ll. 31–32), and "angels [show] him thrones" (l. 1) much like the one glimpsed by the poet of the second "Armageddon." So too the driving refrain in "Recollections of the Arabian Nights" virtually drags the speaker through the surrounding exoticism to behold first the throne and then the face of "good Haroun Alrashid."[6]

Yet in other poems this power, though equally beneficent, is not so efficacious. The emanations from God's throne in the unpublished "Perdidi Diem" dissipate among the surrounding heavenly bodies before they ever reach earth; likewise Love, though mounted on a flying throne in the second 1830 sonnet in his honor, is always encompassed by a cloud of evil. When Love itself becomes this encircling force, as in the first of these sonnets, it can only "mellow" the hostile power within it. In either case this mutual dissipation of moral and physical forces again leaves Tennyson's speaker confronting entropy, a universe gradually losing the ability to save or even reach him.

Tennyson often tied the more munificent image of God to some dying city or civilization: first, as we saw, in "Timbuctoo" and later in some of the *Poems by Two Brothers* like "Persia," "The Druid's Prophecies," "The Fall of Jerusalem," and "Babylon." In 1830 this connection, though more tenuous, still holds. In "The Deserted House" the departure of "Life and Thought" have allowed the surrounding edifice of the body to decay. Though they have taken a "mansion incorruptible" in "a great and distant city," its very distance renders it inaccessible to the grieving speaker. Similarly within "The Dying

Swan," the bird's "death-hymn" seems to transform "the soul / Of that waste place" into another celestial city:

> As when a mighty people rejoice
> With shawms, and with cymbals, and harps of gold,
> And the tumult of their acclaim is rolled
> Through the open gates of the city afar.
>
> (ll. 31–34)

Here again, however, the city is distanced—first in time because of the biblical instruments, next in space within the metaphor, and finally in syntactic remoteness as part of the vehicle of this metaphor. In actuality, the swan's song cannot free it from its own desolate swamp.[7]

All these different attempts to isolate and depersonalize the Other thus prove no more satisfactory than the vatic speaker's attempt to rationalize it within the revisions of "Armageddon." That speaker, however, had grown increasingly identified with an increasingly uncomfortable poet. Within this volume this identification is often disguised by the sheer number of disparate poems and by a mask of bored, philosophical sophistication which renders many of them nearly as derivative as the Byronic lyrics of *Poems by Two Brothers*. Tucker sees this mask as itself masking a psychological withdrawal. He argues that because these lyrics "remained the preserve of the self in proud or ruinous isolation, . . . they lagged behind their creator. Since 'Timbuctoo' Tennyson had known that the poetical character becomes itself in relationship."[8] I would argue instead that Tennyson uses many of these lyrics as tentative, covert, but still daring experiments in just such relationships. Because the speaker of each poem stands at a real but carefully undefined distance from his authorial position, he can manipulate this relationship to explore very different forms of mediation. These speakers, in turn, can test his imaginative powers against situations more dangerous than any he has previously confronted.

From this perspective, the 1830 volume explores systematically two forms of isolation (idealism and introversion) and two imaginative constructs (personification and projection), through all of which Tennyson can confront Ryals' "forces of a hostile world." Tennyson's refusal to commit himself to any of these four possibilities is vindicated by the partial failure of each of them: (1) if the mediator reduces this world into an extension of this newly creative self, he finds that idealism leaves him in solipsism; (2) if he withdraws into some mental center of meaning, he opens his sanctuary to the very outer world he has refused to acknowledge; (3) if he personifies this world, he finds the personification siding with its origins against him; (4) if he projects some aspect of himself against the world, he reduces all the responses of this projection to echoes of his own voice. Tennyson's psyche remains shielded from all these failures; it is only that of the mediator which is walled off, or invaded, or attacked by his own creations. As faithful though powerless mediators, however, these projections can be acknowledged, can be gifted with personal treasures and allowed to display them before an indifferent world.

Tennyson had been toying with philosophical idealism ever since the revised draft of *The Devil and the Lady*. There the Devil questions the reality of the heavenly bodies:

> I have some doubt if ye exist when none
> Are by to view ye–if your Being alone
> Be in the mind and the intelligence
> Of the created. . . .
>
> (II, i, 52–55)

By the concluding poem of the 1830 volume, "Οἱ ῥέοντες," Tennyson seems even stronger in his assertion that man's "dreams are true" simply because he dreams them: "Man is the measure of all truth / Unto himself" (ll. 3–4). At this point, however, he introduces the contrary assertion that reality is not personal vision but flux: "All truth is Change" (l. 4). Finally, he asserts in a subscript that both of the previous assertions are true only relative to that most skeptical of philosophers, Heraclitus.

Such sophism should make us wary of an apparently more straightforward poem of this period, "The Idealist": "I am the earth, the stars, the sun / I am the clouds, the sea" (ll. 9–10). While "the spirit of a man" here claims that he can "weave the universe," he follows Coleridge, Maurice, and Tennyson's own early mouthpiece, the Magus, in excluding from his being "the souls of fellow men and very God" (l. 18). Tennyson's own reservations, however, may go beyond these; he not only fails to include the poem in the 1830 volume, he also undercuts the smugness of the spirit's opening assertion:

> A mighty matter I rehearse,
> A mighty matter undescried;
> Come listen all who can.
>
> (ll. 1–3)

Tennyson attacks a similar smugness much more directly in "A Character." The desire to stand at the center of his universe denies to the figure parodying Thomas Sunderland any possibility of comprehending it, responding to it, learning from it.[9] Having already mastered "the wanderings / Of this most intricate Universe," Sunderland gives them but "a half-glance"; yet like the Idealist, he actually perceives not them but only the self-image in "the bottom of his eye." Because the outer world, even at its most alien, is more accessible to imaginative vision than to habit or preconception, it needs to be taken with greater seriousness than idealism can permit.

If idealism produces self-centeredness, the alternative, contemplating one's own psyche, destroys the center itself. Withdrawal here differs from idealism in that instead of modeling the outer world on his mind, the mediator models a tightly enclosed inner reality upon the domain of the alien Other. Hence the dangers of withdrawal resemble those encountered by earlier recluses. The Kraken, as we saw, must eventually yield to a new manifestation of the Other, the God of "the latter fire." The figure of Hatred, already withdrawn from humanity in her central cave, has her human form further constricted by a golden snake encircling her forehead, which "skims the colour from her trembling lips."

The effects of the outer world on the mediator's withdrawn spirit are often portrayed in snake imagery. Paden, as we saw (pp. 45–50, 136n), has pointed out their obvious phallic associations. Within these poems, however, the snake represents the whole dilemma of introversion, both its goal, self-renewal, and its danger, suffocation. The snake's need to shed its skin every year forms the basis for both the third sonnet on Love and the one which begins, "Could I outwear my present state of woe." In the first of these the speaker, like the Indians he describes, stands as an "awestricken" witness to the travails of Love in its annual quest for rebirth. In the latter sonnet, however, the speaker himself wears "the wan dark coil of faded suffering," like a skin which he cannot "outgrow." Unlike the "sheeny snake" "forth in the pride of beauty issuing" (ll. 5–6), he remains trapped within the mantle of his frozen tears.

This fragmentation of the speaker's psyche into conflicting parts actually blurs the question of whether the fragmentation comes from without or within. This difficulty, in turn, may help explain Tennyson's well-known difficulty with abstractions. Those in *Poems by Two Brothers* may indeed reflect a poor understanding of eighteenth-century personification, but those in "The Poet's Mind," for example, may reflect instead a consciousness so withdrawn that, as Tucker puts it (p. 88), "It is difficult to know whether the poet's grouchiness arises in his sense of alienation from his power source, or whether he deliberately mystifies that source as a means of coping with an audience whose curiosity he both covets and fears." Though the hostile critic is part of an outer world so unfeeling as to be deaf to the poet's inner fountain, he seems able to probe deep enough to destroy it: "It would shrink to the earth if you came in" (ll. 35–37).

Faced with these inroads of the outer world, the mediator, instead of withdrawing, may seek to confront them with yet a second mediating figure, either one called up from this outer world or one projected from his or her own being. The first device, indeed, helps mitigate the gloom of some of the poems we have already discussed. The figure of Love mellowed God's edicts of fear, and angels and the daughters of time pulled back the limits of normal perception for the Mystic. Even in "Supposed Confessions" the infant becomes the temple and birthplace of "the Spirit of happiness and perfect rest," the sanctuary

> Where she would ever wish to dwell,
> Life of the fountain there, beneath
> Its salient springs. . . .
>
> (ll. 54–56)

Such figures grow from earlier supernatural mediators, the diabolical assistant to the Magus in *The Devil and the Lady* and the angelic extension of the speaker's visionary powers in "Armageddon." Yet there the supposedly evil servant worked to guard Amoret's chastity while the supposedly good one seemed more impressed with the forces of Satan than with those of God. Here their literary descendants show an equally paradoxical relation to the two positions between which they mediate In fact, the better they are able to cope with the outside world, the more they seem to side with it. "To J.M.K." and "To a Clear-Headed Friend," for example, seem conventional laudatory pieces, but as mediators both friends grow strangely threatening. Because Kemble's pulpit is likened to "a throne / Mounted in heaven," this surrogate for God himself reduces the speaker to a passive onlooker: "I will stand and mark." Tennyson's "clear-headed friend," J. W. Blakesley, carefully nurtures Truth from his "kingly intellect" until she can combat falsehood just as the angel crippled Jacob. Yet the image, though powerful, so twists both its poetic and biblical contexts that Truth—and hence the friend himself—become types of the god figure crippling frail humanity.

Female figures soon abandon mediation for the teasing evanescent sexuality of Amoret. In the balanced natural oppositions we studied at the beginning of this chapter, we saw the speaker frustrated by the Other manifested in impersonal flux. In the so-called girlie poems, begun in this volume and continued in that of 1832, we see that the personifications of this flux leave him just as frustrated. These sentimental echoes of the Lucy poems evoke what Hartman calls boundary figures, bridges between man and the natural world. Such figures, however, seem to have more on their minds than mediation. The speaker attempts to recapture a kind of natural freedom within the "airy, fairy Lilian," but unable to remain disinterested toward her, he vacillates between love and hate:

> If prayers will not hush thee,
> > Airy Lilian,
> Like a rose-leaf I will crush thee,
> > Fairy Lilian.
>
> (ll. 27–30)

In "Isabel," Tennyson finds his mother's virtues embodied within the natural images of moon, stream, and vine. Yet these subvert her subservient role as wife even as they express it: the "mellowed reflex" rounds out the "wintry moon"; the "clear stream . . . absorbs" the "muddy one"; the "upbearing parasite," while providing support, beauty, and value to Tennyson's father, metaphorically reduces him to a dead "stem." He has ceded his whole identity to his supposedly weaker partner.

In "Oriana" yet another apparently sympathetic woman destroys the speaker. As his true love, of course, she is supposed to support his fight against the Other. Her increasingly ambiguous role, however, soon turns the poem into a prototypically Tennysonian response to violence. Like the Princess, she becomes the focus of the speaker's confusion in the battle: "She stood upon the castle wall / . . . She watched my crest among them all" (ll. 28, 30). When he inadvertently shoots her, like Maud's phantom she becomes no mediator but a threatening god figure, the focus of his guilt: "I dare not think of thee / . . . I dare not die and come to thee" (ll. 93, 96). Like Ettarre, though not as willfully, she brings her Pelleas to a self-loathing which courts self-destruction: "They should have stabbed me where I lay / . . . They should have trod me into clay, / Oriana" (ll. 60, 62–63). As Kincaid describes the process (p. 18), "The repetition of her name in nearly every other line supports this transition from devotion, to hypnotic adherence, to something like terror."[10]

Completing this progression, the mediating figure which most subtly evokes the Other forces the speaker to reject this mediation in favor of direct confrontation. The spirit who "haunts the year's last hours" seems to offer the speaker life, motion, and speech within a landscape in thrall to death. But when we "hear him sob and sigh" to himself as "earthward he boweth the heavy stalks / Of the mouldering flowers," we realize that he uses his vital powers only as ironic testimony to the power of death itself. The second stanza replaces even this vitality with the transience, stagnation, and silence imaged in the dying man. As such it virtually demands of the speaker some human but ultimately futile response:

> My very heart faints and my whole soul grieves
> At the moist rich smell of the rotting leaves,
>> And the breath
>> Of the fading edges of box beneath,
> And the year's last rose.
>
> (ll. 16–20)

The success of even this response is rendered dubious by the refrain's juxtaposition of death with the forces of light, permanence, and vitality evoked in "sunflower," "hollyhocks," and "tiger-lily."

Driven back to personal confrontation, the speakers of other poems find a mediator closer to home, close enough in fact to reflect some aspect of the authorial presence. Like the figures of Moneta in Keats's *Fall of Hyperion* or Rousseau in Shelley's *The Triumph of Life*, these projections can body forth their creator's personality against an animate though hostile world. Yet as Keats and Shelley were well aware, such projections are physically powerless and psychologically deceptive; like Stevens' necessary angel, they appear to humanize this world, but they must themselves admit that humanization has become synonymous with falsification. As Moneta warns,

> Mortal, that thou may'st understand aright,
> I humanize my sayings to thine ear,
> Making comparisons of earthly things;
> Or thou might'st better listen to the wind,
> Whose language is to thee a barren noise.
>
> (II, 1–5)[11]

Such limitations are shared by Tennyson's projections; they either collapse, powerless as the authorial values they embody, or they distort the

Other even as they humanize it. In the first case, the speaker of "Supposed Confessions" projects himself into and shares the plight of the lamb and the ox as they are inexplicably struck down in the midst of an apparently beneficent world. In the second case the same speaker projects a more effective but more dangerous image. In "Truth" he claims to have found a figure complex and self-sufficient enough to humanize a universe of both inner and outer flux: "An image with profulgent brows, / And perfect limbs, as from the storm / Of running fires (ll. 145–47). Near the end of the poem, however, he must acknowledge the danger in such projections: "everywhere / Some must clasp Idols." He too may be reading onto the "depths of death" what in section 108 of *In Memoriam* Tennyson will call "the reflex of a human face," the image of his own longing. With this realization, the prospect of death gives rise to an uninvited projection, probably the most frightening of the many serpents in this volume: "the busy fret / Of that sharp-headed worm begins / In the gross blackness underneath" (ll. 185–87).

In "Hero to Leander" Hero also tries to oppose her imaginative powers to a hostile nature; she begins by projecting herself as a lover against the threatening ocean: "My heart is warmer surely than the bosom of the main" (l. 9). Gradually, however, she makes their love an echo and, she hopes, a substitute for this watery embrace. Then, equally gradually, her metaphor begins to work against her. The savagery of the sea resists her humanization of it and drives her to see her love itself as only an ironic foreshadowing of her lover's death: "And the billow will embrace thee with a kiss as soft as mine" (l. 27). She implicitly yields her own world up to the outer one in her suicidal last line: "Go not yet, / Or I will follow thee" (ll. 110–11).

However unlikely it may seem, Tennyson's conflicts with the outer world are best resolved by another female projection, the desolate Mariana. Recent criticism has questioned the power, even the integrity of this figure: Tucker comments (p. 74), "It is because Mariana herself is so vacant that the atmosphere she exudes is so full."[12] Such interpretations assume an authorial presence encompassing and coming to the aesthetic, if not the literal, rescue of his subject. I would like to reverse this relation. In one sense Mariana is taking upon herself many of the frustrating confrontations with the outer world which continued to plague Tennyson. Trapped deep within the domain of the Other, she must encounter it in the person of a male who refuses to encounter her. By withholding himself just beyond the limits of perception, the lover implicitly accuses her of some moral or sexual failure. With his absence, like that of the throned figures in other 1830 lyrics, she must also confront natural flux in the endless repetition of day and night and in the specific objects (the moss, the latch, the bats, the poplar) which only echo her own alienation.

Yet her lack of physical control over this domain is compensated for by an aesthetic control. Her refusal to respond to anything but a human figure conspicuously absent from the surrounding waste gradually forces this landscape to arrange itself in layers radiating out from her perceiving consciousness: the room, the curtain, the casement, the flower-plots, the garden wall, the sluice, the "level waste." In moving toward her final realization that "he will not come," the poem moves us toward the realization that she is not alienated from some outside focus of meaning but isolated as the creative focus of an otherwise meaningless world.[13]

The Lover's Tale

While he was creating these projections for the 1830 volume, Tennyson was laboring to bring to life another projection, the speaker of *The Lover's Tale*.[14] In this character, however, he was trying not to depersonalize the model but to naturalize it. He was trying to reduce the cosmic distance between authorial presence and Other to a human one capable of being bridged by a mediator who could speak as both poet and lover. Tennyson's ongoing composition is reflected in the number of widely variant drafts: 1828, 1832, and the revision and continuation of 1870. We might bring some order to this diversity if we could isolate some intermediate version of the poem before the privately printed text of 1832.[15] This approach is denied us, however, and for reasons besides the fragmentary condition of the extant manuscripts.[16] The poem, as evidenced by both the 1832 and 1870 versions, never even approaches formal stasis. It seems instead to be repeatedly fragmented by the speaker's constant redefinitions of his own turbulent quest.

These redefinitions are in turn forced upon the speaker by his failure to naturalize the Other, to reduce his adored Cadrilla into the passive object of desire. Instead of assuming new autonomy within a revision, therefore, this mediator is forced to assume it in the second half of his poem. As a creative projection of Tennyson's own creativity, the speaker reshapes the meaning of his life and the form of his poem with every twist of the plot. He first identifies with his beloved, then celebrates her as an extension of the self, then discovers that she is Other and another's, then discovers a new Other in the flux of the natural world, then reshapes this encounter into one with Death, and finally transcends Death in vision.

Herbert Tucker argues (p. 95) that neither the speaker's life nor his poem constitutes a quest: "Nothing happens, in this nonstory, because stasis is its very subject: we might indeed call it a narrative about the paralysis of the narrative faculty." The speaker lumps together all the stages of his apparent quest precisely because his joint subject/object remains the narcissistic intensity of his own imaginative desire: the poem confronts "the most intractable of Romantic obstacles to relation and development: the tendency of desire to displace its object and become an end in itself." Certainly the speaker intertwines Cadrilla and his own psyche throughout the poem, but he does this, I think, in progressively different ways and for progressively different reasons.

Amoret, portrayed by the Devil as a sexual object, grew too alien even for definition. Hence this mediator attempts to equate mediation with identification, attempts to portray his beloved as both a psychological extension of his own self and an external object of intensely physical desire. Their shared childhood allows him to go even Byron one better by subsuming Cadrilla's past and hence her being with his own. This childhood preamble to romantic love, so common in later Tennyson, has usually been seen as an attempt to domesticate sexuality, but here at least Tennyson appears to sexualize childhood, to celebrate the speaker's yearning for incest as a logical conclusion to the Romantic quest for total identification with the beloved. Here the parental figures with whom children normally identify virtually disappear. Cadrilla's mother and the speaker's father are dead from the beginning; her father drowns soon after; and his mother, who raises them both, appears only as an impersonal source of milk. All these relationships so collapse in upon the couple that the speaker can literally claim, "In that I live I love, because I love / I live" (I, 173–74).[17]

This celebration, however, pales beside the imaginative, spiritual, physical union celebrated in the narrative passage which occupies nearly half of the 1832 poem. From the outset of their mountain trek, they, the landscape, and love flow together in an interplay of surging forces: Love "burst through the heated buds, and sent his soul / Into the songs of birds. . . . As mountain streams / Our bloods ran free" (I, 314–15, 319–20). Tucker argues ("Lover's Tale," p. 27) that even these claims "of presence and responsiveness," rest on memory and promise, not on any engagement with the present. Yet from this physical, spiritual, and emotional height, the couple are caught up into an ecstatic and frankly sexual union with one another and with the landscape: they behold

> A purple range of mountain-cones, between
> Whose interspaces gushed in blinding bursts
> The incorporate blaze of sun and sea.
>
> (I, 398–400)

As their ecstatic climb has paralleled the sun's, so their descent unites them again in an afternoon of afterglow:

> the loud stream, . . .
> Parting my own loved mountains was received,
> Shorn of its strength, into the sympathy
> Of that small bay, which out to open main
> Glowed intermingling close beneath the sun.
>
> (I, 419, 423–26)

When they descend further into the darkness of approaching evening and of their cave, they seem only to exchange an expansive love for an intensive one. In this scene, as in that with Juan and Haidee in *their* cave at twilight, the very indifference of nature seems to heighten their passion:

> Methought all excellence that ever was
> Had drawn herself from many thousand years,
> And all the separate Edens of this earth,
> To centre in this place and time.
>
> (I, 538–41)

All this intensity, of course, builds only to Cadrilla's shattering revelation of her love for Lionel. Because Tennyson so often portrayed passionate courtships destroyed by outside opposition, critics like Betty Miller have suggested that from adolescence he feared either sexual consummation or women as individuals.[18] The portrayal here, however, grants to love the benefit of every possible doubt; it affirms quite candidly both the speaker's psychological intimacy with Cadrilla and his explicitly sexual love for her; yet here too love succumbs to some ill-defined but fatal anomaly.

On one level the rejection only extends the speaker's own discovery of a distinction between brotherly and romantic love:

> I was as the brother of her blood,
> And by that name I moved upon her breath;
> Dear name, which had too much of nearness in it
> And heralded the distance of this time!
>
> (I, 548–51)

This discovery, however, parallels a far more disconcerting one that the author makes through him. Both discover that this love is not the selfless dissolution of his being into hers which he has celebrated throughout their journey; nor is it even the "shadowy idealization of the beloved that divides beloved and lover alike," as it appears to Tucker ("Lover's Tale," p. 23); it remains instead an attempt to subsume the beloved physically as well as psychologically. The 1870 revision makes perhaps too explicit the comparison of his love to political domination:

> all the maiden empire of her mind,
> Lay like a map before me, and I saw
> There, where I hoped myself to reign as king,
> There, where that day I crowned myself as king,
> There in my realm and even on my throne,
> *Another!*
>
> (I, 578–83)

Once this mediator realizes that his Cadrilla is not just "another's" but fundamentally "Other," he begins to encounter the same manifestations of natural flux which the Magus of the Trinity draft encountered in the protean Amoret. Having already internalized nature as a mere reflection of his inner joy, however, he lacks the Magus' ability to distance himself from it in moralizing. Instead, as Albright argues (p. 27), "His mind . . . cannot keep itself separate from what it contemplates"; much like young Werther, he now finds himself trapped within a domain of the Other which can only mirror his inner grief. As an earlier speaker found his vision of Timbuctoo shrinking into "mud huts," so this speaker finds himself sitting "within the cavernmouth,"

> And all the fragments of the living rock
> (Huge blocks, which some old trembling of the world
> Had loosened from the mountain, till they fell
> Half-digging their own graves) these in my agony
> Did I make bare of all the golden moss.
>
> (II, 36, 43–47)

Instead of trying to escape from either inner or outer gloom, however, he surrenders to them in a series of visions so vivid that they usurp both the landscape and the remainder of the 1832 text:

> Alway the inaudible invisible thought,
> Artificer and subject, lord and slave,
> Shaped by the audible and visible,
> Moulded the audible and visible; . . .
> The cloud-pavilioned element, the wood,
> The mountain, the three cypresses, the cave, . . .
> Were wrought into the tissue of my dream: . . .
> And in my vision bidding me dream on.
>
>   (II, 101–4, 107–8, 112, 118)

For Clarice Short, the dream is finally dispelled by the intensity of the emotions it evokes.[19] From this psychological reduction it is only a short step to the subconscious progression that Paden (p. 31) sees attending sexual desire in Tennyson: violence, guilt, and the doom of God.

Yet when he draws "the mountain, the three cypresses, the cave . . . into the tissue of [his] dream," the speaker is effectively rehabilitating the model, reconstructing its landscape, and redefining the moral significance of the relationships within it. While his visions contain plenty of violence, guilt, and repulsion, surprisingly little of it attaches to him.[20] When he first swoons upon learning of Cadrilla's love for Lionel, it is Lionel whose image appears more horrible than "some lothly ghastful brow, / Half-bursten from the shroud" (*Poems*, I, 354n; 1832). When Lionel "shrank and howled" at the speaker's declaration of love during the first vision, it is again he who appears grotesque. When the speaker clasps Cadrilla in the second vision, he implies that it is she who shrinks into a skeleton within his embrace. Finally, when the pensive speaker joins the funeral-wedding procession in the third vision, it is they who indulge in the Bacchanalian rout. The newly risen Cadrilla, "my sister and my cousin, and my love," offers this love in a very ambiguous gesture: "One hand she reached to those that came behind" (III, 48). And the speaker fails to win her less out of shame or guilt than out of culpable indecision: "And while I mused nor yet endured to take / So rich a prize, the man who stood with me / Stept gaily forward" (III, 49–51).[21]

Through his reticent detachment, this mediator seems to be consolidating his powers to confront an Other which Tennyson feared even more than feminine sexuality or natural flux: the ultimate loss of death.[22] When the speaker swoons, first after Cadrilla's initial confession and again after their visionary embrace, he seems himself threatened by death. Each of the three visions, moreover, also portrays her as either dead or in the process of dying. Yet within all these visions, the same Cadrilla who had once appeared completely alien now appears a victim, perhaps a fellow victim, of a power alien to them both. The strength of this newly redefined bond may, in its turn, enable the speaker to rescue her from her new bondage. Together these visions build toward a climax like the Boccaccio tale with which Tennyson concluded his 1870 revision.

The failure of this conclusion in "The Golden Supper" has led many critics to interpret the whole Boccaccio story as an afterthought. They point out, first, the many discrepancies between the two openings and, second, the lack of evidence within Tennyson's fragment for Boccaccio's conclusion.[23] There is, however, both internal and external evidence that Tennyson had the Boccaccio story at least in the back of his mind early in the poem's composition. Culler (p. 257n) quotes Tennyson's manuscript note to the 1832 edition suggesting Boccaccio as a possible conclusion. A continuation of part I in Trinity Notebook 18 brings the speaker, full of foreboding, back to the cave where Cadrilla had forsaken him (*Poems*, III, 580–83, ll. 135–49). And Short, while she rejects it as an early source, quotes a fragmentary draft (p. 79) which certainly sounds like the laments of one who has brought his beloved back to life only to lose her to another:

> -! O sav'd yet lost & I
> -en. Have I not
> the skeleton's embrace?
> arm was round thee thrown
> -shrouded jaw was prop'd
> -th? Did I not pluck thee back
> -known land, the valley of dreams
> -ness of the inner tomb
> -ded locks of charnel damps
> -hat exquisite brow

An unpublished stub one page later offers further graveyard imagery:

> -e even one w^d wreathe
> -s blooms for one
> leapt into the crimson dust
> -? It were all too vain
> the stirless eye
> of its thanks—unless
> -, blood forsaken lips
> —to bliss—[24]

Tennyson's speaker, now grown confident of his integrity and his powers, could enter the beloved's tomb, perhaps in the cave they had visited together, and snatch her back from the combined forces of death and petty social restrictions.

That Tennyson may have intended such a confrontation is suggested by these fragmentary drafts. That he never completed it, at least to his satisfaction, may suggest that he could not translate such visionary daring into factual license. Yet this omission may also suggest his discovery that he did not need such a translation in the first place. One of the unused fragments from notebook 8, perhaps again from a scene in her sepulcher, seems to grant an immortality to her image and through it to the speaker as well:

> Fair face! fair form, sole [?sad? *deleted*] tenant of a brain
> Peopled with griefs whose blackness cannot mar
> Your lustre. . . .
> Intense Idea; though I close the lids
> Of mental vision on thee thou dost burn
> As sunlight, through them: Slumber is no veil
> For thou art up and broad awake in dreams,
> O deeply loved: yet like a cruel foe
> Fast-centred in the heart thou hast undone
> Which must exist for ever. Can it lose
> Thy presence, when this head is low in dust?
>
> (ll. 1–3, 9–16)[25]

In such a context, Cadrilla's physical revival may be unnecessary, may even be anticlimactic. All his visions, in fact, move through death to some form of resurrection. Even before the later-added part 3, Tennyson gives hints of this resurrection in the sheer number of the visions. Death never robs the mediating speaker of his will and ability to recreate himself and his beloved for one more confrontation with the Other, one more chance to prove themselves ultimately superior in the very fecundity of their imaginative powers.[26]

Yet their superiority, like that of Mariana, remains primarily imaginative. While not trapped within the authorial presence, they win their dramatic autonomy by drawing power from it. Armed with this power, they can rediscover or recreate an opposable Other from within its own geographical domain. In his proliferating visions, this speaker continually dissolves both this domain and the narrative dilemmas within which it seems to have trapped him. Mariana, on the other hand, establishes within it a sanctuary much like the vatic poet's mountain in "Armageddon" or the Magus' magic circle surrounded by "the glassy arch" of the hostile ocean. Tennyson signals his appreciation of these strategies by returning to them throughout the 1832 volume.

CHAPTER THREE

The 1832 Volume

According to the traditional interpretation of the 1832 poems, Tennyson used art as an escape from the pressures of his society: he created characters distanced enough to keep him from being accused of vicariously identifying with them, and then he placed them in settings distanced enough from Victorian England that they could indulge their aesthetic impulses in safety.[1] The scenario itself is irrefutable. These intensely aesthetic figures do in fact inhabit a series of mystical lands in the West. I would question only the supposed distance between these characters and their settings on the one hand and that between Tennyson and his own psychological landscape on the other. I would argue instead that these settings recreate on their own terms the same threatening outer world that Tennyson was supposedly trying to escape. The characters themselves seem to me outgrowths of the figures who mediated between Tennyson and the domain of the Other within *The Lover's Tale* and the 1830 volume.

As we saw there, such figures created various dilemmas for the authorial presence: if they achieved rapport with this domain, like the Spirit haunting the year's last hours, they threatened him with decay, death, and oblivion; if they remained true to him, they were left equally alienated, equally powerless. Two of these projections, however, offered different but oddly compatible strategies for confronting both this world and the Other who inhabited it. One of these, Mariana, exploited her centered position to distance Tennyson from this world. By creating later mediators as artists capable of erecting their own imaginative defenses, Tennyson in his turn can empower them to reshape an otherwise alien landscape into concentric circles, from within which the Other can be localized and personified. As Tucker puts it (p. 126), "The once-embowered Tennysonian self has by 1832 become self-embowering."[2] Their defense, moreover, does not need to be another mediating figure. It more often stands as some aesthetic structure shielding them from a now-localized threat. If this threat nevertheless overwhelms them, they can emulate the second of these projections, the speaker of *The Lover's Tale*; by shifting the conflict to a new setting, they can win an ethical, aesthetic, though often pyrrhic victory.

Although Tennyson maintains the same strategy within both the 1832 poems and their 1842 revisions, at first he hedges it in ways that critics ever since have found disconcerting. In 1832 he gives so many privileged qualities to his mediators that he cannot resist pulling them back out of their fictional contexts, signaling to us that those same qualities are safe from the fate that threatens the mediator him- or (more often) herself. When his 1832 Iphigenia described her death scene as "One drew a sharp knife through my tender throat / Slowly,—and nothing more" (in place of ll. 115–16), it prompted J. W. Croker's famous rejoinder, "One might indeed ask, '*What more*' she would have?" (*Poems*, I, 486n). The "more" that Tennyson wants, I think, is the perpetual and very personal possession of this embodiment of his own victimized psyche. By giving up this line, along with countless others in the 1842 revisions, Tennyson recreates his mediators as both more limited and more autonomous—limited because they carry only the imaginative powers they need for their particular mission; autonomous because they are allowed to carry the mission out to an end which may end them as figures but which reshapes their landscape and their narrative.

"The Palace of Art"

The most material, most grandly built, yet most vulnerable of these structures is the Palace of Art. It supposedly arises within—and through its own art portrays—a fairy-tale land set at double remove from reality. Yet the palace cannot itself constitute the aesthetic bulwark, if only because the art it displays is haunted by both male and female embodiments of the Other.[3] Surrounding the dais hang paintings of the teachers and poets (including a grimly smiling Dante) against whom the young Tennyson has had to measure himself. All the openings, moreover, reveal sweeping landscapes suggestive of the impersonal, leveling nature at the other pole of Tennyson's universe. Though a few of these landscapes, like that of the English cottage, are habitable, most present "scornful crags," an arid "tract of sand," an "iron coast with windy waves," or "an endless plain" brooded over by thunder. The astronomical speculations included in the notes to the 1832 version add to this spatial vastness an even more threatening temporal flux:

> Regions of lucid matter taking forms,
>   Brushes of fire, hazy gleams,
> Clusters and beds of worlds, and bee-like swarms
>   Of suns, and starry streams.[4]

For all this profusion, what actually accomplishes the Soul's downfall remains far from clear. In 1832 her blasphemous speech occurs not immediately before her fall but much earlier. She is, to be sure, guilty here of a Keatsian sensuousness:

> My vainglorious, gorgeous soul
> Sat throned between the shining oriels,
>   In pomp beyond control;
>
> With piles of flavourous fruits in basket-twine
>   Of gold, upheaped, crushing down
> Muskscented blooms—all taste—grape, gourd or pine—
>   In bunch, or singlegrown. . . .
>
> (between ll. 181–83; 1832)

But it is her "pomp beyond control" which brings her structure crashing down of its own imaginative weight, a weight for which her author seems at least equally responsible: "If the Poem were not already too long, I should have inserted in the text the following stanzas . . ." (*Poems*, I, 450n).

When Croker mocked this "ingenious device . . . for reconciling the rigour of criticism with the indulgence of parental partiality" (*Poems*, I, 450–51n), he unwittingly pointed up Tennyson's relationship not just to his poem but with its heroine. He thus anticipated Tucker's judgment (p. 118) that the "patient soliciting our attention . . . is not the aristocratic aesthete languishing in her palace but the aesthetically torn bourgeois poet who created her." As Tennyson continually invites her back into his own psyche, so he continually invites himself into her palace, loading every rift in it with the ore of his own ostentatiously eclectic imagination. As Shaw puts it (p. 57), "Each element of sublimity—the darkness, the largeness, and the light—is given so much elaboration that instead of being finely faceted . . . it congeals into one general lump." At the end Tennyson leaves the palace so cluttered that his mediator cannot focus on the alien presences within it.

In 1842, spare and symmetrical, the palace reflects in this very order the Soul's artistic power to neutralize the forbidding extremes within it. Shaw complains (p. 57) that "pictures are switched on for a few seconds, then switched off." F. E. L. Priestley, after describing the whole palace (p. 40) as "a carefully constructed isolation ward," goes on to argue that the soul's art fails because she refuses to use it.[5] In fact, however, she is constantly using it in a manipulative but highly effective way. Within her inner sanctuary she is able to reduce the whole tragedy of human social history to a decorative pattern of mutual contradictions:

> The people here, a beast of burden slow,
>   Toiled onward, pricked with goads and stings;
> Here played, a tiger, rolling to and fro
>   The heads and crowns of kings;
>
> Here rose an athlete, strong to break or bind
>   All force in bonds that might endure,
> And here once more like some sick man declined,
>   And trusted any cure.
>
> (ll. 149–56)

These techniques, having triumphed over the universe, evolution, and social change, also neutralize the equally threatening god figures. Plato can be played off against Bacon, Milton against Shakespeare, Dante against Homer, St. Cecilia against Islamic houris, Indian Cama riding on a boat against Europa riding on her bull. To quote Albright (p. 38), Christianity is "demoted to one of . . . several mythologies . . . , chiefly decorative, soothing, an illustration from a child's Bible." Even more effectively, however, these gods, saints, and heroes are frozen by art in a moment of sleep or death (as with Cecilia, the Islamite, and Arthur) or in one of harmless potential (as with Cama, Europa, and Ganymede). The "Maid-mother by a crucifix . . . babe in arm" embodies both aspects of this technique, escaping any challenge from Jesus' teachings in this conflation of his birth and death.[6]

By fragmentation, juxtaposition, stagnation, the Soul has effectively stymied the varied manifestations of the Other. Why then does she fail, and why does Tennyson seem to acquiesce in her failure? Perhaps it is because her aesthetic techniques have produced unaesthetic results; to paraphrase William Cadbury, they have turned the poem itself into a dreary gallery.[7] Hence what nearly destroys her helps redeem the poem; time and change force her to participate metaphorically in scenes like those she has tried to enclose within her palace. The comparison of the Soul to "a traveller walking slow, / In doubt and great perplexity / A little before the moon-rise" (ll. 277–79), echoes the landscape which

> seemed all dark and red—a tract of sand,
>   And some one pacing there alone,
> Who paced for ever in a glimmering land,
>   Lit with a low large moon.
>
> (ll. 65–68)[8]

Yet perhaps she has simply succeeded too well, not just in neutralizing the Other, but in claiming kin with it. In 1842 Tennyson first moves her own claims of godlike indifference to a climactic position where they complete her fragmentation of the Other. Then, in expanding these claims, he makes her reduce a normally dangerous divine immanence to sheer absurdity: Jesus' mission is no longer to the man in Matthew 8 possessed of devils; it is now to the swine into which he exorcised them:

> They graze and wallow, breed and sleep;
>   And oft some brainless devil enters in,
>   And drives them to the deep.
>
> (ll. 202–4)

She, in contrast, has so domesticated the Other that she now includes herself as another of its manifestations: "O silent faces of the Great and Wise, / My Gods, with whom I dwell!" (ll. 195–96). When she is surprised by "white-eyed phantasms . . . And hollow shades enclosing hearts of flame" (ll. 239, 241), she now recapitulates the pattern of "Timbuctoo," where the speaker's imaginative manipulation of God and Devil provoked the disturbing arrival of "keen *Discovery*."

"The Lotos-Eaters"

Unlike the Soul, who fails in her attempt to remain "apart from place, withholding time," an even more unlikely group of mediators succeed through their sophisticated handling of both these categories. The Lotos-Eaters do not even speak until the frame has set them at the outer limits of the Homeric world, sheltered from nineteenth-century English reality. Through the allegorical overtones of the Spenserian stanzas, however, their lethargy seems not an interruption of Odysseus' quest but another tempta-tion blocking progress to the land of the Faerie Queene.[9] For Douglas Bush, the choric song which makes up the body of their poem represents a further debasement of Homeric myth: "These singers who sit down on the shore and melodiously interweave the most delicate observations of nature with the most delicate analysis of modern ennui, these are not a band of tough, hairy, brine-stained Greek mariners eager for food and drink, but an operatic chorus, or at any rate a chorus of college-bred poets."[10] Yet as Kincaid observes (p. 40), "It is a strange fellowship, but one that is difficult to deny." Other studies find them more sympathetic in the 1832 poem; for Alan Grob the 1842 revision of these lines "effectively destroy[s] all sympathy with the lotos-eaters, who regard their own behavior as imitation of the gods."[11]

While I would agree that Tennyson grows more ambivalent toward these mediators during his revisions, I think this ambivalence itself grows out of their increasing imaginative autonomy. As Shaw claims (p. 67), "The mariners' analytical intelligence is constantly at work," and it works harder with each revision. Paralleling the frequently noted pendulum movements between their island and their home,[12] another, more complex movement evaluates both places with ever greater philosophical precision. Yet both movements grow clear only in the final version. Stanzas 1 and 2 contrast island and home only as rest versus work; stanzas 3 and 4 contrast them as a life cycle of fulfillment versus one of hopeless war with transience. Here the earliest manuscript draft ends.[13] In 1832 stanza 5 presents the island as a set of human relationships recreated from the past, but only in 1842 does the newly added stanza 6 present a contrasting vision of domestic relationships threatened by the future.

In each of these comparisons, the Mariners allow themselves a progressively clearer vision of the homeland. What was only "sharp distress" in stanza 2, for example, becomes a prediction of nightmarish alienation:

> surely now our household hearths are cold:
> Our sons inherit us: our looks are strange:
> And we should come like ghosts to trouble joy.
>
> (ll. 117–19)

From this perspective they can envision themselves being forced to assume the role of the Other, to imitate the aggressively sexual Dis invading the sanctuaries of Tennyson's other artists.

In each comparison, however, they can counter such visions with an increasingly active synthesis of their increasingly passive existence. In stanza 1 they find the island landscape an amalgam of high granite walls and deep moss linked only by music; in stanza 3 they find it an amalgam of birth and death linked only by peace. In stanza 5 they replace the here and now with the long ago and far away; in stanza 7 they slow the natural movement of this landscape into rhythmic measure with their drugged perception. In the opening of stanza 8, a passage common to both printed versions, they not only see the landscape through lotos, they transform it into lotos: "Through every hollow cave and alley lone / Round and round the spicy downs the yellow Lotos-dust is blown" (ll. 148–49).

Thus the gradually accumulating stanzas build for the Mariners' island a mythic integrity of its own. Their position beyond the realms of time, space, and human meaning gradually shifts to one of central importance, an importance not just assumed, like that of the Soul, but earned. With the final addition of the revised stanza 8, their fear of turning into the Other suddenly turns itself into a desire. In curious fulfillment of Eve's fatal wish, the eating of this sacred fruit grants the Mariners a close though carefully undefined identification with the Lucretian gods, usually Tennyson's symbol of alienated divinity. This identification in turn transforms the out-of-the-way, dangerous little island into a central, transcendent, invulnerable heaven where they can lie "on the hills like Gods together, careless of mankind" (l. 155). They have found the kind of sanctuary which the Soul had to build. This same identification transforms the few hours before Homer has them dragged back to their ships into an eternity.[14] They have already moved beyond a grudging acceptance of natural process to an ability to "live again in memory, / With those old faces of our infancy" (ll. 110–11). Now, at the end, they possess the divine calm ordinarily granted only to those who "in Elysian valleys dwell, / Resting weary limbs on beds of asphodel" (ll. 169–70).

The callousness which Grob, Hughes, and many others have found in this passage may reflect Tennyson's own annoyance to find them lying "beside their nectar" much like those distant, disinterested, throned figures from the 1830 volume. In this shift of allegiance, however, the Mariners are only following the example set by the Spirit haunting the year's last hours. And just as he did there, Tennyson has again relinquished even rhetorical control over his creations. By so carefully constructing the ground of their physical and moral landscape, he has literally ceded to them the ground on which he might have criticized them. They are, after all, simply living out the escape which he had planned for himself.

"The Hesperides"

That "The Hesperides" is a companion poem to "The Lotos-Eaters" is suggested by their juxtaposition in the 1832 volume. At first glance, however, the relation seems all contrast. While the Mariners sink into lethargy, the Sisters exhort one another to continue their dance:[15]

> If you sing not, if you make false measure,
> We shall lose eternal pleasure,
> Worth eternal want of rest.
>
> (ll. 23–25)

While the Mariners obtain gradually clearer visions of their lost homes, the Sisters strive to keep their threat only a vague possibility: "Guard the apple night and day, / Lest one from the East come and take it away" (ll. 41–42). While the Mariners are reinterpreting the Fall by continuing to eat the lotos, the Sisters are attempting to frustrate it by withholding their golden apples,[16]

> Lest the old wound of the world be healed,
> The glory unsealed,
> The golden apple stolen away,
> And the ancient secret revealed.
>
> (ll. 69–72)

Yet these contrasts, I would argue, are but different means to the same end, the protection of their sanctuary against the Other. We know the Other here as Hercules. We also know, as Christine Gallant argues, that this representative of the male, forward-looking, Olympian gods will break up the female, chthonic, cyclical rhythm which the Sisters have sworn to preserve.[17] But that is our myth; the Sisters are trying to write their own version. Harold Bloom describes them "as poets and as performers, as weavers of an enchantment so sinuous as to block all questers from fulfillment in an earthly paradise."[18] While they realize that out there, "kingdoms lapse, and climates change, and races die" (l. 45), like the Mariners they hope to frustrate the narrative basis of myth by reducing their own situation to stasis.[19] Joseph characterizes the poem (p. 133) as universal change counterpoised against divine immobility. Yet as divinities the Sisters do not rank very high in anyone's pantheon; hence their appeal to some even less efficacious mediators may only echo the appeal of the priestess to her idol in "Timbuctoo."

Matthew Rowlinson suggests that the Sisters create this stasis by creating a naturalized language which displaces "anxiety away from . . . the song and garden of the Hesperides and onto a world at large against which the song is specifically a defense."[20] They control this "world at large"—and Hercules in particular—by giving spatial shape and extension to a vision which other critics have too quickly relegated to the psyche.[21] I would question only the term "naturalized." The undeniable power of their incantation comes not from nature—taken in any sense—but from art, even from the deliberately artificial. A better word for their language would be performative: "They find themselves in their function, and in the mythmaking climate of this poem for them to sing a song about a tree is to bring the tree into being as they form around it."[22] As their dance embodies their song, they so lose themselves in the dance that they, song, and dance together create the same symbolic integrity that concludes Yeats's "Among School Children."

Their movement away from public mythology is thus a movement into some of the sources of myth itself. As Ricks points out (*Poems*, I, 462), the later classical authors and their English editors had already revised this curious tale into realism. For them the golden apples were only the island's flocks, the song a means of guarding these flocks from beasts of prey, and the dragon a protective arm of the sea. To distance his account from such rationalizing, Tennyson distances his setting from the known classical world. An ancient explorer, at the farthest reaches of the African coast, hears disembodied voices which even to him sound like "voices in a dream."[23]

Because the dream was in fact Tennyson's own, he could offer the guardians of his sanctuary some of his own magic. This same device, as we will continue to see, vitiated many of the original 1832 poems. This poem lost even the benefits of revision since Tennyson abandoned it until his son asked for its return. He saved its speakers from the self-conscious prettiness of his other 1832 heroines only by giving them some of his darker qualities. Day may argue (p. 20) that "far from sympathizing with the powers of the Garden, and far from expressing a desire to retreat from purposive moral activity, Tennyson [was] recording anger and moral outrage."[24] Yet as the Lotos-Eaters were "brother mariners," so these singers are sisters—to one another and to him. If Tennyson found a comforting explanation for his own antisocial drives in the black blood of his family, he could also band with these three against the eastern, civilized world.

Together they can all project a secondary mediator, one which appeared both fascinating and taboo in Tennyson's early poetry. In "Armageddon," towering over the "dark pavilions" ranged against "the Lord God,"

a mighty snake
Twined his black folds, the while his ardent crest
And glossy neck were swaying to and fro.

(I, 140–42)

The serpents of 1830, besides their obvious equation with sexual aggression, often strangled the self in solipsism. Yet now that the earlier god figure has monopolized the role of Other, the "redcombed dragon" becomes a valuable ally. Instead of crushing the authorial presence, this dragon protects its sanctuary; it surrounds and guards the tree and its apples, and is in turn surrounded and guarded by the Sisters. Against the threatening figure of Hercules, they have set up their own comfortably fixed but impressively positioned idol. The priestess, investing her lifeless statue with the light of her own "phantasy," may seem an object of pity. The Sisters' fantasy, on the other hand, seems powerful enough to set up their idol as the magical center around which the whole western landscape revolves. From this center they can confront civilization and Hercules on equal terms.

"Fatima"

Fatima belongs to a different story and a different tradition than either "The Hesperides" or "The Lotos-Eaters." As the foster child of Sappho and of Savary's exotic impressions of the Near East,[25] she appears in two distinct genres within the young Tennyson's canon. She becomes, on the one hand, another of the 1830 feminine portraits which Tennyson elaborated for the 1832 lyrics to Eleanore, Rosalind, Margaret, and Kate. Like them the object of bemused authorial speculation, she is freed from both the classical decorum of the Three Sisters and the Victorian propriety imposed on the Miller's Daughter.

Yet she does possess her own voice and the merest hint of a story line, a hint which Tennyson develops in his 1842 description of her frustrations during the previous night. With this plot Fatima also joins the group of forsaken women reliving the plight of Mariana. As such she can use language and only language to urge on a story which has lapsed into stasis. From the parallel in Savary, we know that she may be waiting indefinitely for a lover who dares not come for fear of her husband. She controls this situation, not by establishing her own identity as did Mariana, but by recreating that of her lover. By equating him with the sun and by invoking that equation with incantatory intensity, she redefines the sunrise as the arrival of the lover himself.

Creating the metaphor, however, is easier than dealing with it. The 1833 fragment "Semele" gives a glowing account of Zeus's epiphany from the perspective of a cinder.[26] Like her, Fatima also puts herself in danger of encountering one of Tennyson's most threatening embodiments of the Other. Its very immanence during the preceding night made her crush the gentler symbols of fertility and so reduce the whole landscape to a "long desert in the south." The mere mention of the lover's name turned night into the withering brilliance of day: "A thousand little shafts of flame / Werc shivered in my narrow frame" (ll. 17–18). As the poem moves from night to morning, Fatima's initial equation becomes so literal that instead of the lover's acquiring the power of the sun, the sun itself seems to be preparing for a violent sexual assault:

> And from beyond the noon a fire
> Is poured upon the hills, and nigher
> The skies stoop down in their desire.
>
> (ll. 30–32)

Meanwhile, however, Fatima has borrowed Tennyson's power of embodying passion within the landscape to reshape her own self-image. Changing from withered leaf to passive receptacle drained of her own soul, to moon "dazzled" at the approach of day, she finally meets the challenge actively:

> And, isled in sudden seas of light,
> My heart, pierced through with fierce delight,
> Bursts into blossom at his sight.
>
> (ll. 33–35)

As Tucker points out (p. 151), "Fatima's increasing personification of her beloved in his otherness converges with a rapidly burgeoning sense of personal identity." From an insignificant victim of the Other, she becomes herself the central object of his cosmic desire. This apotheosis at first daunts her:

> My whole soul waiting silently,
> All naked in a sultry sky,
> Droops blinded with his shining eye.
>
> (ll. 36–38)

But her love, buttressed by her own creativity, lets her change her image once again to the one who possesses; she "can reciprocate the godlike overture with her own fierce rejoinder"; "she *is* also that fire, that sun poised in the sky, subject and object all at once."[27] In this role she perceives physical death as indistinguishable from sexual fulfillment:

> I will grow round him in his place,
> Grow, live, die looking on his face,
> Die, dying clasped in his embrace.
>
> (ll. 40–42)

"Mariana in the South"

While all these successful figures may seem likely mediators for Tennyson, we now have to consider the more difficult cases to be made for the apparent failures. Mariana in the South, for instance, never achieves even Fatima's metaphoric union with her beloved. The blinding heat which Fatima reinterprets as desire remains for Mariana an image of sterile alienation: "And all the furnace of the light / Struck up against the blinding wall" (ll. 55–56).

In 1832 Tennyson rescues her from her predicament, but only to cast her in an equally uncomfortable role. He has to keep at least the illusion of distance between himself and some of his more dubious mediators: the Soul playing God, the Mariners on their journey toward addiction, the Three Sisters denying the world salvation, Fatima achieving a cosmic consummation. Mariana in the South, however, remains the passive but intensely sexual object, not of her lover or her story, but of her poem and her poet:

> She praying disarrayed and warm
> From slumber, deep her wavy form
> In the darklustrous mirror shone.
>
> (in place of ll. 30–32; 1832)

The mirror here, reflecting her image back into the authorial psyche, simply reverses the Lover's narcissistic attempt to project Cadrilla as the emanation of his own passion. But this lyric offers no narrative check on such manipulation. Where Fatima rendered erotic the cycle of day and night, Mariana actually subverts this same cycle. The sterile noon is made fertile by the dream of her youth, and the dark night is made luminous by the divine acceptance of her prayer: "the rise / Of moonlight . . . streamed / On her white arm" (in place of ll. 89–96; 1832). Because her figure virtually negates her situation and her story, her poem, instead of portraying her failure, becomes her principal justification.

In 1842, perhaps embarrassed by this imaginative incest, Tennyson not only returns her to her dramatic predicament but implicitly denies the very basis of his involvement.[28] By giving her real letters from a real lover, he can vicariously dismiss her erotic power:

> An image seemed to pass the door,
>   To look at her with slight, and say
>   "But now thy beauty flows away,
> So be alone for evermore."
>
> (ll. 65–68)

This same skeletal plot, however, also offers her a hope of transcending her plight when still another image tells her, "Thou shalt be alone no more" (l. 77). Tucker (p. 144) finds the image "reluctan[t] to specify either sex or death as Mariana's place of rest." But by flinging back the lattice to watch the approaching night, she seems to accept the offer in all its ambiguity: "The night comes on that knows not morn, / When I shall cease to be all alone" (ll. 94–95).[29]

As a response this cannot count for much, but we cannot count on this Mariana for much more. Priestley has pointed out (pp. 52–54) that Tennyson has reshaped the bleak setting as a reflection of her perceiving eye; hence it would be tempting to claim the "images" themselves as her distillation of this setting. Yet in his very attempt to naturalize the refrain, Tennyson subverts her power and perhaps the whole poem. The balladlike rigidity of "He cometh not," as Boyd and Williams argue, freed the first Mariana to inhabit the whole of her—and her poet's—creation. This Mariana, by contrast, seems confined not just to "the South" or to her house but to the end of each stanza, frantically manipulating her supposedly inarticulate moans to match each new role that Tennyson brings to her.

"Oenone"

Oenone eventually transforms her art into an escape rather than a trap, but art is neither her first expedient nor her last. Her mediating power, moreover, comes from no single one of these expedients so much as from an imaginative flexibility like that shown by the hallucinating speaker in *The Lover's Tale.* In fact as her sanctuary lies breached and scarred by successive violations, so her entire poem resembles an archeological site preserving successive strata of mutually destructive mediation.

Oenone is not locked up in a Palace of Art or Moated Grange; nor is she enisled in the Hesperides. Hence we may forget that her first and primal sanctuary is nature itself. Several critics have interpreted what Ricks tactfully calls the poem's "love landscapes" (*Tennyson*, p. 87) as projections of the female body, but their evident eroticism is played off against the cold sterility of "topmost Gargaros" and the hot turbulence of the plains of Troy below. Only by singing from a glen halfway between these extremes, as from the island sanctuaries of the other mediators, can Oenone clothe herself with both natural innocence and human passion. In 1832 Tennyson captures both qualities within the cave to which Paris consigns her:

> Within the green hillside,
> Under yon whispering tuft of oldest pine,
> Is an ingoing grotto, strown with spar
> And ivymatted at the mouth. . . .
> (in place of ll. 71–87; 1832)[30]

This setting, however, shields his mediator from her story much as a similar cave permitted the Lover to lose himself in visions. In 1842 Tennyson lets Oenone encounter her lover in the open: "I sat alone: white-breasted like a star / Fronting the dawn he moved" (ll. 56–57).

The course of the poem, however, portrays the transformation of Paris from lover to one of the many male aggressors in this volume. In 1832 he even suspects that his judgment "may breed . . . sere / Heartburning toward hallowed Ilion" (between ll. 71–87), but in 1842 Tennyson omits this passage and reworks the whole judgment scene as a joint quest for some comprehensible etiology for war.[31] As Paris personifies a larger and less comprehensible world for Oenone, so do the goddesses for him, and so does the mysterious Eris, goddess of strife, for them. Since their proffered gifts encompass the principal motives for war, the goddesses offer Paris the power to localize and appropriate different manifestations of the Other: Herè offers the same power the Mariners coveted in the Lucretian gods,

> who have attained
> Rest in a happy place and quiet seats
> Above the thunder, with undying bliss
> In knowledge of their own supremacy.
> (ll. 128–31)

In the 1832 version, Pallas' offer of wisdom models the human will on the enthroned figure of God in Tennyson's early poetry: "the dark body of the Sun robed round / With his own ever-emanating lights" (in place of ll. 150–

64; 1832). In offering Helen, Aphrodite offers Amoret—and since that fig-ure also embodied "omnipotent Love," she ultimately offers herself.

All these offers, however, are made to Paris; in fact his mediating power grows from his willingness to side with the Other against Oenone.[32] Her sanctuary is raped by the war which follows his abduction of Helen; she is deserted; and as a mediator she approaches those impotent authorial projec-tions like Hero from within the 1830 volume. Tennyson can identify more closely with her than with the Sisters hoarding their apples or with the Mar-iners renouncing their social obligations. Yet can he find a way to project the identification itself?

What he finds is a way to speak through her, not just as victim but as poet. Where the Mariners used choric song and the Sisters choric dance, Oenone uses prayer: "Dear mother Ida, harken ere I die." Prayer to a now-violated spirit of place may seem pathetically ineffectual, but Oenone is praying not for reparation but for a memorial to pathos itself. Tennyson's act of writing the poem becomes her act of "build[ing] up my sorrow with my song," re-capitulating her loss in order to gain some control over it. This goal helps account for the self-consciousness Douglas Bush found in the poem: "We wonder how many pipes he smoked over these delicately contrived embroid-eries of phrase and rhythm, which constantly call attention to their beauty" (p. 204). This sense of interminable delay belongs less, I think, to the pro-cess of composition than to the lines themselves. Although he sees her strat-egy as an evasion, Tucker observes (p. 160) that Oenone is "distanc[ing] herself from the painful narrative facts by idling over a prolonged and irrele-vant introduction."[33] As with the songs of the Mariners and the Three Sis-ters, these lines are intended to reduce action to a stasis of expectation: "and all my heart / Went forth to embrace him coming ere he came" (ll. 61–62).[34]

In one sense, of course, she cannot stop time or the loss that it brings; she sings only "that, while I speak of it, a little while / My heart may wander from its deeper woe" (ll. 42–43). There seems, at this point, only one stasis available to her: "O death, death, death, thou ever-floating cloud, . . . shadow all my soul, that I may die" (ll. 234, 238). Yet here, as Tucker puts it (p. 163), "The judgment of Oenone now recapitulates and supersedes the Judgment of Paris"; her refrain suddenly changes from the plea, "harken ere I die," to the assertion, "I will not die alone."[35] Her growing awareness of her verbal powers has suggested a new goal and a new identity. If the coming war has wasted her once-beautiful sanctuary, she can change roles simply by identifying herself with its new desolation. In Tennyson's source for the poem, the Oenone of Ovid's *Heroides* avenged her loss in petty slander. Tennyson's heroine turns to one of Ovid's more authentically mythic alternatives, metamorphosis. If Paris could ally himself with the Other by appropriating the motives for war, she can ally herself with it by personifying war's effects: "Wheresoe'er I am by night and day, / All earth and air seem only burning fire."[36]

"The Lady of Shalott"

Oenone, whatever role she assumed, stood at the narrative center of her poem. The far more stationary Lady of Shalott controls only the focus of her poem, not its point of view. Ricks observes (*Tennyson*, pp. 79–80) that each section ends with a human voice. Within each of these sections, a shadowy authorial presence confronts his subject from a specific physical and psychological perspective. At the end of each section, the voice of one of his own creations forces him to a new perspective, from which he must reinterpret the central action of the Lady herself.

At the beginning, separate from both the island and the river, his perspective merges with that of the reapers until their cry, "'Tis the fairy," moves him into an imaginative identification with her. In part 2, however, his hovering presence moves with her own psyche beyond the mirror of her art and back toward the world it seems to promise. Her partial renunciation, "I am half sick of shadows" (l. 71), urges him out to search for the embodiment of her desires. Lancelot, as has frequently been noted, replaces the Lady as the concluding rhyme word of stanza 13, but his image has already "flashed into the crystal mirror" (l. 106), and the narrative voice follows it back into her chamber to witness her self-condemnation: "The curse has come upon me" (l. 116). He has been drawn into psychological identification with the Lady; he has sympathetically explored her desires; now, while following her physically through a land stripped of her illusions, he needs to sacrifice this mediator by sending her off on her one-way journey toward death.

At this point in the 1832 poem, however, the details of her dress suggest that Tennyson has taken her out of her story and into his own fantasy world:

> A cloudwhite crown of pearl she dight.
> All raimented in snowy white

> That loosely flew, (her zone in sight,
> Clasped with one blinding diamond bright.)
>
> (between ll. 126–27; 1832)

Even near the beginning, when the reapers are speculating about her nature, he has already entered the castle and decked her out with the same erotic devotion he showed to the southern Mariana and the Soul in her palace:

> A pearlgarland winds her head:
> She leaneth on a velvet bed,
> Full royally apparelled. . . .
>
> (in place of ll. 24–26; 1832)

In 1842 he returns her to her story, but only as what Priestley calls (p. 49) "a legend and a voice, unseen, unknown."[37] Defined almost exclusively by negation, she and her island sanctuary exist in a stasis which forbids communication with a landscape determined by the narrowly two-dimensional flux of the river. Even her voice is audible only across the grain of this spatial and temporal flow, only across the fields at those transitional times in the diurnal cycle, dawn and dusk.[38] Conversely, in her own visions of the random daily procession along the river, the Lady defines Camelot as the focus of everything she is not and has not.

Such mutual incomprehension would seem to deny her any possibility of mediation. In fact Ann C. Colley finds her visions limited in their "metonymic" temporal discontinuity,[39] and Albright claims that the Lover's "breaking asunder of his forest life and refashioning it into a private artifice have [with the Lady] elaborated themselves into a cottage industry" (p. 32). Yet her artifice does succeed in distilling the amorphous and unknowable Other of Camelot into churls, damsels, shepherds, knights, lovers—images which she can capture within her web. In one sense she is undone by her artistic success; her brilliant embodiment of the Other within Lancelot shatters her mirror,[40] her means of isolating his predecessors, and brings her literally face to face with her real enemy:

> She saw the water-lily bloom
> She saw the helmet and the plume,
> She looked down to Camelot.
>
> (ll. 111–13)

Driven from her sanctuary, she seems even more vulnerable than the suddenly militant Oenone, yet several critics have seen her final voyage as somehow positive.[41] Flavia M. Alaya, in particular, sees her reborn as artistic statement in her effect on her audience.[42] Here, for once, a mediator has not only carried the battle to the camp of the Other, she has forced the Other to acknowledge her. In one of the Lover's visionary confrontations with his rival, we remember, it was Lionel who "shrank and howled." Here the Lady produces similar consternation: "they crossed themselves for fear, / All the knights of Camelot" (ll. 166–67).

An even more impressive triumph, however, is Lancelot's reaction. He could, by analogy with Paris, be considered another mediator who has deserted the Lady for the Other; yet as her art has won his initial reality, so now the epitaph inspired by her mysterious presence wins him an incipient humanity. Without participating in Tennyson's dangerous identification with the Lady, he cannot hope to understand her.[43] Camelot, the domain of the Other, admits only the physical and the conventionally spiritual: "He said, 'She has a lovely face: / God in his mercy lend her grace.'" (ll. 169–70). Hence his words, like the whole poem, can only define her negatively; they set up two limits between which she must "live and move and have her being." That she could not do so represents her tragedy; that Tennyson could imagine her vividly enough to celebrate her attempt represents his aesthetic and psychological triumph.

"A Dream of Fair Women"

Perhaps encouraged by the artistic, though pyrrhic, success of the Lady of Shalott, Tennyson began the 1832 "Dream of Fair Women" by identifying himself with the speaker and taking art as his mediator. He even compares the aesthetic invulnerability of the poet to that of a man in a balloon. Memory, however, responds with a company of actual poets much like the intimidating list portrayed by the Soul in her Palace of Art. When this list narrows to an encounter with Chaucer's *Legend of Good Women*, any symptoms of Bloom's anxiety of influence are reinforced by the earlier work's assault on the most vulnerable recesses of Tennyson's psyche. At first he appropriates Chaucer's own aesthetic invulnerability ("the knowledge of his art / Held me above his subject"), but soon he is drawn into the domain of this fictive Other. Within this landscape his 1832 sanctuaries—castles, shrines, vaults, seraglios—are being breached by male violence, and the mediators who inhabit them are being violated and abducted.

Caught between wake and sleep, he first tries to address this horror but then reverts to force:

> And once my arm was lifted to hew down
> A cavalier from off his saddle-bow,
> That bore a lady from a leaguered town.
>
> (ll. 45–47)

Yet such ritual defiance only disguises the similarity between this retreat and the Magus' progression from confrontation into frightened passivity. As these "fancies" are "rounded, smoothed, and brought / Into the gulfs of sleep" (ll. 51–52), sleep itself appears a figure for the defensive introspection which characterized 1830 lyrics like "The Poet's Mind." In this poem, however, sleep works more like the speaker's visionary states within *The Lover's Tale*. It moves the poet to a new, still more secure sanctuary and introduces him to new, still more powerful mediators. Like the Lover, he can now continue the struggle on his own turf and on his own terms.

Even this struggle presents dangers: for the first time he must share his sanctuary with these dream women, and the women, for their part, seem less mediators than embodiments of the Other like Amoret. Yet because the pre-dawn woods ensure an almost pre-oedipal innocence,[44] his inner voice grants him the power to reinterpret adolescent sexual threats as very different childhood traumas. As the Lover transformed Cadrilla from Other into victim of death, so Tennyson discovers that all these figures have been brought to their deaths by some of his own villains: Helen and Cleopatra through male aggression, Iphigenia and Jephtha's Daughter through desertion by a father figure. Their fates still leave them dangerous—now dangerously vulnerable—but assured by his inner voice that "the wood is all thine own," he can wait passively while these apparent victims mediate between him and the forces which they, in death, have successfully overcome.

With this approach Tennyson succeeds in rewriting or, as Bloom would have it, misreading Chaucer, whose *Legend* revels in stories of virtue coming to a bad end. The moral values challenged by the earlier poet Tennyson changes into aesthetic ones. His first view of Helen is of a statue: "At length I saw a lady within call, / Stiller than chiselled marble, standing there" (ll. 85–86). In fact both she and Iphigenia, as purely statuesque victims, seem unlikely mediators. Yet in their stories, as in Oenone's account of her suffering, they carefully position themselves at the center of an elaborately contrived tragic scenario.

The sexual power that Helen has renounced Cleopatra still plays on: "I have no men to govern in this wood: / That makes my only woe" (ll. 135–36). Yet even in life Tennyson's figure has exercised this power, as Albright argues (p. 47), by "describing a love that competes with the natural world, a refuge of passion equal to the refuge of art." Here she can confound temporal progression like the Three Sisters or Oenone; here too she can merge love and death like Fatima: "My mailed Bacchus leapt into my arms, / Contented there to die!" (ll. 151–52). When this sanctuary is violated by that "dull cold-blooded Caesar," she can stage her own death as an elaborate tableau like that of the 1832 Lady of Shalott:

> I died a Queen. The Roman soldier found
>   Me lying dead, my crown about my brows
> A name for ever!—lying robed and crowned,
>   Worthy a Roman spouse.
>
> (ll. 161–64)

Through this speech she shows that composure can transcend violation and even death, that the self can become its own inviolate sanctuary.

The poet's next encounter changes the terms of this mediation but not its results. As Cleopatra has transcended violation and death, so Jephtha's Daughter transcends desertion and death. Like the young Tennyson, she has seen her equation of God and father destroyed when the latter degenerated into an object of disgust and pity. Yet her carefully realized visionary experience allows her to separate the two figures just as the God of her vision "divide[s] the night with flying flame." She can transform her grief into "a solemn scorn of ills," because she can offer her father literal obedience, as had Tennyson, while simultaneously proclaiming her moral and aesthetic autonomy as a divinely elected victim.[45]

Tennyson's response implies that she has brought him to some turning point:

> Losing her carol I stood pensively,
>   As one that from a casement leans his head
> When midnight bells cease ringing suddenly
>   And the old year is dead.
>
> (ll. 245–48)

The verbal echoes of "magic casements . . . in faery lands forlorn" suggest that the bells here function like the verbal bell which wakens Keats in "Ode to a Nightingale."[46] Although Rosamund makes an appearance, Cleopatra's

attacks upon her destroy the artistic integrity of Tennyson's vignettes—and
with them the dream itself. Though he attempts to continue the sequence,
his conscious art fails him by "failing to give the bitter with the sweet"; it fails
to confront the deep traumas that prompted his subconscious reenacting of
the past.[47] Once his mediators have enabled him to overcome these traumas,
such compulsive returns to the past are not only impossible, they are unnecessary.

Overall then, the 1832 poems succeed in their art, and art succeeds in the 1832 poems. The strategies borrowed from "Mariana" on the
one hand and *The Lover's Tale* on the other transform otherwise-sequestered
bowers into either defensive or offensive outposts in Tennyson's ongoing
conflict with the Other. Through his mediators he has overcome natural and
sexual violence, the hostility of a harsh—and the desertion of a loving—
God, even the finality of death. He has so delimited all these forces that both
the outposts and the figures who inform them seem, if not invulnerable, at
least infinitely renewable.

What made him abandon this view was neither the advice of friends nor
the hostile reviews of his poetry, nor even the death of Hallam, but rather the
creation of some disturbing new characters. While St. Simeon and the first
of "The Two Voices" also struggle against outside aggression, they no longer
demurely allow the poet to decide whether and how to identify with them.
Instead they unceremoniously invite themselves into his psyche and use it for
their fortress. That they forced him to reevaluate his earlier strategies is clear
from the new autonomy he granted to his 1832 mediators within his 1842
revisions. Simultaneously, however, he was moving toward an identification
with some very different old men. Like their predecessors, Ulysses,
Tithonus, Tiresias, and Arthur are enclosed by their landscape, but instead
of being enshrined, they are entrapped. Tennyson's new mediators also need
to escape, but instead of escaping from an unknown peril into art, they must
escape from the artificial into the unknown.

CHAPTER FOUR

The 1842 Volume

Perhaps the pithiest evaluation of Tennyson's 1842 volume concludes Ryals' discussion: "The collection is one of the strangest publications ever to come from the mind of man."[1] At one time it may have been singled out as Tennyson's least-qualified triumph, the synthesis of his powers toward which his earlier poetry had pointed and away from which society enticed him with offers of fame, wealth, and laureateship. Examined closely, however, the volume encompasses frantic and diverse experimentations—almost random efforts to escape from the collapse of his earlier synthesis.

Chronologically, the sequence begins with two poems largely completed before Hallam's death, poems which nevertheless reexamine and repudiate the almost solipsistic escape won in the 1832 volume. They in turn prefigure the loss which challenged not just his world-view but the model with which he interpreted it. These same poems also suggest new responses, which Tennyson employs in the narratives and dramatic monologues written immediately thereafter. Yet when Tennyson tries to respond in similar ways to ostensibly public confrontations between aristocratic stasis and lower-class anarchy, his covert involvement transforms them into confrontations with monsters from his own imaginative past. Only when their formal structures reveal the emotional turbulence beneath them do some poems from the late 1830s regain the hard-won integrity of those from the beginning of the decade.

The two poems begun before the fall of 1833, "St. Simeon Stylites" and "The Two Voices," encounter the same two forms of the Other that have threatened Tennyson's poetic landscape from the beginning: a hostile God and a fluid, impersonal nature. In this encounter "St. Simeon" in particular renders itself so grotesque that Tennyson has to dissociate himself from his speaker through irony. Throughout his ordeal, however, Simeon himself strives for the very detachment achieved by his predecessors in the 1832 volume.

In the single most searching analysis of the poem, Tucker also sees it as an outgrowth of 1832: "Tennyson . . . had begun to test such embowered stasis with the dialectics of encounter. We may regard the experimentation with dramatic monologue that began with 'St. Simeon Stylites' as an extension of that development."[2] While we have been interpreting the 1832 poems as celebrations rather than tests, we must accept Simeon's pole as what Tucker ("Monomania," p. 134) calls it, "a denuded and exposed version of the Tennysonian bower," a parody of the Lady's tower, or the Three Sisters' tree, or even the Mariners' island. While all of these are manipulated by their interpreters into places of centered importance, Simeon needs other people as both foils and witnesses to what Tucker calls (p. 131) "his ambition to become not God's humble subject but God's pedestaled object."

In seconding such criticism, however, we should also acknowledge Ryals' warning: "To be sure, we can condemn Simeon, but condemnation is not the most interesting response."[3] According to Kincaid (p. 36), Tennyson assures our ambivalent response to many of these poems when he "removes the solid position from which we can make judgments and then urges on us both the necessity for judgments and their futility." Reaffirming the integrity of his model within his revision, he forces Simeon into the role of mediator by confronting him with a now frighteningly immanent Other. In a passage only added within the margin of the second and more complete Harvard draft, Simeon's God actively rejoices in the suffering of his servants:[4]

> For did not all thy martyrs die one death?
> For either they were stoned, or crucified,
> Or burned in fire, or boiled in oil, or sawn
> In twain beneath the ribs; but I die here
> Today, and whole years long, a life of death.
>
> (ll. 49–53)

Because Simeon must mediate between "the silly people [who] take me for a saint" and an Other as threatening as any in "Armageddon," even his pillar "betwixt the meadow and the cloud" now appears to be another imaginative outpost, deeper (or in this case higher) within the Other's domain than any in the 1832 volume.

And as Tennyson came to identify with another grotesque senex figure while revising *The Devil and the Lady*, so here he endows Simeon with his own powers and fears. In two passages missing entirely from even the second Harvard draft,[5] Simeon admits that he began his lifelong penance to appease not just his God but a series of specters within his own personality. And as in

"Armageddon," the threats posed by God and Devil fuse to produce a single "blot upon the brain / That will show itself without": "I smote them with my cross; they swarmed again. . . . Yet this way was left, / And by this way I 'scaped them" (ll. 170, 175–76). Yet even this "escape" is premature; similar specters continually open up aporias within what Tucker calls (p. 131) "the peculiarly doomed genre" of "autohagiography":

> the evil ones come here, and say,
> 'Fall down, O Simeon: thou hast suffered long
> For ages and for ages!' . . .
>   and oft I fall,
> Maybe for months, in such blind lethargies
> That Heaven, and Earth, and Time are choked.
>   (ll. 96–98, 100–102)

Hence when his audience shouts, "St. Simeon Stylites," he must ask himself, "Can I work miracles and not be saved?" (l. 148). When the angel dangles a crown over him, his fear that he will lose it ("What! deny it now?") expands into a very real fear for his soul: "Ah! let me not be fooled, sweet saints" (l. 209).

Despite his eagerness to accept the miracles attributed to him, he can acknowledge his own mediating power only by turning himself, much like Browning's Bishop, into a relic:

> You may carve a shrine about my dust,
> And burn a fragrant lamp before my bones,
> When I am gathered to the glorious saints.
>   (ll. 191–93)

These very doubts, of course, may seem to change this "when" into an "if," to undermine his claim that "by the warning of the Holy Ghost" he will actually die at "a quarter before twelve." Both Shaw (pp. 104–6) and Ricks (*Tennyson*, p. 111) brood over this penultimate suspension of closure. Yet in *either* case Simeon has won a kind of victory over the Other. If his God, like Godot, refuses to arrive on schedule, he merely acknowledges himself to be the spiteful figure whom Simeon has been propitiating. If he accepts Simeon, he does so on Simeon's own terms, implicitly acknowledging that this madman has not only taken heaven by storm but has remodeled it in his own image.

When Tennyson invites the demons into his mediator's psyche, he wins him increased credibility, but only at a price. The bill does not come due, however, until "The Two Voices," a poem in which, as Ricks puts it (*Tennyson*, p. 105), "the enemy seems to be within the gates." The very figure of the mediator, even as an apparently ineffectual projection, seems to have simply dissolved away. In its absence, the world of the poem shrinks down to an internalized landscape like that of "The Poet's Mind," a landscape whose apparent safety is threatened by some unknowable outer power.

Here the authorial voice, the poem's "I," finds itself sharing the authorial psyche with "a still small voice," a voice different from Elijah's and more troubling—because less raucous—than Simeon's demons. Simeon's opponents, divine or infernal, grew from the male deities of "Armageddon"; this Voice invokes the vaguely female but ultimately impersonal flux which haunted both *The Devil and the Lady* and the 1830 poems. Where the Magus failed to assert his imaginative power against an otherwise tranquil sea, here the Voice claims that the speaker will fail to discover any innate link between imaginative and outer reality:

> Much less this dreamer, deaf and blind,
> Named man, may hope some truth to find,
> That bears relation to the mind.
>
> (ll. 175–77)

The Voice has reduced to relativity every scale—space, time, and complexity—by which to take some human measure of the cosmos:

> Thou hast not gained a real height,
> Nor art thou nearer to the light,
> Because the scale is infinite.
>
> (ll. 91–93)

For Tucker (p. 15), "the virtual absence of context [and] the ultimate passivity of the speaker . . . conspire against the credible formation of [his] character," but for me the variety of his tentative responses ultimately wins him some integrity. On one level he tries, like the 1832 mediators, to localize and so delimit this manifestation of the Other. By the sheer number of his arguments, he forces the Voice to subvert its own identification with flux by returning again and again to stasis. As it harps on the inevitability of death, it picks up the same smug composure which it finds on the face of the corpse lying oblivious to the Ecclesiastian disintegration of his line:

His sons grow up that bear his name,
Some grow to honour, some to shame,—
But he is chill to praise or blame.

(ll. 256–58)

Finally, as the speaker triumphantly points out, the Voice inadvertently echoes one of Tennyson's least-effectual mediators, building death itself into a wished-for stasis much like that in "The Palace of Art":

"O dull, one-sided voice," said I,
"Wilt thou make everything a lie,
To *flatter* me that I may die?

(ll. 202–4; italics mine)

The Voice's Olympian calm also remains vulnerable to the rising emotional intensity which informs the poem's otherwise opportunistic exchanges. The Voice reduces the speaker first to grief, then to anger, then to doubt; but none of these states can find either answer or rebuttal within the Voice's *nil admirari* pose. Hence the speaker can argue from and not against the gaps, inconsistencies, and frustrations in experience:

Heaven opens inward, chasms yawn,
Vast images in glimmering dawn,
Half shown, are broken and withdrawn.

(ll. 304–6)

After looking into the self like the speaker of the "Armageddon" poems, he can venture out like the 1832 mediators into a natural world which the Voice has up until now appropriated as its own.

The poem's principal skirmish, however, is fought over control of the speaker's past. The Voice ties his earlier imaginative success to contingent causes: "It was the stirring of the blood" (l. 159). Hence it denies his claim to have discovered any enduring evidence for human transcendence: "Not that the grounds of hope were fixed, / The elements were kindlier mixed" (ll. 227–28). It even tries to appropriate his imaginative space as relative and thus its own: "Shadows thou dost strike, / Embracing clouds, Ixion-like" (ll. 194–95). The speaker never confronts this relativism directly, but by recreating his earlier imaginative forays, he reaches back in time to confront specters from his own youth:

I found [Death] when my years were few;
A shadow on the graves I knew,
And darkness in the village yew. . . .

> "Omega! thou art Lord, they said,
> "We find no motion in the dead."
>   (ll. 271–73, 278–79)

By acknowledging Death as only "their" Lord, the speaker implicitly re-shapes him. In so doing, he also demonstrates that he has regained the imaginative intensity which both he and the Voice have supposed lost with youth itself. And if thus retrievable, this past cannot remain as much in thrall to relativism as the Voice has been claiming.

The speaker seems quite proud of this daring raid on his opponent's position ("With thine own weapon art thou slain"), but is he at this point assured of victory? The question would not matter except for evidence that Tennyson had reached roughly this point in the poem when he learned of Hallam's death.[6] And at this point the prospects for victory are at least ambiguous. A Kemble letter of 1833 claims that the speaker is "thoroughly floored" by the Voice.[7] Tennyson's ambiguity and Hallam's death may together explain why the continuation of two years later remains one of Tennyson's patently unsuccessful revisions. To satisfy his desperate need for the very mediation that he has lost, he seized upon mediators foreign to both self and Other, the fatuous church-going family and the second voice with its "hidden hope."

To be sure, the family must enter the church through the churchyard, must accept life and community in the context of death. So too the second voice makes no new claims for the cosmos; it only slows down the cycles described by the first voice so that the speaker can participate in the resulting fecundity:

> And forth into the fields I went,
> And Nature's living motion lent
> The pulse of hope to discontent.
>   (ll. 448–50)

Despite such qualifications, however, this conclusion remains far less convincing than those of poems which acknowledge the gap between desire and achievement.

We need at this point to consider more extensively what changes Hallam's death actually produced in Tennyson's poetry. Ricks's discovery of an earlier date for "The Two Voices" seems to support both Arthur J. Carr's claim that much of Tennyson's previous poetry anticipates the catastrophe and Tucker's claim (p. 178) that "the creation of a personal myth of elegiac rescue . . . came to serve Tennyson as a resource."[8] In fact the model we have been tracing seems a virtual back formation from the death itself: a mediator between Tennyson and an already unfriendly universe is threatened, sometimes even destroyed by the incursion of some powerful and inexplicable force from without. So stated, the model seems so strong a defense that we might wonder why the death caused Tennyson as much imaginative trauma as it did.

The trauma, I think, grows from a vulnerability within the model until now hidden even from Tennyson. Hallam the person served Tennyson as an almost perfect mediator, yet among the profusion of Tennyson's mediators we have found none that we could identify as Hallam. Within the model he seems to exist only as the possibility or potential for mediation. Thus by destroying this potential, the destroying agent could proclaim itself immune to any mediation whatsoever. It is not that Tennyson had never confronted strokes of fortune as senseless, random, and irrevocable as that which killed his friend. Yet their very appearance *in poems* meant that poetry had at least the potential for personifying them, delimiting them, reducing them to an Other with whom Tennyson's mediators had already done battle. How was Tennyson to confront in poetry a phenomenon which surpassed his darkest imaginings and then denied the imagination any means of comprehending it?[9]

This question explains why most of the major undertakings in Tennyson's creative life grow not just from Hallam's death but from the poems written immediately after it. Whether eventually incorporated into larger works like *In Memoriam, Maud,* and the *Idylls,* whether printed, often years later, in something like their original form, all the productions of 1833–34 challenge the model itself. Beneath the polished finish and the refined tone, they all betray a blind, groping search for plot, characters, and setting capable of answering an unanswerable question and consoling an inconsolable grief.

Tennyson, for his part, seems to have understood instinctively that his model could again confront some Other if and only if it could conjure up an Other from this central absurdity. Until now the Other has appeared largely unbidden. From now on Tennyson will not only invite it but will actively develop it, as if acknowledging that a victory over anything less frightening than Hallam's death would fall short of both his powers and his needs. If from now on we begin to hear an increasing stridency in the authorial voice, it may grow from Tennyson's unconscious decision to measure the power of the Other by its ability to make him put off his mask of disinterested calm.

In the few personal responses Tennyson wrote immediately after Hallam's death, he abandoned this mask voluntarily. In the place of stridency, therefore, we hear an implicit refusal to admit that any coherent model can encompass his grief. We must postpone until later chapters both the strangely impersonal quatrains which grew into *In Memoriam* and the anguished cry which grew into *Maud*.[10] The remaining lyric, "Break, Break, Break," has often been described as a lyric in search of a voice.[11] I would describe it further as a lyric in search of plot, characters, and setting.[12] An assemblage of people, objects, and places impinges on "the tender grace of a day that is dead," but how, Tennyson does not yet know.[13] The children appear too naive to mediate between the sea and the speaker, yet too innocent to taunt him with the gap between their lot and his. The sea, as in *The Devil and the Lady*, would constitute an obvious Other did it not embody the speaker's confinement, his blind perseverance, and even the voice that he himself cannot "utter."[14] As Ricks puts it (*Tennyson*, p. 143), "The dissociative gulf between the outer scene and the inner pain is one which the sturdy words of reason like *And* and *But* can ultimately only pretend to bridge."

The Monologues

The nearly simultaneous composition of "Ulysses," "Tithonus," and "Tiresias" seems, by contrast, to suggest that Tennyson's model could still win him some precious distance on his personal grief. Mariana may have been more catatonic and Simeon more grotesque, but none of Tennyson's earlier projections has been any more impotent than these three old men. Paden's mask of age, as we saw, interprets such figures as efforts to distance a present sexual trauma; these speakers, fragmented by the past and trapped by the present, may instead reflect Tennyson's own condition unsupported by Hallam. Yet by reducing all of them to the lowest common denominator of existence, Tennyson could win for himself what Hallam's presence alone had given him, the power to create fictional extensions of the self.

Such creativity, however, did not transfer automatically to these creations. In their initial paralysis, they seem to prefigure the nightmare portrayed in an early (though not early-written) section from *In Memoriam*:

> I sit within a helmless bark,
> And with my heart I muse and say:
>
> O heart, how fares it with thee now . . . ?
>
> Something it is which thou hast lost.
>
> (section 4: ll. 3–5, 9)

Like Tennyson's heart, these three seem at first unwilling to discover who or what they have lost and who or what has taken it from them. Ulysses' "much is taken," with its indefinite pronoun and its passive verb, may epitomize this very refusal.

Their refusal, in turn, may explain what has often been dismissed as the author's imperfect control of his still-experimental genre.[15] This apparent breakdown in dramatic form we can relocate *inside* the poems. Our own gradual discovery of character, setting, and plot we can then attribute to the speakers' gradual discovery of their own natures, their situations, and the figures ranged against them. Using their monologues to gain psychological distance on their dilemma, they move from an initial existence as a suffering consciousness to a celebration of their past, to a perception of their present setting, to a redefinition of the other characters in it, to an attempt to re-define themselves against these characters, and finally to a demand for physical escape from them and their world.[16] Within this same process they allow Tennyson to escape his own grief by participating vicariously in their escape. They give him, in short, the kind of dramatic integrity which he could not achieve in his own person.

"Tiresias," because of the fragmentary nature of the 1833 version, remains the most conjectural of the three, but for this same reason it can best serve as the opening paradigm for this process. The first manuscript fragment seems to have been composed even before Hallam's death:

> I wish I were as in the days of old
> Ere my smooth cheek darkened with youthful down,
> While yet the blessed daylight made itself
> Ruddy within the eves of sight, before
> I looked upon divinity unveiled
> And wisdom naked, while my mind was set
> To follow Knowledge like a sinking star,
> Beyond the utmost bound of human thought.[17]

This passage is curious, not just because it contains the famous wish later given to Ulysses, but because it gives so little indication of the speaker. We know only that he is old, unhappy, blind, and bereft of his former inquisitive spirit through some traumatic confrontation.[18]

When we turn to the slightly later set of extant passages, we find a much more coherent sequence, but one which still follows the same progression we have been describing. We gradually learn that Tiresias is counseling a young man to undertake some heroic deed, that they are both in a besieged city, that the city is Thebes threatened by Polyneices, that since the youth is Creon's son and a descendant of Cadmus, he can lift the curse Mars has placed on the city by sacrificing himself. Finally the prophet laments that the "boundless yearnings" of his own heart are not seen as equally heroic, yet he denies that in counseling the youth's death he is really seeking his own.

At first Tiresias claims that time has trapped him in a situation he once could have controlled: the besieged Thebans are only now suffering what age, blindness, and social ostracism have inflicted on him for years. Even worse, in confronting Menoeceus, he is confronting a mocking image of his own younger, more capable self. His triumph within this draft rests on his ability to see his situation as truly dramatic and the characters he confronts as more than extensions of his own personality. As he outlines his plan, he realizes that Menoeceus can mediate for him just as he can mediate for Tennyson.[19] Menoeceus, unlike him, can appease the gods, and he, unlike his still weaker creator, can win for his fellows the freedom he cannot win for himself.

From the perspective of the printed poem, Joseph attributes Tiresias' plight (p. 143) to both male and female manifestations of the Other: "A terrible goddess joins forces with the god of war to ravage Thebes." But Tiresias doesn't seem to blame Mars for the siege in this draft any more than he blamed Athene for his blindness in the earlier one. In guiding this speaker toward a pragmatic response to a delimited situation, Tennyson seems to be guiding him away from cosmic confrontations which neither of them is ready to face. Not until the poem had languished in manuscript for fifty years did Tennyson return to his speaker's "boundless yearnings," yearnings which will earn him both Athene's curse and his own visions of a pagan afterlife.

The speaker who inherits Tiresias' longing "to follow knowledge like a sinking star" also inherits his reticence about the reasons behind this need to escape. Tiresias' physical plight is actually worse than that of Ulysses. We can understand the prophet's grief over his own blindness and that of his scoffing audience, but we may find Ulysses' grief only partially explained by the barren crags, the idleness, the aged wife, the savage subjects. While the poem may conceal a hidden agenda, its argument, like that of "Tiresias," moves forward to confront Ulysses with the far more limited problem of his present confinement. In this context, his opening celebration of his own past stands as a less-than-convincing effort both to escape from his surroundings and to subsume them. While he has criticized his subjects because they "hoard and sleep and feed," he celebrates his own life in many of the same ingestive images: "I will drink life to the lees," "always roaming with a hungry heart," "drank delight of battle," and even "I am a part of all that I have met." This oral self-identification with his world has allowed him to escape the question of his own identity. Yet now that his earlier prowess is inaccessible, how can he succeed in opposing this world, not encompassing it?

He succeeds in part by turning away from his past. Although Ricks argues (*Tennyson*, p. 125) that "past and present leav[e] no room for future," Ulysses makes room for it by turning from fulfillment to longing: "all experience is an arch wherethrough / Gleams that untravelled world" (ll. 19–20).[20] From this perspective, as Linda Hughes has observed, he can discover a number of individuals with whom he must come to terms during his monologue—among them his "own Telemachus."[21] His portrait, though admittedly less than enthusiastic, gives at least a grudging acknowledgment that the boy is not an ironic parody of his own youth but a distinct and ultimately viable personality. This acknowledgment in turn moves the poem one step closer to drama: we have a speaker and a subject—but as yet no audience.

The audience appears as Ulysses addresses his mariners. We do not, of course, discover where they, or Telemachus—or Ulysses for that matter—have been during the first half of the poem. Tennyson, I believe, wanted the mariners to swim into focus as the speaker opened his own perspective wide enough to include them. Through them, in turn, he can reinterpret his past in terms of confronting, not devouring: "Souls . . . that ever with a frolic welcome took / The thunder and the sunshine."[22] In this description, as Georg Roppen has pointed out, his sentence rhythms move from belated qualification to balanced, periodic inclusiveness.[23] The blatant discrepancies between their age and their new hardships, the declining day and their new quest, the alternative possibilities of discovery and death—all these oppositions seem to fuse into a common direction, escape. From the trap in which Ulysses has now found himself, only the way out is clearly visible.

Tithonus' dilemma, unlike that of Ulysses, seems all too evident to both him and the reader. A mere ten lines into his monologue he confronts Aurora as a type of the fatal goddess already confronted by the Magus, the Lover, and Oenone. This dramatic awareness, however, is itself a product of Tennyson's 1859 revision of the poem. The speaker of the 1833 version, here named Tithon, does not even address Aurora until line 15; he cannot differentiate himself from her until she actually leaves him near the end of the poem. In 1833–34 Tennyson himself needed the entire poem to come to terms with Aurora as a new Other appearing in a new context.

It would be tempting to see her either as death carrying off Hallam to a particularly hideous afterlife or as Hallam himself offering Tennyson some particularly dangerous sexual temptation. For Culler, however, "this poem is [not] about Tennyson's love for Hallam, or about immortality, or about the desire for death. It is about a poet who feels his poetic powers failing. . . . Tithonus' marriage to the Dawn is simply the conviction of every great poet in his youth that he is immortal and cannot die" (pp. 87–88). For Tucker (p. 252) Tennyson had grown disillusioned with the Romantic muse herself: "the visionary gleam [Tithonus] sleeps with has become equivalent to common day, just the daily cue to a handsomely executed fade-in." Yet to interpret Aurora as muse is to miss both the qualities she shares with her female predecessors and those which make her more dangerous than any of them. Tucker, we remember, saw the Magus as Tennyson's surrogate, celebrating the pleasurable frustration inherent in any encounter with the force of Doom. But Aurora gives what Amoret, or Cadrilla, or Aphrodite only appears to promise. As such she may represent not the frustration of Hallam's death but the ultimate wish fulfillment which Tennyson creates in compensation for it. The female mediators of 1832 can make only brief and self-destructive forays into the domain of the Other; Tithon has been given a permanent invitation into her bed.[24]

At the opening Tithon can identify himself only in terms of his surroundings. Where Ulysses had once engulfed his world, Tithon has been engulfed by his, transformed into the cold gray glimmer on the eastern horizon before sunrise. As Sinfield puts it (p. 109), his "individual subjectivity appears not as the source of meaning in the world but as constructed *by* the world." E. D. H. Johnson has interpreted Aurora herself as "a Keatsian Ideal of beauty which the poet cannot escape,"[25] and Shaw has compared Tithonus' relation to her to those explored in several of Keats's odes,[26] but Tennyson may be borrowing this particular metamorphosis from Keats's attempt at natural magic in *Hyperion*. There the sun god, balked in his effort to open the day before its appointed hour, reclines in a celestial sulk along the eastern horizon:

> And all along a dismal rack of clouds,
> Upon the boundaries of day and night,
> He stretch'd himself in grief and radiance faint.
>
> (I, 302–4)

In this posture he is approached by Coelus, one of the oldest of the immortals, whose generation has been overthrown by the Titans even as they are now being threatened by the upstart Olympian gods. While he criticizes Hyperion's ungodlike (i.e., human) display of emotion, Coelus reveals that he has lost so much of his own personality that he has become a mere voice: "My life is but the life of winds and tides, / No more than winds and tides can I avail" (I, 341–42).[27]

Tennyson develops this same dilemma, in which personality implies transience and immortality implies petrifaction, as the central realization of his mediator Tithon. Like the Lady of Shalott and Oenone, however, Tithon can win Tennyson this realization only by assuming both these contradictory states and being destroyed by them. His mortal transience has left him reduced to a state of changeless potential, "a white-haired shadow roaming like a dream / The ever-silent spaces of the East" (ll. 8–9). His discovery of other modes of existence must depend on his growing understanding of Aurora; yet *because* she has so freely given herself to him, this understanding is itself dependent on his loss of her. With her he can do no more than feel her encircling arms and see her tear-filled eyes; only as she leaves, as the dawn rises up from the predawn glow, can he see her as a whole:

> Once more the old mysterious glimmer steals
> From thy pure brows, and from thy shoulders pure,
> And bosom throbbing with a fresher heart.
> Thy cheek begins to bloom a fuller red,
> Thy sweet eyes brighten slowly close to mine,
> Ere yet they blind the stars. . . .
>
> (ll. 30–35)

Yet here she breaks away, not just from decrepit mortality, but from the kind of cold, static immortality that Keats confronted in the Grecian Urn.[28] McSweeney points out (p. 64) that "Eos is a nature goddess and her immortality is that of natural process,"[29] and Albright (p. 109) that "Dawn, like youth . . . , must change itself every day into the full sun at which no man can gaze." From Tithon's perspective, she *is* dawn only in leaving him; she can return to him only on "silver wheels," that is, in a grayish state of half-being much like his own.

This new vision of her as distinct, alien, physically distanced wins him and Tennyson a renewed self-awareness like that acquired by Ulysses. And as Ulysses came to confront Telemachus as a separate person, so now Tithon comes to perceive his own past self as a separate entity. The 1860 version states this separation even more bluntly:

> with what another heart
> In days far-off, and with what other eyes

> I used to watch—if I be he that watched—
> The lucid outline forming round thee. . . .

(ll. 50–53)

For Michael Greene (pp. 293–300), Tithonus never manages to grow beyond these erotic memories, but Tucker (p. 250) counters that these constitute "Tithonus's willful fall out of love with the process he is describing." From the spatial, temporal, personal distance he has gained on his original theophany, he comes to see that Aurora assumes her immortal glory only from a literally mundane perspective. In the heavens she must remain a departure; only on earth can she be a consummation.

Tithon's subsequent plea to return to the earth has often been contrasted with Ulysses' quest for life, just as that quest has been seen as a covert longing for death. I argued earlier that Ulysses' obsessive hunger for escape made the alternatives of life and death irrelevant; they remain so for Tithon as well, but for different reasons. Now that Tennyson has learned from his mediator that his deepest desires remain ontologically, not just physically, contradictory, he has no more interest in Tithon's fate than in that of the Lotos-Eaters, or the Three Sisters, or Oenone. Tithon's case differs from theirs only in that they sought a stasis which was threatened or actually destroyed from without; he, like the earlier, weaker Mariana, remains trapped in a very similar stasis. In this context, his discovery of Aurora's nature represents not only the one significant event of the poem, but *as* an event his one significant challenge to his fate.

This pattern we have been tracing—progressive realization of self, of surroundings, and of conflict—serves both Tennyson and his mediators, yet in severely limited ways. Like the escapes of his speakers, his own escape from the consequences of Hallam's death exists only as potential. The speakers are psychologically too close and physically too far removed to offer him any practical remedies. From an aesthetic perspective, this psychological proximity also holds a mixture of advantages and drawbacks. In fact Tennyson measures his own distance from these creations in the wildly different ways he chooses to revise the three poems.

"Ulysses," for example, we have considered as a finished product, in part because of the appearance of the earliest, Harvard draft. Inscribed with unusual care on two sides of a page, it leaves little doubt that the poem began and essentially remained the fruit of a single creative outburst, a single flash of identification with another suffering yet creative psyche. Yet the Heath

Manuscript version, written a few weeks later on 20 October 1833, contains some significant additions, including some of the poem's more famous lines. Considering the additions separately, we find that rather than emphasizing any one aspect of Ulysses' psychological journey, they focus the journey as a whole: both "I will drink / Life to the lees" and "always roaming with a hungry heart" intensify the speaker's desire to consume his past. "I am a part of all that I have met" signals his awareness of his present fragmentation. The reference to Telemachus, itself added on the next folio of the Harvard manuscript, forces him to define himself against the people around him. The evocative description of the sea at twilight broadens his perspective on his physical setting. Finally his possible landing on "the Happy Isles" gives his escape a clearer, if no more realistic, goal.

By intensifying Ulysses' desire for escape without making it any more realistic, all these additions undermine his dramatic objectivity in the very act of creating it. Hence they reinforce our suspicion of some hidden agenda, some unspoken identification between speaker and poet.[30] Because these three mediators have shared so much of Tennyson's loss, there seemed no need to posit any authorial presence within their poems. Here, however, such a presence reappears in the gap between Ulysses' tolerable, if rather boring existence and his exaggerated revulsion from it.[31] The poem's burden of unspeakable, inconsolable grief may suggest that some force within it is making Ulysses respond, not to his own situation, but to Tennyson's confrontation with an Other who refuses to be mediated, challenged, even understood. Yet if Tennyson acknowledged the source of Ulysses' grief and his own share in it, he would deny any hope of escape for either himself or his speaker. This unconscious authorial blindness may explain the poem's physical and moral tunnel vision—it may also render the explanation almost trivial.[32] Ulysses himself may be blind to the moral consequences of his decisions; yet his creator, obsessed with "the need of going forward and braving the struggle of life" (*Poems*, I, 613), would have lost interest in anyone remotely resembling Telemachus.

"Tithon," as we saw, also possessed more immediacy than its revision, "Tithonus." Because Tennyson seems to grope toward autonomy along with his 1833 speaker, Tithon's recollection of his past union with Aurora appears all the more intense and his present rejection of her all the more sudden and violent. By the time Tennyson revised the poem in 1859 for Thackeray's *Cornhill Magazine*, he had gained a new psychological and moral perspective on both figures, but the nature of that perspective seems open to critical dispute. Arthur Simpson, Jr., claims that by attributing the gift of immortality to Aurora herself, Tennyson makes her responsible for Tithonus' fate.[33] Linda Hughes, on the other hand, argues that the now-weeping Eos appears more sympathetic while Tithonus, since he now admits that he requested immortality, appears responsible for his own fate.[34] Both positions may in fact be right: *because* Tennyson no longer identified so completely with Tithon's compulsive desire to escape from his tragic stasis, he could explore dispassionately the shared responsibility for it. Although thirty years may seem like a long time for Tithonus to wait for a dramatic identity, the few weeks separating drafts of "Ulysses" proved insufficient to win him an escape from the authorial presence. As we will now see, a mediator could also wait too long.

Tiresias, taken up again after a full fifty years, faces a different and ultimately more damaging threat. While no longer serving as a mask of age behind which the young Tennyson could lament his loss, the prophet is overwhelmed by a poet nearly his equal in years and now even more eager to use him as a mouthpiece. The revision returns to the confessional cry of the earliest draft, "I wish I were as in the years of old." This Tiresias, however, is made to sound suspiciously like the Ancient Sage as he rationalizes that his "wont / Was more to scale the highest of the heights" (ll. 26–27) and that when he surprised Athene, he was really only looking for a bit of shade. The self-justifying complaints finally approach the petulance of "Locksley Hall Sixty Years After" when he rails against the failure of the audience to hear "my counsel that the tyranny of all / Led backward to the tyranny of one" (ll. 74–75). Tiresias and his poem recover their own voices only at the end, where he is allowed to envision in Elysium an escape from life more heroic and more creative than any Tennyson could consciously entertain for himself, even within "Crossing the Bar" or "Merlin and the Gleam":

> the wise man's word,
> Here trampled by the populace underfoot,
> There [is] crowned with worship. . . .
> while the golden lyre
> Is ever sounding in heroic ears
> Heroic hymns. . . .
>
> (ll. 165–67, 172–74)

As Tucker puts it (p. 206), Tennyson is here articulating "the boundless prophetic yearning to join the gods as an equal . . . in a rich lyricism that would rank as a triumph of imagination from any poet, much less a poet in his seventies."

"Morte d'Arthur"

As a narrative largely based on Malory, the "Morte" would seem a less promising vehicle than the monologues for letting Tennyson speak through individual mediators. In reality this form permits its characters to speak to and for him more directly than any since Hallam's death. By opposing the characters, it also juxtaposes the corresponding desires within Tennyson, enclosing each within its fictional context. As in the monologues, each character's awareness of self and surroundings grows with his unfolding narrative.

At first, for example, we see Bedivere as a part of the symbolic landscape, the means by which Arthur is moved from the role of a warrior king to that of a dying man within the shell of a dying faith, "a broken chancel with a broken cross" (l. 9). Even Bedivere's refusal to throw Arthur's sword away remains inarticulate until his soliloquy by the mere, where he reveals that he is holding onto this symbol of Arthur to mediate between him and a flux like the sea in "Break, Break, Break" or *The Devil and the Lady*. In lying to Arthur, however, he inadvertently admits the very truth which he has tried to hide from himself. In claiming to hear only "the wild water lapping on the crag" (l. 71), he acknowledges that he cannot mediate retroactively. As a mocking relic of the realm's past glory, Excalibur proves just as useless for Bedivere as did Telemachus, or Menoeceus, or Tithonus' past self for the speakers of those poems.

When he is forced to throw his past away, he can transfer his commitment to Arthur himself, but when Arthur then deserts him, he is finally driven to articulate the alienation experienced by all these speakers:

> But now the whole ROUND TABLE is dissolved
> Which was an image of the mighty world;
> And I, the last, go forth companionless,
> And the days darken round me, and the years,
> Among new men, strange faces, other minds.
>
> (ll. 234–38)

These lines, in this context, make their own case for inclusion within the title of this study. Bedivere, whom Kincaid has described (pp. 212–13) as too stupid to understand the meaning of his poem and too inarticulate to express it, is here forced to bewail Tennyson's loss of another Arthur. Simultaneously, this same character bewails his own eviction from the sanctuary of Camelot and his unmediated encounter with the Other in the "other minds" of the "new men" who inhabit the wasteland outside. Yet in this encounter he also becomes, as Tucker says (p. 341), "a Higher Critic of Arthurian legend, both a last citizen and a first witnessing guide to the Camelot that is never built at all and therefore built forever."

The autonomy Bedivere wins through this grief is limited not by any authorial presence but by the other figure who shares his story. It is, after all, Arthur who has first usurped Bedivere's own identity and then thrust it back upon him. These conflicting demands arise from Arthur's two conflicting quests, the first for understanding and control of his situation, the second for his own autonomy as a mediator. Through these quests, which include but reinterpret Bedivere's experiences, Arthur effectively challenges Bedivere for the role of protagonist.[35]

In his first speech Arthur seems to be putting his past behind him:

> I think that we
> Shall never more, at any future time,
> Delight our souls with talk of knightly deeds,
> Walking about the gardens and the halls
> Of Camelot, as in the days that were.
>
> (ll. 17–21)

Yet even this admission seems curiously guarded—how could he even consider engaging "in talk of knightly deeds" with men whom he has just acknowledged to be dead? His decision to throw away Excalibur may thus be tainted with as many implicit reservations as was Bedivere's refusal to do so. On a deeper level, he, Bedivere, and the author seem to join their voices in celebrating a sanctuary for the authorial presence much like the glen in Ida or the islands of the Hesperides and the Lotos-Eaters. The narrative portrait of Arthur, "who, with lance in rest, / From spur to plume a star of tournament, / Shot through the lists at Camelot" (ll. 222–24), matches the romantic, recuperating Arthur within the portrait which decorated the Palace of Art.

Like the Soul in that poem, however, Arthur is ruefully viewing his edifice from without. Ricks criticizes the "Morte" (*Tennyson*, p. 138) because the vivid landscape jars with the formalized characters. For me, Arthur in particular gains an almost modern immediacy precisely because he finds himself just as distanced from Camelot as does Tennyson.[36] The landscape, in turn, gains immediacy because through Arthur, as through Bedivere, Tennyson confronts it as the domain of an Other manifested in impersonal flux. To quote Culler (p. 103), "Tennyson well knew how to invoke the barrenness of the landscape in order to express the desolation of the heart."

Whereas Bedivere failed to oppose Arthur's sword to this flux, Arthur uses Bedivere to impose human form upon it. Toward this goal Arthur, like the speakers of the dramatic monologues, must redefine his relationships. He must see Bedivere, no longer as simply "the latest-left of all my knights," but as one who "wouldst betray me for the precious hilt" (ll. 124, 126). But by coopting Bedivere as a mediator, as Tennyson has coopted him, Arthur succeeds in personifying the Other; he forces "the wild water lapping on the crag" (l. 71), like the sea confronting the Magus, to confess its own femininity: "But ere he dipt the surface, rose an arm / Clothed in white samite, mystic, wonderful" (ll. 143–44). Not content with this triumph, Arthur then commands the three Queens to mediate between him and the sea on his final voyage.

More blatantly than Ulysses, Tithonus, or Tiresias, Arthur manipulates his situation and his companions to win any escape by any means. Yet this escape, with its flight to Avalon, cannot convince Malory (XXI, 7). Tennyson's manuscripts, as Marcia Culver points out, reveal he had serious problems with it. The first draft ends with the arrival of the barge and the cry of the three Queens; "there is no hint here of the myth of Arthur's survival and return; missing also is the King's final speech to Bedivere on the power of prayer and the ultimate good of God's unknown purpose."[37] By finally indulging in such consolation, however, Tennyson also grants to Arthur an autonomy beyond that achieved by either Bedivere or the speakers of the monologues. Bedivere's autonomy was restricted to speech, and theirs remained poised on the penultimate brink of escape. Arthur may be passively borne to the shore by Bedivere, borne off he knows not whither by the three Queens, and borne into irrelevance by a changing world he no longer understands. Yet he *does* escape, and even in his piously Victorian speech from the barge, he effectively shrugs off the weight of the metaphysical quandaries with which Tennyson, through Bedivere, has burdened him. While he expands the bald "pray for my soul" of Malory's Arthur, Tucker finds "The old order changeth" "about as comforting as the speech of Oceanus that [it] condense[s]" (p. 342). At best Arthur's spiritual laissez-faire converts those whom Bedivere had seen as Other into potential mediators. As Arthur hopes to be cured by others in Avilion, so the world's problems must be solved by "new men, strange faces, other minds."

Both Bedivere and Arthur seek the same goals, confront the same incidents, even reach many of the same conclusions. Yet in trying to coopt one another as mediators, they clash at almost every point. And it is the creation of such opposition which may define Tennyson's inadvertent achievement in moving from monologue to narrative. The dichotomy which Ricks sees between setting and character may thus arise from the paradox that the setting is shaped by each character, while the character himself exists only as a force shaping setting, action, and other characters into an ultimately partial fiction.

In creating this species of narrative, Tennyson virtually anticipates the process by which Browning was later to combine monologues into a multi-faceted single poem. Tennyson's narrative stands as ostensibly single but constantly in danger of being unraveled by characters too much at odds to remain comfortable even within the same story. As I will try to show, this narrative technique came to dominate Tennyson's later poetry. Before that time, however, he would need to win a very paradoxical ambivalence: enough assurance of his own power to wrestle these larger forms into shape; enough tolerance of his characters' autonomy to let them reshape these same forms in potentially incompatible ways.

Walter Nash interprets Tennyson's later addition of the framing "Epic" as an attempt to transfer the solemnity and importance of Arthur's death to all death in contemporary Victorian England.[38] For all its skill, however, the frame parallels other disconcerting decisions of the mid-1830s: the decision to tidy up "O that 'twere possible" for a keepsake album, for example, or to tie *In Memoriam* lyrics together with pat refrains.[39] Here in "The Epic," as Tennyson is ostensibly establishing the relevance of Arthur's mediation for contemporary England, he is simultaneously trying to distance it from his own imaginative universe. By contemplating Arthur's passing from across the wassail bowl as the parson, or the speaker, or even the disgruntled poet, Tennyson can avoid contemplating it as Bedivere or Arthur himself. He can thus turn a cry for escape into a forum on the possibility of return. Hence when Arthur reappears in the speaker's dream, even though now dressed "like a modern gentleman / Of stateliest port," he implicitly validates Bedivere's treasonous concealment of the sword and undercuts the knight's final realization that "the true old times are dead" (l. 229).

Most of the poems begun in the mid-1830s also attempt to mediate between Tennyson's loss and the larger social world. They fail, according to many critics, because they reject personal feelings in favor of public facility. Within the context of this chapter, however, we can argue that they fail instead because they remain too deeply felt, because Tennyson's sense of loss undermines his intended escape from it, because supposedly stock characters in supposedly public genres suddenly find themselves confronting Others or playing mediators within Tennyson's own highly inappropriate scenario. Of all these genres, the English idylls can best encompass these internal struggles, since their formal conventions exist only to be broken through.

The various kinds of "public" poems written in the 1830s—political lyrics, popular tales, ballads, love sonnets, domestic idylls—all embody a typically Tennysonian dilemma: simultaneous fears of social change and of entrapment within social class. Behind this public front, however, social change disguises the incursion of impersonal flux, and upper-class norms reflect the response of some male figure, either the sanctions of a hostile God or the advances of a seducer. In their ostensibly public laments for lost values and institutions, moreover, many of Tennyson's mediators find themselves being coopted by their creator. Instead of being acknowledged as fellow artists like the embowered women of 1832, they are subsumed as fellow sufferers, haunted by the same losses which have haunted all Tennyson's mediators after Hallam's death: nostalgia for an irretrievable glory, isolation within a hostile space, doubts before an unknown future. Because Tennyson will neither liberate these characters—even in revision—nor acknowledge his involvement with them, most of them remain trapped between the social dilemmas of their poems and the monsters of their author's psyche.

The political poems of 1842, for example, seem to form a rather diffuse collection of *In Memoriam* quatrains, all espousing Tennyson's rather timid philosophy of gradualism. If we compare the poems written before and after Hallam's death, however, we find within these parameters an ominous change. Throughout even the fifty-some stanzas of "Hail Briton," Tennyson is able to maintain a coherent comparison of England's present potential anarchy with the more principled social dissent in the Puritan and Glorious Revolutions of the seventeenth century. By the time of "Love Thou Thy Land," this straightforward political analysis yields to metaphorical anarchy:

> pamper not a hasty time,
>   Nor feed with crude imaginings
>   The herd, wild hearts and feeble wings
> That every sophister can lime.
>
> Deliver not the tasks of might
>   To weakness, neither hide thy ray
>   From those, not blind, who wait for day,
> Though sitting girt with doubtful light.
>
> (ll. 9–16)

Beneath the impersonal sententiousness, we find ourselves again within the private universe of our model, but for once the model cannot restore order because Tennyson cannot decide who will play the mediator and who the Other. Within this universe, the middle-class speaker adopts the posture of a hostile God chastising the oppressed masses, while these same masses are simultaneously threatening him with chaotic natural flux. By translating this psychological anarchy into a metaphorical one, Tennyson completely undermines the poem's theme of cautious, balanced progress.

In another set of poems these same dilemmas produce not catachresis but an apparently facile sentimentality. What we can call the popular poems of the 1842 volume include legends like "Lady Godiva" and ballads like "Lady Clara Vere de Vere" and "The Lord of Burleigh." Tennyson's covert identification with Godiva has already been pointed out by Culler: "When . . . we read the lovely description of her tender, shrinking modesty, her sense of shame, her reluctance to reveal her beauty to the world, then we realize . . . that Tennyson was getting ready to publish once again" (p. 111). Culler argues that in this context the four-line contemporary introduction "is not, as Leigh Hunt says, to inform us how casually Tennyson writes his poetry but to . . . [show] the poet mingling with grooms and porters, as Lady Godiva did" (p. 112). In this company, however, Tennyson also stands trapped between those who have transformed Coventry with modern technology and the city's past, which lives only by countering change with legend. And in the legend this dilemma recreates itself in terms somewhat broader than Culler's. Tennyson assumes the role of the high-born maiden, not just as reclusive artist but as a mediator caught between two contradictory manifestations of the Other: her aristocratic, socially repressive husband and her lower-class, sexually threatening subjects.

While the poem ostensibly celebrates Godiva's wifely chastity and the docile loyalty of her subjects, the imagery portrays her journey as a progressive degradation to the level of sexual object: from her husband's toying with her earring, to her erotically portrayed disrobing, to her literal reenactment of the archetypal nightmare of discovering oneself naked in a public place. Tennyson's description of Peeping Tom as a "low churl" would seem to challenge his usual association of lower-class anarchy with feminine personifications.[40] Yet Godiva passes him by unaware, so preoccupied is she with the sexual assaults made on her by the architecture of her husband's city:

> The little wide-mouthed heads upon the spout
> Had cunning eyes to see: the barking cur

> Made her cheek flame: her palfrey's footfall shot
> Light horrors through her pulses: the blind walls
> Were full of chinks and holes; and overhead
> Fantastic gables, crowding, stared. . . .
>   and all at once,
> With twelve great shocks of sound, the shameless noon
> Was clashed and hammered from a hundred towers.
>   (ll. 56–61, 73–75)

Even though she has "built herself an everlasting name" (l. 79), this mediator has been vicariously violated by the until-now-inanimate surrogates of her husband's aristocratic power.

In a balladlike poem dealing specifically with class conflict, we might expect a more direct relation between Tennyson's public and private fears. Yet "The Lord of Burleigh," like "Godiva," succeeds only in its nightmarish portrayal of aristocratic privilege as male sexual aggression. The supposed landscape painter has planned to surprise his new bride by substituting his baronial hall for the peasant cottage he promised her. Yet the otherwise banal trochees take on a sinister insistence when the apparent detour on their journey is perceived by reader and victim as the entrance of a bewildered animal into the increasingly narrow confines of a trap:

> While he treads with footstep firmer,
>   Leading on from hall to hall.
> And, while now she wonders blindly,
>   Nor the meaning can divine,
> Proudly turns he round and kindly,
>   "All of this is mine and thine."
>   (ll. 51–56)

Though he expects this revelation to open the trap into the spacious vistas of the aristocracy, both his title and his sexual demands upon her merge into a parasitic force draining her vitality:

> So she drooped and drooped before him,
>   Fading slowly from his side:
> Three fair children first she bore him,
>   Then before her time she died.
>   (ll. 85–88)

His order that she be buried as a peasant "that her spirit might have rest" establishes him as a male Aurora and her as a female Tithonus, a human figure trapped within the specious freedom of an inhumanly demanding sexuality.

Lady Clara Vere de Vere seems to will what the Lord of Burleigh accomplishes by accident, the destruction of a peasant lover:

> A great enchantress you may be;
> But there was that across his throat
> Which you had hardly cared to see.
> (ll. 30–32)

In this role she seems to justify Ryals' inclusion of her within the circle of Tennyson's "fatal women."[41] Though Ryals rightly feels that she and similar figures in this volume have dwindled to unthreatening stock characters, her own guilt appears before her like a vengeful God: "There stands a spectre in your hall: / The guilt of blood is at your door" (ll. 42–43). Thus haunted, she lapses like the Soul in her Palace from a manifestation of the Other into its victim:

> You pine among your halls and towers:
> The languid light of your proud eyes
> Is wearied of the rolling hours.
> (ll. 58–60)

The plan of social action Tennyson prescribes for her is no more convincing than the Soul's self-prescribed exile in her "cottage." Instead we see both figures trapped like Burleigh's wife within a castle, within a moribund aristocracy, and within the subconscious associations of a socially ambivalent poet.

The English Idylls

Love in the context of class struggle is treated more openly in another, much-underrated set of poems, the English Idylls. They are underrated, I suspect, because the class conflicts portrayed, instead of merely undermining some conventional formal pattern, are allowed to force the poems into apparent formlessness. They usually consist of casual, aimless conversations filling up an action as inconsequential as going on a picnic or "Walking to the Mail." We can rescue these subjects from triviality most easily if we examine the implications in Tennyson's own term "idyll."

As J. W. Mackail long ago demonstrated, Tennyson was deliberately imitating Theocritus' effort to broaden the mythical and aesthetic traditions of classical Greece to include the diffuse population of the Hellenistic empire.[42] Implicit in this double focus is the hypocrisy of using a still picture of timeless pastoral life to disguise an effort to manipulate social change. Tennyson removes the hypocrisy by making that paradox the theme of these poems. While the equally bleak alternatives of social change and social stasis may undermine the pastoral harmony of the settings, these settings themselves cast the dilemma into personal immediacy. Within this immediacy Tennyson's model and the figures within it can again reassert themselves.[43] Even more radically, these same settings portray both model and figures as debased by society into ludicrous, though still frightening caricatures.

"Audley Court," for example, with its picnic and pastoral singing match, seems the most anachronistically Theocritean of the set, but the entire idyll is built up of class conflicts: the farmer's son versus the idle aristocratic speaker, the frustration with social inequity in Allen's song versus the deliberately decadent eroticism of the speaker's, the busyness of the port versus the stagnant stillness of the pastures within the now-empty estate, even the "griffin-guarded gates" of Audley Court versus the library, "old Sir Robert's pride," now dispersed at auction. Like Arthur and Bedivere, each of these speakers sees his partner as an Other attempting to incorporate the speaker's sanctuary into its domain. Only by agreeing to disagree can they hold these contraries together for the defined space of this holiday.

June Steffensen Hagen has analyzed the pains Tennyson took with the concluding landscape, pruning the Keatsian lushness of the early drafts into an indefinitely delayed closure which encompasses speakers and natural objects, imagery and sound within a liminal harmony.[44] The reasons for Tennyson's pains grow clearer in the present context. The landscape itself is the poem's mediator of last resort, and as the speakers' truce extends only to this holiday, so the conclusion holds the otherwise conflicting elements within a nominally spatial, but ultimately verbal suspension:

> as we sank
> From rock to rock upon the glooming quay,
> The town was hushed beneath us: lower down
> The bay was oily calm; the harbour-buoy,
> Sole star of phosphorescence in the calm,

> With one green sparkle ever and anon
> Dipt by itself, and we were glad at heart.
>   (ll. 82–88)

Similar antagonisms render "Walking to the Mail" even more disjunctive, but the split here grows not between characters but within them. Until the end, for example, John exists only as a straight man for James. Yet as a visitor whose principal memories of the district are ten years out of date, he also serves as a measure of the dilemma underlying all these analyses of social change. Passage of the 1832 Reform Bill, which Tennyson favored, was supposed to bridge the gap between classes. Here reform coalesces into a malignant Other, somewhere between a daemon and a poltergeist, who presides over the dissolution of a noble family.

In a series of apparently disparate portraits, we see Sir Edward Head's fear of the Chartist movement become "a morbid devil in his blood / That veiled the world with jaundice" and ultimately drove him abroad. We see his wife, "the daughter of a cottager," shrivel as if cursed from a beautiful and gracious girl to a shrew, caught "betwixt shame and pride, / New things and old, himself and her" (ll. 52–53). In addition to these manifestations of the Other, we also see a lower-class parody of it. Sir Edward's tenant, so affected by this aristocratic malaise that he punishes a youngster caught fishing on his master's land, finds himself "haunted by a jolly ghost, that shook / The curtains, whined in lobbies, tapt at doors, / And rummaged like a rat" (ll. 28–30). This poltergeist even accompanies him as he tries to leave: "'Yes, we're flitting,' says the ghost" (l. 35).[45]

James now recalls how he and his college roommates dragged a pregnant sow up to their rooms and there lived off her farrow. This grotesque self-revelation we can interpret as either poor students preying on the rich farmer or as upper-class students preying on a barnyard animal. And as the "jolly ghost" parodied the Other, so now the sow, "as never sow was higher in the world," parodies one of Tennyson's favorite mediators, the high-born maiden. As a sort of high-breeding matron, she is exploited and denied any future for her progeny by the lower classes. James's image of the sow as Niobe even identifies him as a descendant of Tennyson's vengeful god figures. To quote Culler (p. 124), "the more we hear of James the less we like him."

This welter of serious and parodic figures is mediated not by the landscape but by the almost monosyllabic John:

> What know we of the secrets of a man?
> His nerves were wrong. What ails us, who are sound,
> That we should mimic this raw fool the world,
> Which charts us all in its coarse blacks or whites.
>
> (ll. 94–97)

John suggests here that by rejecting the "world's" social stereotypes, by acknowledging their link with Sir Edward, the two can keep from being possessed by his personal Other. If John's mediation seems rather too glib, we must remember that the hostile forces which other mediators have had to delimit he encounters as *almost* harmless parodies.

Here Tennyson has been able to juxtapose so many conflicting attitudes only by embodying the conflicts within his authorial voice. In "Edwin Morris" he can reintegrate at least his present self within the speaker. In so doing, however, he must fragment the poem into a series of warring genres, each embodying a different version of the model, each reflecting a different period in his creative and romantic life. The first genre, a microcosmic idyll within the speeches of Edwin Morris himself, echoes the Lover's early conviction that he can enlist his beloved Cadrilla to mediate between him and virtually any experience. Ricks's edition (II, 141n, 143n) points out that most of Edwin's encomiums are borrowed from discarded descriptions of Rose, the Gardener's Daughter, a figure Michael Timko defines as the willingly passive recipient of the speaker's upper-class affection. With Rose, Tennyson could show sensuality in the service of sentiment—reconciling time and landscape to and through human love.[46] So with his beloved, Edwin can actually shape the diurnal and seasonal cycles into a constant progress towards closure: "daily hope fulfilled, to rise again, / Revolving toward fulfillment" (ll. 38–39).

The subsequent conversation, however, sets Morris as the thesis of a dialectic, opposed by the mindless male chauvinism of "the fat-faced curate Edward Bull" and then, if not synthesized, at least evaluated by the speaker in what Ricks aptly describes as an "implicit criticism by T[ennyson] of his earlier poetic manner" (*Poems*, II, 144n):

>   something jarred;
> Whether he spoke too largely; that there seemed
> A touch of something false, some self-conceit,
> Or over-smoothness. . . .
>
> (ll. 72–75)

At this point, however, the speaker stops mediating between these incompatible claims for love and poetry. Instead he tries to mediate between Tennyson and the domain of his particular Other, the forbidden aristocratic world of the Tennyson-d'Eyncourts and Rosa Baring. To woo *his* beloved, Letty Hill, the speaker borrows the pretentious metaphor of her social class. As the Hills have aged their new money by investing in an ancient castle, so he tries to take it and the girl by storm. Unfortunately, in one of the funniest and saddest passages in Tennyson, the medieval model shifts from "The Knight's Tale" to the barnyard chase in "The Nun's Priest's Tale." Tennyson seems to parody his own fondness for piling up parallel structures as, without syntactic break, he transforms an accumulation of passion to an accumulation of ludicrous but hostile onlookers:

> She turned, we closed, we kissed, swore faith, I breathed
> In some new planet: a silent cousin stole
> Upon us and departed: "Leave," she cried,
> "O leave me!" "Never, dearest, never: here
> I brave the worst:" and while we stood like fools
> Embracing, all at once a score of pugs
> And poodles yelled within, and out they came
> Trustees and Aunts and Uncles.
>
> (ll. 114–21)

While the speaker has not fallen before the hostile stronghold in battle with its hostile lord, the bathetic reduction of the Other to "pugs and poodles" has not lessened their collective power.[47] "The rentroll Cupid," "that was a God, and is a lawyer's clerk" (l. 102), can still thwart the speaker's love and drive him to flee by night.

In fleeing, the speaker brings us to the narrative present with yet another shift in genre. As we have moved from idyll to debate, to romantic narrative, to mock-heroic parody, so now we glide into Wordsworthian retrospection.

> For in the dust and drouth of London life
> She moves among my visions of the lake,
> While the prime swallow dips his wing, or then
> While the gold-lily blows, and overhead
> The light cloud smoulders on the summer crag.
>
> (ll. 143–47)

As Pattison says (p. 78), however, nature here "becomes problematical and ambiguous." Despite the flowers, the speaker's memories are not of dancing daffodils, and the smoldering cloud suggests that the landscape, instead of mediating between his present and his past, hides its own unresolved trauma. The trauma in turn casts its pall upon the poem's opening characterization of this past as "my sweet, wild, fresh three quarters of a year, / My one Oasis in the dust and drouth / Of city life!" (ll. 2–4). Instead of a Romantic reflection reshaping the past, this poem becomes an uncontrolled compulsion to relive it.

    In its compulsive return to Tennyson's creative and emotional past, "Edwin Morris" leads us naturally to two better-known retrospective poems from the late 1830s, "The Vision of Sin" and "Locksley Hall." While no more successful than their predecessors, these otherwise disparate works merit our serious attention because in them Tennyson makes a serious effort to reevaluate his own career.

In "The Vision of Sin," for example, Tennyson evaluates the alternatives to his stoic self-denial in the face of loss: loss of Hallam, of Rosa, and now (since the poem seems contemporaneous with "Love and Duty"), loss of Emily Sellwood. The poem is supposed to portray a youth being initiated into a full-blown orgy and, after countless repetitions, withering away to the "gray and gap-toothed man" whose nihilistic song makes up the penultimate section. This moralistic reading, however, ignores an immense temporal and spatial gap. The youth exists only in the palace and the old man only in the inn of age, disease, and death. The youth seems never to age, while the old man seems never to have been young. By reducing everyone to bodies in his first incarnation and skeletons in his second, this apparent vice figure also reduces into irrelevance all the sexual threats associated with social class: "Madam—if I know your sex, / From the fashion of your bones" (ll. 182–83). In short he begins to change into a covert mediator, confronting the same aristocratic manifestations of the Other confronted by Godiva and the speakers of "Clara Vere de Vere" and "Edwin Morris."

We should remember, however, that when Tennyson's mediators triumph too conclusively over one manifestation of the Other, they risk encountering it in some far more frightening form. In theory, of course, these appearances of God remain problematical only for the sinful world of this poem. In reality, they repeat similar incursions of the Other in Tennyson's earliest poetry. By covertly identifying with this mediator, therefore, Tennyson must relive through him a whole series of these encounters: guarding the fountain of inspiration against some hostile critic in "The Poet's Mind," or distancing the supernatural conflict within "Armageddon," or accepting the freedom offered by an equally ominous dawn in "A Dream of Fair Women."

The dawn here may dramatize less "a crime of sense avenged by sense that wore with time" than a mediator for the mature Tennyson being enveloped within a primitive universe from his creator's past. Within this universe invisible voices pronounce incomprehensible judgments and the ultimate power speaks in an unknown tongue. The "answer pealed from that high land," however, resembles no single early symbol so much as the equally inarticulate blast from the quarry which "answers" the millennial visions of "The Golden Year." As Tennyson's poetic vehicles carry his mediators from confrontation into attempted escape, the Other insinuates that these supposedly "new" sanctuaries are really part of its old domain.

"Locksley Hall" establishes that past love can prove just as disorienting as past lust. In fact June Steffensen Hagen finds the speaker himself fearful that, "if love made him a poet originally, the removal of love will take away his ability."[48] I would question only her claim that the poem recreates his quest to renew the dried-up springs of his own imagination. I would instead follow F. E. L. Priestley's observation that the speaker imagines Amy's future so vividly that he reacts to each projected scene as if it were fact.[49] It is the troubling nature of these projections, in fact, which render this speaker one of the most troubling of the poet's mediators.

According to most interpretations of the poem since Rader, Tennyson is using this speaker to reorder his life after his rejection by Rosa Baring.[50] This interpretation helps explain the speaker's compulsion to caricature Amy's husband, like the nouveau riche Hills, as a pathetic travesty of the Other:

> What is this? his eyes are heavy: think not they are glazed with wine.
> Go to him: it is thy duty: kiss him: take his hand in thine. . . .
>
> Like a dog, he hunts in dreams, and thou art staring at the wall,
> Where the dying night-lamp flickers, and the shadows rise and fall.
>
> Then a hand shall pass before thee, pointing to his drunken sleep,
> To thy widowed marriage-pillows, to the tears that thou wilt weep.
>
> (ll. 51–52, 79–82)

In both vision and poem the hand is clearly the speaker's, pointing like the parody of a mediator at this parody of the Other. And yet the vividness of his own vision drives him to interrupt both these sections with outbursts of frustrated rage: "Perish in thy self-contempt!" (l. 96); "Better thou wert dead before me, though I slew thee with my hand!" (l. 56).

Amy's role has already undergone two changes: from mediator as her love gave meaning to his universe to unworthy ingrate as she rejects him, to pitiable victim as she discovers her husband's true nature. Now, as the wife of "Another," Amy changes like Cadrilla into a real—not a parodied—manifestation of the Other. Priestley points out (pp. 518–19) that the speaker sidles around the couple's sexual relations with greater discomfort than can be explained by authorial or public prudishness. Yet if he avoids envisioning her as the embodiment of female sexuality, he cannot avoid envisioning the results:

> Baby lips will laugh me down: my latest rival brings thee rest.
> Baby fingers, waxen touches, press me from the mother's breast.
>
> (ll. 89–90)

Even as the speaker contemplates Amy's transferring her love from him to her child, he must acknowledge his continued dependence on her. Like Edwin Morris, he has used his love to transform the spatial and temporal discontinuity within these later poems into a projection of the couple's own desires:

> Love took up the glass of Time, and turned it in his glowing hands;
> Every moment, lightly shaken, ran itself in golden sands.
>
> (ll. 31–32)

Yet every early couplet opens with a spatial or temporal modifier: "'Tis the place," "Locksley Hall," "Many a night," "Here about the beach," "When the centuries," "When I dipt into the future," "In the spring," "Then her cheek." In order to affirm his own youth, he must continue to affirm Amy as mediator and the hall as their shared sanctuary; yet by rejecting him, by proclaiming herself Other, Amy shows *him* to be the interloper on *her* time and *her* space.

His difficulties in establishing his own spatial and temporal ground are reflected in Tennyson's own difficulties in finding an appropriate place and sequence for his visions. Ricks points out (*Poems*, II, 120–21n) that lines 11–16 and 121–30 originally constituted a single flashback, an effort to feel again "the wild pulsation" that he had lost with Amy. Then, since he had to acknowledge that her loss had "left [him] dry, / Left [him] with the palsied heart, and left [him] with the jaundiced eye" (ll. 131–32), Tennyson moved the entire visionary passage forward to line 11. Then, since the passage now delayed the speaker's initial compulsion to pour out his unrequited love to the wind and waves, Tennyson finally cut it in two by repeating lines 15–16. Priestley observes (p. 520) that the speaker has more trouble imagining his own future than Amy's. All this shuffling suggests that once evicted from his former sanctuary, this mediator cannot find a home even for his visions.

The speaker's efforts to find at least a rhetorical locus for mediation may account for several of the poem's less popular features: the thumping trochees, the end-stopped couplets, the poorly defined audience, the hyperbole, the self-conscious airs of self-importance. The imaginative constructs he opposes to Amy—from annihilation to sexual fulfillment on some tropical island—inadvertently parody some of those employed by Tennyson's earlier mediators. Even his final vision of the future seems no more compelling than any of his earlier ones. Our sense of hope, and perhaps the speaker's as well, grows rather from the sheer imaginative exuberance he displays throughout the poem. Through it he finally affirms, not necessarily the future, but at least the continued possibility of imagining it.

This affirmation of exuberance, however, cannot offset our impression that this poem—and the whole volume—are running downhill. When Tennyson tries to bypass the model as his sole means of bodying forth internal conflicts, he loses the implicit decorum which it established between author and mediator, tenor and vehicle. Altieri (p. 298) celebrates the stanzas on evolution in *In Memoriam* for their deconstruction of language from abstract thought to inarticulate cry. To appreciate "Locksley Hall" and the poems of the late 1830s, we need instead to listen for their *over-rhetorical* cry. We need to hear within its apparent bombast the kind of personal anguish Tennyson was expressing much more directly in the lyrics which would become *In Memoriam*. Finally we need to hear within this cry a series of implicit admissions: that he has lost the protective distance between himself and his vulnerable mediators; that his supposedly public world is metamorphosing into a procession of Others from his own past; that repressing the loss of Hallam has so diffused loss within this imaginative universe that he no longer knows where to look for mediation or what kind of mediation to look for.

Such an appreciation cannot restore these poems to the artistic level Tennyson had achieved at the decade's beginning. It can suggest, as it seems to have suggested to Tennyson, that such rhetorical overkill could be made dramatically useful. In both the "Morte" and the English idylls he juxtaposed attempts at mediation so incompatible that they tore apart the fabric of their shared poem. After roughly five years of wrestling with the intensely personal *In Memoriam*, he would be ready to structure *The Princess* as a conflict, not just between mediators but between rhetorical campaigns to take control of the poem itself. Within those rhetorical constructs, however, we will find descendants of these characters from the late 1830s—frightened, vulnerable, strangely sympathetic extensions of their frightened, vulnerable, and strangely sympathetic author.

CHAPTER FIVE

In Memoriam

Of the poems in the 1842 volume, only "Break, Break, Break" confronted Hallam's death with any degree of directness, and even there the poem's setting, characters, and argument were thrown into an anguished indeterminacy. The great repository of direct confrontations is, of course, *In Memoriam.* As Timothy Peltason describes the poem, "The unique self and the unique moment rise up . . . in the space of memorable individual lyrics that refuse . . . to be read as preparations for 'the one far-off divine event' to which the creation and the poem both move."[1] Yet the immediacy of individual sections within the finished poem belies the difficulty Tennyson had in achieving this goal.

The reasons for his nervous, almost compulsive indirection grow from the same dilemma we analyzed in the last chapter. Hallam's death had effectively called into question the validity of Tennyson's model. It exposed most of his mediators as projections of his own psyche, projections whose power grew either from the same friend whose loss they must now mediate or from a psyche devastated by this loss. The loss itself, as we saw, refused to be brought into an imaginative landscape where it could be personified and so confronted.

Hallam, moreover, presented special problems of his own. Alive he may have acted less like a mediator than like the guarantor of the possibility of mediation. Dead he became the object of Tennyson's desire, what Peltason (p. 15) calls "not a vivid presence, but a vivid absence." T. S. Eliot noted early that Tennyson's "concern is for the loss of man rather than the gain of God."[2] But throughout Tennyson, objects of desire are rarely mediators. Either male (Paris and Lancelot) or female (Amoret and Cadrilla), they remain manifestations of the Other, sources of frustration at best and devastation at worst.

While we found hints of this dilemma in some of the other poems from the early 1830s, similar hints do not appear within the *In Memoriam* lyrics until several years later. Before then we can see only the careful efforts to avoid the dilemma altogether. Though often topical, the earliest-written sections carefully choose their topicality at the edge of Tennyson's central grief. With a rhetorical indirection rivaling that of "Ulysses," they never focus directly on Hallam, on his loss, or on the personal and philosophical consequences of it. Moreover they move almost precipitously toward closure. Only in an early stage of the Trinity Butcher's Book, where Tennyson assembled a formal progression from loss toward redress, could he consider delaying closure long enough to consider this loss directly.

Even there the lyrics employ considerable indirection. Because in death Hallam seems to have leagued with the Other, Tennyson vacillates between enshrining him within the past and relying upon several provisional mediators. Though at first these mediators are barely animate, they establish what Ulysses, Tithonus, and Arthur have already established, proof that Tennyson has not lost his power to project. Their growing success in confronting the Other only brings it back in some new and more frightening form. Yet the most frightening of these, Nature, seems to trigger Tennyson's realization that its power to frighten grows from a personification which the earlier mediators have tried to foist upon it. After this point, each new incursion upon Tennyson's newly reordered universe promotes his paradoxical faith that the incursion itself will create opportunities for mediation.

His very success finally drives him to question whether his stronger intimations of Hallam's mediating presence are themselves only projections of his own stronger imaginative power. But as he comes to perceive a rhythm between his openness to these intimations and their arrival, he comes to perceive Hallam not as an object committed to loss but as a being dependent on Tennyson to fulfill his potential. Here, in perhaps Tennyson's most desperate dilemma, his revisions produce a mediator whose increasing presence does not imply increasing autonomy. In fact Hallam can mediate only to the extent that Tennyson can speak through him.

In discovering this power, Tennyson goes on to discover another: in fleshing out the skeleton of his elegy, he can move in spirit through the individual stages, not just of his poem, but of his grief as well. Hence he can reaffirm, perhaps more successfully than Wordsworth through his myriad revisions of *The Prelude*, that to explore loss with sufficient imaginative power is to oppose the power of loss itself.

We can trace this process accurately because of two excellent bibliographical studies: the variorum edition by Susan Shatto and Marion Shaw[3] and the analysis of the early manuscripts by Joseph Sendry.[4] Together these works give, if not a complete, certainly a much clearer picture of the poem's composition. In the process, they shatter two assumptions upon which many interpretations still rest: first, that the poem's final order reflects roughly the order of composition (i.e., that Tennyson moved from writing gloomy lyrics to writing hopeful ones), and second, that he moved from writing occasional, dramatic lyrics to more reflective, philosophical ones. We have long known that neither of these assumptions held up in detail—have known, for example, that both Dark House sections (7 and 119) were added after the first trial edition of 1850. Yet these manuscript studies show that Tennyson denied dramatic objectivity to his earliest-written sections by closing them within his personal dilemma and by rigorously pointing them toward some final solution to it.[5]

At every stage and on every level, even the completed poem reflects this tension between the conflicting desires to effect and to delay closure.[6] On the highest level, for example, the whole poem works to encompass its major patterns, be they the skeletal structure of the Christmas poems or the alternating of expansion and contraction which J. C. C. Mays has posited.[7] On a lower level, the fourth line of every stanza, its rhyme reaching back toward the first, works to tie the stanza into a microcosm of the whole sequence.[8] The very first stanza, itself composed originally as a motto, still serves as a self-contained paradigm for the hundreds which will follow:

> I held it truth, with him who sings
>   To one clear harp in divers tones,
>   That men may rise on stepping-stones
> Of their dead selves to higher things.
>
>   (1: 1–4)

Other early-written sections show a similar, often less qualified drive toward closure. The Christmas lyric section 30, for example, portrays the family reaching toward religious consolation: "They do not die / . . . Nor change to us although they change" (ll. 22, 24). Instead of allowing the family to mediate for him, Tennyson insists on imposing some often transcendent conclusion upon himself and his potential mediators. None of these closures adequately prefigures those offered in the final sections of the poem; in fact the obvious differences among them suggest that no single conclusion can or is meant to supplant any other. Each section, in other words, strives toward an autonomous standing as a microcosm of the whole process. As Ricks has observed (*Tennyson*, pp. 121–22), these early lyrics are *too* resolved to permit Tennyson to confront his deepest grief. Tennyson himself will later describe them as "short swallow flights of song" and his grief as itself "given in outline and no more."

In another early section, 18, we find a revision which captures this delay of closure through context. The present first stanza stood originally at the end:

> And yet 'tis something here to stand
> Where he in native earth is laid,
> And from his ashes may be made
> The violet of his native land.[9]

Only in later revisions does this consolation lead first to the hopeless conjecture that Tennyson can exchange his own life for Hallam's and then to the realization that his spirit "slowly forms the firmer mind" without any clearly defined hope.

To assemble a collection of such would-be microcosms would be inviting chaos; yet Joseph Sendry has shown (pp. 45–48) that as early as the Trinity Notebook of c. 1834 Tennyson was trying to group the ten sections then written: he balanced contrasting situations (for example, the embarkation versus the arrival of the ship); he began one section from the previously unqualified conclusion of another; he severed the section on Lazarus, 31-a and 31-b, into its component and hence partial claims; he even used refrains like the one repeated in sections 9 and 17: ". . . I shall not see / Till all my widowed race be run" (9: 17–18 and 17: 19–20). When Tennyson later claimed that he had not contemplated arranging the sections "till he discovered he had written so many," he may have been admitting that this material was proving more refractory than he had anticipated.

According to both Sendry and the editors of the variorum edition, the next stage in Tennyson's composition is represented by the Huntington and Sellwood manuscripts. While these critics do not use either manuscript to speculate about Tennyson's intentions,[10] there is evidence that both predate the Trinity Butcher's Book and that both contain not a coherent ordering but a rough grouping of related lyrics.[11] From them we can draw further inferences about where Tennyson was taking his lyrics and, equally important, where they were taking him.

Sendry describes the Huntington manuscript (p. 51) as a new approach both to Hallam and to the nascent poem, "a larger, looser gathering of reflections on metaphysical and religious matters . . . not tied to concrete situations or local settings." By shedding the limitations of a particular occasion, these lyrics begin to grope toward some shared but still very tentative context. If we then interpret this context as part of Tennyson's continuing attempt to resolve the tension between immediate and suspended closure, we can discover not only links between the adjacent sections but a rhythm produced by their sequence.

Because this manuscript contains several lyrics finally numbered in the 40s and 60s, for example, we might speculate that Tennyson was exploring the possibilities for reunion implicit in his assumption that Hallam's spirit continued to exist in some higher state. Yet because Tennyson claims that *all* his imaginative projections can transcend space and time, he is forced to accept the integrity of each separate possibility. Consequently the dialectic which Andrew Fichter finds throughout *In Memoriam* seems to be inaugurated by the strings of consecutive sections within the Huntington manuscript.[12] Each partial, contingent conclusion produces a contrary, often ironic answer in the following lyric. This process, however, far from suggesting a direction for the poem, projects an endless series of bifurcations.

Emily Sellwood's transcriptions repeat the patterns of the Huntington manuscript, but where that set echoed the philosophical speculations of "The Two Voices," hers reaches further back to the more personal quandaries of "Supposed Confessions." Each of the earlier-written Christmas lyrics, we remember, had ended with a strong affirmation: the original fusion of sections 31 and 32 in the Trinity notebook, for example, had paralleled the serene faith of Lazarus' sister with that of Tennyson's own. But as the later division of this poem left section 31 containing Tennyson's unanswered questions, so the new poems added here, while not actively attacking the family's conventional piety, work to reconcile it with a position simply *assumed* to be different: "O thou . . . / Whose faith has centre everywhere, . . . / Leave thou thy sister when she prays" (33: 1, 3, 5). In his earlier poetry, Tennyson had been almost callous about expending fictional mediators in his struggle with the Other; but first Hallam refused to fit conveniently into his model, and now he hesitates to cast his own sister into a sacrificial role she would fit all too well.

Thus section 34, instead of disputing her assurance "that life shall live for evermore," simply relegates it to the second line and then proceeds to contemplate the world called forth by its denial:

> This round of green, this orb of flame,
> > Fantastic beauty; such as lurks
> > In some wild poet, when he works
> Without a conscience or an aim.

> What then were God to such as I?
>   'Twere hardly worth my while to choose
>   Of all things mortal, or to use
> A little patience ere I die.
>
>   (ll. 5–12)

The random generation of new sections from their opposites suddenly leaps out as a metaphor for the creative power of an indifferent deity. In this blasphemous parody of the poet as the imitator of God's creative powers, Tennyson discovers that the Other has been imitating him all along. He has created an imaginative bulwark against a loss he conceived of as some power from outside. Now the power has appeared, formed in his own image by the imaginative faculties which he invoked to keep it out.[13]

The verbs in this vision do suggest Tennyson's use of what Harry Puckett has called the subjunctive imagination: "What then were God to such as I? / 'Twere hardly worth my while to choose. . . . 'Twere best at once to sink to peace" (34: 9–10, 13). Because these are all conditions contrary to fact, they would confront him only if he lost his faith that "life should live for evermore." The subjunctive imagination thus grants the power of exploring conflicting, often frightening possibilities without committing the self to any one of them. Tennyson's affirmation of art and artful purpose in nature actually requires him to imagine their absence.[14] As a balance to Puckett's persuasive reading, I would only expand my earlier qualification of Johnson: the "what if's" which distance the vision are the same "what if's" which have invoked it in the first place. As Tennyson probes deeper into both the cosmos and his own psyche, their apparent pledge of imaginative immunity lures him into confrontation with the most frightening specters of the poem.

It is in this context that Tennyson turned to the composition of the Trinity Butcher's Book (hereafter referred to as T.MS). He had by now identified at least some manifestations of the Other and some techniques for containing them, but the escapes from the specters of one lyric consistently embroiled him with those of another. The device he needed now was a more comprehensive, architectonic one—an ordered progression for all the lyrics now written and a heuristic for adding and positioning any new ones. The ordering in T.MS broke down, to be sure, since the manuscript had to be replaced in 1842 by the Lincoln Butcher's Book (hereafter L.MS), but in its original conception it stands, I shall argue, as the single most important influence upon both the shape and the content of the completed poem.

Shatto and Shaw report (p. 12) that T.MS contains seventy-eight sections, but "that Tennyson's practice was usually to copy only one section on to the recto of each leaf, leaving the lower half and the verso of each leaf blank." If we test this assumption by examining the placement of the twenty-nine sections known to exist before the composition of this butcher's book, we discover that only three appear elsewhere than the upper recto.[15] There are sixteen apparently new lyrics occupying the upper recto, but only five of these appear before section 78.[16] This arrangement supports three separate conclusions: first, that the extant early-written manuscripts, while usually not containing first drafts, may contain most of the sections written up to the time of their compilation; second, that several poems appearing late in the sequence were composed between that time and the compilation of T.MS; and third, that the ordering of these later poems was thus more problematical, an assumption borne out by their subsequent reordering in the later Lincoln Butcher's Book.[17]

If we grant all these conclusions, at least provisionally, we can posit a separate compositional stage, one which I shall call T.MS-1, between the rather nebulous individual collections in the Sellwood and Huntington notebooks and the "completed" T.MS. Indeed this last form may not represent a stage at all but, as Shatto and Shaw argue (p. 14), a decision to abandon this butcher's book because the poem had unexpectedly grown beyond its limits.[18] The forty-four poems either already extant or appearing sequentially on the upper recto folios of T.MS may represent, by contrast, an *ordered* series of already polished sections which Tennyson copied into a new butcher's book on the assumption that he could bring the work to publishable form with only limited revision.

Examining the series, we may be surprised to discover how closely a collection roughly one-third as long as the printed text could prefigure its shape, particularly in the middle sections. In its principal divisions, however, this stage seems to recapitulate the imaginative rhythm of Tennyson's early career. Initially, the even divisions enshrine Hallam as the goal of Tennyson's imaginative quest into some golden age of the past or some transcendent existence after death. The odd divisions, on the other hand, drive Tennyson to identify with provisional mediators, mediators which often succeed in escaping or delimiting the still nebulous specter of Hallam's loss. Subsequently these mediators either desert Tennyson for the Other or inadvertently resurrect it in a new form. Yet amid the fear and frustration accompanying these successive betrayals, Tennyson usually discovers the basis for a new and more powerful mediation. To appreciate the rhythmic alternations within this larger progression, we must now examine its individual divisions in some detail.

In the first division (sections 1, 3, 9, 17, 18, 19), outside forces move toward the passive poet. Within the opening sections of T.MS-1, Tennyson appears too passive to undertake any quest. The optimistic quatrain which comprises section 1 probably stands as an epigraph for the whole process, not as its beginning.[19] Within the sections on detached pages, a procession of more-or-less hostile forces moves actively towards the nearly paralyzed speaker. His very passivity suggests that as an Other, Hallam's loss may be toying with him, appearing now in one incongruous form and now in another: in section 3 he is besieged first by an officious personification of his own grief and then by the random motion of a mechanistic Nature; later, in section 21, he will be mocked by a series of scornful passersby.

In sections 9 and 17, as he waits for the arrival of Hallam's body, the approaching ship seems an inanimate mediator toward which he can reach out "in spirit":

> My blessing, like a line of light,
> Is on the waters day and night,
> And like a beacon guards thee home.
>
> (17: 10–12)

Yet the ship's safe arrival, even if due to Tennyson's imaginative intercession, is more honestly evaluated in the following lyric: "'Tis well, 'tis something. . . . 'Tis little" (18: 1, 5). Section 19 suggests—as the lyrics interpolated within this sequence will later make clear—that the ship, the forces driving it, and Hallam's body are all manifestations of an impersonal Other. As such they render irrelevant Tennyson's blessing and coopt all his imaginative powers: "The Wye is hushed nor moved along, / And hushed my deepest grief of all" (ll. 9–10).

In the second division (sections X, 22, 21, 38), his escape into the past calls up the Shadow of Hallam's death. Since the present Hallam "sleeps or wears the mask of sleep," Tennyson next turns to a past Hallam for what *appears* as mediation. While Henry Kozicki can argue that the completed poem does confront the terror of the past,[20] these sections turn the past into an escape. Just as the 1832 volume provided the authorial projections of 1830 with the security of a world of art, so here Tennyson transforms their shared existence into an Edenic golden age. But Hallam soon proves to be less a key to this retreat than the object for whom Tennyson has come to look. This is, I think, the first stage of the poem's composition to which we can apply Ryals' claim that *In Memoriam* refuses to accept the reality of loss.[21] It is here, individually and with virtually no appeal to authority, that Tennyson begins testing the possibility that the friendship of two transient humans was and could remain as significant as any other aspect of the universe.[22] In section 22, for example, he defines the four-year relationship as one of perpetual beginnings: the two "from April on to April went, / And glad at heart from May to May" (ll. 7–8).

For the moment, however, his will to enshrine the past and the beloved object is not matched by a corresponding imaginative hold on either. Whereas fictional mediators like Ulysses and Tithonus could recreate their lives in order to reinterpret them, Tennyson's own "passion for the past" here produces a patently artificial construct. As such the pastoral world "of Arcady,"[23] like the cozy mental landscapes of the 1830 volume, seems to call up another incursion of the Other, "the Shadow feared of man." Beneath this "Shadow," the "altered skies" of section 38 (the first extant lyric within T.MS proper) rob Tennyson's carefree progress with Hallam of both goal and direction: "With weary steps I loiter on, . . . / My prospect and horizon gone" (ll. 1, 4).

In the third division (sections 13, 28, 30, 31, 32, 33–4, 36), his encounter with his family's faith calls up the specter of a purposeless cosmos. Having failed to recapture or even reimagine the past Hallam, Tennyson turns back to less capable but less challenging mediators, the apparently inanimate Christmas bells of section 28. Even these, however, can offer a transition from the artificial past to the actual present. They evoke enough associations with Tennyson's past and his surroundings that he, like Faust on hearing the Easter chorus, can renounce suicide for patience. More important, they also allow Tennyson to look, again like Faust, for present comfort from human voices. They call him to undertake a new imaginative quest for mediators among those members of his family who are trying, like him, to make sense of a Christmas without Hallam.

Given the early composition of most of these sections (28–36), their relatively late appearance in T.MS-1 can be only partially explained by Tennyson's more active role within them. The rest of the explanation we have already analyzed within the Sellwood manuscript: Tennyson's celebration of his sister's piety leads quickly to his own suicidal confrontation with a godless universe modeled on his own imagination. In section 36 he gains distance on this Other by positing "the creed of creeds" as "more strong than all poetic thought." Ultimately, however, his creed must offer some more immediate restitution for his loss.

In the fourth division (sections 41–46), religious doubts make him plead for more unmediated communication with Hallam. To win such restitution, he reinterprets as pleas for visionary communication his more philosophical speculations from both the Huntington and Sellwood manuscripts (41–46). James Kissane has roundly criticized these visions as lacking any firm religious tradition.[24] Yet Tennyson's heaven may be less a theological than an imaginative failure. Like his Edenic golden age, this invocation fails for reasons besides his compulsion to make Hallam the end and not the means of his quest. In fact Tennyson cannot really visualize a Hallam who can fulfill his own cosmic potential and still satisfy Tennyson's very personal needs. If Hallam's spirit continues to "rise from high to higher" (41: 3), will Tennyson's be "evermore a life behind"? Will both sleep till the end of time and reawaken together (43)? Will Hallam be susceptible to information from earth, or will he even care to hear of his former friend (44–46)? Like all Tennyson's mediators, Hallam cannot achieve even a heaven based on wish fulfillment without risking psychological infidelity.

In the fifth division (sections 48, 51, 60, 61, 66, 68, 71), philosophical doubts open the possibility of some relationship with the dead in fictional parallels and dreams. The implicit conflicts within Tennyson's desires may explain the subsequent set of demurrals: Section 48, for example, not daring to "trust the larger lay," reduces the mediating power of poetry to "short swallow flights of song." Section 51 may explain this limitation when it questions Tennyson's longing for contact with the supernatural mediator he has created. In section 41 Tennyson complained that Hallam had "turn'd to something strange" (l. 5); he now muses whether we do "indeed desire the dead / Should still be near us at our side" (ll. 1–2).

Such demurrals apparently cause him to distance within the past this draft's closest encounters with visionary experience.[25] In the newly added section 71, sleep has "forged at last / A night-long Present of the Past / In which we went through summer France" (ll. 2–4). Yet by surrendering himself to this inner experience, Tennyson has paradoxically captured a far more objective image of the past than he could from the metaphorical manipulations of section 22. The preceding section, 68, includes his first admission—still only in dream—that his own youth had been less than the paradise of lost innocence.[26] After dreaming of "a trouble" in Hallam's eye, he identifies it as "the trouble of my youth / That foolish sleep transfers to thee." (68: 15–16). This admission presents Hallam for the first time as a true mediator instead of an object. The whole sequence, moreover, suggests that the more he encompasses Hallam within his own imagination, the more Hallam gains that unexpected aptness of response which establishes him as an independent spirit.

In the sixth division (sections 73, 74, 75), doubts about the power of art reveal the value of the poem as a recompense for loss. As we should now expect, even such provisional success can only be followed by doubt. Sections 73–75, all copied from earlier manuscripts, vent his frustration at being unable to capture and thus preserve Hallam's unrealized potential in his poem. The sequence mirrors King Arthur's refusal to let Bedivere preserve the realm's glory in Excalibur; yet Tennyson captured in the "Morte" the very elegy which he renounces in its moral. Here too even his denial that his poem can win lasting fame implicitly acknowledges its potential as artifact. Only after his dream-encounters with Hallam's spirit can he openly consider whether his elegy, like the artistic bastions of his 1832 mediators, might itself compensate for the loss it portrays.

In the seventh division (sections 78, 80, 82, 83, 85), the loss of Hallam to seasonal change prompts him to reach toward Hallam through it. Again it seems no coincidence that the following section, 78, should put most starkly the dilemma posed by Tennyson's growing success in allaying these losses. During the family's celebration of the second Christmas after Hallam's death, he is driven to ask, "Can grief be changed to less? / O last regret, regret can die!" (ll. 16–17). How can he come to terms with his loss of Hallam without simultaneously surrendering the loss to the inhuman Other lurking within time and change? He confronts these powers, in fact, by his very placement of this section. While the lyrics which became the second and third Christmas sections appeared with the first in earlier drafts, their position there did not suggest the new use he now makes of them as markers for seasonal cycles.

Until now most of Tennyson's landscapes have alternated between the Edenic sanctuary in section 22 and the hellish domain of the Other in section 3. This Christmas poem, however, signals his acceptance of both spatial and temporal relativity. In section 83, for example, he can now participate in seasonal change, not to escape loss but to accept it as a means of renewal:

> O thou, new-year, delaying long,
>   Delayest the sorrow in my blood,
>   That longs to burst a frozen bud
> And flood a fresher throat with song.
> (ll. 13–16)

Evocations of nature and natural change also insinuate themselves into the following sections, 85 and 102. More than even Tennyson's dreams, these seem to arrive at their own times, on their own terms, and for their own purposes.[27] Even their scattered and changing placement within the poem suggests that they come when Tennyson can let them come. And as a chastened Romantic, Tennyson can let them come to the extent that he stops attributing all incursions from without to the Other. These incursions of nature offer neither redress nor consolation for Tennyson's loss; yet they *can* mediate if he refrains from dictating either the times or the ends of their mediation.

The central position of section 85 makes all the more unfortunate the loss of its opening folio. There is good evidence, however, that the complete lyric included both Tennyson's claim that his was "a friendship as had mastered time" (l. 64) and his immediate admission that he was torn between seasonal change ("Summer on the steaming floods") and the fixity of his loss ("My prime passion in the grave").[28] Within this tentative context, Hallam's "whisper," "I triumph in conclusive bliss, / And that serene result of all" (ll. 91–92), would mediate a central dilemma of the entire poem.

In this context Hallam might finally become a far more conclusive mediator than the provisional figures Tennyson has turned to until now. Yet even if section 85 were meant to stand—like section 95 in the completed poem—as the visionary centerpiece of T.MS-1, it remains far more tentative than its later counterpart. To begin with, it is not definitely Hallam who speaks but rather "my old affection of the tomb, / A part of stillness" (ll. 77–78). And in the first lines of the extant T.MS text, Tennyson doubts whether he has had a dialogue at all:

> So hold I converse with the dead;
>   Or so methinks the dead would say;

> Or so shall grief with symbols play
> And pining life be fancy-fed.
>
> (ll. 93–96)

In the eighth division (sections 102, 105, 91, 88, 108, 112), the spatial boundedness of Hallam's spirit causes the lyrics of the third year to lose purpose and direction. With the partial failure of section 85 as a center-piece, both the third year of the cycle and T.MS-1 as a formal document begin to lose their focus. Until this point the upper recto sections have appeared in dark ink written in a firm hand with their stanzas evenly spaced. Beginning with the following section, 102, they begin to share the more tentative appearance of the sections which will come to be interpolated earlier in the manuscript.

This textual uncertainty, moreover, reflects Tennyson's conception of the poem itself. The seasonal progression following the third Christmas poem duplicates the previous one, and Tennyson acknowledges as much when he later moves two of the sections, 88 and 91, back a year. Even more significant, this cycle seems not to progress so much as to revolve around a central gap, the absence of some mediation more definitive than that Tennyson conjectures in section 85. All of these poems admit at least indirectly their need for visionary communication; they encourage it, they set conditions for it, yet with provisional sour grapes they claim they would question it should it occur.

The metaphorical fluidity of section 91, for example, leaves us uncertain whether Hallam is to mediate between Tennyson and natural change or whether natural change is to mediate between Tennyson and Hallam. We know only that Hallam is asked to appear as earthly potential in the spring and as fulfilled spirit in summer: "beauteous in thine after form, / And like a finer light in light" (ll. 15–16). In section 108, on the other hand, Tennyson dismisses as his own projection the visionary encounter he has just been pleading for:

> What find I in the highest place,
>   But mine own phantom chanting hymns?
>   And on the depths of death there swims
> The reflex of a human face.
>
> (ll. 13–16)

Then, concluding the T.MS version of this same poem, the skepticism is itself replaced by another indirect plea for vision: "Yet how much wisdom sleeps with thee."

Since section 112 is the last which definitely came from a prior manuscript, we cannot extend beyond it our hypothesis that in T.MS-1 previously composed sections were compiled on the upper recto of each leaf. These recto sides continue with five self-consciously melancholy attempts at a conclusion, three of them subsequently canceled. When Tennyson entered section 125, "There rolls the deep," on the next leaf, he may have been demoting T.MS from a completed, or even completable text to an intermediate draft which he had to recopy, with the interpolated sections given their own leaves, into the Lincoln Butcher's Book.[29]

If we contrast the *kinds* of poems in this version with those represented among the almost ninety sections which came to be added, we find our clearest refutation of the critical assumption that the most deeply felt of the lyrics were composed first. In fact the most intense sections of *In Memoriam*, those most often reprinted in "edited" anthology versions, come most often from the sections added after T.MS-1. If we remember the patterns of the earliest-written sections, however, we may be less surprised. We have argued that the overlapping functions of T.MS reflected Tennyson's struggle with both closure and suspension. We can now see in those functions his resolution of the struggle. The manuscript may have begun life as a fair copy, but it fulfilled itself, perhaps to Tennyson's surprise, as a heuristic device.

Dolores R. Rosenblum argues that "*In Memoriam* records no process beyond that of its own unfolding";[30] indeed it may have unfolded itself within the precise physical confines of T.MS. The increasingly codified structure and the increasingly dense context may have actually created new occasions for mediation, occasions which were in their turn incorporated into that same context. The pattern of T.MS-1 may not be convincing to us—perhaps it did not remain so even to Tennyson—but most important to Tennyson it *was* a pattern, a pattern that moved, however awkwardly, from paralyzing grief toward calm, from loss toward fulfillment, from question toward possible answer. As such it gained value less from its coherence than from its very presence.

We can see the value of this presence in the image through which Tennyson dismisses his own lyrics: "short swallow-flights of song that dip / Their wings in tears and skim away." In a broader sense all the early-written sections had been forced to skim the emotional surface of Tennyson's grief, simply because they had to reach calm and closure within the short lyric flight open to each. The pattern suddenly opened by T.MS-1, however, offered many resting places, in themselves far from any ultimate destination, but at a now-measured, now-achievable distance from it.

Tennyson described his own compositional practice to Knowles in these self-effacing terms: "The general way of its being written was so queer that if there were a blank space, I would put in a poem."[31] Blank space could be had, however, on any fresh sheet of paper. We should focus instead on the writing at the top of every recto leaf, writing which both physically and psychologically delimited the space between one leaf and the next. It was in precisely this way that the skeleton of T.MS-1 delimited, nurtured, and shaped every addition to the developing poem.

It is in turn this cycle of mutual reinforcement which ultimately validates the poem's structure. This structure, as we saw, carries no authority as a chronological narrative of Tennyson's changing emotions, and T.MS-1 is itself only slightly more unified than the nearly random sequences of the earlier collections. Tennyson in all probability could have ordered it better; he certainly could have rearranged its lyrics and those added later into a more coherent poem than the one we now possess. He refused, I think, less from laziness or even incompetence than from a sense that many of the deepest evocations in the poem owed their very existence to its present structure. Hence we too should accept the poem *as* it is and for *what* it is, a record not of the historical but of the atemporal process of creation, a reflection, not of the order in which Tennyson wrung gain from loss, but of the *way* he wrung it.

The T.MS-1 draft, as we have seen, omits most of the lyrics in three significant blocks within the final text: the beginning (sections 1–8), the middle (49–59), and the end (92–epilogue). In the opening poems Tennyson explores his own refusal to accept the reality of his loss, in the middle poems he explores what appears a purposeless, godless universe, and at the end he explores his encounter with visionary experience and its implications. Each one of these explorations, I would argue, could only be undertaken within the structure and progression furnished originally by T.MS-1.

The most curious fact about the poem's opening is how late it was actually written: sections 2, 4, 5, and 6 do not appear until L.MS; the introductory stanzas and the concluding twelve lines of section 1 not until the trial; sections 7 and 8 not until the first edition. In all of these, I think, Tennyson is returning with a new courage to redefine his initial state of mind. This was, he now implies, not the passive response to outer forces with which he opened T.MS-1 but a deliberate rejection of mediation, a turning inward like that described in "The Poet's Mind" of the 1830 volume. Those parts of the authorial presence not already destroyed with the beloved object are enclosed within a sanctuary carefully separated from an alien but otherwise unknown universe.[32]

As Tennyson draws nourishment from his loss, for example, so the yew in the second section sends its roots down to "net the dreamless head." Unmoved by the life and change around it, it incorporates into itself the stasis of death. When he longs "to fail from out my blood and grow incorporate" with the yew, he is, according to Tucker (p. 380), "figur[ing] Hallam's absence through repeated images of clasping, grasping, and embracing what is emphatically not Hallam, . . . a series of substitutes for the confidant who will not hear or answer." The yew, however, does not stand between Tennyson and some Other. Instead its "stubborn hardihood" mirrors the same imaginative isolation which Tennyson hopes to achieve.[33]

The opening line of section 4, "To sleep I give my powers away," may also appear to move out of the self, but in reality it fragments the authorial presence into an internal landscape where the "I" and his heart find themselves helplessly adrift within "a helmless bark": "O heart, how fares it with thee now. . . . Something there is which thou has lost" (4: 5, 9). Yet just as Tennyson's 1830 efforts to draw inward fragmented the self into warring factions, so here Tennyson's question initiates a retrogression he cannot stop. Even the heart is commanded to open and reveal *its* contents: "Break, thou deep vase of chilling tears." When the dream itself is broken up, the will too revives, but as yet another fragment it cannot restore the psychological unity lost with Hallam.

As the landscape of the Poet's Mind hedged it against the rationalism of the critic, so the "words" of section 5 "half reveal / And half conceal the Soul within." But where that tidy sanctuary was fed by a fountain of inspiration, here the authorial presence remains in such disarray that it needs the "mechanic exercise" of composition to drug it into a semblance of harmony. Here poetry, instead of communicating, offers the Soul the kind of hermetic protection that song offered to the Daughters of the Hesperides: "In words, like weeds, I'll wrap me o'er, / Like coarsest clothes against the cold" (ll. 9–10). Instead of delaying the arrival of Hercules, however, poetry here shrouds Tennyson from the "cold" domain of the Other he must confront before he can regain the source of his inspiration.

Much has been made of Tennyson's belated composition of sections 7 and 119 as contrasting visits to Hallam's London lodgings; the first of these, however, may also grow out of its context in L.MS. Although Tennyson's attempt to enter the dark house echoes the self's guilty attempt to turn inward, he has now enlarged his sanctuary to include, if not the beloved himself, at least his loss. Only when he is himself denied entrance is he at last forced to confront time and space as controlled by the Other, "the long unlovely street" and "the blank day" of a world without Hallam. This world in turn becomes bearable only within the context of the following ship poems. Even though the interpolated sections within this group qualified the value of the ship as a mediator, it offers more imaginative potential than Tennyson's vision of the urban dawn in section 7.

If these opening sections portray an imaginative quandary, they also portray an imagination more active—and more dangerous—than that in the opening of T.MS-1. Having stationed various barriers between the authorial presence and the domain of the Other, Tennyson begins experimenting with forms which can mediate between them more powerfully than in T.MS-1. But just as in T.MS-1, the more powerful the mediation, the more threatening the Other it invokes. The growing intensity of these confrontations can be seen in the additions to virtually every group: the ship poems, the evocations of his shared past, the encounters with his family, and the conjectures on Hallam's future state. This last group in particular, by creating abstract mediators almost at will, seems almost to invite the subsequent incursions of cosmic entropy: in section 47, for example, Tennyson justifies one vision of reunion solely by asking, "What vaster dream can hit the mood / Of love on earth?" (ll. 11–12).

Even in T.MS-1, we remember, the group was followed by a series of demurrals, doubts about the truth of poetry and the value of ghostly visitations. In his additions to T.MS Tennyson continues to brood over these issues. Section 49 plumbs the depths of a sorrow supposedly unavailable to artistic expression. But his new confidence in song as a conjuring device conjures up section 50 in L.MS. The theological speculations of the Sellwood manuscript spawned the image of an uncontrolled imagination as the trope for a directionless cosmos; here Tennyson himself is troped as a machine in the process of breaking down:

> Be near me when my light is low,
>   When the blood creeps, and the nerves prick

> And tingle; and the heart is sick,
> And all the wheels of Being slow.
>   (ll. 1–4)

The Other as entropy has here invaded the sanctuary of the authorial presence, but the same structure which produced this invasion also controls it. From such imaginative disintegration Tennyson cannot possibly achieve either psychological or aesthetic closure within a single section; he can only ask Hallam's mediating presence "to point . . . on the low dark verge of life / The twilight of eternal day" (ll. 14–16). But within the context of L.MS Tennyson has already taken this poetic and psychological road, has already attained the dawn it points toward. Section 50, in turn, reinterprets its immediate successor. Section 51, we remember, opened with what remained in T.MS-1 a very disconcerting question: "Do we indeed desire the dead / Should still be near us . . . ?" (ll. 1–2). The preceding section has now made such mediation a necessity. The opening of the final quatrain, "Be near us," now echoes the repeated entreaty, "Be near me," which in section 50 held out Tennyson's only hope of sanity.

Each section added to T.MS after section 51 explores the most negative implications of its immediate predecessor. Not until L.MS, however, can Tennyson bring himself to realize that since his hopes for the cosmos derive from "the likest God within the soul," he must ask whether "God and Nature [are] then at strife" (ll. 4–5). His discovery that "of fifty seeds / She often brings but one to bear" drives him to "call / To what I feel is Lord of all"; yet in section 56 he is answered instead by a Nature who denies any connection with human values: "A thousand types are gone: / I care for nothing, all shall go" (ll. 3–4). Again, however, the same structure which led him to this confrontation offers an escape from it. Tennyson is expanding what is by definition only the middle of his poem. Now that he has already seen beyond it, he can transfer the resigned withdrawal of section 57, "Peace, come away," from the end of the whole poem in T.MS-1 to this much bleaker, but much more contingent subsection of it.[34]

At this point L.MS offers another discovery beyond that of context, the discovery that this definitive statement on the amoral impersonality of Nature is made by a very talkative personification. The further the Other's message departs from Tennyson's individualized human norm, the more closely the Other cleaves to this norm within the poetic context. We have already witnessed the birth of several other impersonal personifications: the women whose sexuality troped natural flux, the god figures who either confronted or deserted Tennyson within his adolescent poetry, their secular descendants of 1830, the male intruders of 1832. Even within T.MS-1, the "inhuman" universe of section 34 grew from the brain "of some wild poet" while section 3, with its "murmurs from the dying sun," portrayed inanimate objects as crying out against entrapment, desertion, and death. Within these later-written sections Tennyson comes to see, though not in one unequivocal vision, that the Other which supposedly destroyed his mediators has itself taken form as one of their number.

He does discover the inverse of this paradox, again within L.MS, in the one unequivocal vision of section 70. If the apparent Others are merely creatures of his own imagination, then the very responsiveness of Hallam's spirit may suggest that it too lacks objective reality. Such doubts drive him to envision Hallam, "to paint the face I know," against the gloom. The gloom, however, yields a very different vision:

> crowds that stream from yawning doors,
> And shoals of puckered faces drive;
> Dark bulks that tumble half alive,
> And lazy lengths on boundless shores.
>
> (ll. 9–12)[35]

While Hallam finally arrives uninvited, "beyond the will," to redeem Tennyson's nightmare, the nightmare itself has grown from his compulsion to define Hallam as a goal instead of a mediator. Within this definition, anything not Hallam or anything changeable must appear as Other—as unnatural, monstrous, or grotesque. The Shadow can thus replace Hallam as Tennyson's boon companion, and Nature can manifest a deep personal commitment to her doctrine of blind change.

This discovery in turn reinterprets the temporal relativity implicit within the seasonal cycles of T.MS-1. In accepting this relativity, Tennyson actually reverses the compulsion which produced the nightmare of section 70. Instead of defining everything not Hallam as Other, he defines every incursion not definitely Other as potentially Hallam. By moving section 91 from the third to the second year within L.MS, Tennyson acknowledges even sooner that he must accept Hallam in whatever form he appears. Because he is conceived of, asked for, and perceived in response to the changing needs of the changing Tennyson, Hallam as an abiding spiritual presence can actually grow with him.[36] Section 91 invited a spirit virtually indistinguishable from some natural phenomenon; the three sections inserted after it in T.MS use this new openness to construct a powerful invitation to vision.

This invitation makes the gap within the "completed" T.MS even more obvious than it appeared within T.MS-1. And yet this gap itself speaks eloquently not just to the authenticity of the eventual vision but to the power of the realization which prompts it. Section 70 exposed the danger of commanding Hallam as he had been; the intervening sections invoked him in new forms and new situations; yet until now Hallam, like all of Tennyson's other mediators, has been grounded less in religious, philosophical, or aesthetic faith than in need. Tennyson has worked to recreate him from the sheer intensity of his own yearning. In these last invitations, however, Tennyson must admit that need alone cannot compel mediation; it can only open him to the potential for mediation in whatever incursions choose to appear.

This context forces us to reverse the common question about the date of the experience described in section 95. Instead of asking how Tennyson could retain so vivid a sense of Hallam's presence nearly eight years after his death, we need to ask why he could not achieve this visionary union before then. The answer, I suspect, is that the vision owes not just its emphasis but its very existence to the gradually intensifying invitations which precede it. Collectively these form not a sufficient but a necessary condition, a sine qua non for the experience itself.[37]

The actual experience in section 95 has been analyzed so often and so well that here I need only explain how it confronts Tennyson's epistemological quandary. The doubt which "cancels" his trance is the doubt that "the living soul" and "that which is" may all be aspects of the self; but now Tennyson can offer a dramatic resolution instead of an epistemological one. If the self can contain an "Aeonian music" guiding the universe, and if it can perceive an equally harmonious interchange of day and night, life and death, within the surrounding landscape, then its visions may claim the authority of more publicly accepted forms of revelation. Shaw defines the inclusiveness of this affirmation: "As Tennyson is drawn by the mystic 'breeze' into a spiritual world completely subject to imaginative power, he is not retreating into a subjective metaphor but into a concrete universe. . . . Instead of using the objects as human metaphors which project animate qualities into the non-human world, Tennyson summons up the impersonal world of things."[38]

The affirmation, in turn, marks yet another stage in Tennyson's relationship to Hallam. Tennyson's increasingly aggressive search for mediation has been alternately checked and rewarded throughout the poem. Now that his paradoxical fusion of impetuosity and receptivity has produced Hallam, he can receive him on equal terms. As Hallam's appearance affirms the power of Tennyson's visionary quest, so Tennyson's visionary power affirms the reality of Hallam's appearance. When he assumes such imaginative responsibility for Hallam, he also redefines the meaning of mediation itself. Because Hallam can mediate only to the extent that Tennyson can speak through him, he remains dependent on Tennyson to fulfill his potential. In rendering moot the question of Hallam's ontological status, Tennyson thus renders moot the question of who is mediating for whom.

Shaw reads this imaginative power back into the whole poem. The salvation Tennyson discovered, he argues (p. 163), is that "the soul's power to create its world finally overcomes the poet's intellectual despair." Yet because Tennyson's desires, as Eliot argued, focused on personal relationships, salvation for him could only mean tangible interaction with Hallam. And because visions like that in section 95 come only fortuitously to even the greatest mystics, he could achieve this salvation, but he could not hold it.

The necessary transience of his victory explains an ending which has often been seen as something between a confusion and an embarrassment.[39] While many of the individual sections are impressive, they apparently retreat to the pattern of the earliest-written lyrics in their mutually inconsistent drives toward closure. All this inconsistency, however, overlies a uniformity in pattern which seems to me the poem's deepest conclusion.

We have traced Tennyson's consuming desire for some tangible human relationship, his creation of mediating figures, their apparent transformation into spectral creatures of the Other, his discovery that these specters were also of his own creation, his growing conviction of Hallam's abiding presence, and his subsequent suspicion that it too is only his imaginative creation. Finally we have seen his possession of Hallam as the one mediator in his poetry whose increasing power does not imply increasing autonomy. The concluding sections, however, never really show this mediation in action. Instead of affirming any one incarnation of his model, they imply that the actual progression from one to another constitutes an aesthetically valid way of confronting and formulating experience.

In one section after another Tennyson seizes some immediately troubling experience, manipulates it into an affirmation of his continuing relationship with Hallam, and then, before his claim can encounter opposition, drops it for some new perception. In so blatantly denying any real sense of an ending, Tennyson may only be reaffirming the same creative process he has won in the last score of sections. For Puckett (pp. 110–11, 122) the poem finally endorses neither a conclusion nor a theory but a myth to be lived. I would take this interpretation a step further, claiming that the actual process of creation and amplification constitutes the poem's real conclusion, the real insight Tennyson has won from his loss.

Such an interpretation accounts for the near absence of correlation between the poem's order of composition and its final order. Tennyson obviously needed to work through many sections before he discovered the viability of his peculiar creative method; yet once he discovered it, he could move "back" into any previously composed section, could experience it again and capture yet another aspect of it in poetry. As Albright has remarked about the dramatic monologues (p. 120), it is "as if Tennyson's final consolation were to become a spectator of the operations of his own genius." While Fichter argues (p. 421) that the physical length of the poem and the length of its composition set up time as a reality which cannot be transcended, Tennyson here turns time against itself. It is not simply that he could keep Hallam alive in the immortality of his poetry, or that, as E. D. H. Johnson argues, he could rediscover his inspiration in the process of writing about Hallam. It is rather that the act of moving within this rhythm of perception, response, control, and rejection opened up the most diverse kinds of mediation between Hallam's spirit and his own—past and present, near and far-off, familiar and august.

As no one of these sequences really invalidates any earlier one, the whole poem exists for both Tennyson and the reader in a perpetual imaginative present. In summing up and evaluating Tennyson's past incarnations of his model, *In Memoriam* ultimately rejects none of them. Just as it preserves Hallam, the loss of Hallam, and the recovery from that loss, so it preserves, reformulates, and celebrates Tennyson's creative past as a powerful resource for the future.

CHAPTER SIX

The Princess

"Yet for creation, Tennyson's truthful hopes needed to meet his truthful fears . . . and it was exactly this which in the years of *The Princess*, 1845–47, he could not bring himself to do. What is wrong with *The Princess* stems from its innumerable evasions." For Ricks (*Tennyson*, p. 189), the subjects evaded include social reform, women's rights, geological time, the death of Hallam, inherited madness, paternal violence, even the anxieties of possible marriage—all of them reduced to political or biographical irrelevance within the metaphorical and mythic context of the poem.[1] That the implicit threats are reinterpreted by context is undeniable. But is the reinterpretation here evasive?

In fact, what Ricks sees as the vehicle of evasion embodies all the features of the model within which Tennyson, so we have argued, confronted his deepest fears as a man and a poet. As John Killham, Ryals, and Joseph (pp. 89–94) have noted in very different contexts,[2] *The Princess* returns us to familiar ground: we find again a high-born maiden isolated and then besieged within her tower; we find a hero venturing on forbidden territory ruled by a cruel, manipulative woman; yet we find these conflicting versions of the model embodied within a single poem.

In fact this long intersubjective narrative demands the simultaneous use of several different perspectives. Tennyson has identified with the Magus' attempt to protect a woman he can neither believe nor comprehend. He has identified with the Lover's discovery that the Cadrilla he saw as an extension of his own spirit was already pledged to another. He has identified with more militant male protagonists, whether confronting the castle of Sleeping Beauty or rebuffing the hauteur of Lady Clara Vere de Vere. He has even identified with the passive Tithonus, sexually wasted by the woman who promised him immortality. But he now must enter far more sympathetically into the soul of Ida, allowing her to portray the Prince, his father, and the whole male-dominated setting of her story as different manifestations of the Other.

Likewise Tennyson has already looked through feminine eyes at the threatening intrusions of Lancelot, Hercules, and Paris. He has spoken through various female victims of male tyranny in "A Dream of Fair Women." He has even worked to redeem another feminine figure enclosed within a castle, the Soul in her Palace of Art.[3] Now he must also allow the Prince to justify his own intrusion upon Ida's property and person, must even allow him to portray her changing before his eyes into one of the supernatural despots from Tennyson's adolescent poems.

Tucker describes this strategy as one of containment: "A textbook Victorian compromise, the poem avoids taking a position on a hotly debated issue by taking up any number of positions, letting reciprocally ventilated views cool each other off, and leaving affairs pretty much where they stood. . . . *The Princess* . . . has the diplomatic and anonymous air of a committee report" (pp. 351–52).[4] I think such reductionism underestimates both the cost and the consequences of this new authorial toleration. If earlier mediators proved unable or unwilling to confront some new manifestation of the Other, Tennyson showed little compunction about sacrificing them to it. Here, however, he cannot sanction such authorial tyranny as a self-validating imaginative process. While he may play off the ideological extremists against one another, he must grant ever greater powers to the two figures at the poem's center. When he does so, however, he discovers that both Prince and Princess are using their new autonomy to escape this center, to free themselves from the poem's claustrophobic fairy-tale setting.

The poem's formal structure is not usually seen as threatening. Eileen Tess Johnston argues persuasively that *The Princess* equates "melee" with exploitation and "medley" with cooperation,[5] but often the very tidiness of the poem's structure becomes itself a means of exploitation. In Tennyson's 1832 poems, we remember, a setting which the frame described to us as both remote and insecure was redefined by a similarly beleaguered figure as both central and protected. There we never bothered to ask about the chemical dependence of the natives in lotos land, or the insomnia of the Sisters' dragon, or the job security of the gardener on Shalott, or the potential loss in property value faced by Mariana's landlord. Here the same device, multiplied many times over, raises just such troubling questions about the secondary figures whose lives are being so radically redefined.

If we analyze the poem's intricate Chinese-box construction from the outside in, we are forced to consider the human cost of the imaginative telescoping through which Tennyson projects a mediator who in turn projects a mediator of his or her own. Here we encounter beleaguered figures seeking to escape their own narrative situations by creating and manipulating narrative boxes interior to them. We find Tennyson shaping the outermost level of *The Princess* to escape (Ricks) or contain (Tucker, pp. 352–56) the dilemmas facing him as a Victorian poet. Here the holiday setting tames the awesome industrial revolution into a series of games and demonstrations. Here he can give himself the time and space to evaluate the aristocratic traditions he cherished against the more progressive attitudes of what remains for the narrative moment a crowd of jovial townspeople.[6] Here, finally, he can burlesque the "great poem" he had been urged to write by rendering it in the undergraduate "genre" of serial narration.[7]

What is escape for Tennyson, of course, creates potential conflict for his creations. Revolution remains a real fear for the Tory member's eldest son, and the friends' debate on feminism threatens to turn a garden party into an at least verbal war. Their story, however, provides the same escape for them that they have provided for Tennyson. In it, the masses appear only as anonymous bodies to fill classrooms or fight tournaments. In it, the whole woman question can be reduced to a fairy tale of one recalcitrant woman. Even the fairy-tale form itself can embody their conservative values: it champions social stability, rewards humility, relies in short on the comfortable cliché of a fixed human nature.

We might assume that the characters within the fairy tale proper would have no further interior story to manipulate; yet their actions, and in particular their language, suggest otherwise. In fact Tennyson extends his earlier poetics into narrative simply by expanding the covert struggle for point of view in the 1832 poems and the "Morte d'Arthur."[8] As Arthur and Bedivere wrestled for imaginative control over their story, as the 1832 heroines reinterpreted and redirected their own myths, so these characters place themselves at the center of Tennyson's model, arrange the other characters around them, and prod their story to fulfill their potential as heroes or heroines. Cyril sees himself in a college prank, Blanche in a vendetta against men, the old King in a military campaign, and Gama in a steady state where nothing happens at all.

They each shape their speeches, not just into an individual style, but into a rhetorical pattern appropriate to each story. And the more rigid the pattern, the more self-contained the story, the more success they seem to enjoy. At some moment, however, each pattern and each story must confront the existence of others. And to emphasize such moments, Tennyson usually breaks the narrative flow with a long speech during which the character being enlightened stands speech-less. Their individual moments of physical stasis signal their new vulnerability to a plot suddenly more complex than they had anticipated. Yet even as the poem thwarts their often-ludicrous efforts to control it, it uses them to threaten the two leads with intimations of the Other which seem to speak through them.

Thus besieged, Ida constructs her college as a bastion of nineteenth-century feminism in the midst of what she tries to portray as an anachronistic medieval setting. The Prince, as both character and narrator, tries to encompass within the compendious structure of idyll the very discontinuity upon which Ida is insisting. Despite their conflicting efforts to escape the rhetorical and psychological collapse of the other characters, both Ida and the Prince suffer a collapse so traumatic that Tennyson seems to be punishing them for the dangerous autonomy of their mediation. At this point, however, he must reaffirm his imaginative investment in them and grope with them toward some possible resolution to the anarchy of their joint creation.

To evaluate both the anarchy and its resolution, we need to examine the characters who shape it, from the minor roles through the more inclusive ones played by the Prince and Princess. Gama might seem an unlikely beginning, if only because he seems unwilling and unable to manipulate anyone. In reality his speeches are cleverly designed to blunt all forces threatening the small circle of his own lethargy. His opening, given only after he has delayed the Prince's petition for a full three days, revels in discontinuities of its own. Betrothals are equated with crop failures; expressions of sympathy and good will are set at naught by the wills of others; his own feigned efforts at understanding these forces are dissipated in word play:

> Awful odes she wrote, . . .
> But all she is and does is awful . . .
>   they that know such things—I sought but peace;
> No critic I—would call them masterpieces:
> They mastered me.
>
> (I, 137, 139, 143–45)

Yet when he tries to break up the tourney between his sons and his would-be son-in-law, he speaks "vainlier than a hen / To her false daughters in the pool; for none / Regarded" (V, 318–20).

Gama's fall from authority may also mirror his fall from authorial favor during the course of the poem. Unlike the major characters, who seem to win increasing respect, Gama may start out sharing his attitude, if not his motivation, with Tennyson. Most of his speeches within part 1 appear in the 1839 Harvard draft, where his mock terror before his militant daughter parallels the mock-heroic status which Tennyson, according to Killham (pp. 161–68), was planning to award her. Gama's later collapse into impotent anger may thus signal Tennyson's own implicit acknowledgment that neither the Princess nor her poem can remain fit vehicles for humor.

The contrast between Gama and the Prince's father is mirrored in the two letters they address to Ida on the night of Gama's capture. Gama writes his in a tortured network of relative clauses, the other writes in imperatives:

> You have our son: touch not a hair of his head:
> Render him up unscathed: give him your hand:
> Cleave to your contract. . . .
>
> (IV, 387–89)

The Prince, who has dismissed his father's militant chauvinism as merely a convenient foil for his own prank, must now realize that their actions spring from very similar assumptions. To Ida, on the other hand, the King's arrival must appear as frightening as the threatened arrival of Hercules to the Three Sisters. Yet when his game of war turns real, the girl he has considered a "colt" easily breaks him, silences his speeches, and reduces him to grim sign language: "the King in bitter scorn / Drew from my neck the painting and the tress, / And held them up" (VI, 93–95).

Even though Blanche is not seen until the end of part 2 and does not appear on stage until part 4, she and the old King embody the ideological split which dominates the poem's beginning. Her proto-Darwinian imagery may sound surprisingly close to the old King's: "The plan was mine. I built the nest . . . / To hatch the cuckoo" (IV, 346–47). As Killham points out (pp. 248–49), however, her speech suggests neither evolution nor her opponent's rough-and-tumble propagation but Lyell's pessimistic theory that natural selection was diminishing an originally bountiful creation. For Blanche the good times and good people are being shaded out or pushed out:

>   a noble scheme
> Grew up from seed we two long since had sown;
> In us true growth, in her a Jonah's gourd,
> Up in one night and due to sudden sun:
> We took this palace; but even from the first
> You stood in your own light and darkened mine.
>
> (IV, 290–95)

Blanche's obsession with natural entropy aligns her with two equally unattractive agents of the Other to whom Tennyson had been inexorably drawn in *In Memoriam*: "O Sorrow, cruel fellowship . . . / What whispers from thy lying lip? . . . 'all the phantom, Nature, stands . . . / A hollow form with empty hands'" (3: 1, 4, 9, 12). Like these precursors, Blanche may offer the poem's clearest vision of the flux threatening both physical and human nature. Hence Tennyson feels compelled to "crush" her, like them, "upon the threshold of the mind."[9] Ida's later acceptance of a few of the wounded, for example, prompts Blanche to insinuate that she is yielding to the blind power of sexual attraction: "These men came to woo / Your Highness—verily I think to win." But it is this cynicism, more than all the men's appeals, which drives Ida to transform her mentor's cherished college into a hospital.

Even the most stereotyped members of the older generation, Blanche and the King, occasionally let the voice of some threatening power speak through their blustering threats. The friends of the two leads, on the other hand, present them with a more dangerous—because subtler—challenge. Exposing other versions of the story as self-serving fictions, they offer to mediate between the leads and these fictions. But when they claim that their particular mediation must suffice, they tempt the leads to adopt their own limited role in—and limited perspective on—the world of the poem. In the process these friends change from partial mediators to would-be role models. Since they seek to usurp the center of Tennyson's own model, the leads must finally dismiss them as particularly devious manifestations of the Other.

Hence Blanche and her daughter Melissa, despite all their differences in temperament, share a reciprocal relationship. Where Blanche reveals the truth through a torrent of verbal deception, Melissa does so by her silence. When Blanche backs into discovering the disguised men, the narrative slows to dramatize the closed circle of her sexual obsession: "Girls?—more like men! . . . girls, like men! . . . very like men indeed. . . . Why—these—*are*—men . . . and you know it" (III, 27, 39, 42). But where Blanche has uncovered Melissa's secret through her blushes, Melissa's silence uncovers Blanche's secret to Ida. As Melissa debunks the fictions of others by accident,[10] so she never deliberately imposes her own fictions on anyone. Because neither she nor Florian has a story to protect, their union, while sensual, is compared to that of two dewdrops, which "on the petal shake / To the same sweet air, and tremble deeper down, / And slip at once all-fragrant into one" (VII, 53–55).

Florian's own distrust of hypocrisy is occasionally more assertive. He sees Ida as "crammed with erring pride" (III, 86), but he also attacks Cyril's attempt to flatter Psyche: "Have you learnt / No more from Psyche's lecture, you that talked / The trash that made me sick, and almost sad?" (II, 370–72). As Ricks claims (*Tennyson*, pp. 191–92), however, Florian remains a portrait of Hallam drained of the vitality Tennyson found so troubling in *In Memoriam*. Tennyson could continually recreate Hallam in the image of his changing needs, but it is Florian's very lack of assertiveness which tempts the Prince to deny the vitality latent within his own nature. Hence in learning to assert himself, he must learn to reject Florian's criticism of Ida, must implicitly reject him as a model and Melissa as a mate:

> The crane, I said, may chatter of the crane,
> The dove may murmur of the dove, but I
> An eagle clang an eagle to the sphere.
>
> (III, 88–90)

Although Florian's lack of identity causes the Prince to call him "my other heart, and almost my half self," it is Cyril who proclaims himself the Prince's alter ego:

> I have no sorcerer's malison on me,
> No ghostly hauntings like his Highness. I
> Flatter myself that always everywhere
> I know the substance when I see it.
>
> (II, 388–91)

And it is in fact the other pair, Cyril and Psyche, whose stories the Prince and Ida find more persuasive, complex, and troubling as models for their own.[11] Cyril's story, as we said, is of a college prank, a medieval panty raid. As a nominalist among gullible idealists, he sees Ida's goals, her college, education itself, in fact, as mere opportunities for hypocritical flattery toward the women, amusement for his friends, and financial (perhaps sexual) exploitation for himself.[12] He even describes his wooing of Blanche as a kind of rape:

> I forced a way
> Through solid opposition crabbed and gnarled.
> Better to clear prime forests, . . .
> Than hammer at this reverend gentlewoman.
>
> (III, 109–11, 113)

However shallow a modern reader may find Cyril, within the poem he incorporates both the temptation and the threat embodied in the aggressive males of 1832. As a curiously sympathetic rake, he fuses the roles of Paris and Hercules. The Prince is to see him as a model, reducing Ida's castle to a mere caricature of the Other's domain. The women may see him as either seductive mediator or militant Other—he cares not which.

By his blatant rhetorical manipulation, Cyril brings others to question the efficacy of language itself; yet when he is forced to abandon his story of the risqué college prank, he is forced to question his own rhetorical powers. He does indeed regain Psyche's child through persuasion, but he does so "battered by the battle." Where he had earlier threatened in jest "to roar, / To break my chain, to shake my mane," (II, 401–2), where he had almost deliberately scattered the women by throwing off his disguise, he like the old King must now admit himself vanquished by the "Lioness / That with the long locks play[s] the lion's mane" (VI, 147–48).

As Cyril for the Prince, Psyche stands as a possible role model for Ida, but she does so as a teacher and a mother, not a lover. This dual role makes Psyche unique among the secondary characters. Once these others see the inadequacy of their narrative and rhetorical constructs, most of them lapse into silence and near oblivion. Psyche, however, comes to this realization early. As Ida's chief assistant she has just concluded an impressive opening lecture when,

> as when a boat
> Tacks, and the slackened sail flaps, all her voice
> Faltering and fluttering in her throat, she cried
> "My brother!"
>
> (II, 168–71)

After using verbal third degree to make her break her vow to Ida, the disguised males break their own promise to depart. She is then exposed by Melissa, berated by Blanche, bereft of her child by Ida, and finally brought from her former academic eloquence down to an incoherent cry, "Mine—mine—not yours, / . . . give me the child" (VI, 124–25).

This new role of distraught mother has its own appropriate rhetorical pattern, the lament:

> My one sweet child, whom I shall see no more!
> For now will cruel Ida keep her back;
> And either she will die from want of care, . . .

> Or they will take her, they will make her hard,
> And she will pass me by in after-life
> With some cold reverence worse than were she dead.
> (V, 80–82, 87–89)

Through this lament, Psyche shapes part 6 into domestic melodrama just as she had earlier shaped part 2 into social didacticism. Both of the models for mediation which she offers to Ida prove exclusive, unrealizable, and hence false. Ida is left to modify and reconcile them even as she forgives Psyche herself.

Although the minor characters seek to coopt both Prince and Princess, Ida appears the more obvious target. She is wanted by the old King as a breeder of grandchildren, by Gama as a dutiful daughter, by Cyril as a means to his marrying money, and by the Prince as the sum total of everything he is not. Yet more threatening than any encircling army and more insidious than the infiltration of her college is the shape which these minor characters give to her story. Whether medieval, romantic, or modern, it bears the classic form of the fairy tale. Whether or not Tennyson's specific source was the tale of Turandote, as Killham argues (pp. 200–228), Ida's desire for independence can only win her the role of potential villain. As the traditional haughty princess, she will be forced to marry some highly undesirable man and will be considered lucky if he turns out to be better-born and better-natured than first suspected. At best a change of heart may be forced upon her: the old King, priming his son for the final battle, assures him that "a lusty brace / Of twins may weed her of her folly" (V, 453–54).

Killham (pp. 161–68) explains this role as the reflection of Kemble's anti-feminist attitudes at the time Tennyson was composing a draft of part 1 in 1839, but we may need to qualify his argument that Tennyson's conception of his heroine changed between this date and the resumption of writing in 1845. Certainly there is a great gulf fixed between the caricatures of Ida in the early Harvard draft (H.Nbk 22) and Hallam's claim in the *Memoir* (I, 248) that his father "considered her as one of the noblest among his women." Yet this draft never reaches the point where Ida is presented. Tennyson, moreover, must have been working toward the final marriage from the very beginning. The mysterious Prince in the Persian tale could love a virago and undergo trials for her beauty, but Tennyson knew that however much improbability his nineteenth-century audience could swallow, they would not accept any union that was not psychologically convincing.

The later Berg manuscript, dated less than a year before the poem's publication, may present a more accurate picture of Tennyson's attitude.[13] Virtually a fair copy of the first book, it skips several passages of the second, third, and fourth, contains a rough working draft of the fifth, very little of the sixth, and some of the more lyric sections of the seventh. By itself it might suggest that Tennyson was simply creating his poem as he went along. Yet there may be considerable significance in its principal omissions, Ida's two long self-revelations on the field trip (III, 181–271) and the general attack upon the victorious Ida which constitutes most of part 6. Coming between the first draft and the still-incomplete first edition, this manuscript suggests that throughout both the poem and the process of composition, Tennyson had not fully come to terms with his heroine. When the Prince rationalizes that "she wears her error like a crown / To blind the truth and me" (III, 95–96), his confusion may reflect that of his creator. We may seem to have left Tennyson standing on the outside of his Chinese-box poem, increasingly distant from the characters in each successive layer. Yet during its composition, he seems also to have locked himself within the unexpressed desires of the two figures standing at the poem's center.

From this internalized perspective, Ida seems as physically and psychologically embattled as the mediators of the 1832 poems—the Marianas in their house, the Soul in her palace, the Sisters on their island, or the Lady of Shalott in her tower. Before the battle the Prince fears lest within it "a smoke go up through which I loom to her / Three times a monster" (V, 124–25). Yet as he arrives encompassed by male deceit and male aggression, he must from the very beginning "loom to her" as a monstrous Other. Like her precursors, Ida mediates his aggression through both the physical bastion of her college and the roles it opens for her. Like them too, she protects within this sanctuary the vulnerable traits of the authorial presence: Tennyson's love for art and personal freedom, his hatred for class oppression and parental tampering with young love. Though Ida's roles parallel the versions of the story acted out by the minor characters, they differ in being self-consciously artificial. Those characters accepted their fairy-tale world as a given; Ida actively challenges its identity as the domain of the Other by erecting a series of deliberately incongruous defenses within it.

As with the Soul's Palace, the physical bastion of Ida's college is the most impressive but least effective of her defenses:

> Far off from men I built a fold for them:
> I stored it full of rich memorial:
> I fenced it round with gallant institutes,
> And biting laws to scare the beasts of prey.
>
> (V, 380–83)

Yet of the many statues in and around her castle, those threatening physical violence deter invasion no better than the castle itself.[14] The figure of Tomyris dunking the head of Cyrus into a bag of blood, embossed on the valves of the entrance, may contribute to the Prince's nightmarish impressions of the final tourney (V, 355–56). Yet where Ida sees a powerful warning in the figure of Actaeon sprouting horns after gazing on the naked Diana, the Prince sees the spreading horns only as a fence to be climbed (IV, 184–88). Likewise the whole male trio passes calmly under the shadowy woman rising over the menacing sign at the gate (I, 207–8). Florian, spying on Ida's court-martial of the disguised men, even puts his head under that of Holofernes, newly severed by the victorious Judith (IV, 207–8).

Perhaps sensing her failure to win transcendence through myth, Ida searches for patterns in specific places and times within the real world and its real history.[15] Standing between the statues of Miriam and Jael to watch the final battle, she absorbs some of their religious fervor. Calling the roll of the heroines in the sculpture gallery of her hall, she can convince her students, and even the disguised Prince, that "to look on noble forms / Makes noble thro' the sensuous organism / That which is higher" (II, 72–74). The very cruelty of history arms her with examples of suttee, infanticide, and foot-binding; and these in turn, because they introduce social patterns so unrelated to the actual story, succeed in stymieing most of the male characters. By blaming the Prince for these irrelevant instances of female persecution, by thus forcing him to reenact vicariously all these incursions of male violence, she denies his efforts to set up a romantic encounter between two individuals.[16]

Finally her statues, besides shielding Ida from the threatening fairy-tale world, hold out to her the possibility of escaping it altogether. Those of the muses clearly transcend the frenetic activity beneath them, and Ida is compared, in fact compares herself, to them. At the opening of part 2, for example, the muses' heads are "touched / Above the darkness from their native East" (III, 5–6), and less than one hundred lines later the Prince describes his beloved as "a Memnon smitten with the morning sun" (III, 100). Again, when Ida's court is threatened by the army of the Prince's father, the melee of frightened women in the court is dwarfed by "the placid marble Muses, looking peace."

Like the Soul in her palace, Ida has used aesthetic form to transcend the outer world of her poem; like the Soul she also finds it increasingly difficult to transcend this form itself.[17] While she has successfully avoided the models offered her by the secondary characters, she now submits to what was originally only a means of her mediation. Hence the stony fixity of her imprint on life becomes a desirable quality for life itself. As she contemplates her sculpture gallery, it is natural for her to equate the stoicism of the women represented with the rigidity of the statues themselves—and natural then to counsel her supposed novices, "Ye are green wood, see ye warp not" (II, 61). On her field trip she climbs a mountain much like those ascetic mountains of death and morning which trap the maid in the famous idyll she is to read later in the poem. When she notices "the bones of some vast bulk that lived and roared / Before man was," she remarks, "As these rude bones to us, are we to her / That will be" (III, 279–80). Yet in both these instances, although she attempts to merge with cultural or evolutionary change, she is actually modeling herself on the fixed form, idol or skeleton, which natural changes are destroying.[18]

After once failing to achieve the composure of the muses, she can later watch the battle from between Miriam and Jael, "among the statues, statue-like" (V, 499). When she comes down to tend the wounded of her victorious army, the girl in whom "grace and power . . . with every turn / Lived thro' her to the tips of her long hands, / And to her feet" (II, 24–27) is now accused of being "flint," "steel temper[ed]," "stiff as Lot's wife."[19] In her triumph she even orders statues made of her victorious brothers, a command which avoids the problem of seeing them as male intruders, but which simultaneously turns them into idols, before which the vitality of nature is to be sacrificed:

> dames and heroines of the golden year
> Shall strip a hundred hollows bare of Spring,
> To rain an April of ovation round
> Their statues, borne aloft, the three.
>
> (VI, 48–51)

This effort to delimit the Other through idolatry may remind us again of the Priestess in "Timbuctoo."[20] Yet as the vatic speaker endowed her idolatry with mediating power, so here Tennyson comes to free Ida from the metaphorical idol within which she has imprisoned herself. First the sight of the apparently dead Prince causes a shudder; then "her iron will was broken in her mind; / Her noble heart was molten in her breast" (VI, 102–3). Later, when she is about to be reconciled with Psyche,

> Down through her limbs a drooping languor wept:
> Her head a little bent; and on her mouth
> A doubtful smile dwelt like a clouded moon
> In a still water. . . .
>
> (VI, 251–54)

The reference to water ties these images to earlier ones of objects finally yielding to the current. In the half-serious parody of the fortunate fall which concludes part 3, she is carried back down off the mountain by the river as she will be carried back into life by the even stronger current of her own emotions. Before the battle, she is still able to stand "like a stately pine / Set in a cataract on an island-crag, / When storm is on the heights" (V, 336–38). When she does yield her castle, though not herself, she echoes this image: "I stagger in the stream: I cannot keep / My heart an eddy from the brawling hour" (VI, 301–2). Her final surrender to the valley shepherd is prefigured by that of the speaker in the last intercalary lyric: "I strove against the stream and all in vain: / Let the great river take me to the main" (ll. 12–13).

Her wound, however, is far from healed. When the Prince's unconscious state allows the now-omniscient narrator to move into Ida's psyche, we can see that she, betrayed by her allies, has come to see herself as embodying the whole feminist cause; she is now imaged as a sanctuary like the one she has just abandoned. The men thus become types of male violence and their entrance into her castle becomes a rape: "To them the doors gave way / Groaning, and in the Vestal entry shriek'd / The virgin marble under iron heels" (VI, 329–31). While the other men and women quickly reject these sexual stereotypes, Ida, trapped again within her now-violated castle, faces a new storm:

> void was her use,
> And she as one that climbs a peak to gaze
> O'er land and main, and sees a great black cloud
> Drag inward from the deeps. . . .
> so fared she gazing there;
> So blackened all her world in secret.
>
> (VII, 19–22, 26–27)

No longer sufficient for her escape to other worlds, her imagination sees the encroachments of male sexuality as a force "blackening" the world which entraps her: "blank / And waste it seemed and vain" (VII, 27–28).[21]

That Ida yields up her college may be due to the efforts of the other characters. That she fails to yield up herself is certainly due to the ineffectuality of her would-be lover. The Prince, to be sure, is almost as besieged by the other characters as Ida. Yet with neither Ida's fire nor her nobility, he can only endure their patronizing interference with feckless passivity: Cyril accompanies him to improve his vision, the old King follows to compel him first to marry and then to fight, and Ida dismisses him with an insult which for her should have been a compliment: "'Poor boy,' she said, . . . / 'To nurse a blind ideal like a girl'" (III, 198, 201).

The reasons for this inadequacy, though long debated, are most often attributed to Tennyson's ambivalence about either creating or speaking through an aggressively male character. The ambivalence, however, may also be seen as artistic. Because Tennyson, like Browning, is turning an "objective" narrative into an intersubjective tissue of visions,[22] his narrator must present both these visions and his own; he must make his story multifaceted, ambivalent, paradoxical enough to encompass them all.

The effeminacy of which Ida and critics ever since have accused him may thus grow from his patient, apparently passive acceptance of the voices and goals of the more active characters around him.[23] Like Tennyson's amorous heroes, from the Magus to the Lover to Tithonus, he expects mediation from a woman whose sexuality soon identifies her with natural flux. But the "blind ideal" that the Prince follows, while it forces him to accept Ida's own frightening self-image, offers one possibility of combining this acceptance with his own purpose. Ida has fashioned her castle to mediate the Other she has always seen manifested in the Prince. While waiting passively within its confines, the Prince fashions a rhetorical strategy to mediate an Other he comes to see manifested in Ida. This strategy—with its eclecticism, its intermittent lapses into stasis, its self-conscious, occasionally self-indulgent awareness of tension—becomes both his own signature and that of the poem as a whole.[24]

The evident links between this strategy and idyll go back again to Mackail's analysis of the form as a means of giving pluralistic Alexandrian society an etiological home within the myths of classical Greece. Certainly a poem which its author subtitled "A Medley" must be equally pluralistic, yet the idyll is hardly the favorite form of most of the characters. Hence this form might better be restricted to the particular vision of the Prince, a vision which characterizes and accounts for the particular artistic success of the first half of the poem. The "something . . . that seemed to wrestle with burlesque" would then characterize other responses to conflict within the poem, responses which threaten and finally overthrow the Prince's vision and the Prince himself.

Though the frame refers to this vision as "burlesque," "grotesque," "false sublime," I would follow Kincaid (p. 61) in softening such descriptions. Even within the first draft the Prince's vision itself softens the old King's fit of temper, Gama's pathetic puns, the host's barnyard joke, and Cyril's mocking. Where Ida revealed her imaginative power by finding temporal and ethical incongruities within her story, the Prince reveals his by finding unforeseen harmony in incongruity. As the speaker in "Armageddon" held the conflicting supernatural forces at imaginative arm's length, so this speaker carefully balances conflicting forces within the monstrous image of Ida presented in part 1. He presents her as tall, imposing, even almost supernatural, but with an intense vitality which offsets her stated intention of kiln-drying the new arrivals.

So too the Prince accepts Ida's much-burlesqued university as a given:

> [We] scarce could hear each other speak for noise
> Of clocks and chimes, like silver hammers falling
> On silver anvils, and the splash and stir
> Of fountains spouted up and showering down
> In meshes of the jasmine and the rose:
> And all about us pealed the nightingale,
> Rapt in her song, and careless of the snare.
>
> (I, 212–18)[25]

The clocks striking midnight may signal the beginning of a new era as the three intruders enter, but his description works as idyll because, like the conclusion of "Audley Court," it holds together past and future, art and nature, beauty and the threat of violence within a momentary suspension. The half-visible setting remains unrealized but unlimited potential, and they in their disguises retain the possibility of participating in Ida's world.

Like part 1, part 2 closes with another of the Prince's idylls, a description of their first evening as students. Here too we find a long series of conflicts held in suspension: the seriousness of some students against the frivolity of others; their carefree pastoral amusements against their worries about the future; the three intruders, "muffled like the fates," apart from the scene yet threatening it by their very presence; Melissa "hitting all we saw with shafts of gentle satire"; and finally Ida herself, filling the chapel with "six hundred maidens clad in purest white" as a bastion of virginal feminism, yet embellishing her hymns with an aggressively sexual accompaniment:

> the great organ almost burst his pipes,
> Groaning for power, and rolling through the court
> A long melodious thunder. . . .
>
> (II, 450–52)

What holds these confused and conflicting purposes together is the implicit claim of the Prince's idyll to a value and meaning above any one of them, above any possible resolution of them that the plot could offer.[26]

The Prince's urbanity has thus been able to perceive the sexual vitality dormant within Ida and her college, but this very vitality finally proves more than his urbanity can handle. Well before she allies herself with Arac and the outside forces of oppression, her strategy for escaping this oppression casts her in roles in which she must appear as Other to her necessarily ingenuous lover. And as Ida by sheer force of will keeps appropriating more of the conflicting roles in the story, she keeps usurping the carefully distanced synthesis of the Prince's idyllic vision. When she mimics the god figures of Tennyson's adolescence, dressing as an oriental deity and toying with a tame leopard, she reduces her lover to one of his famous seizures:[27]

> The Princess Ida seemed a hollow show,
> Her gay-furred cats a painted fantasy,
> Her college and her maidens, empty masks,
> And I myself the shadow of a dream,
> For all things were and were not.
>
> (III, 169–73)

While this failure of identity does counter his "desire to kneel" and submit to her pretensions, it also gives rise to his progressive failure as interpreting narrator.[28] Ida, surrounded from without and infiltrated from within, may also have lost control of her story, yet even in her impotent isolation she comes to personify the masculine violence directed against her. As the Prince loses his active role, on the other hand, he can deny Ida's power only by validating the whole scene as a nightmarish phantasmagoria:

> The Princess with her monstrous woman-guard,
> The jest and earnest working side by side,

> The cataract and the tumult and the kings
> Were Shadows. . . .
>
> (IV, 540–43)

Yet when he tries to act on these shadows by fighting for her hand, he only brings on seizure and the conviction that he is lost within the domain of this preternatural Other: he "seemed to move in old memorial tilts, . . . doing battle with forgotten ghosts" (V, 468–69). Ida has escaped this medieval past vicariously through her visions of the future. The Prince, his inclusive narrative structure now torn asunder by conflicting obligations, sees himself here as an English Connecticut Yankee, trapped in the very anachronism she has just left. Already psychologically defeated, he makes the physical battle, fought in a curious waking seizure, reenact his own death wish: "she sees me fight; / Yea let her see me fall" (V, 505–6).[29] And fulfilling his own prophecy, he abandons his active and narrative roles simultaneously: "dream and truth / Flowed from me; darkness closed me; and I fell" (V, 530–31).

The collapse of the Prince and Princess makes up two separate accounts; their triumphant union makes up a single account of physical, psychological, even stylistic sharing. More than ever each needs the other as a mediator; yet by couching this request *indirectly*, each allows the other to see mediation as an opportunity for personal fulfillment. By opening their separate visions to include one another, they humanize a formal pattern which has remained until now an impersonal means of oppression. In the battle, for example, the Prince had tried unsuccessfully to "make of my dream / All that I would." Now, waking in Ida's presence, he can invite her to become the woman he has imagined instead of the one he has perceived:

> If you be, what I think you, some sweet dream,
> I would but ask you to fulfill yourself: . . .
> Stoop down and seem to kiss me ere I die.
>
> (VII, 130–31, 135)

In the ensuing kiss, the personification of passion so usurps the languorous Prince, the closing of their spirits so preempts that of their lips, that tenor becomes subsumed in vehicle. From this point on both characters seem happy to let their author impart a sophisticated verbal eroticism to the hesitant gestures of two nervous and inexperienced lovers:

> She stooped; and out of languor leapt a cry;
> Leapt fiery Passion from the brinks of death;

> And I believed that in the living world
> My spirit closed with Ida's at the lips.
>   (VII, 140–43)

Ida's reliance on her author may seem both embarrassed and embarrassing, but in context it remains necessary. We have tried to trace a metaphorical coherence in the petrifaction and subsequent melting of her self-created metaphorical prison; yet the almost sadistic ferocity of the verbal attack mounted against her in part 6 may well justify Kincaid's impassioned defense (p. 73): "They are out to kill her." Ultimately, this attack may come from Tennyson himself, grown increasingly threatened by the growing imaginative autonomy of his erstwhile mediator.

Hence part 7 may celebrate Ida's reconciliation, not just with her Prince but with her author.[30] This reconciliation in turn may inform the following comparison of Ida's transformation to the birth of Venus. As the psychological has just usurped the physical in the description of their kiss, so now a change in Ida's mood resonates into an erotic splendor hardly appropriate to any Victorian or even medieval maiden. What one early critic saw as psychological incongruity,[31] however, may represent Tennyson's acknowledgment of Ida as a sexual presence that can now mediate instead of threatening:

> lovelier in her mood
> Than in her mould that other, when she came
> From barren deeps to conquer all with love; . . .
> Naked, a double light in air and wave.
>   (VII, 147–49, 152)

This vicarious use of language prepares us for the anomaly of Ida *reading* the two love poems. Such indirection makes no explicit demands on either partner; instead it offers a carefully distanced model for both. In addition it allows Tennyson to offer his own recompense for both leads' earlier efforts at poetry. The Prince's falsetto delivery burlesqued the sentimental conceits in his swallow song; Ida's obsession with fixity destroyed the organic basis of her metaphor. In her triumph song, her cause grew from a seed into a tree, but then hardened into a kind of fortress with "an iron nature" and "fruits of power" which drop much like bombs. Even more reprehensible, by attacking the lyrics of part 6 Ida attacked their implicit yearning for fulfillment.[32]

Here her first lyric selection, "Now Sleeps the Crimson Petal," clothes their love in an eastern immediacy of desire just as Tennyson has clothed her in a nakedly classical beauty. Killham (pp. 213–17) notes its similarity to early Tennysonian fantasies of exotic enclosed gardens, fantasies embodied in the disguised invasion of the Prince himself. But that story, as we have seen, was clouded by the threat posed by the male aggressor to the sanctuaries of the 1832 heroines. Only here can Ida, at one remove, explore for him, at two removes, the union of alienated seeker and besieged citadel.[33]

As the first song achieves their joint aspirations to lyric intensity, the second achieves the Prince's idyllic vision. Like his earlier efforts it holds tensions in suspension, but now it can encompass the fierce purity of Ida's ideals without lapsing into paralysis. Instead its seductively insistent rhythm only eddies back to the beloved on her mountain in order to surge forward: "And come, for Love is of the valley, come, / For Love is of the valley, come thou down" (VII, 183–84). To Ida, the idyll grants the supernatural power she yearned for to escape her fairy-tale role: "Would indeed we had been . . . / Giants living each a thousand years, / That we might see our own work out" (III, 250, 252–53). She now is able "to glide a sunbeam by the blasted Pine, / To sit a star upon the sparkling spire" (VII, 181–82).

But it is because even the personification of love shuns these feats, "nor cares to walk / With Death and Morning on the silver horns," that Ida must move down. The physical freedom of her disembodied state exists only to permit her to abandon it with decorum. Ida's fall into the stream threatened not only her life but, worse, her dignity; the maiden here can "let the torrent dance [her] down" and need fear only that she may "like a broken purpose waste in air." Rolfe comments, "To illustrate the material by the immaterial is rare in figurative language" (p. 184n), but materiality is what the maiden and Ida herself are both gracefully permitted to assume.[34]

It is fitting that Ida's liberating power spills out, not only into the imagination of her creator but into the concluding frame. The characters in the prologue employed an idyllic balance of tensions much like that in the Prince's own narrative. In the conclusion they may seem only to close up each successively larger Chinese box until Tennyson can put the lid on the whole poem: the fairy tale ends in expectation of a royal marriage; the seven narrators succeed in comfortably "killing" a summer's afternoon; the jolly peer, Sir Walter, wins over the people for another year; and Tennyson, both in story and frame, reaffirms the status quo against social discontent at home and political revolution across the channel.

I would argue, however, that this formal enclosure has been sabotaged. The Prince and Princess, instead of dissipating their powers trying to mediate one another, have jointly projected an almost visionary state. Although the apocalyptic androgyny of this state transcends the conflicts inherent within Tennyson's model, they use their vision as a means of mediating an Other lodged within the restrictive norms of their story. By breaking through their fairy-tale setting, they have broken up the story itself.[35] They have broken up the group of friendly debaters into a collection of musing individuals. They have forced the "compiler" of the poem to answer his friend's criticism of France by echoing their own personal vision. Finally, they have allowed Tennyson to break up, not only the contrived little world of the holiday outing, but the fixed norms of the so-called real world as well:

> gradually the powers of the night,
> That range above the region of the wind,
> Deepening the courts of twilight *broke them up*
> Thro' all the silent spaces of the worlds,
> Beyond all thought into the Heaven of Heavens.
>   (Concl., 111–15; italics mine)

The vision glimpsed by these two fictions within the fiction of a maker of fictions has cast doubt on all the more conventional realities of the conclusion.[36]

CHAPTER SEVEN

Maud

The great critical dilemma concerning *Maud*, encompassing and surpassing even its warmongering conclusion, is the relation between Tennyson and the poem's speaker. While roughly half the Tennyson critics see the speaker as madman and half see him as mouthpiece, they seem to agree unanimously that, as Philip Drew argues at some length, Tennyson cannot have it both ways at once. If the speaker has recovered his sanity at the end, then not only must his opinions be able to stand on their own, they must be stylistically differentiated from his earlier ravings; they cannot appear only as Tennyson's private obsessions breaking through the pretense of dramatic disguise.[1] If, on the other hand, the ravings are only dramatically valid, they should not seem as close as they often do to Tennyson's jingoistic poems to the editor of the *Times* in the early 1850s.

Probably the majority of modern critics find the speaker's psyche too damaged to project any truly positive emotion. Roy Basler, James Waltar, and Jonathan Wordsworth, among others, see his actions and attitudes throughout the poem as dominated by a childhood oedipal trauma.[2] According to them he transforms his love for his mother into a hatred, first toward his father for destroying her through his suicide and then toward those two father surrogates, Maud's father and brother. They, after all, had caused his family's ruin and were conveniently available to taunt him with it. Since Maud, according to Basler (p. 146), represents the objects both of his love and his hatred, his response to her can only repeat his compulsive response to the original trauma.[3] All these analyses posit a character far less willing and able to cope with his world than was Tennyson himself. As the speaker comes later to be haunted by Maud's specter, so he remains himself, Ricks claims (*Tennyson*, p. 246), a familiar spirit to be exorcised by his creator.

Yet if we admit that the speaker is a psychological monstrosity, how can we account for Tennyson's description of him (*Poems*, II, 517) as "raised to a pure and holy love which elevates his whole nature," or how account for the consensus of generations of readers that the poem is a celebration of love? In fact *Maud* is not just a love poem, but one that Tennyson's friend Sterling rightly called "the finest love chant . . . in the whole compass of English Literature."[4] And the speaker himself, for all his failings, stands as the consummate love poet among Tennyson's characters. Alone among them he can fulfill the Romantic goal of recreating himself, his world, and his beloved.

In so doing he virtually redefines the powers and functions of the mediator. While many of his predecessors have delimited the Other within some human figure, only the speakers of the English idylls and "Locksley Hall" have had to personify the diffuse, impersonal reality of contemporary England. When they confronted the family of their upper-class beloved, moreover, this hostile power destroyed the metaphorical world they had constructed around her. This speaker not only traces all the evils in his world back to the family which has destroyed his, he then manages to reshape a portion of it into the one figure who can mediate for him. He then turns himself, his world, and for one moment even her family into reflections of her. The speaker in *The Lover's Tale* attempts his metaphorical transformation only after Cadrilla has deserted him. The Prince and Princess do reshape the world of their poem, but theirs is a fairy-tale world to begin with and they are already royalty within it. This speaker, by contrast, completely transforms a contemporary, tawdry, stifling situation over which he has no physical or social power.

Through this speaker, in turn, Tennyson may escape the dilemma in which all these critics have placed him; he may conceivably have it both ways at once. In *Maud*, I would argue, he found a poetic vehicle which could take him where he himself could no longer go and a speaker who could make claims for him that he himself could no longer make. By choosing a mediator with both the emotional need and the metaphorical power to shape his beloved as the only goal in his life, Tennyson could affirm the transforming power of "a pure and holy love" to an age which had already cast aside all the conventional bases for such an affirmation. Through this surrogate he could systematically prepare the only epistemological ground upon which he as a Victorian poet could celebrate love with an Elizabethan breadth and grandeur.

In order to understand why this speaker could offer Tennyson what a more conventional, apparently more accomplished mediator could not, we need to return to the tangled, often problematic genesis of *Maud* itself. There we quickly discover that throughout most of the compositional process, the supposedly dramatic voice of this speaker remained indistinguishable from the lyric voice of Tennyson himself. While both the precise time and the motivation are matters for debate, it is certain that "O that 'twere possible," written shortly after Hallam's death, grew into the completed monodrama. What is perhaps the earliest draft of the poem contains only six stanzas, the first three nearly identical to those of the final text.[5] The lyric alternates between what will become part 1 of *Maud*, filled with her songs and laughter and their pastoral trysts in the twilight, and what will become part 2, with the speaker driven by some unknown shame, haunted by a shadow ("Not thou but like to thee") and lost in an urban wasteland of equally driven strangers. The second version of the poem, reentered into the Heath Manuscript in the fall of 1834, adds to the speaker's lost idyll a reference to the "garden by the turrets / Of the old manorial hall."

George O. Marshall, Jr., offers several convincing parallels between the Shadow of the beloved here and ghostly appearances of Hallam in early-written sections of *In Memoriam*.[6] Beyond this, however, critics have not successfully explained why Tennyson's own loss of Hallam metamorphosed into the winning and subsequent loss of a wealthy girl by a paranoid neurotic. Rader argues (pp. 97–98) that for Tennyson the love of this girl resembled his love for Hallam in that both transcended mere lust. Yet such a parallel, in fixing the genesis of Maud herself at 1833, neglects Carr's equally valid argument (p. 51) that all the manifold dramatizations of Hallam's death in effect repeat earlier expressions of some far less palpable loss. The living Hallam, relatively late in a long line of mediators, existed principally as a sanction for the process of mediation. With his death, Tennyson created the old men of the 1842 volume to reaffirm the process itself. In "O that 'twere possible," on the other hand, he creates this image of the beloved to reaffirm the goals of mediation.

Although Tennyson's desire for and fear of romantic love is obvious in much of his early poetry, "O that 'twere possible" stands as his earliest celebration of a mutually fulfilling relationship. Yet as far as we can see, Tennyson had no opportunity for such a relationship. At most he could only have been fantasizing here about some future winning and losing of Rosa Baring, whose hall garden at Harrington is supposed to be the original of Maud's.[7] Neither, however, does this lyric fit completely Paden's pattern (p. 74) of desire, guilt, and punishment. The past fulfillment is too passionately celebrated and the present loss connected to it by too tenuous a thread of personal responsibility. Instead, as a psychological self-analysis, the poem might better be read *backwards*: The speaker's desolate present would represent Tennyson's equally desolate present, the creation of an indifferent world and a mediator who has now forsaken both it and him.[8] The scenes of past fulfillment, both the "woody places" of the first draft and the "Manorial Hall" of the second, would represent less the lost Edens of "William Morris" and "Locksley Hall"[9] than Tennyson's challenge to the future, a projection of the only conceivable recompense for his present suffering.

If the city here epitomizes the domain of the Other, the Phantom can only epitomize the Other itself. At first just as implacably nebulous as its counterparts within *In Memoriam*, it soon reveals how insidiously it can play upon the imaginative shaping which Tennyson has already given it. In particular it echoes Tennyson's own ironic success in subsuming and hence destroying a series of earlier mediators. By reducing his angelic visitor to the Spirit of Fable within "Timbuctoo," Tennyson cleared the way for the incursion of keen Discovery. Within the second vision of *The Lover's Tale*, the speaker transferred his despair to Cadrilla so completely that she shriveled into a wraith much like the one haunting this speaker. So here this phantom, "not thou, but like to thee," taunts Tennyson with his own complicity in the beloved's transformation. It leaves him haunted not only by the genesis of this blot upon the brain but by the dim awareness that for years he has been inadvertently working to call it forth.

As with the landscape, however, the Phantom's ability to torment Tennyson suggests the means by which he can escape it. Marshall suggests (pp. 228–29) that the ghosts within *In Memoriam* embody both Hallam's loss and Hallam's continued presence. The parallels he draws between these two poems may suggest that this Phantom can also embody or, better, disembody both the absence of the beloved and the reality that she must become. Hence, in keeping with my attempt to read the lyric backwards, I would argue that it is the "real" girl of the poem who represents a photographic negative of the Phantom.

Rader, we remember (p. 99), saw this girl as an emotional substitute for Hallam. Indeed it would be absurd to argue that before Hallam's death Tennyson could have written the anguished cry in the third stanza:

> Ah Christ, that it were possible
> For one short hour to see
> The souls we loved, that they might tell us
> What and where they be.

Yet if Tennyson's quest for such a mediator predated Hallam, it may have forced on the chosen women a role more complicated than simply substituting for Hallam's loss. In part Maud grows, as Rader claims (p. 100), from a composite of Rosa Baring, Sophie Rawnsley, and Emily Sellwood; in part, however, Tennyson may have sought out, courted, and molded these three into poetic form as part of an already complex interaction between his own psyche and this once-again female mediator. He may even have pursued these women because he needed to ground within the real world the distanced, shadowy, often schematic mediator who had once protected him from it.

Between "O that 'twere possible" and Tennyson's decision to begin *Maud* proper in 1854, we can identify at least three intervening compositional stages: (1) an expanded version of "O that 'twere possible" published in 1837;[10] (2) a "shell" lyric, probably composed shortly after Hallam's death, but now imbedded within section ii of part 2;[11] and (3) "Go not, happy day," originally written in 1849 as one of the intercalary songs for the third edition of *The Princess*.[12] While tangential to the speaker and, in the case of the shell lyric, very problematic, all these three, like "O that 'twere possible," are impassioned, personal, lyric utterances.

The next compositional stage, however, substitutes a male speaker in place of a female beloved as the principal mediator, a male aristocrat in place of a female phantom as the Other, and the aristocrat's estate in place of the city as the Other's domain. To analyze these changes in form, persona, and point of view, we need to explore their first coherent appearance within a manuscript draft. In her edition of the poem, Susan Shatto has posited this draft as composed of only five sections: "Birds in the high Hall-garden" (I, xii); the already-composed "Go not, happy day" (I, xvii); "I have led her home" (I, xviii); "Strange, that I felt so gay" (I, xx); and the first four stanzas of "My life has crept so long" (III, vi). Shatto points out that while "O that 'twere possible" does not appear in Harvard Notebook 30, the sequence is structured around it.

Noting the presence of the Brother, the Suitor, the dinner, and the speaker's recovery of sanity and purpose, she argues (pp. 3–7) that the sequence "constitutes a *Maud* in miniature." Yet her earlier description of the poem's beginning as a set of love lyrics seems equally apt:[13] the duel has yet to be described or even prefigured; the first three lyrics celebrate the winning of Maud and even the last one regains her in vision; finally in all of them she is clearly distinguished from her nouveau riche context. What we may have "in miniature" is a compositional strategy parallel to the one we traced in *In Memoriam*. There Tennyson's first-written lyrics spanned the whole progression from mourning to consolation; here the comparable stage fulfills the romantic quest begun in the 1833 lyric. If Rosa, Sophie, and Emily came to embody aspects of that beloved, Tennyson's return to the lyric may suggest that none of these, particularly Emily, could encompass her. The return may further suggest that as a now-unavailable fusion of aristocratic allure and middle-class devotion, she could be recreated and rewon only if first returned to the realm of her poet's imagination.

The next phase of composition, again like that in *In Memoriam*, allows Tennyson to explore slightly more dangerous territory. In "So dark a mind within me dwells" (I, xv) and "O let the solid ground" (I, xi), the quest itself displays its obsessive power to demand a response, even if self-destructive, as a condition of self-worth. The next addition, "Maud has a garden of roses" (I, xiv), forces Tennyson to question his initially tidy separation of Maud from her social setting; she now appears, "like a precious stone / Set in the heart of the carven gloom." Perhaps because of his traumatic experience with Rosa, he here begins to transform the temporal split between the beloved and the Phantom in "O that 'twere possible" into a psychological split between Maud the beloved and Maud the representative of her family.[14] While he needs to give the beloved an identity and a setting independent of her later emanation, he also needs to confront her with some new manifestation of the Other. As Tennyson finally realized with Hallam's death, without an Other mediation has no meaning.

The next clearly defined compositional stage is so defined by Tennyson himself. Trinity Notebook 36 contains a sequence of fair copies comprising roughly two-thirds of the final version and numbered in Tennyson's own hand.[15] We can obtain the clearest picture of this draft by listing the sections *missing* from it. From part 1 these include iii, on his ghostly vision of Maud's face; vii, on his dream of their betrothal; viii, on Maud in church; x, on his jealousy of his new rival; xiii, present in part but missing his encounter with and reflections on the brother; xvi, on the brother's departure; xix (a section added only in the second edition), on the brother's return and Maud's account of her past; and xxi, on the rivulet carrying Maud's rose. From part 2, section iii on the news of Maud's death replaces the portrait of an urban wasteland like that in iv, "O that 'twere possible," and in v, the mad scene, the stanzas on the father do not appear. Even though the plot is already intact, this draft gives us less of the condition of England, less of the brother, much less of the suitor, and overall less concern with a continuous, as opposed to an implied, narrative.

What does the speaker gain and lose with the various additions which constituted the first and then second editions? We might expect that his sharper pictures of Maud's garish upper-class world have sharpened his ability to define and hence delimit both the Other and its domain. Yet if these revisions offer the speaker more dramatic autonomy, Tennyson fights this autonomy just as hard in *Maud* as he did in its two immediate predecessors. In *The Princess* even the leads expended most of their ingenuity subverting the structure within which Tennyson had enclosed them. In *In Memoriam* each incursion of the Other and each response of a mediator became a new opportunity for authorial control. In *Maud* the additions do not really draw the speaker into a deeper commitment to the demands of his fictive world. Instead, as Rader and later Martin (pp. 384–99) have shown, they draw him progressively deeper into Tennyson's fears, insecurities, and hatreds. As a virtual projection of the authorial presence, he meets each additional incursion of the Other with the same a priori patterns of response already explored by the speakers of "Edwin Morris" and "Locksley Hall."

If these later additions do expand the speaker's potential, it must be his potential for incurring and experiencing pain; Tucker (p. 408) notes that the "revisions show the poet . . . generalizing [erotic] grief into a malaise whose cultural specificity . . . widens its appeal beyond the power of narrative explanation." First, the additions reveal that his invocation of Maud depends on the same powers and grows from the same fears as his hatred of her family. Second, they reveal that when his love and his beloved are overwhelmed by hatred, these same powers turn against their host. Only at this point does Tennyson hint that his cozy identification with this now-self-destructive speaker is causing him some discomfort. He resumed the poem, as we saw, by winning the girl and thus fulfilling the thwarted desires embodied in "O that 'twere possible." He wrote the penultimate mad scene "in twenty minutes" late in the process of composition.[16]

What, besides self-expression, did the speaker offer Tennyson to compensate for the psychological costs of this identification? He shares the vulnerability of Tennyson's 1830 projections, but unlike the heroines of 1832, he has no sanctuary from which to mediate. Like his disturbed and disturbing counterpart in "Locksley Hall," he has been evicted from his childhood Eden, and his present "empty house" resembles nothing so much as Mariana's grange,

> Where I hear the dead at midday moan,
> And the shrieking rush of the wainscot mouse,
> And my own sad name in corners cried.
>
> (I, 259–61)

Unlike Mariana, however, he exhibits no centered and centering consciousness from which he could identify and confront the Other. He gives way instead to outbursts of violent love alternating with outbursts of equally violent hatred.

Culler finds this same emotional alternation the mark of the whole subgenre of the monodrama.[17] It is through his use of monodrama, in fact, that the speaker transforms himself from an authorial liability to an authorial asset. In this poem, according to Priestley, we know the speaker's psyche with certainty, the physical action and other characters only unreliably and second hand; the principal conflicts arise less between characters than within the speaker's psyche; these conflicts structure themselves into an *internalized* setting pitting the garden (Maud, civilization, hierarchy) against the wood (the speaker, nature, equality, violence); more internalized than the dramatic monologue, this format does not allow even mute characters on stage during any but the last two speeches.[18] In fact one of the speaker's lamentations in the madhouse could be extended to cover the entire poem:

> For I never whispered a private affair
> Within the hearing of cat or mouse,
> No, not to myself in the closet alone,
> But I heard it shouted at once from the top of the house.
>
> (II, 285–88)

Yet if the speaker conceives of his poem as a closet drama—in the more literal sense of being created, not simply read, in private—this conception may be less a sign of weakness than a means of mediation. Having thus blocked out the incursions of any threatening audience, either within or outside of his poem, the speaker can transform each individual section into an exclusively verbal sanctuary. Yet he avoids the solipsism of Tennyson's 1830 figures by placing these sections immediately before or after some offstage encounter.[19] If the internal in *Maud* controls the external, it is less because we do not know what happens physically, as Priestley claims, than because the speaker uses Tennyson's intensely subjective model to shape the meaning of his world. Having established himself as the focus of his world, he can construct each section as a verbal artifact which simultaneously embodies and defines its own content. From within it he can pass judgment on the actions of all those around him and weigh the response he should take in return. He may be, as Tennyson admitted (*Poems*, II, 517), "an egoist," but he is an egoist to good purpose.

As the speaker finds his sanctuary reduced to the verbal artifact of each lyric, he finds his means of mediation reduced to image and metaphor. To quote James Killham, "the hero's sensory world is over-brilliant, exaggeratedly alive. . . . He is, for example, unusually responsive to scents and sounds, as well as to colours."[20] From the very beginning the speaker's choice is never *whether* to shape the hostile domain of the Other through language but only *how*. And when he is confronted by Maud herself, his choice is never whether to respond to her rationally or imaginatively but only *which* of the many interpretations he places upon her he will believe. Like *In Memoriam*, the poem begins by opposing the transient object of individual desire to the powers of the outer world. As these powers knock down one of the speaker's imaginative constructs, he throws up another in its place until a supposedly alien reality, almost as if from fatigue, offers him a human response he can work with. Albright generalizes (p. 166) that "the world of Tennysonian myth is dominated . . . by the kinetic singer who can alter and invigorate his environs, by the world-deranger who can impress himself on the landscape he beholds."

At the poem's opening, the speaker's metaphors demonstrate their ability to control his world, but the speaker demonstrates his inability to control his metaphors:

> I hate the dreadful hollow behind the little wood,
> Its lips in the field above are dabbled with blood-red heath,
> The red-ribbed ledges drip with a silent horror of blood,
> And Echo there, whatever is asked her, answers "Death."
>
> For there in the ghastly pit long since a body was found,
> His who had given me life—O father! O God! was it well? . . .
>
> But that old man, now lord of the broad estate and the Hall,
> Dropt off gorged from a scheme that had left us flaccid and drained.
>
> (I, 1–6, 19–20)

This has been read persuasively by several critics, most recently Chris R. Vanden Bossche, as a scene of brutal though unfocused sexual violence.[21] The imagery, however, is more oral than genital, as though rape and cannibalism came to much the same thing. Maud's father, like a leech, gorges on his family until they are left "flaccid and drained." His daughter had a "sweet purse-mouth when my father dangled the grapes" (I, 71). Yet "a company forges the wine / . . . And chalk and alum and plaster are sold to the poor for bread" (I, 36, 39). Throughout these early stanzas, ravenous forms and immeasurable forces prowl the crevices of the text like the bears stalking Christopher Robin around the London sidewalks.

Although the speaker has the vehicle and the means for mediation, he remains too bound up with the fragmented authorial presence to use them. Like the poet within the very first sections of *In Memoriam*, he can only watch his world splitting into an anarchic image of his own psyche. And as Tennyson needed Hallam, so this speaker needs some secondary figure to mediate for him. Unfortunately, he refuses to admit either this need or the possibility that Maud could fill it:

> Faultily faultless, icily regular, splendidly null,
> Dead perfection, no more . . .
> From which I escaped heart-free, with the least little touch of spleen.
>   (I, 82–83, 87)

Of course he has not escaped at all—yet it would be as incorrect to say that he calls her to him as to say that she comes of her own accord. The growth of their love remains a mystery to them both, to their author, and finally to us as well.

The mystery begins, quite fittingly, within his dream of section iii. Here, even before he admits to himself his need for someone or something beyond his own misanthropy, he opens himself in sleep to the possibility that Maud might detach herself from her hostile world. And as if in response, her emanation appears, simultaneously descending from the hall and arising from the depths of his own subconscious:[22]

> Cold and clear-cut face, why come you so cruelly meek, . . .
>   and ever as pale as before
> Growing and fading and growing upon me without a sound,
> Luminous, gemlike, ghostlike, deathlike, half the night long.
>   (I, 88, 93–95)

This oxymoronic specter seems to displace death from its previous context and to fuse it with light, with Maud, and with the speaker's only hope for fulfillment. As Robert E. Lougy has noted,[23] it functions much like Keats's image of Moneta in *The Fall of Hyperion*:

> deathwards progressing
> To no death was that visage; it had pass'd
> The lily and the snow; and beyond these
> I must not think now. . . .
>
> (I, 260–63)

In both contexts, the rival associations of light and death together suggest a reality transcending either. The preternatural power of both visions may thus reflect not just the speakers' fragmentation of a being they fear to encounter as a whole, but the stubborn refusal of their visions to be known, to be seen through.

This speaker's acceptance of his vision is hardly immediate. He tries in fact to flee from it back into the comforting darkness of nature:

> I could bear it no more,
> But arose, and all by myself in my own dark garden ground, . . .
> Walked in a wintry wind. . . .
>
> (I, 96–97, 99)

Here again he feels the gravitational pull drawing all things down to the sea, death, and burial: "the scream of a maddened beach dragged down by the wave" (I, 99). Opposed to this pull, however, he rediscovers Maud's glimmering light in the aurora and her fusion of light and death in "the shining daffodil dead, and Orion low in his grave" (I, 101).[24] Here, just as in her visionary appearance, death is qualified by hope; the deaths of the winter constellation Orion and the daffodil, a flower that in *The Winter's Tale* "take[s] the winds of March with beauty," betoken the fulfillment of later spring.

Within section v, the same mysterious power which has brought her specter to him now allows him to reach out to her. She already appears physically distanced from the Other: she walks "in the meadow under the Hall"; she sings, not of the tawdry commercial present, but of the glorious martial past. To be sure, he can confront her only in a form as fragmented as that of her specter.[25] Even in spirit he can only

> move to the meadow and fall before
> Her feet on the meadow grass, and adore,
> Not her, who is neither courtly nor kind,
> Not her, not her, but a voice.
>
> (I, 186–89)

Yet this admittedly compulsive response allows him to duplicate the ends, if not the means, of the Prince's inclusively idyllic vision. From the most evanescent and peripheral of Maud's qualities, he can assemble an image which the "real" Maud is coming, as if by magic, to follow.

He may indeed be gaining control over the mediating power which until now seemed to originate somewhere outside him. Yet as his power grows more manifest, its nature, means, and extent grow proportionally more baffling. To claim that the visions reveal Tennyson indulging in unearned pathetic fallacies overlooks the fact that most of the visions are more troubling than sentimental. To claim that the speaker exercises from the beginning a Svengali-like power over Maud's will overlooks Kurata's perception that Maud has yet to offer him a single gesture of friendship, much less attraction.[26] To claim that Maud and the hall are "imaginary" seems silly, if only because it lumps these perceptions together with the speaker's later illusion that he has been buried alive. Yet to claim that his imagination merely responds to Maud's own desire "to be reconciled" may understate his growing power. He can find Maud in places and actions which affect him—and can find within *her* apparently random details which affect us as well. In sum this power, always partial, works in equal measure upon him, upon Maud, upon the setting, and—not least—upon the reader.

Section vi embodies the clearest demonstration of this power: the speaker has met Maud again "at the head of the village street"; she has given him her hand, smiled, and reminded him of the times they played together as children. The speaker's subsequent meditations reveal that he has indeed won this sign of her affection. Yet he has done so, not in spite of time and setting, but through his sensitivity to them. After he meets Maud "when the sunset burned / On the blossomed gable ends," he preserves this light through the night, less as his previous ghostly vision of her than as the warm glow of potential love:

> And thus a delicate spark
> Of glowing and growing light
> Through the livelong hours of the dark

> Kept itself warm in the heart of my dreams,
> Ready to burst in a coloured flame;
> Till at last when the morning came
> In a cloud, it faded, and seems
> But an ashen-gray delight.
>
> (I, 204–11)

Like many Romantic heroes, the speaker cannot sustain his night visions into the day. His noons are haunted by moaning ghosts and shrieking mice, emanations much like those tormenting Mariana or the Soul in "The Palace of Art." Yet as we discovered in the very first section, he can live only in a world either shaped or distorted by this restless imaginative energy. He must make his choice, not between vision and reality, but between vision and vision. To this point such relativism has been draining him of all purpose; here for the first time he cooperates with it to *make* his vision of Maud as valid and as important as he chooses. He can, he discovers, shape his universe around her:

> If Maud were all that she seemed,
> And her smile had all that I dreamed,
> Then the world were not so bitter
> But a smile could make it sweet.
>
> (I, 281–84)

All along the speaker has been establishing the ontological credibility of his visions by testing inner projections against outer ones, those of the night against those of the day, those of Maud as his beloved against those of Maud as embodiment of her family. Suddenly, however, the last of these visions threatens to overwhelm all the others. His sight of the "young lord-lover" with Maud in section ix so engulfs her within the domain of the Other that it nearly engulfs his vision of her within the encircling dark. His earlier glimpse of her at sunset had glowed through the night; his glimpse of her here produces only

> a sudden spark
> Struck vainly in the night,
> Then returns the dark
> With no more hope of light.
>
> (I, 326–29)

Faced with this dilemma, he divides his mediating powers between invoking Maud and denouncing her world. His vindictive attack on the suitor ends by reducing the speaker himself to "a wounded thing with a rancorous cry / At war with myself and a wretched race" (I, 363–64). But his plea to "the sweet heavens" for some sign of Maud's favor wins him an opportunity to celebrate her while indirectly blocking the threatened incursion of her family. In section xii, when Maud and the speaker enact the silent ritual of courtship in his woods, they shape a subtle contrast between bourgeois noise and the silence of aristocratic gesture. The natural purity of the lilies balanced against the hinted passion in the daisies turned up by her step, the offer and acceptance of a formal kiss on the hand, the speaker's wonder at the unaffected stateliness of one so young—all these set up a norm which the attempted visit of her "aristocratic" suitor can only parody. *His* "calling" is announced by the snarling of a "royal" King Charles spaniel; it is passed along by the onomatopoetic cawing of the rooks, which desecrate Maud's own name in the process:

> Birds in the high Hall-garden
>   Were crying and calling to her,
> Where is Maud, Maud, Maud?
>   One is come to woo her.
>   (I, 436–39)

Only the speaker's power can mediate this cacophony into a celebration of his beloved as the object of all the world's desire.

When the brother temporarily withdraws to London, the speaker finally commits himself to action. And here, characteristically, the control he pleads for is not over Maud, but over the unreliable agents of his own power:

> Catch not my breath, O clamorous heart,
> Let not my tongue be a thrall to my eye,
> For I must tell her before we part,
> I must tell her, or die.
>   (I, 567–70)

His celebration of Maud's acceptance in section xvii is similarly indirect, a show of power less over her than over time and space. He first commands the day to "go not . . . / Till the maiden yields," and when she does, he spreads her blush over at least three points of the compass. Yet the glowing ships, red cedars, and red men hold in common not so much a color or a flower as a word, a word which he bestows on his beloved and graciously shares with the rest of creation:

> Rosy is the West,
>> Rosy is the South,
> Roses are her cheeks,
>> And a rose her mouth.
>
> (I, 595–98)

Section xviii, ostensibly a meditation after walking Maud home, explores a further extension of their relationship. While Culler (p. 209) concludes from the speaker's epithalamium and from his mood of calm fulfillment that their love has been consummated,[27] he may underestimate the speaker's imaginative freedom to reinterpret Maud's nature and role almost at will. Near the end of section xviii the speaker can wish that no dreams frighten her "maiden grace." In section xx he can praise "Maiden Maud" for her everyday dresses. In section xxii he can describe her as "Queen lily and rose in one." Just as section xviii is both prothalamium and epithalamium, just as "Come into the Garden" is both invitation and aubade, so Maud herself, like the "snow-limbed Eve" both here and in *Paradise Lost* (IX, 270), is simultaneously both virgin and lover.

In his synthesis of these conflicting images within a single figure, he shows his final strength as Tennyson's mediator. He has desired his beloved desperately enough to obliterate any conflict between desire and reality.[28] He has invoked her powerfully enough to charm her to him. Here he glorifies her convincingly enough to reconcile an otherwise hostile world to and through her image. Because he had less to lose than Tennyson, he could risk more. In the very depths of Tennyson's own despair, as Ann Colley has argued (pp. 37–40), he could look beyond the solace of solipsism to the fate of his brothers Septimus and Arthur; *his* plight could get worse. The speaker, however, not only begins mad, he learns to celebrate his condition:

> what care I,
> Who in this stormy gulf have found a pearl
> The countercharm of space and hollow sky,
> And do accept my madness, and would die
> To save from some slight shame one simple girl.
>
> (I, 639–43)

In celebrating Maud as his countercharm to an otherwise impersonal universe, the speaker is not renouncing madness. He is redefining it as his only means of giving ultimate importance to what an "objective" observer would dismiss as a "simple girl."

Shaw, from the perspective of the poem's conclusion, links the speaker's love and his madness rather differently:

> The hero discovers that if the ostentatious visions of the great love lyrics are illusions, they are illusions of [a] transforming beauty that ennobles him. It is as if the insanity and violence that conspire against the marvelous visions at the center of *Maud* express the hero's own tragic fears about the vast pretentiousness of these visions, and so purge the fears and preserve the poem's transforming power intact. (p. 191)

I would question both the word "illusion" and the connection drawn between it and the poem's tragic reversal. To label something an illusion implies a kind of objective vantage which Tennyson and the speaker steadfastly refuse to give us. If we refuse to see *with* and not just through the speaker's madness, we must also refuse his vision of Maud—and she, as the poem works to establish, is a vision worth affirming.

Shaw's interpretation, however, raises a significant challenge to my own: If the speaker's constructs grow from power and not from illusion, why does this mediating power fail him in the end? The best answer, simply put, might be that it does not fail him; instead he fails it. His language, which has saved him from himself, cannot save him from his own hypocritical misuse of it. He often claims, for example, that he can praise Maud only by dissociating her from her family. In order to make the brother a literal scapegoat, he must make her the child of a grotesque immaculate conception, "only the child of her mother." Kincaid in fact traces his sickness (p. 113) to his refusal to acknowledge that "Maud is one with her brother," who himself "is both animalistic and tender." Yet beneath his ostracism the speaker envies the brother, not for his tenderness but for his animalism. In the very act of winning Maud from the domain of the Other, he is sidling past her. Like Tennyson's fickle mediators of 1830, he is covertly trying to identify with the Other even as he combats it.[29]

For J. L. Kendall it is in section xx that "the subversion of the hero's imagination is complete. . . . [He has persuaded Maud] to nickname her brother 'The Sultan' (I. xx. 790). But then, ironically enough, he proceeds to nickname Maud his 'queen.' . . . He cannot help associating possession of Maud with the acquisition of material wealth and that wealth with the impulse toward aggression."[30] Indeed the whole garden scene represents a trap of his own making. Pauline Fletcher, in her analysis of Victorian poetic land-scapes, has noted that the Tennysonian narrator leaves Eden and returns only to find it "private property."[31] But here he is drawn back to the garden because it *is* private property. While waiting for Maud in section xxii, he looks past her toward the dancers dancing in tune and the "young lord lover" sighing "for one that will never be thine." He has almost reduced her to a pawn in his own love-hate relationship with the upper class.

Within this lyric, however, he confronts and partially transcends this obsession by appropriating its metaphorical context. His invocation of the flowers was parodied by Lewis Carroll as fatuous personification; yet when he claims that "the soul of the rose went into my blood," he translates both his passion and the world's aristocratic disdain into a botanical debate of which he is the sole privileged interpreter. Through the heraldic significance of rose and lily, he can celebrate Maud in Renaissance conceits as their queen, their sun. Where Maud had attempted to redeem the courtly code through the immediacy of gesture, the speaker invokes its metaphorical source to the same end.[32]

The flower images, however, carry the seeds of their own destruction. The speaker's image of death as sexual consummation has often been seen as yet another Elizabethan conceit:

> the planet of love is on high,
> Beginning to faint in the light that she loves
> On a bed of daffodil sky,
> To faint in the light of the sun that she loves,
> To faint in his light and to die.
>
> (I, 857–61)

By the end of the lyric, however, the speaker has come to take both death and eros far more literally:

> My dust would hear her and beat,
> Had I lain for a century dead;
> Would start and tremble under her feet,
> And blossom in purple and red.
>
> (I, 920–23)

For Shaw (p. 184), Tennyson "has given to the blood and the flower the terror of the lover's darkest imaginings." For Albright, "his emotion slips out of him, grows huge and shifting, an attribute of the cosmos" (p. 25). We might be tempted to reply that the image is more focused than either critic admits, that Tennyson saves it from conventional necrophilia only by making the dead not the beloved object but the throbbing phallic speaker himself.

This link between imaginative, sexual, and aggressive power may carry him back to the self-destructive progression in *Poems by Two Brothers*: aggression, violence, and the Doom of God. Earlier his language endowed all the males surrounding Maud with the physical, social, and sexual power of the Other: the brother is an "oiled and curled Assyrian bull"; the father (later to be "a gray old wolf") is "a wretched swindler"; the suitor's grandfather "crept from a gutted mine . . . / And left his coal all turned into gold / To a grandson, . . . / Rich in the grace all women desire" (I, 338, 340–42). Earlier the speaker's vituperation guaranteed him the hostility of these men without depriving them of their power. Now, by covertly invoking these same monstrous figures, he calls forth the brother himself. In this context, his pathetic question in the madhouse—"Who told *him* we were there?"—may be more rhetorical than he wants to admit.

This invocation echoes the speaker's equally unconscious, equally self-destructive invocation of Maud's phantom. After the duel he prays, "Powers of the height, Powers of the deep, / . . . comfort her though I die." He receives his answer in the following section with the news of her death. But "the ghastly Wraith of one that I know" has already "glided out of the joyous wood"—not only before Maud's death, but even before her "passionate cry" at her brother's murder. In the earliest version of "O that 'twere possible," this specter stood divorced from any specific guilt as the mocking projection of the Other as loss. While Tennyson pleaded for knowledge of the dead, "where and what they be," he was given a "type of pain," which "mixes memory with doubt."

Although it now embodies not loss or doubt but guilt, this phantom remains credible because the speaker's perceptions of it parallel Tennyson's own myopic perception of distant objects as blurred, fading, reappearing: it can "stand, / A shadow there at my feet / High over the shadowy land" (II, 38–40). Earlier the speaker envisioned Maud "growing and fading and growing upon me without a sound." But there, like Tennyson throughout his life, he could turn a visual weakness into an imaginative strength: though the earlier vision seemed to come from without, he could assimilate it. Now, however, guilt has fragmented his psyche just as grief fragmented Tennyson's in the early sections of *In Memoriam*. Hence, while he recognizes this vision as only "a lying trick of the brain," he must acknowledge the stubborn corporeality it shares with the shell and the ring: it is "a hard mechanic ghost," "that abiding phantom cold," "the shadow still the same."

Even more devastating, the speaker must also acknowledge that where he had earlier conjured up a mediator from the domain of the Other, he has now allowed her to escape, not back to her old domain, but to one more frighteningly alien than any in Tennyson: it "never came from on high / Nor ever arose from below" (II, 82–83), but "comes from another stiller world of the dead, / Stiller, not fairer than mine" (II, 308–9). Although as implacable as any manifestation of the Other, it remains a locus for the mediating power he once superimposed on the world, a power which has deserted him as unworthy and now watches him impassively from without: the brother "may take her now; for she never speaks her mind, / But is ever the one thing silent here" (II, 305–6). This silence may be fit retribution for the speaker's earlier refusal to give his mediator the autonomy she needed to save him. Despite Maud's adolescent rebellion against her family's wishes and values, Dorothy Mermin dismisses her as "a cipher."[33] Maud's only real language throughout part 1 has been that of significant gesture: an averted look, a blush, a song, a handclasp, a smile. Hence we should feel the justice of the Phantom's refusal to communicate even through gesture. It stands instead as the side of Maud he has ignored, a silent, implacable embodiment of blood vengeance.

Now that his own powers have forsaken him for emanations like the Phantom, the world of the Other "beats" its way into their place even within the madhouse: "The hoofs of the horses beat, / Beat into my scalp and my brain" (II, 247–48). The same world which has broadcast his former whispers ("Who told *him* we were there?") is deaf to the present grief: "It is that which makes us loud in the world of the dead" (II, 264). Yet even his voice, as Lougy points out (pp. 420–22), is still not specifically his own but part of the general gabble.[34] He can use this voice only to

> cry to the steps above my head
> And somebody, surely, some kind heart will come
> To bury me, bury me
> Deeper, ever so little deeper.
>
> (II, 339–42)

Since his plea is for death, not mediation, it is providentially neither granted nor even answered from the expected quarter. Instead Maud's spirit comes to him in the form that he had feared to contemplate in "O that 'twere possible":

> like a silent lightning under the stars
> She seemed to divide in a dream from a band of the blest,
> And spoke of a hope for the world in the coming wars—
> "And in that hope, dear soul, let trouble have rest,
> Knowing I tarry for thee," . . . .
>
> (III, 9–13)

Neither the nature of this visit nor the motives for it are any clearer than those ascribed to Ida's love for the unconscious Prince. Even within Tennyson's model, the visit may represent the response of some new mediator to a fragmented authorial presence, or the return of the speaker's own mediating powers, or even the metamorphosis of the phantom from Other to mediator.[35] We know only that here, as in section 95 of *In Memoriam*, the mediating vision can come only to one open and confident enough to celebrate the experience.

In this very celebration the speaker seems to have regained much of his verbal power. He can characterize the Czar as an essentially linguistic villain, a manipulator of language, "a giant liar."[36] He, by contrast, shapes the conclusion of the first edition into a handsome synthesis of virtually all the poem's imagery:

> And now by the side of the Black and Baltic deep,
> And deathful-grinning mouths of the fortress, flames
> The blood-red blossom of war with a heart of fire.
>
> (III, 51–53)

Here the oral threat posed by the devouring Other in the opening is transformed into his own implicitly sexual aggression. Here his heart, reduced in the madhouse to "a handful of dust" and resurrected into a "passionate heart" earlier in this section, is transformed into the blazing communal passion which now subsumes him. Here the flowers—the symbols first of human values, then of Maud herself, then of blood vengeance—are transformed into his means of burning out of a life he hates and toward a reunion with her.

Tennyson felt impelled to dilute this conclusion with a verbally passive addition: "I embrace the purpose of God, and the doom assigned"

(III, 59). Even in the first edition, as the cannon speaks only in the inarticulate roar of destruction, so the speaker eagerly surrenders his individual voice to that of mass violence: "I stood on a giant deck and mixed my breath / With a loyal people shouting a battle cry" (III, 34–35). He may thus be repeating his earlier surrender to the "idiot gabble" of the madhouse. Kennedy argues (pp. 175–76) that this return to the inarticulate undermines his supposed cure, and Lougy (p. 409) that now "we see the real face of madness staring at us, especially terrifying because it alone believes itself to be sane." Overall, however, I think commentators have overstated the importance of the conclusion both for the poem and for Tennyson. It should be seen neither as the remedy for an ironically presented "love," nor as the ironically presented descent from individual madness into mass hysteria; it should be seen instead as a narrative and ideological second best. Though such an interpretation may frustrate our craving for dramatic climax, we should remember that it is Maud's name which appears as the poem's title; the speaker's name appears nowhere.

In forsaking speech in favor of action, the speaker is only following the example of Tennyson's male mediators in the 1842 volume: Ulysses, Tithonus, Tiresias, Arthur, and the speaker of "Locksley Hall." All these have nearly lost their identity in some relationship with a woman; all talk their way to an awareness of their present situation and the people ranged against them; then all commit themselves to some physical escape. For Ulysses, Arthur, and later Tennyson himself, to sail out into the ocean entails danger, probable death, but certain confrontation with some ultimate reality. As a goal for this speaker, the Crimea may exist only as a remote place where he can strike out against the monsters of his own psyche without hitting his neighbors. His escape differs from those of 1842 only in this: Where those men were all running away from some woman, he thinks he is running toward one.

How valid this hope is we can best determine by comparing it to the similar visionary quest in *In Memoriam*. Both poems owe their origins to the same loss; both confront similar manifestations of the Other in their quests to mediate that loss. The greater optimism of *In Memoriam* lies not so much in its conclusion as in the different basis of its visions. There Tennyson was willing to discover and abide by whatever conditions could win him some mediating presence. Here the speaker exists as Tennyson's means of reaching back toward a mediating presence initially defined as unattainable. Thus the speaker must invoke, body forth, and celebrate a figure which he cannot, by definition, keep alive. Even his image of Maud awaiting him after death cannot carry complete authorial or even dramatic conviction; it cannot be more than what he himself calls it:

> it was but a dream, yet it yielded a dear delight
> To have looked, though but in a dream, upon eyes so fair,
> That had been in a weary world my one thing bright;
> And it was but a dream. . . .
>
> (III, 15–18)

CHAPTER EIGHT

The 1859 *Idylls of the King*

"Vivien"

The more closely we examine Tennyson's approach to his great Arthurian opus in the mid-1850s, the stranger the whole proccss appears.[1] Catherine Barnes Stevenson argues well for Merlin's place within the long line of bardic and prophetic figures through whom Tennyson denounced his age.[2] Yet the particular Merlin story which Tennyson chose, the seer's seduction and enchantment by Vivien, seems more like a footnote to the Arthurian world than an entrance. The action takes place far from Camelot, and neither Arthur, Guinevere, nor Lancelot ever appears within it. And while Southey's account makes Merlin more actively lecherous and Vivien more actively manipulative than in Malory,[3] neither seems capable of serious development, much less dramatic interest.

The earliest manuscript drafts, even in their jumbled and probably incomplete condition, are actually both well developed and suggestive—yet not in the ways we might expect.[4] The extant passages include a description of Vivien (c. ll. 237–48), her request for the charm (c. ll. 267–335), Merlin's denial and her song (c. ll. 354–91), his tale of the charm's origin (c. ll. 553–630), his description of its text (c. ll. 666–83), her very general attack on the knights who accuse her (c. ll. 690–96), his muttered condemnation of her (c. ll. 808–22), her tearful reply (c. ll. 838–84), and Merlin's relenting (c. ll. 890–91). The story itself moves more straightforwardly toward its climax than it does in the printed text, but it is certainly a curious beginning to what Tennyson's friends and admirers hoped would be the definitive version of the Arthurian epic. Here we discover an old man being mentally enslaved and physically seduced by an unscrupulous young woman.

Missing from these sketches are the implicit contrast between Arthur's court and Mark's, Arthur's imperviousness to Vivien's flattery, Merlin's fame as Arthur's material and imaginative architect, and finally his recollections of the founding of the Round Table—in short, virtually the entire Arthurian setting. What background the story does provide—Merlin's tale of kings, pirates, and enchantments—ties it more closely to the jumbled fairy-tale world of *The Princess* than to anything else in Tennyson's canon. If he was turning away from the contemporary relevance of *Maud*, he was turning not so much to any historical or literary context as to the conflicting figures and forces within his own model.[5]

    Maud itself hints at the very different conflicts which will generate its successor. Rader, we remember (p. 114), saw that poem as growing out of a sexual obsession, exorcising the more violent passions aroused by Rosa Baring in favor of the more spiritual love offered by Emily Sellwood. To me, the speaker's invocation of Maud remained one of the healthiest and most clearly sanctioned of his emotional outlets. Yet his early image of her "lying [in] splendid whoredom," while eventually canceled, foreshadowed the pervasive image of women in the *Idylls* as predatory manifestations of the Other. The manuscript sketches for "Vivien" in particular, though still far from the idyll's printed form, come dangerously close to its central obsession.[6] What may be the earliest-written scrap reads, "She along the ground / Writhed toward him."[7] The pervasiveness of sexual threat throughout the 1859 *Idylls* has often been linked to themes and obsessions in Tennyson's earlier poetry.[8] Even within the 1833–34 "Morte d'Arthur," we can find his mediators confronting the Other manifested as both female and flux. There, we remember, Bedivere hopes to protect the phallic Excalibur from what he sees as the impersonal depths of the mere. Arthur, however, is willing to sacrifice it in return for the personal, feminine response of the water's resident spirit, the Lady of the Lake.

We can only speculate about why Tennyson still saw the Arthurian world as sexually threatening and why he felt compelled to explore this threat so thoroughly. Had the long-repressed sexual glamour of Rosa Baring begun again to work in his subconscious? Had the domestic comforts of his now-six-year marriage begun to appear as a sexual threat of their own? Had the forty-seven-year-old poet discovered that desire, so long a psychological given, had to be consciously, artistically evoked? Had sexuality itself come to seem the only available form for an Other which, since Hallam's death, had become ever more difficult to personify? Whatever the reasons or combination of them, Tennyson's Camelot of 1856 had become less a literary public domain than a domain contested by a feminine Other and whatever mediators Tennyson could bring against her.

While Arthur and Guinevere would eventually assume the principal roles in this contest, his earlier Arthurian portraits had made them too complex to fit neatly into his model. Arthur, though England's king, was also Guinevere's husband. Guinevere, though Lancelot's lover, was also England's queen. By the time of "Guinevere" and "Elaine," Tennyson was ready to exploit the pathos inherent in these contradictory roles. For now, however, he needed figures more open to almost allegorical treatment. He needed to have virtue win its argument with sexual license; yet he also needed to have his virtuous mediator lose his battle with this seductive embodiment of the Other. While sacrificing Merlin, as he had already sacrificed the Lady of Shalott and Bedivere among his Arthurian mediators, he could still protect the values within the poem's shadowy authorial presence; he could reaffirm his own vulnerable ideals in the face of their evident impotence in the world around him. As a microcosm for the failure of Camelot itself, Merlin's fall offered a ready-made *a fortiori* argument: If ideals alone could not save this man and this society, then how much less could they be expected to save the men and the society of nineteenth-century England?[9]

Tennyson had to accept this carefully limited defeat in accepting the outline of Merlin's seduction within his sources. By hedging it about with additions, he hoped to confine it to the same hollow oak which held his now-paralyzed mediator. His compositional strategy thus recapitulated the strategies of spatial delimitation within his model. Yet his revisions, which were to turn a paragraph in Southey into an idyll of almost a thousand lines, also turned this idyll into a battle for imaginative control of the whole setting. The early drafts are set in a contextual limbo because only the values of the two combatants are givens. All other details become not just the focus of their debate but the focus of Tennyson's own additions to this text. He adds background, in other words, only in the process of developing the perspectives of his two leads. As Merlin defensively tries to reinterpret the imaginative creations of his opponent, Tennyson's additions must likewise redirect a poem which is being taken in unforeseen and discomforting directions.

We can see this process exemplified if we turn from the fragmented drafts of "Vivien" to Tennyson's first attempts to string them into a continuous narrative within Huntington Manuscript 1326. This draft begins to oppose "the True and the False," the ostensible theme of the 1859 *Idylls*; yet at this point truth and falsehood are *very* hard to distinguish. Most of the norms provided by the wider Arthurian world are still missing. In fact our only extended glimpses of this world in the manuscript are the opposed speeches which serve as proof texts for both Merlin and Vivien. Piqued by Merlin's tactless reference to her reputation at court, Vivien turns on the institution as a hotbed of sexual license and hypocrisy: husbands returning after a year's absence to discover newborn additions to their families, lovers sleeping together before marriage, saintly Sir Percivale consorting with a witch in a graveyard, Lancelot and Guinevere the object of scandal and gossip for the whole realm, and finally Arthur himself a self-acknowledged cuckold.

Merlin's responses to these accusations grow more indignant as each mounts an increasingly open attack on his ideals, yet these responses also grow more qualified as he must grant more of her circumstances: the "illegitimate" child was not even the wife's; the couple did spend the night together, but innocently; Sir Percivale may have succumbed to a momentary temptation; Guinevere's affair cannot be denied, only excused because she originally mistook Lancelot for Arthur; and Arthur "wouldst against thine own eye-witness fain / Have all men true and leal, all women pure" (ll. 791–92). What is this last defense but a kinder version of Vivien's own description of him, "crowned King, coward, and fool"?

The court, in other words, cannot serve as a sanctuary, even one as vulnerable as Oenone's glen or as flawed as the Soul's Palace. Its meaning, like that of the entire setting, depends upon the values of its interpreter. As David Staines has shown, most of Vivien's examples owe less to Malory or any other medieval source than to Tennyson's own "poetic license."[10] Such license, however, merely reflects the author's covert collaboration with Vivien as she works for the right to exist in *her* version of Camelot, not the more traditional one of her adversary.

Tennyson's subsequent additions, both within and after the Huntington draft, attempt to build a historical, social, moral setting which can contain Vivien, can allow his mediator to dismiss her as a "harlot" and her charges as mere spite. Yet instead of thus delimiting the Other, these additions only reveal the origins of both figures in myth, in Tennyson's disconcerting early poems, and in the darker regions of his own unconscious. By calling upon the powers she shares with her counterparts in his early poems, Vivien can call up equally dark, equally irrational forces both within Merlin and within his vision of the setting they share.

Tennyson found Vivien so problematic a figure that in Malory even her identity remains in doubt. Sometimes singly, sometimes as a group, the Ladies of the Lake forge and receive again Arthur's sword, are beheaded by Balin, steal Lancelot from his mother's arms and raise him. Since Tennyson had already assigned the first of these roles to the Lady of the Lake in his 1833 "Morte d'Arthur," he tried here to deprive the disreputable Vivien of her sisters' magic.[11] Yet thirty years later, as Gordon Haight has shown (pp. 557–64), Tennyson would use some dubious Welsh etymology to transform her into Poetic Inspiration within his autobiographical testament, "Merlin and the Gleam."

I would argue that her imaginative power is equally evident here. Like her descendants throughout the *Idylls*, she draws on her heritage as a "fatal woman," particularly on the power she shares with Amoret, to embody what Joseph calls (p. 124) "the universe conceived of as a woman." Yet Vivien draws also on a tradition older than Tennyson's Keatsian prototype. Like Eve, Satan, Duessa, and Cleopatra, she possesses an "infinite variety" which charms the artist even as it threatens the man.[12] Like all these villains she is able to clothe herself in a scene and embroil herself in a plot. As Albright puts it (p. 52), "She is the superior magician, the superior image maker, because she can govern the internal emblems, the interpretation of language." From the very first manuscript sketches Vivien is able to breathe some life and suspense into a static form (a derivative of the Theocritean singing match) with Merlin's stasis as its conclusion.

In the poem's earliest draft, for example, the world of Merlin's fairy tale stood as his own creation. To convince Vivien of the danger of the charm, he tells her its history: how a king marries a wife who drives his whole realm mad for her beauty; how he finally finds "a little glassy-headed hairless man" so ascetic that he knows a charm to render her invisible to all save the king. To the seer in his story, like those in Tennyson's earlier poetry, asceticism meant power: since he never

> owned a sensual wish, to him the wall
> That sunders ghosts and shadow-casting men
> Became as crystal, and he saw them through it,
> And heard their voices talk behind the wall,
> And learnt their elemental secrets, powers
> And forces. . . .
>
> (ll. 626–31)

The vision, however, gains this power by "seeing through" and hence vitiating all human goals and desires. When Merlin himself is faced with a similar norm of "use" without fulfillment, he is driven to deny his similarity to the king (and implicitly the seer) in his own story:

> There lived a king in the most Eastern East,
> Less old than I, yet older, for my blood
> Hath earnest in it of far springs to be.
>
> (ll. 553–55)

In later additions to Merlin's story, Vivien exploits this subliminal conflict, reinterpreting the story and applying it to him in ways so subtle that he acts on the reinterpretations without ever having to accept them. She interrupts him to deny the good faith of the characters involved, implying that all ages share the corruption she has posited in present society. In an added conclusion Merlin is made to admit that the seer, offered the grateful King's reward, "went back to his old wild, and lived on grass, / And vanished, and his book came down to me" (ll. 647–48). Finally, in the shortest but most significant addition, Merlin is made to deny the resemblance Vivien claims to see between him and the ascetic seer: "Nay, not like to me."

As this capitulation implies, Merlin develops out of the most subjective and hence most vulnerable of Tennyson's mediators, the visionary. Stevenson argues ("Druids," pp. 19–20) that as heir to an "inward" vision, Merlin also inherits his predecessors' temptation to flee from social responsibility. Kemble's 1833 prose sketch of the projected "Ballad of Sir Lancelot" (*Poems*, I, 545) describes the knight as dismissing Merlin's criticism and "flooring" him "since his propensities are no secret, and since he very well knows what will become of him in the valley of Avilion some day." Joseph notes (p. 127) that his closest counterpart, the Magus in *The Devil and the Lady*, is also besotted with a young woman who finds him odious. He too harangues her on chastity—without ever applying his moral to himself. He too laments that he cannot penetrate another consciousness—without realizing that the outer world is itself a product of consciousness, others' and his own.

Fred Kaplan argues that Vivien herself exists only as the dark side of Merlin's imagination, the power that destroys instead of creating.[13] Yet the ascetic alternative facing both Tennyson and his mediator, a future without Vivien, proves just as menacing in its sterility. Through Merlin's dilemma Tennyson may be exploring the real problems of exiling from his own art the sexual energy on which he may already have grown aesthetically dependent. Paden, we remember, identified the Magus and other old men in Tennyson's youthful poems as his mask of age. In Merlin Tennyson may instead have created, if you will, a mask for middle age. The superannuated Merlin may exaggerate and hence distance Tennyson's very real fears that the ascetic goals deemed appropriate for one of his years were not worth the sacrifices necessary to achieve them.

Apart from this fairy-tale world, the setting is virtually absent from the early manuscripts. Not until after the Huntington draft does Tennyson draw the implied contrast between Merlin's surreptitious journey with Vivien to "the wild woods of Broceliande" and his earlier visit with Arthur: "It was the time when first the question rose / About the founding of a Table Round" (ll. 408–9). While Merlin tries to appropriate this spirit of place for Arthur, chivalry, and idealism, he leaves it rooted in the narrative past and in the murky realm of nineteenth-century forays into Celtic legend.[14] Vivien can then exploit this limitation to redefine their shared setting within the actual present. Throughout Tennyson both forest and storm have been charged with sexual power,[15] and by arousing and manipulating the unacknowledged storm of passion in Merlin, Vivien actually transforms these woods from a sanctuary of Victorian chivalry to her own personal domain.

The violent storm at the end, Vivien's oath on her veracity, the lightning bolt that barely misses her, her flight for safely into Merlin's arms, his revelation of the charm and subsequent slumber, her weaving of the charm until "in the hollow oak he lay as dead"—the entire sequence forms such an obvious metaphor for sexual surrender that even some perceptive Victorian readers saw it as such: FitzGerald nicknamed this idyll "the naughty one," and even while the poem was in manuscript, "James Spedding wrote to T[ennyson] objecting to Merlin's seduction by Vivien" (*Poems*, III, 393).

Yet Vivien, I think, is playing for more than Merlin—indeed for nothing less than sexual domination over the setting itself. She has turned the storm from an omen of danger to one of desire; she has turned the bolt from a divine judgment to an invitation to further intimacy; now the metaphors suggest that she has turned the seduction itself into a rape of the entire landscape:

> Till now the storm, its burst of passion spent,
> Moaning and calling out of other lands,
> Had left the ravaged woodland yet once more
> To peace; and what should not have been had been.
>
> (ll. 959–62)

The further she extends her domain over the landscape of Tennyson's model, the more she blocks the power of his mediator to define and so limit her. As she slips from ingenue to vamp, to courtly lover, to wronged maiden, the reader is kept wondering not just whether she will win but what identity she will assume next. She begins practicing upon Merlin, "fancying that her glory would be great / According to his greatness whom she quenched" (ll. 215–16). And in triumph she not only assumes his glory, she effectively reverses the consummation of "Leda and the Swan" by putting on "his knowledge with his power." Although in a manuscript draft she lies in protesting to Merlin, "I will use no glamour on thee," she is correct in her claim that possessing this power is more important to her than using it. For the power resides less in the charm itself than in the credence she has already won from Merlin in order to gain it. She thus achieves, not just the roles she practices, but the power to change roles at will. She transforms herself, more completely than any of Tennyson's other fatal women, into one of the shape-shifting specters who haunt medieval romance.

That this imaginative anarchy bothered Tennyson is evident from the final additions he made to the idyll, both in late drafts for its original publication and again fourteen years afterward. For the first edition we are given not just Merlin's account of the stag hunt, but his fame as Arthur's architect, builder of "his havens, ships, and halls." Yet the more we are allowed to see the height from which Merlin falls, the more we are forced to see the tenuousness of his original position. Though not added until 1873, his prescient visions of "a doom that ever poised itself to fall . . . and the high purpose broken by the worm" are already implicit in the 1859 text. As some of the 1859 additions on the court were meant to glorify Merlin as mediator, others seem meant to delimit Vivien as Other, to fix her place much as she has fixed his. Her attempt on "the blameless king" and the knights' merriment at her failure together give her an initial stamp of intellectual as well as moral triviality, but in forcing readers to share Merlin's impression of her as "a gilded summer fly," Tennyson has also forced them to participate vicariously in his seduction.

His later additions prove no less ambiguous. He actually planned another whole idyll, "Balin and Balan," to introduce (and hence define) Vivien, but in 1873, when she threatened to usurp that story as well, he moved the introduction to the beginning of "Merlin and Vivien" itself. There we learn that she was "born from death . . . and sown upon the wind" (ll. 44–45). We learn that she was then corrupted by the treacherous King Mark and that she now goes to Camelot to expose the truth about Arthur's ideal, the "old true filth, and bottom of the well." We learn that she dares this undertaking because "Hate, if Hate be perfect, casts out fear." Such a genesis may give her a stature worthy of Merlin's opposition, but it also gives her a satanic intensity until now reserved for male embodiments of the Other. Hard as Tennyson works to pin her down, she can at least taunt Merlin with *his* inability to do so: "I think, / However wise, ye hardly know me yet" (ll. 352–53). By the time he does know her, carnally or otherwise, it is he who has yielded up his identity and she who has incorporated it into her own.

Tennyson's last thoughts on Merlin turn out to be no more conclusive than those on Vivien. In the "Holy Grail" idyll of 1869, as Galahad prepares to sit in the Siege perilous, Tennyson again departs from his sources to offer what he meant to be the *public* explanation of Merlin's sudden disappearance:

> In our great hall there stood a vacant chair,
> Fashioned by Merlin ere he past away, . . .
> And Merlin called it "The Siege perilous,"
> Perilous for good and ill; "for there," he said,
> "No man could sit but he should lose himself:"
> And once by misadventure Merlin sat
> In his own chair, and so was lost. . . .
> (ll. 167–68, 172–76)

The Siege perilous Tennyson himself glosses as "the spiritual imagination" (*Poems*, III, 469), and Stevenson argues ("Druids," p. 19) that "both the charm and the chair symbolize the esoteric, even lethal, knowledge that the prophet-bard possesses."[16] The evident dangers of surrender to such an imaginative power seem to reinforce Fred Kaplan's interpretation of Vivien as only the embodiment of its presence within Merlin. Yet we saw that within "Vivien" it was she who reduced him to her own imaginative fiction. We might better see the passage from the "Grail" as Tennyson's ruefully tardy warning to himself. Just as the Siege perilous here turns back upon and envelops its creator, so Tennyson's *Idylls* gain reality almost at the expense of his conscious control. And just as Vivien usurped first Merlin's vision and then his identity, so within Tennyson's expanding poem ever more active personifications of the Other are seizing imaginative control of their stories, shaping them to their own visions and their own needs.

"Enid"

While I have been arguing against Betty Miller's claim that "Vivien" dramatizes only Tennyson's blinding fear of female sexuality, the fears it does dramatize may be even more frightening. Hence we should not be surprised to find in Tennyson's next-written idyll, originally entitled simply "Enid," a violent reaction to the first. In the place of apparently rational argument, he gives us a sentimental portrait of selfless devotion and undeserved suffering. In the place of physical stasis, both before and after the charm, he gives us Geraint's blind obsession with physical violence. In place of a reliance on dialogue, he gives us Geraint's command of silence.

Searching for parallels among the characters, readers are quick to note the substitution of truth for falsehood, Enid for Vivien. But other possible parallels complicate this one. Geraint's jealousy, for example, can be seen as overcompensation for Merlin's credulity. Or, to reverse the pairs, his demand for total commitment proves just as pernicious in its seriousness as does Vivien's demand for commitment in its hypocrisy. Finally Enid's acceptance of these demands echoes Merlin's tolerance of Vivien, both revealing the dangers of passivity. In short by changing *all* the parameters of his first idyll, Tennyson has surrendered the possibility of any simple opposition between truth and falsehood in the second.

When we turn to the manuscripts for help in unraveling this complexity, we find them curiously unhelpful. The notebooks, although full of snippets with some interesting variant readings, are simultaneously too far from and too close to the printed text—too far in that they are too jumbled to permit many firm conclusions about the sequence of composition, too close in that, apart from one very compressed account of Geraint's return to the court with his future bride, they show that Tennyson already had a firm hold on his story and on the extensive changes he would make in the *Mabinogion* tale of "Geraint Son of Erbin."[17]

Within his source the freedom of shaping one's world, won so dearly by Vivien, is freely bestowed on all. The court and Guinevere in particular may be models of gentility without the sexual shortcomings which Tennyson and *his* hero find there. But for all this the Welsh Geraint is sanctioned in abandoning the court, in doting on his wife, in dragging her off on his quest, in denying her the right to speak, and in making her herd his captured horses. He wins similar approval for only grudgingly accepting the hospitality of Arthur and for plunging back into another series of adventures as soon as he is cured of his wound. In the same way, the "morally neutral" Sparrow Hawk is sanctioned in oppressing Enid's father,[18] Doorm in pleading for her love, the Little King in opposing Geraint's journey through his realm—in short, if the court has its customs, Geraint has a right to his and his antagonists to theirs. Geraint is the story's hero, not because he is morally superior, but because in the inevitable clash of customs, he makes his prevail by force of will and arms.

Within his early drafts, Tennyson seems to discover that bringing order to this story is far easier than discovering its meaning. He can blacken the unmannerly figures Geraint encounters on his journeys, present Enid as innocent victim both before and after her marriage, bring Arthur in at the end rather than the middle, criticize Geraint for abusing his wife—and yet the physical action of the story still does not develop its psychological themes. Indeed Geraint's journey in the second half constitutes one long effort to avoid the misunderstanding which prompted it. In a sense Tennyson's manuscript jottings remain workmanlike efforts to grind out the plot while he continued to ponder its implications for his model.

Some of these implications are present in embryo within two manuscript passages, both of which stand out by their completeness and their early position within what seems the first of the notebooks (H.Nbk 35). The first is the bedroom scene where Enid bewails her husband's uxoriousness (ll. 69–108); the second is Geraint's search for lodgings and his discovery of Enid in her ruined tower (ll. 251–344). Together these passages define a confrontation, like those in the "Morte" and *The Princess*, between two potential mediators who see each other as Other.

In "Vivien" the initial tableau did not appear in the drafts until Tennyson had delineated the couple's physical standoff. Here the primacy of this tableau suggests that Tennyson has now realized that such a confrontation produces its own stasis. The opposed symbols he captures within it—speech and silence, clothing and nakedness, violence and passivity, wake and sleep—virtually determine the meaning of the subsequent action. He can now reproduce the raw adventures and formulaic dialogue of *The Mabinogion* as Enid's realistic impressions of a loving husband inexplicably transformed into another of Tennyson's tyrannical god figures.

For a modern reader, Enid's impressions not only appear realistic in this scene, but remain so even after the couple's reconciliation. Tennyson does change to criticism the admiration shown Geraint in *The Mabinogion*; yet throughout his "quest for honor where no honor can be gained" Geraint still appears entirely too heroic. Paul Zietlow attributes his boorishness to Enid's very passivity: though sexually true, "she behaves falsely, for she lacks the inner strength to communicate to him the truth that she clearly sees."[19] More consonant with Tennyson's underlying obsession is Arthur Wayne Glowka's sexual interpretation of Enid's falsity. He argues that her choice of the "faded silk," while ostensibly submissive, is both knowingly and unconsciously subversive. Although it recalls Geraint's past rescue of her, it also convinces Limours and Doorm that she is unloved and hence sexually available.[20] If Tennyson was too easy on his "hero," he may have been covertly identifying with Geraint's response to Enid as threatening sexual force.

This same fear may shape the second developed manuscript passage, particularly in relation to the sections which follow it in Harvard Notebook 35. Here Geraint's quest to avenge Guinevere's insult becomes itself transformed:

> So the sweet voice of Enid moved Geraint . . .
> > who thought and said,
> "Here, by God's grace, is the one voice for me."
> > (ll. 334, 343–44)

The following passages, however, describe his continued fascination with Enid, her courtship by Limours and Edyrn, and (from the second journey) the attacks of the brigands and the amorous advances of Limours and Doorm. Enid is hardly a kindred spirit to Vivien, but in the earliest drafts of this idyll she evokes unwillingly the kind of sexual obsession Vivien has to work for. Geraint's behavior changes only because on the first journey he is under her sexual spell while on the second he is fighting against it. On this second journey, in fact, part of his prowess seems to grow from his ability to read correctly the obsession of every character except his wife.

Tennyson's covert identification with his erring hero is further suggested by the absence of any objective measure of Geraint's mistake until the second notebook (H.Nbk 71) and, in some cases, until the first full draft (T.Nbk 30). Only in these do we find full descriptions of Arthur's hunt, of the insult done Guinevere's maiden, of Edyrn's account of his reformation at court, and of Arthur's criticism of Geraint's self-appointed quest. From this new geographical perspective, we can see that the realms through which Geraint journeys are obsessed with sensuality, violence, and deceit precisely because they are removed from the influence of the court. Geraint escapes their influence on his first journey only because he represents the court; by removing himself from it to his own lands, he surrenders to his wife; by carrying her off to the "common sewer of his realm," he sinks immediately to its level.

The completed "Enid" does not resolve Tennyson's ambivalence toward Arthur's court, but it does establish this institution as a test of the spatial assumptions of Tennyson's model. As in "Vivien," the couple struggle for control over the setting; this struggle, however, is not between mediator and Other but between two mediators. Unlike Arthur and Bedivere, they do not try to force their partners into the role of mediator. Instead, by claiming to inhabit incompatible versions of Tennyson's model, they claim that they alone can mediate for their author. Since they deny that they may need mediation themselves, the only role left open for their partners is that of Other.

Geraint, like the Three Sisters and the Lotos-Eaters, implicitly affirms that mediation depends upon the integrity of some physical sanctuary. They set up court in what they hope will remain the inaccessible East; he initially is all too willing to let the court and Guinevere shape his values and his quest. But even when he turns against her, he continues to see human nature as fundamentally controlled by physical and social place. If Enid dons her newly restored dress, she will grow proud in her own newly raised station. If Guinevere dresses her, Enid will absorb the court's values. If Guinevere and the court have grown corrupt, then Enid, being so clothed, may have incurred "a taint in nature." If so, she can be made clean and Geraint's own again by being removed to his own country. If she still, as he hears her confess, longs for an adulterous love, then she must be dragged still farther away—off into the wilds.

Against a husband who must find his sanctuary within the real world, Enid defiantly insists on finding hers elsewhere. Like the Soul in her Palace of Art, like Ida in the deliberate anachronisms of her own palace, like the Lover in his visions, Enid implicitly claims that she exists on a level of reality different from that of the outer world. Like the speaker in *Maud*, Geraint falls in love with a voice;[21] later he will be enraged by a voice. Yet rightly understood both voices are saying the same thing—that the values she shares with the authorial presence are preserved in a sanctuary beyond the reach of fortune: "Thy wheel and thee we neither love nor hate." Safe within this sanctuary, she cannot be tempted by Guinevere's worship of love, flattered by Geraint's uxorious attention, or wholly alienated by his subsequent abuse. In her self-defined role as mediating wife, she can acknowledge Geraint only as a reflection of her values: "I cannot love my lord and not his name." To be anything else, he must be Other.

The revised idyll thus grants its characters sufficient autonomy to reduce all communication between them to a grotesque mummery of violent and misinterpreted gestures. Yet both Tennyson and his source were committed to giving the story what became the only happy ending among the 1859 *Idylls*. Thus he had to make both characters acknowledge that their mutually exclusive models remained individually inadequate. Geraint, associating the Other with its domain, sees this domain impinging on his marriage, corrupting his wife, usurping every nook of the landscape through which he drags her. Yet only after being wounded "secretly" by one of Limours' followers can he realize that his human antagonists, instead of powers from without, are what John D. Rosenberg has called "extensions of [his] own erotic obsession with Enid."[22] Only after being "awakened" by another forbidden cry from Enid does he realize what Merlin never did—that the individual who flees the court to escape his forebodings of the Other actually carries the Other along with him.

Enid's realization is more paradoxical. Unlike Maud, who could break the silence imposed on her only with "a passionate cry" at her brother's death, Enid learns in time that to be faithful to her husband she must simultaneously thwart the bully leading her toward their mutual destruction. Only when this bully lies unconscious can she call for mediation with the force which brings her husband back to his physical and ethical senses. In this cry she acknowledges that even her sanctuary cannot remain impervious to the domain of the Other. After Doorm slaps her, she finds herself as helplessly imprisoned as the Lord of Burleigh's intended:

> Then Enid . . .
> Sent forth a sudden sharp and bitter cry,
> As of a wild thing taken in the trap,
> Which sees the trapper coming through the wood.
> (ll. 718, 721–23)

It is true, of course, that while Geraint returns to the court a changed man, the court to which he returns has itself changed. Guinevere has stayed behind and Arthur, who earlier confined himself to organizing sporting events, is now showing Geraint how to achieve social justice. It would be tempting to equate this, Arthur's first appearance in the nascent poem, with Tennyson's decision to resolve his ambivalence by splitting the court into two institutions. To the extent that it followed Arthur, Camelot would prove a true sanctuary, embodying a selfless devotion to king, country, and lady. To the extent that it followed Guinevere, it would remain the domain of an aggressive, sexually destructive Other.

Such a resolution, however, assumes a coherent image of both principals—and we find that even here Arthur embodies as many ironies as does the court itself. First of all, his criticism of Geraint merely redirects Geraint's original charge that Arthur himself had been neglecting his social duty. Second, that criticism was itself a hypocritical excuse to escape the "evils" of the same court in whose name Arthur is about to purge his realm. Third, those evils ultimately prove more fatal than the external ones which Arthur has left the court to fight.

Many of these ironies lie hidden within Tennyson's previous portrayals of Arthur. Tennyson tried for over fifty years to make him his ultimate mediator. Yet in "The Palace of Art," the "Morte," and "The Epic," Arthur appeared something less than heroic, whether tended by weeping queens in the Soul's tableau, carried to meet them by Bedivere, or returning "like a modern gentleman" in the narrator's dream. In these poems he embodied not just his namesake, Arthur Hallam, but loss itself.

Within the three manuscript sketches for the *Idylls*, this association with loss continues.[23] Within the prose fragment he seems as vulnerable as Kubla Khan in Tennyson's probable source. As he is surrounded by his court and dwarfed by Camelot, so Camelot itself, like Kubla's pleasure dome, is threatened with invasion, undermined by the caves, and set within a long-vanished land. In the allegorical sketch Arthur is more militant but no more successful. As "Religious Faith" he keeps losing the wives, that is, churches, in which this faith must be embodied. The play scenario, while sketching many scenes of the finished *Idylls* in a form original with Tennyson, seems to accord Arthur a curiously minor role. He arrives late, after Modred and the Lady of the Lake have already defined their mutual antagonism. He marries Guinevere after the introduction of Elaine and only one act before Lancelot and Guinevere are discovered by Modred and Nimue. Throughout he acts less like the founder of Camelot than like one celebrating its demise in a series of hopeless but heroic gestures.

"Guinevere"

It was, I think, to rescue Arthur from this tissue of ironies that Tennyson began writing "Guinevere." Arthur was to remain a surrogate for his real-life namesake, but instead of re-enacting the ritual of Hallam's departure, he was to begin demonstrating the mediating potential which Tennyson had claimed for his friend throughout *In Memoriam*. In trying to build "Guinevere" as a eulogy for the realm's glory, however, Tennyson was suddenly forced to demonstrate that the *Idylls'* ultimate mediator could confront effectively the *Idylls'* ultimate incarnation of the Other. Since both Malory's *Morte* and his own affirmed that Arthur had already lost the war, Tennyson could allow him to win this particular battle only by reinterpreting the battle between Merlin and Vivien, raising Arthur's moral and rhetorical superiority to the point that Guinevere, not Merlin, lay paralyzed and "lost to . . . name and fame."[24]

Both biographical and manuscript evidence suggests that Arthur's "triumph" over his queen was in fact the idyll's earliest-written section. On July 9, 1857, Emily found the final three lines on her plate as a strange and, one hopes, tongue-in-cheek birthday present:

> But hither shall I never come again,
> Never lie by thy side; see thee no more—
> Farewell!
>
> (ll. 575–77)[25]

The earliest continuous manuscript draft, Harvard Notebook 36, opens with Arthur's cries of personal anguish, then weaves them into a continuous monologue, then inserts lines 450–93 on the social order Guinevere has destroyed, and only then returns to the events preceding Arthur's arrival. Within this same manuscript sequence, Guinevere appears first as the focus of Arthur's personal loss, then as the focus of social anarchy, and only then as a character with her own desires and dreams.

With its compositional importance reflected in its climactic position within the completed *Idylls*, Arthur's speech has probably done more to damn the poem and its author than anything else Tennyson wrote. Much of our revulsion, however, arises from a conflict between the stance which Arthur is made to assume and the emotions he is made to express. In his position of physical, rhetorical, and moral superiority, Arthur is inevitably transformed from a mediator to one of the god figures of the adolescent poems. As an implacable father left Tennyson's early exiles haunted by a pervasive yet unspecified guilt, as St. Simeon's implacable God left him "one slough and crust of sin," so this implacable manifestation of the Other makes Guinevere mother to every evil within the world of her poem:

> The children born of thee are sword and fire,
> Red ruin and the breaking up of laws,
> The craft of kindred and the Godless hosts
> Of heathen swarming o'er the Northern Sea.
>
> (ll. 422–25)

Underlying and ultimately undermining this stance, however, are emotions characteristic of the weakest and often least effectual of Tennyson's mediators: the speakers of "Locksley Hall," "Edwin Morris," and *Maud*. In what the early manuscripts portray as a primarily sexual code, Arthur claims that he could have domesticated Goethe's *Ewig-Weibliche*: "For indeed I knew / Of no more subtle master under heaven / Than is the maiden passion for a maid" (ll. 474–76). Yet in blaming what seems to us an inevitable failure entirely on Guinevere, Arthur becomes another uncomprehending witness to an incomprehensible world, sinking into diatribes against a materialistic society which has lured his high-born beloved into the arms of one of her own class. We saw in "Locksley Hall" that Amy, by betraying the speaker's love, robbed him even of his past. Likewise Arthur, deprived of his assurance that Guinevere had once truly loved him, cannot shape any concept of self except one bewitched by an illusion.

The most immediate and earliest-written lines of his speech stand as grotesque efforts to define himself against her: first the bizarre birthday present; then "I forgive thee, as Eternal God / Forgives" (ll. 541–42); and finally "mine own flesh, / Here looking down on thine polluted, cries / 'I loathe thee'" (ll. 551–53). Yet he fears that she will expose even his desire for some spiritual reunion as simply another illusion: "Leave me that, / I charge thee, my last hope" (ll. 564–65). In the first manuscript draft, these lines were preceded by "Let no man doubt the folly of the King / Nor doubt that like a child he loves her still" (Pfordresher, p. 954). Here the self-doubt of "Edwin Morris" and "Locksley Hall" grows to the intensity of Tennyson's own comparison of himself to a child in *In Memoriam*, "An infant crying for the light: / And with no language but a cry" (54:19–20). Arthur's speech fails primarily because he must betray but cannot acknowledge the vulnerability he has inherited from his creator.

Because Guinevere remains silent while Arthur is betraying his ignorance of her efforts to repent, she remains "not mine / But Lancelot's." In actuality she remains not so much Lancelot's as irrevocably Other. From her earliest appearances within Tennyson's poetry, she has possessed the sexual potential, if not the sexual aggressiveness, of fatal women like Amoret or Vivien. Ryals points out that in the 1832 lyric "Sir Launcelot and Queen Guinevere," her emblems of springtime fertility gradually break free from the chaste bonds which have until now confined them.[26] The last stanza even suggests that her provoking innocence becomes as dangerous for her future lover as her sexuality will become for her husband:

> A man had given all other bliss,
> And all his worldly wealth for this,

> To waste his whole heart in one kiss
> Upon her perfect lips.
>
> (ll. 42–45)

In Lancelot's song, later canceled from that poem, he has so far yielded to the enticement of May and Guinevere that his invitation to "bathe with me in the fiery flood" caused J. M. Kemble, in copying the lyric for a friend, to warn "for the sake of my future clerical views and Ælfred's and Sir L's character, I must request that it be kept as quiet as possible" (*Poems*, I, 549).

The sketches for the *Idylls* broaden Guinevere's association with the Other conceived as change. In the prose fragment she represents no more than a "sumptuous" accessory to Arthur's glory, but in the allegory, even while personifying the Christian churches, she remains the enigmatic object of male desire: Arthur puts her away and then returns to her; Modred pulls her from the throne, perhaps, as in Malory, in order to make her his queen. The play scenario, equally critical of Guinevere, also associates her exclusively with men. Modred has a "cringing interview" with her even before Arthur's arrival. Her journey to Arthur, her rejection of Lancelot's diamonds, the discovery of her and Lancelot together, her final meeting with Arthur—all suggest that her very nature is shaped and reshaped by male desire and male guilt.

The first two idylls simply expand on this characterization. Merlin excuses her adultery because she had originally mistaken Lancelot for Arthur. Vivien, however, reflecting court opinion, presents her as both an object of scandal and the object of the courtly song attributed to Lancelot. Finally Geraint, as we saw, begins and completes his first quest under the spell of her romantic fantasies.

Since Harvard Notebook 36 mingles sketches for Arthur's speech with those for Guinevere's following soliloquy, it is not too surprising that she rather spinelessly accepts his definition of her:

> The shadow of another cleaves to me,
> And makes me one pollution: he, the King,
> Called me polluted; shall I kill myself?
>
> (ll. 613–15)

Tennyson signals his ambivalence toward her subsequent reform by relying heavily on Malory for her address to the nuns and by summarizing the rest of her life in eight lines. Even in her death he is only grudgingly generous. As late as the Trinity fair copy (T.Nbk 38), he simply lets her die, allowing the abbess she replaces to pass "to where beyond these voices there is peace." Despite the inked-in revision awarding this peace to Guinevere herself, voices within him were still clamoring for her condemnation.

Because of the number of manuscript fragments, each of which seems to presuppose the others, we cannot even begin to conjecture which passage in "Guinevere" Tennyson composed next. We can, however, establish that they were confined to her dialogue with the Novice and her subsequent reveries, roughly lines 127–398. Where Arthur defined her as blind to his spiritual order, now the Novice seeks to define her as fatal to his society. At this point, however, the Queen's appeal to "the world and all its lights / And shadows" (ll. 341–42) moves the debate from morals to manners. In so doing she invalidates the Novice's invidious comparisons of Lancelot to Arthur and of the "sweet lady" before her to "the sinful Queen." Even more important, for probably the first time in the poem's composition, Guinevere has begun to argue back. Perhaps Tennyson felt that Arthur's already-composed chastisement would neutralize her persuasive appeal. More likely he was simply admitting a need for some dramatic conflict.

Both his admission and his need, however, remain far from simple. Since the time of Hallam's death, Tennyson has had to admit that he needed to cultivate the Other as a sine qua non of both his model and his creative process. In revising the 1859 *Idylls*, he has already had to find almost diabolical power in one whom he had hoped to dismiss as a common harlot; he has had to admit an equally alien sexual power in the most submissive of his heroines; now he must allow the ostensible source of all evil in his poem to assume perhaps the most dangerous autonomy of all. Guinevere does not win any arguments, but in merely stating her case she projects a gracious, compassionate humanity which subverts Arthur's vision of her and of his own mission.

Guinevere's argument with the Novice reenacts the familiar contest between mediator and Other for control of their world. While the Novice's obtuse naiveté may win her this argument, it loses her any real claim even to the Camelot of the past. Pfordresher (pp. 30–31) feels Tennyson has deliberately distanced her stories of Arthur's origins by changing the early first-person drafts to secondhand accounts told to her by her father. Even in their earlier form, however, these stories reflect her own self-conscious celebration of presexual childhood. Some of the wonders are drawn from *Keightley's Fairy Legends*, others from Tennyson's early excursions into fantasy within *The Devil and the Lady* and "The Coach of Death." The Bard, whose ego-

tistical sublime rivals that portrayed in "The Poet," sings Arthur's life from
birth only up to his marriage. All these childhood associations in turn render
the stories and the Novice herself irrelevant to psychological or social maturity.[27]

Guinevere's dialogue with the Novice only calls into question her role as
the object of others' judgments; the reveries which Tennyson composed at
roughly the same time let her present her world as a perceiving subject. In
asserting her own version of origins against that of the Novice, she also reasserts her former role within Tennyson's early lyrics, reasserts her claim that
the springtime of the realm must have been a sexual one. Here the latent
sensuality in the Novice's stories literally blossoms into a world where desire
reverses all moral polarities. She and Lancelot ride

> under groves that looked a paradise
> Of blossom, over sheets of hyacinth
> That seemed the heavens upbreaking through the earth.
>
> (ll. 386–88)

This reversal may be meant to dramatize her perversity in associating the
journey with her guide instead of with the king who organized it. Yet this
stately progress toward a marriage with an aristocratic and virtually unknown
groom awakens disconcerting echoes of "The Lord of Burleigh." There the
heroine's journey, turning unexpectedly into the great hall, confined her to a
life of misery and an early death. Here Guinevere may only "sigh to find her
journey done," but despite all her rebellion, marriage to Arthur has led her
inescapably to a very similar confinement within the walls of the nunnery.
Arthur's speech forced him to relinquish the role of mediator for that of
Other; the reverie which precedes it allows Guinevere to relinquish her
identification with Tennyson's fatal women and to ally herself with the high-
born maidens at the other end of his polarized feminine spectrum. Besides
being high born, Guinevere now finds herself locked away from her love and
from an outside world that can neither understand nor accept her.

Within a fallen kingdom and a retrospective idyll, "the holy house at
Almesbury" may appear largely irrelevant, but in this setting Guinevere has
asked that the "peaceful sisterhood, / Receive, and yield me *sanctuary*" (ll.
139–40; italics mine). In the context of her identification with Tennyson's
other mediators, it may be something more than coincidence that she uses
the same word we have used to describe the base of the mediator's power. As
she and the Novice contested the past, they also contest the meaning of
sanctuary itself. And as the Novice's definition of an asexual past came to

appear childish, so her definition of sanctuary as the sterile absence of human emotion finally reduces mediation to the kind of solipsism which Tennyson examined and found wanting within the 1830 poems.

This far more sympathetic image of Guinevere is bolstered by the last-written section of the idyll, the opening flashback. Harvard Notebook 36 does not even hint at such a flashback: Guinevere's flight to the nunnery precedes her request for asylum in line 137; the details of Modred's usurpation are given in full by the Novice following line 197; and Guinevere, before her reverie, does not refer to her vow never to see Lancelot again but instead wishes she had never seen him at all. Yet once Tennyson had confined his fallen heroine within two alien sets of social and spiritual norms, he felt free to explore the reasons for her fall in a retrospective passage like those in "Vivien" and "Enid."

Unlike Malory's Guinevere, secure in her adherence to the code of courtly love, this Guinevere does not ignore guilt. Instead she internalizes it within images much like those associated with Tennyson's fully developed highborn maidens. The "grim faces" plaguing her resemble the "white-eyed phantoms" and "hollow shades" plaguing the Soul in "The Palace of Art." Guinevere's dream of a ghostly something moving toward her from the setting sun echoes the simile of the "great black cloud" "expunging the world" of Ida after *her* attempts to shape that world have failed. These ghosts resemble even more closely the "shoals of puckered faces" which haunt Tennyson in *In Memoriam* as he tries "to paint / The face" of Hallam. In all these cases, Tennyson uses specters to chasten a mediator too closely identified with him to confront in a more objective way.

Indeed Tennyson foists off on Modred the objective villainy within this flashback, leaving Guinevere struggling against a love portrayed as too strong to resist:

> at the last she said,
> "O Lancelot, get thee hence to thine own land,
> For if thou tarry we shall meet again. . . ."
> And Lancelot ever promised, but remained,
> And still they met and met.
>
> (ll. 86–88, 92–93)

When discovered, she does not worry about her fate, like Malory's heroine, but about her shame; and the lovers make their escape in a poignantly understated reprise of their original journey to Arthur's court: "then they rode to the divided way, / There kissed, and parted weeping" (ll. 123–24). Guinevere shares with Maud and with Enid the ability to shape her life into a series of graceful and significant gestures.

The printed idyll, virtually the reverse of its order of composition, seems itself structured in loose imitation of *Paradise Lost*. It first lures readers into sympathy with a character destined to become the ultimate villain and then forces them to participate in that character's realization of guilt.[28] Guinevere has laid such a strong hold upon Tennyson, however, that like Blake's Milton he was of her party "without knowing it." Being of Guinevere's party could lead Tennyson to one of two alternatives: either identifying with her covertly as Other or identifying with her openly as a covert mediator. In the first alternative Tennyson would be preserving his model at the expense of his place within it. Instead of hiding at the center, shielded from the Other by some protective mediator, at least part of him would confront the world of Camelot and its guardian king from without.

In the second alternative he would be preserving his place within a model whose very meaning and raison d'être were under siege. Tennyson's mediators, of course, have remained under siege almost by definition, but now, by including two such contradictory figures among their number, Tennyson has pushed the paradox inherent in *The Princess* and "Enid" to the point of absurdity. There the partners only appeared to one another as Other, and their conflict resolved itself into harmony when this appearance resolved itself into reality. Here, however, neither Arthur's grudging confession of his love nor Guinevere's belated confession of her guilt can bridge the gap which yawns between them and swallows up the world of their story. Because Tennyson did not want to accept the disturbing consequences of either of these alternatives, because he did not want even to acknowledge the dilemma which they together constituted, he left the idyll itself in a similar state of irreconcilable tension, torn between its heroine's original integrity and the essentially alien demands which force her to renounce her past, her nature, and—ultimately—her life.

"Elaine"

While it is tempting to assume that the writing of "Guinevere" virtually committed Tennyson to "Elaine"—the second "true" to balance his second "false"—Hugh Wilson points out that the cameo of the Queen sitting beside Enid and Vivien may originally have made "Guinevere" the centerpiece in a triptych, the concluding portrayal of a woman's journey from falsehood to truth.[29] Thus when Tennyson accepted Woolner's request for an Elaine idyll, he may have been less interested in rounding out a preconceived pattern than in confronting the troubling challenges to his model implicit in the first three idylls and "Guinevere" in particular.

While his choice of the Elaine story circumvents many of these challenges, it occasions his first head-on confrontation with Malory in over twenty years. "Vivien," as we saw, grew from a two-sentence reference, "Enid" from a completely different tradition, "Guinevere" from a meeting not in Malory at all; but "Elaine" stands as one of the best-focused, best-developed stories in the *Morte*. Without ruining it Tennyson dared not change the psychological realism, the tragic inevitability of the plot line, the grandeur bestowed on all the characters whatever their moral status, and the concluding sense of waste which made mockery of poetic justice. Yet this evenhanded relativism would challenge his model just as severely as the dramatic and psychological claims of the already-written idylls. Tennyson could not let his mediating heroine burn with a love "hotter" than either Vivien's or Guinevere's; he could not let Arthur praise Lancelot for his steadfast rejection of Elaine; he could not let Arthur know Lancelot's identity and so honor a deception which grew out of an adulterous love; he could not criticize Guinevere for her jealousy while ignoring her adultery.

In trying to trace Tennyson's simultaneous efforts to preserve and change his story, we must fall back on the sole early manuscript extant. Held at the University of Virginia, it contains roughly half the poem. The first of the two best-developed sections runs from the beginning to line 139. It includes Elaine's vigil with the shield, the refusal of Lancelot and Guinevere to attend the diamond jousts, and their subsequent dialogue. Yet this first draft omits Arthur's discovery of the diamonds and many of Guinevere's subsequent references to him. The second passage runs roughly from line 1264 to line 1362, including the reading of Elaine's letter, her burial, and an early draft of Arthur's conversation with Lancelot. That these two sections might have come most easily to Tennyson should not be surprising. Both the second and the second half of the first grow directly out of Malory, while Elaine and her embroidered shield-cover match the Lady of Shalott and her web. Although the Lady had poisoned Tennyson's attitude toward Camelot, even in the muted revision of 1842, the passages following Malory echo his celebration of the courtly love ethic. The first passage, then, seems to juxtapose the inner intensity of Elaine with the outward splendor of the court. In the second passage both Elaine's letter and Lancelot's speech acknowledge the impossibility of reconciling these forces.

This narrative frame, probably in Tennyson's mind since the play scenario, seems used as a given, a juxtaposition of initial illusion and hypocrisy with their tragic consequences. Yet the insoluble conflicts within this scenario allow Tennyson to transform Malory's uncritical enthusiasm for his characters into wistful eulogies for human potential stymied by human desire. Like the equally tragic outcome of *Maud* or the Queen's final humiliation before her husband, this frame allows Tennyson to render his mediators more problematic and the Other more human than he could have otherwise. His subsequent additions, first to this manuscript and then to the Trinity fair copy, show him tracing the parallel movements of Lancelot and Elaine from initial optimism to final surrender. They show him analyzing both Arthur's fatal blindness and the almost sadistic power over others which it produces. Finally, they show him renewing his earlier confrontation with Guinevere and with the troubling role he had assigned her in the late-written flashback of her idyll.

The remaining sections of the Virginia manuscript, *very* roughly in order of their composition, include the following scenes: Lancelot's arrival at Astolat, Elaine's falling in love with him, her request that he wear her favor, her request to nurse him, her presentation of the diamonds, her care for him, her plea for his love, her sense of approaching death, her request for a final journey to Camelot, her defense of Lancelot against her father's charges, and the journey itself. Only two sections, Lancelot's account of the victory at Mount Badon and a very rough sketch of his presentation of the diamonds, shift the focus away from the couple's relationship. This manuscript, in fact, focuses singlemindedly on that relationship as a means of discovering the very limited potential for mediation open to Elaine. In the new context of Malory's court, for example, her castle cannot retain the kind of mysterious force radiated by the Lady's island or Enid's ruined tower. Unlike the Lady's magic web, Elaine's shield-cover with its romantic embroidery of "her own wit" can exist only as what Russell M. Goldfarb calls a sexual fetish.[30]

By reversing the sequence of temptation and fall in "The Lady of Shalott," however, Tennyson can let Elaine succumb early to Lancelot "with the love that was her doom." He can then stretch out the Lady's final voyage into a series of initiatives which transform a passive victim into a high-born mediator moving boldly to confront the Other in the now alien domain of the court.[31] Elaine's magic, unlike the Lady's, grows from her determination to transform her "doom" into victory:

> Then came on [Lancelot] a sort of sacred fear,
> For silent, though he greeted her, she stood
> Rapt on his face as if it were a God's.
> Suddenly flashed on her a wild desire,
> That he should wear her favour at the tilt.
>
> (ll. 352–56)

Her determination to practice this magic upon Lancelot transforms him as well. From a destructive agent of the Other so unwitting that he can preach the Lady of Shalott's elegy, he grows into the sympathetic protagonist who carries and finally collapses under the moral burden of his story.

In creating this role for Lancelot, Tennyson has few precedents to draw on. Lancelot cannot be allowed to follow the lead of his namesake in Malory, justifying his adultery with an appeal to the courtly love ethic, boasting of his refusal to take physical advantage of Elaine, and then winning the consolation of Arthur's speech on the hardships of sexual incompatibility. Yet neither can he reassume the role of spineless male victim whose heart is about to be "wasted" by the Guinevere of Tennyson's early lyrics.[32] His enigmatic appearances in both versions of "The Lady of Shalott" suggest that Tennyson still does not know where to have him. Hallam Tennyson claimed that "my father loved his own great imaginative knight, the Lancelot of the *Idylls*,"[33] and the poet himself claimed (*Memoir*, I, 457) that he had composed "Lancelot's Quest of the Grail in as good verses as I ever wrote, no I did not write, I made it in my head, and it has now altogether slipt out of memory." And yet Tennyson virtually ignores this character for some twenty-five years.

To find where and why the Lancelot figure has been hiding during this time, we need to remember that even his offstage presence in "Guinevere" transformed Arthur into one of Tennyson's railing, forsaken lovers. In *Maud*, "Edwin Morris," and "Locksley Hall," the speaker can see himself defeated by large social forces because his rival—with "drunken dreams," "educated whisker," or "rabbit mouth"—is so contemptibly insignificant. Yet Arthur, and through him Tennyson, has lost his love to the one "reputed the best knight and goodliest Man." This phrase, plus the glowing descriptions of Lancelot at Astolat and at the jousts, should evoke some curious echoes from

In Memoriam: echoes of Arthur Hallam beloved of Tennyson's sister, at gracious ease among all levels of society, potentially powerful enough to "uplift the earth / And roll it in another course" (113: 15–16). Given Tennyson's sense of loss and betrayal at his death, given the astonishing variety of sexual metaphors Tennyson used to describe their relationship throughout *In Memoriam*, we may be justified in complicating the parallel commonly drawn between the two Arthurs. Whatever their causes, the implicit connections between Lancelot and Hallam may have effectively suppressed any references to Lancelot until Tennyson found an appropriate context to explore them.

The "Elaine" idyll proves appropriate because it gradually opens for Tennyson a new means of transforming an aggressively masculine agent of the Other into a projection of authorial vulnerability. In *The Princess* he could identify with an ineffectual hero whose seizures reduced the sexual relationship to one between mother and child. In *Maud* he discovered that neurosis could in fact attract a high-born beloved. Here, in the Virginia manuscript of "Elaine," he discovers that Lancelot's physical and sexual invincibility, while initially threatening, leads inevitably to a psychological paralysis characteristic of Tennyson's most cloistered figures.

Elaine awards Lancelot divine protection during her opening reveries in her tower: "here a thrust that might have killed, but God / Broke the strong lance, and rolled his enemy down, / And saved him" (ll. 25–27). Lancelot's reply to Guinevere's fears for her reputation bespeak an equal self-assurance: "My worship of the fairest is allowed by all men" (Pfordresher, p. 611). In this manuscript he next appears at Astolat, where he seems to Elaine "the goodliest man / That ever among ladies ate in hall" (ll. 253–54). (Significantly lines 244–52, describing how his divided loyalties had "marked his face," appear only as an afterthought later in the manuscript.) From this point in the first draft Lancelot appears progressively more passive.[34] His celebration of Arthur's victory at Mount Badon and his courtesy to Elaine only prompt her to offer him her favor. Then the omission of the entire tournament scene makes his wounded condition after line 812 appear a direct consequence of his disguise.

Lancelot's appearances within this manuscript parallel the early appearances of Guinevere; both exist principally as objects of desire. The kiss he gives Elaine and his realization of her love are both described, but his response to her declaration is only sketched in with lines borrowed from the defense of his conduct which he will later make over her body. While Tennyson includes the ending of this speech, he has yet to see it as the crux of

Lancelot's moral dilemma. Only in the nearly complete Trinity manuscript does he modulate from Lancelot's initially boastful request for Elaine's reward, "What I will, I can" (l. 912), to "what I can I will" (l. 969), and finally to this admission of impotence: "More than this I could not; this she would not, and she died" (l. 1314).

In the Virginia manuscript Lancelot does not even analyze his feelings until the roughed-out drafts of his final soliloquy. Originally this soliloquy moved from the wish "would she had drown'd me there" (l. 1401) to the prayer "may God, / . . . send a sudden angel down / To fling me deep in that forgotten mere" (ll. 1412, 1414–15). This neurotic yearning for stasis and oblivion, besides completing Lancelot's descent into powerlessness, also allows him to express similar yearnings in his creator. Here Lancelot not only embodies the wasted potential of Hallam, he also mediates between Tennyson and the sorrow within *In Memoriam* which threatens to "drown / The bases of my life in tears" (49: 15–16). This complex pattern echoes that of the "Morte," where Tennyson could identify with both Bedivere losing his king and Arthur forsaking his world for the apparently sterile waters of death.

Indeed the tragedy inherent in Lancelot's sexual prowess allows Tennyson to see Arthur's tragedy in terms beyond those of sexual betrayal. Arthur's efforts to control social and sexual morality in "Guinevere" identified him with Tennyson's early god figures; here, however, he wins the empathy necessary for mediation even as his power to mediate declines. If his treatment in the Virginia manuscript is sketchier and more hesitant than that of Lancelot, it is so because Tennyson had to search even harder for ways to make Arthur both impressive and completely ineffectual.[35] Predictably, the ways he finally developed in the printed text appear here as two different kinds of revisions: those which displace Arthur's mediating power within the past and those which portray this power lodged within his blind, unyielding presence. The first revisions render his mediation ironic; the second revisions measure it by the difficulty other characters encounter in stepping around him.

Tennyson first displaces this power when he inserts Arthur's discovery of the diamonds (ll. 33–76) between the accounts of Elaine's vigil and the lovers' scheme. Here Arthur can act as an individual in ways he cannot once he is trapped within the seething mass of serpents carved upon his throne at the joust. Despite his physical control here, however, he cannot escape an ironic tangle which anticipates the idyll's central irony: the diamonds, lost

along with life itself in a private feud, are captured by Arthur as "they fled
. . . to the tarn" (l. 52). They are made by him the measure of chivalric
prowess, perverted by Lancelot into tokens of an adulterous love, and finally
lost back to the water when Guinevere's private quarrel with Lancelot drives
her to fling them into the stream. The last passage is absent from the Virginia manuscript, but this conflation of the Malory stories of Elaine and the
Diamond Jousts is foreshadowed as early as Tennyson's play scenario:
"Guinevere throws away the diamonds into the river. The Court and the
dead Elaine."[36]

After inserting the account of the diamonds, Tennyson expands the following dialogue of Guinevere and Lancelot to emphasize the vulnerability
implicit in the mythic stature which Arthur has just been granted. His sun
may still be high, but its very height makes him irrelevant to his realm and to
Guinevere in particular: "But who can gaze upon the Sun in heaven? / . . .
The low sun makes the colour" (ll. 123, 134).[37] With such comparisons
Guinevere deposes Arthur in favor of Lancelot, and in so doing shows that
the king and his code now exist not as a viable alternative but as an obstacle
to be avoided. In "Guinevere" she celebrated Arthur's vicarious existence as
"the conscience of a saint / Among his warring senses" (ll. 634–35); here
she points it up as a weakness which Lancelot can exploit through his disguise:

> how meek soe'er [Arthur] seem,
> No keener hunter after glory breathes.
> He loves it in his knights more than himself:
> They prove to him his work . . . .
>
> (ll. 154–57)

"Trustful," "faultless," "true," "a moral child"—these epithets imply not
just the necessity but the ease of deceiving Arthur; yet, all unknowing,
Arthur combats the couple's deception more effectively here than in his self-
righteous speech at Almesbury. By refusing to suspect either, he tortures
both. Significantly, the Virginia draft of his final speech to Lancelot contains
a hint of suspicion:

> would to heaven—
> Because the people say wild things of thee
> W^h for my sake & thine I not believe
> My fault perchance to dream the best of men.

> While the world howls the worst—but w[d] to God
> Thou couldst have loved this damsel . . .
> (Pfordresher, pp. 720–21)

Not until 1873 is the suspicion softened to an observation on "the homeless trouble in thine eyes" (l. 1354). As early as the Trinity manuscript, however, this very blindness allows him to give Guinevere both the ill news that Lancelot is wounded and the "good news" "that Lancelot is no more a lonely heart" (l. 599).

Yet as Arthur unknowingly destroys the couple's self-gratifying courtly code, he just as unknowingly helps them to achieve a heroic aestheticism equally antagonistic to him but strongly identified with the Tennyson of the 1832 volume. The flashback in "Guinevere," as we saw, endowed the Queen with tragic stature as she wrestled with the conflicting demands of her overpowering love for Lancelot and her duty toward husband and realm. Hence we might be surprised by her very fragmentary development within the Virginia manuscript of "Elaine." It appears, however, that Tennyson had to come to terms with her all over again, had virtually to rediscover the process of enclosure he had developed in "Guinevere."

In truth the enclosure proves more difficult here because here Guinevere defines more of her own values. As we just saw, she ignores questions of her duty to Arthur in her first appearance within the Virginia manuscript and reduces them to social conventions within the revision. Since the story offers no vehicle for denouncing such unrepentance, Tennyson does not confront her again until her interview with Lancelot late in the manuscript. There, convinced that her own plot has cast him into the arms of a younger rival, she must re-evaluate the claims of her husband and her lover:

> Have I for you, my lord, so many years
> Done wrong to him whom in my heart of hearts
> I still acknowledge nobler?
> (Pfordresher, p. 704)

In his first draft Tennyson moves quickly to her reaction within the play scenario, her decision to fling the necklace into the river. But as the extensive revisions of this passage delay the decision, Guinevere is forced to make ever more elaborate, more devastating comparisons between her own beauty and that of the younger woman she thinks has replaced her.

In the later Trinity manuscript, Tennyson implies that the same disguise which apparently lost her Lancelot's love has also undermined her role as queen. The courtly code which she and Lancelot have created now confronts her as the deformed offspring of their love. "The old dame [who] came suddenly on the Queen with the sharp news," the knights "pledging Lancelot and the lily maid," the servant of the house "laughing in his courtly heart" at "the trembling shadow of her lace"—all these taunt her with the implicit claim that her own vows of love and secrecy were never anything more than the lust and intrigue into which they have now degenerated.

Yet just as in "Guinevere," after establishing the inevitability of her suffering Tennyson can grant her the autonomy which again challenges his model and her role within it. When Arthur gives her the "good news" of Lancelot's new love, the Trinity manuscript allows her a fitting response:

> "Yea, lord," she said,
> "Thy hopes are mine," and saying that, she choked,
> And sharply turned about to hide her face,
> Past to her chamber, and there flung herself
> Down on the great King's couch, and writhed upon it,
> And clenched her fingers till they bit the palm,
> And shrieked out "Traitor" to the unhearing wall,
> Then flashed into wild tears, and rose again,
> And moved about her palace, proud and pale.
>
> (ll. 602–10)

The very tensions between her self-chosen roles of queen and lover bring her to a quivering stasis which transcends the shallow aestheticism of either. Again as in "Guinevere," suffering comes to vindicate whatever values are attached to it.

Tennyson's later revisions also celebrate Guinevere, but now more indirectly by undercutting the integrity of her rival. As the best-developed character within the Virginia manuscript, Elaine seemed there to justify her fantasy in the very attempt to make it reality. The revisions, however, begin to explore the darker corners of that fantasy. In Malory the nature of her desire is all too obvious; whether Lancelot agrees to become her husband or her paramour is all one with her. Tennyson's tortured revisions of their dialogue may reflect considerable prudery, yet the epigrammatic death wish in which her plea is finally cast, "I have gone mad. I love you: let me die," may reflect a realization that the "innocent" lily maid is guilty of something more decadent than sexual passion. The nature of this guilt is first suggested in the inserted description of Lancelot's appearance. Here the idol whose face she gazed at "as if it were a God's" is described as "marred . . . and marked." The language moves through Byron and back to Milton's fallen Satan, whose "face / Deep scars of thunder had entrenched" (I, 600–601).[38]

As Tennyson weaves the strands of his story together in the Trinity manuscript, almost all his new references to Elaine associate her with willfulness, death, and the court. While in one sense Gawain is introduced there to contrast his courtly decadence with the rustic innocence of Elaine, in another sense the lessons he offers she has already learned on her own. By the time she prepares for her burial journey, her newly added remarks on his flattery and the Queen's pity make it clear that the court which has become alien to the tortured Guinevere has become home to her. As Stevenson puts it (pp. 13–14), "Elaine fashions herself into Guinevere's competitor"; her bed is "the virginal analogue not only of the marriage bed but also of the adulterous bed on which the Queen 'dies' with Lancelot." Elaine is yielding to Lancelot in death the body which he refused to possess in life. In so doing she so complicates her role that we cannot determine whether she has been corrupted by the domain of the Other, or whether she has transformed the court into a potential sanctuary.[39] Even the manuscript evidence remains ambiguous: The Virginia manuscript concludes with her letter, "I thank my God to witness that I died / A maiden clean in heart and deed." These lines have been canceled through.

The metaphor of Elaine's going home may itself embody Tennyson's ultimate response to Malory. Stylistically he captures quite brilliantly Malory's laconic amalgam of disparate details, often joined simply with the word "and." At times, as in his description of Guinevere's suffering, he seems uncharacteristically willing to let the story reach its own narrative and thematic ends. At other times, however, he distills these juxtapositions down to the intensity of "I have gone mad. I love you: let me die," or "More than this I could not; this she would not, and she died." Here death and stasis become not just the conclusion of narrative action but its antithesis.

And indeed the action of "Elaine" goes nowhere, or, better, goes back to where it began: Elaine's final "home" in court is itself the goal of her childhood fantasies; Guinevere returns to Lancelot to beg and receive his forgiveness; Lancelot longs to return to the watery realms remembered from his abduction by the Lady of the Lake. The diamonds, cause of familial strife, recreate it. Then they too return, literally to the water from which Arthur rescued the "glittering crown" and metaphorically to the dead Elaine as Guinevere hurls them past her barge while trying to keep them from her.

This circular movement grows in part from the compositional process itself. Tennyson initially created the Virginia manuscript as a frame within which he could work out thematic rather than narrative consequences. And as in other works where he used this technique—*The Princess* and parts of *In Memoriam*—these consequences assert a meaning beyond their stories. Ida reached beyond her fairy tale to move us with its stifling conventions; so too these characters, each frozen by different tensions at different points in the action, leave us with a sense not so much of a completed narrative as of the overwhelming individual cost of staying in place.[40]

CHAPTER NINE

Longer Poems of the 1860s

Although certainly not the results of some predetermined plan, *Enoch Arden, Aylmer's Field*, and "Lucretius" can all be seen as reactions to the 1859 *Idylls*. There Tennyson's exploration of a world obsessed with sexual desire had led him into increasingly dangerous sympathy with characters who challenged both his model and their roles within it. Hence the first two of these poems work to shore up different aspects of the model itself. *Enoch Arden* creates an almost suffocating propriety as the apparently secure sanctuary for the apparently conventional characters within it. *Aylmer's Field* replaces the appealing sexual women of the *Idylls* with a monstrous father figure out of *Maud*, an embodiment of the Other as sexual repression. Because overdefining one aspect of these poems brought the model itself back into jeopardy, Tennyson structured "Lucretius" as an attempt to trace sexuality back to its most elemental form, an attempt to learn whether Venus was more threatening as vengeful goddess or as impersonal flux. When he returned from these poems to the *Idylls*, he may have learned new means of confronting the issues raised within them; he may also have discovered that these issues simply could not be escaped.

Enoch Arden

At first reading, Woolner's story must have seemed to Tennyson an opportune escape from royalty to fishermen, from dalliance to the work ethic, from adventure to fettered patience, from seduction to stoic renunciation. Yet other background might lead us to predict some troubling cracks in the poem's middle-class veneer. Well before the *Idylls*, the mediators of Tennyson's longer poems have challenged, wisely or foolishly, the ruling ideology of their poetic context. The speaker of *The Lover's Tale* transforms his poem from a romance to a visionary phantasmagoria. Ida breaks through successive definitions of self and society imposed on her by successive layers of plot. Tennyson in *In Memoriam* achieves less a goal than the ability to recreate the process of searching for one. The speaker of *Maud* just barely keeps his hatred of laissez-faire society from blocking his discovery of love. Finally Geraint and Enid both court destruction by refusing to accept the other as embodying different social values. In *Enoch*, however, these incongruities seem to manifest themselves formally—in plot, setting, and tone.

Despite their lack of a "local habitation," I believe that these formal incongruities constitute a new manifestation of the Other, a coherent though complex challenge to the poem's sanctuary of conventionality. On the most schematic level, this challenge reshapes the apparent significance of the plot. P. G. Scott, perhaps extrapolating from Philip Drew's analysis of *Aylmer's Field*, observes the wanton manipulation of time, in which Enoch's seven years of marital happiness pass in a single sentence, his ten years of shipwrecked solitude earn a paragraph, yet his momentary glimpse of Annie, Philip, and the children receives almost seventy lines of minute detail.[1]

Against this flexibility, however, we must set the poem's almost mathematical symmetry. For Priestley (pp. 76–77), it falls neatly into quarters, the first treating Philip, Enoch, and Annie; the second Philip and Annie; the third Enoch; and the fourth Philip, Enoch, and Annie. Scott points out (p. 19) how early illustrations emphasized the parallels of Philip's slinking away after seeing Enoch and Annie, and Enoch's slinking away after his glimpse of the family in Philip's house. Finally Maurice Montabrut notes the mathematically logical parallels both in Annie's promise to be "little wife unto them both" and in the death of Enoch's third child, conveniently replaced with Philip's first.[2] We might even conclude that the poem's plot contains a fixed set of relationships which can be and in fact are filled by almost random combinations of characters.

While several critics note the peculiar helplessness of these would-be mediators,[3] this formal flaunting of human time and human values suggests that they may be even more cruelly treated: the ultimate value they all place on individual people and relationships may prove to be only wishful illusion. While Kissane sees Enoch's forcefulness and Philip's patience as contrasting halves of Tennyson's own nature,[4] all these characters may be more aptly divided by their success in mediating the natural process which so undermines their ideals: Philip remains blissfully unaware of its existence; Annie perceives but suppresses it; Enoch first follows it unconsciously, then tries to thwart it, finally accepts and comes to embody it.

While not as bullying in his manner, Philip seems as psychologically myopic as Dostoevsky's man of nature. Confronting a brick wall, he simply walks around it without questioning the necessity of its existence. This attitude makes him a consummate (because an unconscious) opportunist: if Annie is Enoch's, she cannot be his; if thwarted in love, he can succeed in trade; if Enoch's children are poor, he can befriend them; if they call him Father Philip, he can become their father in fact; if Annie is apparently a widow, she is apparently his to court; if town gossips impugn his motives, he can appeal to Annie to prove them honorable.

Annie herself appears more sympathetic only because she is more passive. As she plays wife to both Enoch and Philip to satisfy them both, so she marries each to satisfy each in turn. Her inability to run the store or even to keep their last child alive during Enoch's absence seems to excuse her increasing reliance on Philip. Yet this apparently innocent progression moves in vague causal relation to a more sinister one, her increasingly vigorous denial of a perception verging on second sight: her sense that in converting their home into a store Enoch is building her scaffold, her prediction that she will never see his face again, her inability to pick him out aboard ship, her vision of him "under the palm tree," her hearing first the "footsteps . . . beside her paths" and finally the "whisper in her ear" during the early days of her second marriage. All these premonitions prove true, but she misinterprets the vision as a sign of Enoch's death and she forgets the sounds in her fascination with her new baby.

Thus she and Philip are brought by either willed or innate blindness to the smug tableau in which Enoch glimpses them through Philip's window. Several modern critics have emphasized the guilt implicit in Tennyson's comparison of Enoch here to a thief, but even the most narrow-minded Victorian reviewers may have placed the guilt, or least the shame, more accurately on the couple inside the house. Tennyson may have never actually justified Enoch's silence to Queen Victoria by arguing that his revelation would have rendered the baby illegitimate.[5] Yet to the extent that these characters honor the marriage bond—and its preservation has already cost each immense pain—both Annie and Philip would be as horrified to see Enoch as Enoch is crushed to see them. And the "shrill and terrible cry" he fears "to send abroad" would indeed prove a "blast of doom" much like the doom of God which Paden has seen hanging over the erotic desires of the young Tennyson. If Philip and Annie remain happily blind to the Other which invades the sanctuary of their home, they appear deluded to Enoch and unconsciously hypocritical to the reader.

In one sense, of course, Enoch's knowledge makes him guilty of an equal, if more complex hypocrisy. In another, however, he has never completely accepted the goal of a secure domestic sanctuary, has all along defined himself less by his family responsibilities than by his occupation. Thus the proffer of a passage may be an "answer to this prayer" in more than an economic sense; it may allow him to embark on a carefully undefined search to fulfill a series of equally undefined desires.[6] In this search, he recapitulates and pushes to their often frightening conclusions the searches of several of Tennyson's other mediators. Besides the women from 1832 who establish their sanctuaries at the limits of the known world, another group longs for a similar island paradise just over the horizon. The song of the Three Sisters to Hanno, the destination of Ulysses on "the Happy Isles," Arthur's "Island valley of Avilion," the cloud toward which Tennyson and Hallam steer in the dream voyage of *In Memoriam* 103—all these parallels foreshadow Enoch's own dissatisfaction with the domestic here and now. His situation differs from these others only in that he is allowed to experience this island goal.[7]

Once marooned, however, he reenacts the plight of an entirely different group of mediators, those sequestered within a sanctuary suddenly transformed into the domain of the Other.[8] In fact he experiences the disastrous future feared by all Tennyson's solitaries but usually reserved for a mythic frame beyond the confines of their poems: the death of Ulysses' mariners, the death and damnation of Ulysses himself, the metamorphosis of Tithonus. Enoch's island projects the particular form taken by this particularly formal Other, what Priestley (p. 78) sees as an inhuman denial of the human warmth he seeks. Its sights and sounds press in upon him as if to subsume his identity, and its impersonality colors even his attempt to escape it in visions of home. These, while they begin as comfortable re-creations of the past, take on a prophetic strangeness, "a phantom made of many phantoms" (l. 598). "The smell of dying leaves / And the low moan of leaden coloured seas" (ll. 607–8) bespeak less his past than his future alienation.

The story of his rescue breaks into this internal change, but only to offer an external measure of its progress:

> Downward from his mountain gorge
> Stept the long-haired long-bearded solitary,
> Brown, looking hardly human, strangely clad,
> Muttering and mumbling, idiotlike it seemed,

> With inarticulate rage, and making signs
> They knew not what. . . .
>
> (ll. 632–37)

In the crew's terror we can read the impossibility of Enoch's return to the sanctuary of the past. We also can read, however, a new role and a new power. Where other famous rescues have emphasized the glories of unspoiled nature or the traumatic confrontation with civilization, here Enoch's steadfast yearning for home leaves us with the crew's initial impression of him as a vatic figure closer to Gray's Bard than to Crusoe, Gulliver, Juan, and other literary castaways.[9]

In fact Enoch must carry the same burden of forbidden knowledge as Tennyson's other visionaries. The Magus and the speakers of "Armageddon" and *The Lover's Tale* are nearly paralyzed by a vision of the Other too frightening for those around them to contemplate. The Prince's seizures allow him to see through Ida's pretensions but leave him powerless to challenge them. The speaker's constant awareness of Maud's Phantom literally drives him mad. Within *In Memoriam* Tennyson's quest for Hallam can produce both the mystic union of section 95 and the nightmare vision of section 70. More recently, within the 1859 *Idylls*, Merlin's premonition of what Tennyson will call "death in all life and lying in all love" allows him to see through Vivien's affection but breaks his will to do so. Geraint's vision of Enid as "no true wife" grotesquely misinterprets her nature but accurately foretells her effect on men. And Arthur's sudden vision of his wife's infidelity reduces him first to the hysterics of Tennyson's rejected lovers and then to ghostlike insubstantiality.

While Enoch's new visionary powers may suspend Tennyson's obsession with sexual desire in the *Idylls*, they reach even more disquieting visions. If he has looked "too far into the sea," he comes to see less the predatory nature of Keats and *In Memoriam* than a twentieth-century image of the abyss. His quest for home patterns itself on a movement from panorama through mist and confusion to a specific vision at once objective and subjective. As his scanning the horizon has finally produced a sail, so "his fancy [fleeing] before the wind returning" offers at first "the dewy meadowy morning-breath of England" (ll. 656–57). But then, as he disembarks, "a sea-breeze" narrows his view of the once familiar landscape to a strange echo of his vision of it while on the island:

> On the nigh-naked tree the robin piped
> Disconsolate, and through the dripping haze
> The dead weight of the dead leaf bore it down.
>
> (ll. 672–74)

After he learns from Miriam that his past is indeed irretrievable, he repeats this same visionary progression. He first mounts the same hill which has already witnessed two earlier exchanges of Annie. In those cases the hill seemed only a convenient setting for what the characters saw as unique human relationships. Now, however—because it encompasses the incongruity of these repetitions and the juxtaposition of waste, heath, woods, and Danish barrow—the hill offers him a panorama like that from his island. From this height he perceives not just his surroundings or the "thousand memories" of his past but an impersonal natural change which has till now operated apart from the consciousness of individual characters. Enoch's identification of it as Other, like similar revelations in late Hardy novels, creates both spiritual grandeur and physical tragedy.

When he is drawn from this panorama to the narrowed vision of his loss through Philip's window, Enoch endures an encounter with the forbidden more immediate than any granted to Tennyson's other solitaries: "thence / That which he better might have shunned, if griefs / Like his have worse or better, Enoch saw" (ll. 735–37). The vague syntax here mirrors the unlocalized aura of guilt brooding over the entire scene. Enoch himself is torn between the conflicting roles of criminal and agent of retribution, but he realizes that either role would cast him, with the vindictive Arthur, as the personal agent of an otherwise impersonal Other. While Tennyson's earlier mediators have sought to personify the Other, Enoch realizes that the cost of such mediation has become betrayal. During his last lingering year of life, his paradoxical duty as mediator becomes the very paralysis which until now he has fought to escape.

As the bearer of a vision in which sacred institutions seem mere forms and individuals seem mere counters to fill them,[10] Enoch actually carries the weight of guilt and suffering which Tennyson's old men only allude to in acting out their mask of age. On his deathbed he can subdue the garrulous Miriam Lane with the same hypnotic stare through which the Ancient Mariner subdued the Wedding Guest—and for the same reasons. Both, through some undefined fault of their own, have passed through retribution to a revolutionary insight into the cosmos and man's place within it. We may measure the difference between Romantic and Victorian poems in the difference between their protagonists' responses. The Mariner feels compelled to reveal his insight to "one in three"; Enoch feels compelled to hide his: "Tell her that I died / Blessing her, praying for her, loving her. . . . / And say to Philip that I blest him too" (ll. 874–75, 882). Montabrut (pp. 72–77) sees all the ironic denials of Enoch's goals as a hidden plan to woo him from earthly to heavenly fulfillment. Yet the conventionality of his final message, when set against the nihilism of the insight which prompts it, suggests that the poem has surrendered to the *non-dit* in a sense very different from that of Montabrut. The gap between Annie's world and Enoch's has grown, not just too wide to be mediated, but too wide even to be expressed.[11]

Now that the process of life has destroyed Enoch's reason for living, his dying cry, "A sail," may betoken either his rescue from this process or only a recapitulation of it. To *this* world, however, he dare not speak or be seen. Though he permits his children "to see me dead, / Who hardly knew me living" (ll. 884–85), he can reach Annie only in the lock of hair, the reassuring token of their past bond. Much as the Lotos-Eaters feared that on their return they would prove "ghosts to trouble joy,"[12] so here even his "dead face would vex her after-life." Indeed the costly funeral which ends the poem, both ridiculed as a sop to Victorian materialism and praised as an ironic testimony to Enoch's suffering, may instead represent a kind of exorcism, a communal effort to lay to rest a man who had seen too much and the disquieting intimations of his vision.

Aylmer's Field

Although most critics try to see *Aylmer's Field* as a companion poem to *Enoch Arden*, sharing both a volume and a story line suggested by Thomas Woolner, most of them must admit that the two make strange companions. It may be wiser to see the second poem as a reaction to the first— much as the first was a reaction to the 1859 *Idylls* and each of these was a reaction to its predecessor. Having created Others which proved first dangerously sexual and then dangerously impersonal, Tennyson returns to a concrete, violently antisexual figure earlier associated with the Tennyson-d'Eyncourts and the family of Rosa Baring.[13] After he has portrayed love and religious values either mocked by an aristocratic society or rendered inadequate by social forms, Tennyson moves to assert the integrity of love and the power of religion against a tyrannical, aristocratic father. To preserve this integrity, he denies his mediators any autonomy and his Other any hint of psychological complexity: Sir Aylmer coexists with the domain of his hall, and the lovers' sanctuary is so fragile that they can recognize and declare their love only after this love has been pointed out simultaneously to them and their adversary.

That Tennyson circumscribed the love story *in order* to identify with it seems clear from the preeminence he gave it in his principal working draft, Harvard Notebook 41. Apart from the descriptions of the main characters, the earliest *and* most coherent passages dwell on the delicate flowering of this love in lines 95–249, followed by the account of their last meeting, lines 413–31. Only then does he turn to first sketchy and then fuller drafts of the more painful, more dramatic scenes: their discovery, Aylmer's rage, and Leolin's impassioned interview with his brother.

Even in the early drafts, however, Sir Aylmer and the social repression he embodies overshadow the sanctuary left to the lovers: Edith's whimsical transformation of each cottage into "a nest in bloom" is opposed by the rocky solidity of the hall; her struggle as a "hunted creature" casts her father as the hunter, "draw[ing] the cordon close and closer toward the death" (ll. 499–500);[14] even the comparison of her to "a mystic star between the less / And greater glory varying" dims beside the image of Aylmer as diabolical Other, "beneath a pale and unimpassioned moon, / Vext with unworthy madness, and deformed" (ll. 334–35).[15]

In fact these supposed mediators are granted their only identity and value through the mediation of the narrative itself. If the Other in *Enoch Arden* worked through the form, mediation here works through a voice which exists apart from story, characters, or even speaker. If, as Montabrut claims, *Enoch* explored the "unsaid," *Aylmer's Field* explores the "said." Critics have accounted for the poem's reflexive language as simple overwriting, as generic parody, as personal obsession with the subject, or as calculated manipulation of stylistic effects. Using the last approach, Priestley (pp. 94–98) produces a subtle and sympathetic reading in which conflicting styles shape our complex and changing attitudes toward the characters. To me, however, the poem seems more stylistically homogeneous and less objectively controlled than Priestley sees it.

While Ricks (*Tennyson*, pp. 283–84) is certainly correct in identifying the fictive source of the poem as the cripple who betrayed the lovers' letters to Aylmer, his absence—indeed the absence of the whole historical frame from the manuscript draft—suggests that even this gesture at narrative distance was an afterthought. We hear not the voice of an embittered eighteenth-century rustic but that of a nineteenth-century Prufrock: a worldly, supposedly cynical speaker fearful that his supposed audience may prove more cynical than he is, a speaker embarrassed by his story but even more by his covert involvement in it.

Even the first-composed passages on the lovers take the form of an imaginary dialogue, convulsively knotting themselves in rhetorical questions and presupposed reactions: "What lovelier than her, / His only child . . . ?" (ll. 22–23); "And might not Averill . . . / Somewhere beneath his own low range of roofs, / Have also set his many-shielded tree?" (ll. 46–48); Edith . . . shone like a mystic star . . . / We know not wherefore" (ll. 70, 72, 74); "or else he forged, / But that was later, boyish histories / Of battle . . . sketches rude and faint, / But where a passion yet unborn perhaps / Lay hidden" (ll. 96–98, 100–102); "And how should Love . . . follow / Such dear familiarity of dawn? / Seldom, but when he does, Master of all" (ll. 128, 130–32).

Whose voice are we hearing? Perhaps Tennyson's discomfort at having to celebrate what his story cannot dramatize may have forced him to adopt the converse of the *erlebte Rede* of Boyd and Williams. For them (pp. 582–89), "Mariana" spoke its heroine's unspoken fears and longings in words which in other circumstances *might* have been hers. Here the lovers' worth is expressed in a style of which they remain by definition incapable. Because Tennyson knows that the style can belong to no one else, that he has had to step in as the mediator of last resort, he hides his involvement within a voice that he never used before or after.

What integrity this voice fails to give the lovers, they cannot win on their own. Their final meeting is, as Priestley says (pp. 99–100), pathetic and moving, but principally because Aylmer seems to have enlisted the forces of nature against them: their words are drowned by the wind roaring in the pine and their tears diluted by the "careless rain of heaven." Leolin's sleeping vision of her call to him proves only an ironic reversal of *Jane Eyre*, a call not to fulfillment but to suicide. The letters that she could not send are pathetically summed up in the letter telling him of her death. His letters to her achieve their only power by torturing their unintended audience: Sir Aylmer "read; and tore, / As if the living passion symbolled there / Were living nerves to feel the rent" (ll. 534–36).

The rest of the poem, and Averill's sermon in particular, considers whether such mediators may exert through their suffering a force otherwise denied them. Here, as Philip Drew points out, narrative and elapsed time suddenly merge: poem and sermon collapse into one another as joint linguistic defenses against a threatening society.[16] The Harvard manuscript suggests that Tennyson had real trouble both taking up and relinquishing the pulpit. After a long lacuna skips over the couple's final entrapment and subsequent deaths, the manuscript resumes with the prelude to the sermon, followed by compressed sketches for the first section (ll. 647–721), followed by this same section in nearly final form. Though the manuscript concludes with a number of stubs, the second half of the sermon with its references to the French Revolution (ll. 735–97) may have been an afterthought contemporaneous with Tennyson's decision to set the poem during this period.

Despite this last gesture at historical distance, the preacher himself is never given any contextual distance from his creator. Averill has no history (apart from a vague reference to having been jilted), no real emotions except anger, and no future after he stops speaking. Tennyson's evident proximity to the poem's narrator had demanded a rhetorical decorum within which he could glorify the lovers, appease the reader, and apologize for the story itself. Speaking through Averill, however, Tennyson could not resist the temptation to take out his hatred of the Tennyson-d'Eyncourts upon the now hapless Aylmers. He then entangled the couple in a suffocating web of biblical texts, vicariously destroying his preacher father in the very act of following his example. Enoch, presented with a similar opportunity to pronounce the doom of God, chose instead a self-destructive silence. Averill, by translating paternal tyranny into a divine prerogative, implicitly joins the Aylmers and the Arthur of "Guinevere" as yet another agent of the Other.

"Lucretius"

Like these two long domestic idylls, "Lucretius" uses a visionary figure to explore the dangers in any religious system. Enoch's laconic stoicism left open the gap between his conventional piety and his realization of an amoral indifference underlying apparently sacred institutions. Averill blindly called up the power of religious curse to destroy a society he saw as evil. The nightmare visions of Lucretius have been variously interpreted as the dark side of the world-view expressed in *De Rerum Natura*, the repressed libido of Everyman, the definitive refutation of nineteenth-century positivism. All critics, however, extol the historical accuracy of Tennyson's portrait.

Yet Harvard Notebook 37 suggests that the visions themselves are both more central and more subjective than we might have expected. While the manuscript entries are scattered, it seems at least suggestive that the first recto passage opens, "Catch her goatfoot." Other early fragments include his vision of Sylla's blood sprouting Hetairai, his description of the sun as blind to human need, and his encounter with the nymph and satyr from their appearance to his decision to play the Roman in suicide.[17] Regardless of whether these visions are appropriate to the historical Lucretius, they suggest that Tennyson's failure to circumscribe asexual forms of the Other has brought him back to his exploration of desire in the 1859 *Idylls*. When he created Guinevere as an implicit challenge to his model, he may have implicitly committed himself to "Lucretius." The poem stands not just as Tennyson's frankest portrayal of sexuality but as his most direct attempt to reach an accommodation with the source of desire, Venus herself.

Often associated with the fatal woman of Ryals, the fatal goddess of Joseph (pp. 140–41), and the sinful queen of Betty Miller, Venus challenges Tennyson's model by refusing all attempts to delimit her, even the attempt to describe her as undifferentiated flux. In particular she assaults the whole concept of sanctuary, already undermined in *Enoch Arden* and shrunk into powerlessness in *Aylmer's Field*. Lucretius may celebrate his feasts "under plane or pine / With neighbors laid along the grass, . . . / Affirming each his own philosophy" (ll. 213–14, 216), yet the very subjectivity of such communion shrinks his own sanctuary to the confines of the self. In borrowing the defense taken by the introspective lyrics of 1830 and the early stanzas of *In Memoriam*, Lucretius opens himself to a similar fragmentation. Standing inside and outside his psyche, Venus baffles all his efforts to appease her:

> Is this thy vengeance, holy Venus, thine . . . ?
> My tongue
> Trips, or I speak profanely. Which of these
> Angers thee most, or angers thee at all? . . .
> Nay, if thou canst, O Goddess, like ourselves
> Touch, and be touched, then would I cry to thee. . . .
> Ay, but I meant not thee; I meant not her.
> (ll. 67, 73–75, 80–81, 85)

Since Lucretius is so tortured by his obsessive vision of Venus as wronged woman, why can he not see her for what he "knows" her to be, "the all-generating powers and genial heat / Of Nature" (ll. 97–98)? This question has already been answered by Joseph (p. 142): Lucretius "has been an artist as well as a philosopher. . . . As such, as a lord of the five senses despite his ascetic intentions, he needs the *sensuous* Venus to inspire his work. . . . And this is the trap that a fatal goddess sets for him (the same trap that Eros in *Death in Venice* sets for a later proud artist)." It is also a variation on the trap set for Tennyson by Guinevere. Less sympathetic than the Queen but equally necessary, Venus blurs again the distinction between Other and mediator.

Faced with this new threat to the bases of his creativity, Tennyson turns the entire poem into a study of the sources, controls, and dangers of the poetic process. In so doing he also turns it into a singleminded reevaluation of this theme in "Locksley Hall," *In Memoriam*, and "Vivien." While the later-added introduction claims that his wife's poison robbed Lucretius of "his power to shape," the early-written visions make it clear that this loss bears no relation to his power to create. In these visions we see the same untamed imaginative power that tormented Tennyson after the death of Hallam. There too, he worried that he had become like "some wild Poet, when he works / Without a conscience or an aim" (34: 7–8); or perhaps like

> that delirious man
> Whose fancy fuses old and new,
> And flashes into false and true,
> And mingles all without a plan?
>
> (16: 17–20)

Hence all Tennyson's revisions, within and after the Harvard notebook, find some context which can encompass Venus as mediator and Other, muse and destroyer. His invocation of her as the "genial heat / Of Nature," for example, appears in the manuscript soon after a three-line sketch of the breasts of Helen scorching him with their flame. In this context it appears a deliberate effort to depersonalize her aggressive sexuality. As Lucretius' work has dispelled the mythic horrors of Hades, has "stay[ed] the rolling Ixionian wheel" (l. 260), so he tries to dispel his personified visions within another late-added vision of inanimate process: "they fly / Now thinner, and now thicker, like the flakes / In a fall of snow" (ll. 165–67).

Through all of these revisions, however, Venus asserts an autonomy beyond any contemplated by Tennyson's other characters. Instead of assuming a better-defined, better-motivated identity, she exploits her anomalous roles as psychological, personal, and cosmic power; she presides over an anarchy where contradiction no longer counts for anything, where normally separate, normally incompatible manifestations of the Other coalesce into nightmare.

Lucretius' dream of the "flaring atom stream," for example, simply transforms itself into that of the equally volatile Hetairai. Then this visionary sequence is in turn attributed to "some unseen monster [who] lays / His vast and filthy hands upon my will" (ll. 219–20). The devouring spirit who threatened the speaker in *Maud* here finally assumes tangible, if not visible, shape. "Locksley Hall" compared "a hungry people" to "a lion creeping nigher." Here these images of social anarchy invade the psyche as "crowds . . . in an hour of civic tumult" break in upon the "council hall" of Lucretius' higher faculties.[18] Finally his "settled sweet Epicurean life" is modeled on the "sacred everlasting calm" of the gods and so collapses with them into the flux of natural process: "If all be atoms, how then should the Gods / Being atomic not be dissoluble" (ll. 114–15)?

Lucretius' inability to mediate this nightmare has been attributed to his positivistic refusal to admit personality and teleology into his universe. Expanding the parallels with *In Memoriam*, however, we could also attribute the tragedy to his refusal to follow the compositional process of his creator and fellow poet. Tennyson was willing to accept whatever conditions would help him to regain, reshape, redirect the spirit of his dead friend. Lucretius, by contrast, neglects the duty of every visionary mediator to wrestle with the sexual emanations of his atomistic cosmos in Blakean spiritual warfare. In hopes of ending his torment, Lucretius opts to end his life.

Though he describes his suicide as a stroke for freedom and human dignity, the description of it Tennyson added after the Harvard manuscript entraps his speaker in two telling ironies. The first Lucretius himself must acknowledge when his wife tells him that the monster he sees prowling the outer world is only a chemical administered out of misguided human affection. The second irony remains buried in his final soliloquy. He has been fatally cold to his wife, has recoiled at his visions of lust, and has refused to accept them as his own. As Hughes points out (*Glass*, p. 226), this same man now sees his suicide as a Dis-like rape of the personified spirit of tranquillity:[19]

> I know thou surely must be mine
> Or soon or late, yet out of season, thus
> I woo thee roughly, for thou carest not
> How roughly men may woo thee so they win.
>
> (ll. 269–272)

With this unconscious hypocrisy, Lucretius joins Enoch, Averill, Geraint, and Arthur as another mediator who has at least been tempted to side with the Other. In the two preceding narratives, this temptation undermined or at least muted the overt theme of the poem. Lucretius' failure, however, was acknowledged as an aesthetic success by the critics and by the poet himself: "What a mess little Swinburne would have made of this." As a success, the poem opened up new strategies for confronting his Arthurian material.[20] The blurring of inner and outer realities may have destroyed Lucretius, but they showed Tennyson that he could amplify the symbolic devices of *Maud*, "The Vision of Sin," and "A Dream of Fair Women." They showed him that his creation of layered, overlapping fictions within *The Princess* was not as clumsy as his critics had claimed and he himself had come to admit. For the multiple visions of both the Grail and the forces set against it, the visions of Lucretius seem to have been a curious prerequisite.

CHAPTER TEN

The 1869 Idylls

"The Holy Grail"

In its completed form, "The Holy Grail" presents a startlingly new perspective on many of the problems raised by the 1859 *Idylls*. Merlin's story celebrated the ascetic old man whose charm had neutralized a queen's beauty, and now an equally ascetic faction seizes control of the court. The Novice prated of a golden age in which Arthur's realm was full of natural magic "before the coming of the sinful Queen," and now another nun prays to bring back the miraculous Grail and "heal the world of all their wickedness" (l. 94).[1] Thus if "Elaine" showed Tennyson the injustice of blaming the collapse solely on Guinevere, then this idyll, following it both in date of composition and in narrative sequence, offers Camelot at least the ironic possibility of a reprieve.

As Pfordresher points out (p. 36), early in 1862 Tennyson knew that the Grail idyll belonged between "Elaine" and "Guinevere." Yet the new perspectives it offered constituted the principal block in Tennyson's efforts to expand *The True and the False* or even to link them with "the old Morte." Despite Tennyson's protests that his disbelief in the Grail would "incur[] a charge of irreverence,"[2] he may have needed the poems of the 1860s to shore up that very skepticism. Together these suggested that the kind of mediation offered by Percivale's sister was not only doomed from the outset but was itself another manifestation of the Other. Enoch, Averill, and Lucretius were also tempted to bring moral censure upon an often sexual anarchy, but the two who yielded to this temptation transformed themselves into unwilling agents of oppression.

It is thus not surprising that Tennyson would seek out a narrative context in which the judgmental Grail faction appeared as grotesque as Vivien, their opposite number, and much less sympathetic than the now-humanized Guinevere. This context, perhaps the catalyst which allowed him to begin the idyll, has been preserved within Harvard Notebook 38 in a form different from the drafts of Tennyson's earlier poems. More complete, more certain in its direction than the manuscripts of the 1859 *Idylls*, this one nevertheless appears for the most part in prose, as if Tennyson wanted first to capture the elusive Grail material within a viable plot. Without the stories of Bors or of Percivale's childhood love, this plot is actually tighter than that of the finished idyll. The interlocutor Ambrosius appears much less, in part because he is not needed. Instead Percivale's almost uninterrupted dramatic monologue moves from the court, through his Grail quest, and back to the court where Arthur confronts him and the other returned knights. The monologue itself portrays Galahad's purity with the same contempt that modern critics show for the early "Sir Galahad" lyric. Here, "cr[ying] out in a shrill voice" to Arthur (Pfordresher, p. 735), the figure later described by Percivale as "the bright faced boy knight" seems a younger incarnation of St. Simeon Stylites.

The same draft, however, also encompasses the visions of Percivale, his sister, Galahad, Lancelot, and Arthur—and while the characters have been only sketched in, the visions themselves stand virtually complete. The fact that both Lancelot's and Arthur's are already in verse may imply, as Pfordresher argues (p. 37), that they represent the sections which Emily describes her husband as composing months before even this draft. The sudden appearance of verse, however, also suggests heightened inspiration at the time of composition, whenever it may have been. While Tennyson seems unconcerned about the relation of vision to visionary, the narrative impartiality of the prose draft gives all these visions the same kind of priority as those in "Lucretius."

Indeed the visions can be identified more specifically with the powers of the Other which have been encroaching upon Tennyson since adolescence:[3] a presence blinding, burning, and hostile when it confronts Lancelot as he opens the door at Castle Carbonek, yet one hopelessly distant when it flees before Galahad, leaving Percivale stranded on the shore.[4] We can link the first manifestation with Paden's doom of God or with the forces emanating from the more secular god surrogates of 1830. The second resembles those same forces when withdrawn: as the idol fails the supplicating priestess in "Timbuctoo," as the "one fair face" ever flees before the mariners in "The Vision," as Knowledge moves ahead of Ulysses "like a sinking star," as the wounded Arthur leaves Bedivere stranded on a different but equally alien shore.

The disappearance of this power brings back another dilemma of Tennyson's early poetry, the entrapment of the self within natural flux. In Percivale's "temptations," when one natural form after another collapses "into dust," he must recapitulate the plight of Tennyson's earlier mediators as they contemplate the collapse of the "heavenly" Timbuctoo into "mud huts," or compare a past paradise with the bleak urban landscape of "O that 'twere possible," or envision time's power to "draw down Aeonian hills" in *In Memoriam* 35, or ponder what cosmic irony has compelled Enoch's faithful Annie to turn bigamist.

Confronting such visionary emanations of the Other, Tennyson revised the prose draft to distance or even discredit them. The expanded role for Ambrosius, with his common-sense skepticism about the Grail visions and his vicarious sorrow for Percivale's sacrifice, has prompted Ryals to see him as a surrogate of Arthur and his values.[5] The addition of Bors humanizes the Grail by granting a vision of it to one too concerned with Arthur and Lancelot to seek it. The addition of Percivale's childhood love appeals to similarly human, even domestic values, here set in opposition to the Grail. Crabbe (pp. 54–58) justifies this added section by pointing out its similarities to the earlier temptations of Percivale: pastoral landscape, castle, beautiful woman, offers of love and power. Yet when combined with Percivale's admission that "all men, to one so bound by such a vow, / And women were as phantoms" (ll. 564–65), the similarities in these two accounts may hint that both are describing the same experience. Instead of letting Percivale see life *sub specie aeternitatis*, as Tennyson saw evolution in *In Memoriam*, the Grail quest may simply corrode his perception of all reality into the sterile cynicism of "The Vision of Sin."[6]

Other manuscript additions compromise the reality of the Grail visions themselves. Lancelot's account of the two lions confronting him at Castle Carbonek, borrowed from Malory, is now rendered suspect by Bors's account of being rebuffed by him in his madness, "For now there is a lion in my path" (l. 643). Lancelot's whole voyage may have been not an escape from madness but a delusion caused by it. An even more obvious method of distancing Tennyson himself acknowledged with considerable pride: "He pointed out the difference between the five visions of the Grail . . . according to [the questers'] own peculiar natures and circumstances" (*Poems*, III, 464). As many critics have since noted, each character sees what he or she expects to see.

In one sense, Tennyson's additions may attribute the visions to group hysteria, another instance of certain characters' predilection for demanding mediation from embodiments of the Other. Percivale now sees his vision not just in Galahad's company but through his eyes: "His eye, dwelling on mine, / Drew me, with power upon me, till I grew / One with him, to believe as he believed" (ll. 485–87).[7] Galahad in turn is inspired by Percivale's sister in what Buckler describes (p. 55) as a "cabalistic ceremony in which defenseless youth . . . is raped by an embodied psychosis . . . , divesting him of his own identity and . . . planting the seed of herself in him":

> She sent the deathless passion in her eyes
> Through him, and made him hers, and laid her mind
> On him, and he believed in her belief.
>
> (ll. 163–65)

Arthur now passes judgment on them all: "one has seen, and all the blind will see" (l. 313).

In another sense, however, the new links between character and vision in these manuscript additions fill the characters with some of the power inherent in the visions themselves. Galahad in particular grows, if not in humanity, at least in a spirituality like that wielded by Averill in his sermon. He now tells Percivale that the Grail has never left him since the initial vision: "And in the strength of this I rode, / . . . and in the strength of this / Come victor" (ll. 476, 480–81). Indeed Galahad grows not just into Arthur's equal, as Charles Tennyson has noted,[8] but into a curiously Miltonic parody of him: "One will crown me king / Far in the spiritual city" (ll. 482–83). With the prayer attributed to Lancelot in Malory, "God make thee good as thou art beautiful," Arthur hopes to foster his own values in Galahad. Yet as several critics have pointed out, Galahad implicitly denies his authority by addressing him as "Sir Arthur." He receives his passion for the Grail quest from Percivale's sister in a parody of Arthur's coronation in the soon-to-be-written "Coming." He instills this passion within Percivale in much the same way that the newly crowned Arthur will imprint himself on his knights. Galahad further mimics Arthur in his unknown origin and in the vision of his passing. The stormy sea over which he pursues the Grail echoes both the sea which washed Arthur up "between Bude and Bos" and the apparently lifeless water over which the dying Arthur is borne in the "Morte."
This storm at Galahad's departure, while present in the prose sketch, is consistently tied to the visions themselves within the final version. Bors in his vision hears "the hollow-ringing heavens sweep / Over him" (ll. 675–76). Lancelot, coming "in my madness to the naked shore," encounters

> So loud a blast along the shore and sea,
> Ye could not hear the waters for the blast,
> Though heapt in mounds and ridges all the sea
> Drove like a cataract. . . .
>
> (ll. 793–96)

All the other failed questers, when questioned by Arthur, "spoke but of sundry perils in the storm" (l. 758). And Arthur himself tells Percivale that he feared for his safety,

> So fierce a gale made havoc here of late
> Among the strange devices of our kings;
> Yea, shook this newer, stronger hall of ours,
> And from the statue Merlin moulded for us
> Half-wrenched a golden wing. . . .
>
> (ll. 726–30)[9]

Percivale has already found the destruction extensive: "when we reached / The city, our horses stumbl[ed] as they trode / On heaps of ruin" (ll. 712–14).

Tennyson accounts for this connection in a note: "It was a time of storm when men could imagine miracles" (*Poems*, III, 478n). The storm may indeed offer naturalistic and psychological explanations for the visions—yet not, I think, within the context of this poem. The printed text leaves us instead with the clear impression of a single preternatural force which sweeps over the realm. To some it appears only as storm, to others as vision. Even among the visionaries, only some are holy. Others like Lancelot rely on an intensity more Byronic than Christian to achieve an experience which critics as early as M. W. MacCallum have recognized as one of the most vivid in the entire idyll.[10] Indeed the very parallels we listed between Galahad's career and Arthur's may suggest that the cosmic forces which once supported his kingship have now deserted him and his realm.

Arthur can and does oppose the Grail visions with his own, and we must acknowledge both Tennyson's claims about their centrality and the obvious parallels between Arthur's visions and Tennyson's. Yet this passage cannot offset the rest of the idyll. For one thing, Arthur's condescending comparison of himself to a "hind . . . / Who may not wander from the allotted field" (ll. 902, 904) suggests that his visions do not satisfy even him. For another thing, the two kinds of vision grow inseparably from the same source within Tennyson's psyche. The trancelike descents into the self which

Arthur describes are the same ones which in "Armageddon," "Timbuctoo," and *In Memoriam* produce the closest parallels to the Grail visions. Tennyson may with good reason fear them and seek to qualify them, but he cannot renounce them without renouncing the uncontrolled imaginative seizure which, according to his son, produced the poem itself.

Tennyson is thus driven to reassign his original repudiation of the Grail to the blind, self-serving Gawain. Arthur tries to maintain that only a few individuals may pursue individual salvation while the rest must link theirs to the salvation of the realm.[11] Yet he can no longer bind them, as he boasts of having done in "Guinevere," "to reverence the King, as if he were / Their conscience, and their conscience as their King" (ll. 465–66). McSweeney sees Arthur here (p. 122) as moving from moral vindictiveness to the naturalism of Tristram. I would rather see him extending a progression begun in "Elaine." There the Queen's dual role as mediator and Other left him the unknowing measure of social anarchy. Here, by contrast, he admits that he cannot control, judge, or even understand the forces now shaping his destiny as man and as king. Instead he must affirm an imaginative freedom, whatever its consequences, as the prerequisite to both secular and spiritual vision:

> For every fiery prophet in old times,
> And all the sacred madness of the bard,
> When God made music through them, could but speak
> His music by the framework and the chord;
> And as ye saw it ye have spoken truth.
>
> (ll. 872–76)

This late-added admission of visionary relativism makes ironic all the late-added trappings of his kingship: the dim rich city, the gate engraved with his wars, the amplified description of his hall and his place within it. This same admission, however, allows him to mediate between Tennyson and his poem. Like the mediators of the 1830 volume or of *In Memoriam*, Arthur projects the authorial presence so fully that he stands impotent before the world of his poem. In this idyll's last line, "I knew not all he meant" (l. 916), Percivale may indeed be pronouncing a belated self-judgment,[12] but in the context of Arthur's own last line, "Ye have seen what ye have seen," Percivale may only be acknowledging that neither he nor Arthur, nor Tennyson, nor the reader can now reach any conclusion beyond tautology.

"The Coming of Arthur"

In one sense, Tennyson turned to "The Coming of Arthur" because writing "The Holy Grail" had committed him to expand *The True and the False* into a larger work. In another sense, however, the Arthur of the "Grail" needed a new definition and a new genesis. That idyll, as we saw, had bonded him more closely with his creator but separated him from any vestige of control over his realm and his story.

In studying the "Coming" as Tennyson's exploration of both these goals, we are fortunately able to reconstruct a preliminary stage in his conception of the work. Although Wise, as Pfordresher explains in his introduction (pp. 40–42), has effectively butchered Tennyson's first jottings, an early draft is split between the Ashley manuscript collection in the British Museum and the Stark collection at Texas. While this draft in turn breaks off at line 423, the story is brought to a rapid conclusion in a canceled passage of the Berg manuscript at the New York Public Library. Together these three omit a full third of the final version: most of the historical background, all the references to the Romans, Arthur's battle against the rival kings, the whole coronation scene, the phantom ship, Merlin and the infant Arthur enveloped in fire, Merlin's riddling denial and his song, Leodogran's dream, the vows, and the knight's song at Arthur's wedding. Instead this version of the wedding shows Arthur

> founding on his marriage morn,
> And binding by strait vows to his own self
> The glorious order of his Table Round
> True men, to serve as models for the world
> And be the fair beginnings of a time.
> (Pfordresher, p. 117)

Gray postulates that Tennyson wrote the idyll, like its companion piece the "Morte," from the inside out, through the three progressively less visionary birth narratives out to the public, quasi-historical frame.[13] In fact, this manuscript, like others of the *Idylls*, presents a story more straightforward than the final version, a story of Leodogran's discovery of Arthur's past and Arthur's search for his own future as a mediator.

The perceptive and often similar analyses of this idyll by Kincaid and Gray fit this draft very well. Kincaid sees the "Coming" (pp. 158–63) as an object lesson in epistemology, and Gray (pp. 2–6) sees it as a quest for truth in which "people create and destroy their own reality." Both point out that Bedivere's effort to be factual simply casts more slander on his king; both agree that when Bellicent speculates on Arthur's supernatural origins, she demands not just Leodogran's assent but his active participation in the process of mythmaking. Though this early version lacks his dream, it still justifies Kincaid's claim that Leodogran must himself become an artist. As Rosenberg puts it (p. 91), he has at the end no more objective reason for surrendering his daughter to Arthur than he had to begin with.

We may complement these interpretations by examining the draft from Arthur's perspective. Here the opening idyll stands as Tennyson's effort to grant his principal mediator a stature and pedigree at least the equal of Galahad's. Subsequent additions, however, implicitly acknowledge that Arthur has until now been associated not with active mediation but with a retreat into the sanctuary of the self. In earlier-written idylls he has been seen and defined through the needs and desires of other characters. Accounts of his past and the realm's have told more about their speakers than about the King himself. Guinevere's picture of the cold, self-contained figure at the end of her progress reflects her already fixed love for her companion. Lancelot's account of Arthur's twelve battles measures the gap he sees between himself and his own potential. Some of these recollections involve magic: the chase of the phantom hart described by Merlin, for example, and the early wonders described by the Novice. But this magic also implies a similar escape, not just to the childhood of the realm or of the speaker, but to some imagined past of the authorial self. We seem almost to be hearing echoes of the knightly games and tournaments which, according to the *Memoir* (I, 4), the young Tennysons organized at Somersby.

In this early draft of the "Coming," Arthur remains the object of such magical childlike visions. Rosenberg argues (p. 44) that he gains some "borrowed venerability" from his association with Merlin and Bleys, but from the time Merlin catches him up to the time he "has him crowned,"[14] we never see Arthur *doing* anything. Without the coronation, the battle, or the vows taken by the knights and Guinevere, this draft leaves him again as the shadowy object of others' needs or desires. In his one extended speech he even questions his own identity:

> What happiness to reign a lonely king, . . .
>   for saving I be joined
> To her that is the fairest under heaven,
> I seem as nothing in the mighty world.
>
>   (ll. 81, 84–86)

The characters who invoked Arthur's past in the earlier idylls—Merlin, Guinevere, and Lancelot—have all toyed with letting him mediate between them and the "mighty world," but they have all rejected him to their own sorrow. Now Arthur, given his first chance to escape from Tennyson's past and Merlin's magic, immediately reaches out, not for another mediator, but for the "fairest of all flesh on earth." He chooses the one figure who must seem Other to the spiritual mission he shares with the authorial presence.

To give Arthur an identity and a plan for this mission, Tennyson added the historical background, the coronation, and Leodogran's dream within the *Holy Grail* volume of 1869; later he added the battle,[15] Lancelot's pledge, the marriage vows, and the knights' song within the 1873 Library Edition. All these work in one sense—but in other senses they remain unconvincing. They do allow Arthur to compete with Galahad on his own terms, but during both the coronation and marriage ceremonies, as Arthur stands surrounded by his half-real, half-allegorical followers, he seems self-consciously posing for a group portrait to authenticate the august event.

Considered more broadly, this habit of Arthur's accounts for much of what Rosenberg describes (pp. 134–35) as the tendency of the *Idylls* to symbolize themselves. This progressive mythmaking began in "The Holy Grail," where Merlin's disappearance, presumably unknowable to the court, was attributed to his sitting in the Siege perilous. But in the "Coming," if Arthur is proleptically defining his authority against Galahad's, he is also proleptically defining his mission as mediator against what he wants us to see as its inevitable failure.

He sees in battle "the smallest rock upon the farthest hill / And even in high day the morning star" (ll. 98–99)—but he seems to do so *in order* that he may be shrouded in mist for that "last, dim, weird battle of the west" ("Passing," l. 94). He pledges "deathless love" for Lancelot and later tells Guinevere, "I love thee to the death"—in part so that their adulterous love may come to make his life something he does "not greatly care to lose" ("Guinevere," l. 492). He binds his knights with vows which Tennyson struggled to articulate through several drafts but finally cancelled (Pfordresher, pp. 101–3), leaving them represented only by their pathetic recapitulation in "Guinevere." He surrounds himself with the three queens, whose only purpose, Bellicent admits, is to "help him at his need" (l. 410). The sword he receives from the Lady of the Lake is inscribed "Cast me away" (l. 309), and Merlin must admit that Arthur came "from the great deep" (l. 410) only so that he can return to it. "The sun of May" descends on the King at his wedding so that "the moony vapour rolling round the King" can shroud him from Guinevere "till himself became as mist / Before her, moving ghostlike to his doom" (ll. 597, 600–601). Finally Leodogran's dream opposes two visions, one where a "slope of land" is clear but the King a phantom, and another where "the solid earth became / As nothing, but the King stood out in heaven, / Crowned" (ll. 441–43). What can this dream foreshadow except the fatal incompatibility of Arthur and his realm?[16]

Even within the "Coming," Arthur can neither secure his own sanctuary nor identify the Other he is to confront. As in the final draft of "The Holy Grail," however, whatever control he loses over the story he gains over the authorial presence at its center. *In Memoriam*, I think, offers an even closer analogy for Arthur's new mode of being. There Hallam's spirit moved deeper within Tennyson's psyche even as it mediated, like the "rolling air," between him and the created universe. Though haunted by the fear that he was merely communing with some aspect of self, Tennyson finally found validity in the very process through which he could create new forms for the relationship as others became suspect. In the "Coming," I think, this Arthur achieves an even closer bond with Tennyson. He may fail to mediate between poet and poem, but through these failures he becomes, as it were, a co-creator of the motifs which bind the accounts of his failure into an aesthetic success.[17]

"Pelleas and Ettarre"

Since "Pelleas and Ettarre" may be the first test of Arthur's new stance outside the narrative context of his own poem, our lack of manuscript evidence is particularly frustrating. We cannot even be sure that Tennyson composed "Pelleas and Ettarre" before "The Passing of Arthur." A virtually final version of "Pelleas," however, does appear in proof alongside a significantly incomplete draft of the "Passing." Of the manuscript drafts, the most interesting has left us only tantalizing hints of its nature. Harvard Notebook 39 contains five page stubs which David Staines has quite convincingly described as a missing prose draft of "Pelleas."[18] From the appearance late in the draft of the first letters of "Gawain," we can surmise only that the draft broke off somewhere between his arrival and Pelleas' discovery of him and Ettarre. The importance of this draft in the composition of the poem is heightened by the proximity of the first verse draft to the final text.

In our speculation about the poem's origins, we are helped only by two fragments from Texas—one a full page, one much less—which seem independent of the missing prose draft. Either they preceded it or they added incidents not included within it. The first fragment moves from Pelleas' winning of the tourney to his first encounter with Ettarre's knights (c. ll. 160–215), and the second describes Pelleas' dream (c. ll. 493–509). Both suggest that, apart from Ettarre's interview with the Queen (ll. 169–78), the missing prose draft may have prefigured the story's final form.

Such proximity may be all the more notable given the distance between these drafts and their source in Malory. Tennyson had read the Malory tale to his wife and Mrs. Cameron in 1859, "with a view to a new poem,"[19] but in the intervening ten years it suffered a sea change. Most of Malory's story is told from Gawain's point of view. He sees Pelleas' prowess in overthrowing Ettard's knights, wonders at his submission to them, sorrows at his account of Ettard's cruelty, offers to help him (IV, 20–22), and yet immediately woos her himself once inside her castle. Even Malory, with his penchant for admiration, can find little to praise in Gawain except his sexual stamina: he "lay with her in that pauelione two dayes and two nyghtes" (IV, 23). We might expect Tennyson, given his previous practice, to have further blackened the character of Gawain, but his Gawain appears less evil and less important than Malory's.

Tennyson's version, by refusing to identify with any of the participants, dramatizes the consequences of Arthur's withdrawal from his poem. In fact Arthur seems to avoid effective mediation of any kind. Though he has already confessed in "Enid" to "having looked too much through alien eyes" ("Marriage," l. 891), he here knights Pelleas without testing him because "there were those who knew him near the King / And promised for him" (ll. 14–15). He also rigs the tourney so that Pelleas may commit himself irrevocably to a woman dismissed by Guinevere as no better than "an ant." Pelleas may refuse to hear Percivale's assurance that the King is true, but to him Arthur has been far falser than Gawain and Ettarre or Lancelot and Guinevere. At the end of the idyll, the latter pair graciously allow him to accuse them; Arthur, as he has been throughout most of the idyll, is nowhere to be found.

Yet just as the irony in "Elaine" grows from Arthur's obtuse presence, so the irony in this idyll grows from Pelleas' pathetic efforts to imitate the absent mediator at its center.[20] He admits as much in his naive apostrophe to his imagined beloved:

> I love thee, though I know thee not.
> For fair thou art and pure as Guinevere,
> And I will make thee with my spear and sword
> As famous—O my Queen, my Guinevere,
> For I will be thy Arthur when we meet.
>
> (ll. 41–45)

He pleads for knighthood to further this desire, and later reproaches Ettarre for mocking "his vows and the great King." Even after finding her with Gawain, he refuses to slay them because "the King hath bound / And sworn me to his brotherhood" (ll. 439–40). Only when "maddened" does he conclude that "we be all alike: only the King / Hath made us fools and liars" (ll. 469–70).

Pelleas, however, proves less an imitator of Arthur than a cheap imitation; where Arthur is pervasively likened to the sun, Pelleas "felt the sun / Beat like a strong knight on his helm, and reeled / Almost to falling from his horse" (ll. 21–23). He is much happier in shadowy lighting, looking "through the green-glooming twilight of the grove" (l. 32). From this perspective he falls in love with Ettarre because "the beauty of her flesh abashed the boy, / As though it were the beauty of her soul" (ll. 74–75).

Reed remarks (pp. 102–3) that in Ettarre Pelleas receives a Guinevere in a more sinister sense than he intended. Yet Ettarre is really no Guinevere; she is no more an Other than Pelleas is a mediating Arthur. Instead of an intrusive presence which resists being personified or delimited, Ettarre is fixed in artificially brilliant lighting from the moment he first sees her: "A vision hovering on a sea of fire, / Damsels in divers colours like the cloud / Of sunset and sunrise" (ll. 50–52). If Pelleas represents Arthur's sunlight dimmed to the chiaroscuro of the forest, Ettarre represents Guinevere's beauty reduced to a gaudy, Pre-Raphaelite imitation of a medieval painting. Unlike Stevenson's interpretation of Elaine as artist, Ettarre exists only as artifact.[21]

Rosenberg has observed (p. 71) the implicit comparison of Ettarre's castle to her body: first closed and inaccessible, then open and violated. The "hortus conclusus" has often served as sanctuary for Tennyson's female mediators: the Soul's Palace, the castle at Shalott, Ida's college, Maud's garden. These women have often been driven from their sanctuary by some incursion of the Other. But as Ettarre is neither mediator nor Other, so her castle, closed to Pelleas, is open to all comers; when he enters, he finds it not violated but empty. The bower where he does find the couple, far from being secret or even sheltered, lies in an open field. Tennyson cannot even portray her finally awakening love: "he that tells the tale / Says that her ever-veering fancy turned / To Pelleas" (ll. 482–84).[22]

Pelleas' change from mediator to avenging Other may seem to parallel the changes of Arthur in "Guinevere" and Averill in *Aylmer's Field*. In this context, however, it too remains only a parody:

> O towers so strong,
> Huge, solid, would that even while I gaze
> The crack of earthquake shivering to your base
> Split you, and Hell burst up your harlot roofs
> Bellowing. . . .
>
> (ll. 454–58)

Browning used this as a proof text to compare his poetics to Tennyson's: "I should judge the conflict in the knight's soul the proper subject to describe: Tennyson thinks he should describe the castle, and effect of the moon on its towers, and anything but the soul."[23] Though Browning's comparison has been criticized for ignoring the explicitly sexual imagery, Pelleas' metaphorical displacement does sound mechanical, his soul itself as hollow as he has found her castle. Tennyson has often exploited the sexual overtones of similar scenes where a mediator discovers his beloved to be "Other" than he had imagined her: the discoveries of Cadrilla's engagement, of Maud's wealthy lover, of Guinevere's adultery, of Annie's bigamy. The self-consciously oedipal progression of this scene, however, is reinforced by a multitude of details: Pelleas' naiveté, his apparent lack of any parents, his stance before Ettarre's castle like a hurt child pleading for his mother, his acceptance of Gawain's paternal advice, his discovery of the primal scene itself, even his surrender of his sword. Instead of dramatizing Pelleas' awakening into the world of sexual experience, the scene reconstructs the basis for childhood neurosis.

This infantile regression undercuts Pelleas' attempt to renounce mediation for the power of the Other. By renouncing his passion for Ettarre, by dismissing the body itself as only a hollow shell, he tries to transform himself into a preternatural voice. He identifies himself to Lancelot first as a scourge and then as a personification: "I am wrath and shame and hate and evil fame" (l. 556). But the body he has rejected still has weight enough to make him probably the worst rider in Arthurian literature. As he is introduced, we remember, even the heat of the sun nearly unhorses him. Here exhaustion pulls him off his "weary steed" and leaves him helpless under Lancelot's foot. Finally, as the Red Knight in "The Last Tournament," he lets drink cast him "heavily to the swamp" in a slow-motion fall upon which Tennyson lavishes six lines of mock-epic simile.

His grotesque failure to "blaze the crime of Lancelot and the Queen" may suggest that he dismisses too quickly both the realm and the two figures he holds responsible for its demise. While Lancelot and Guinevere remain more dangerously Other than either Pelleas or Ettarre, they also remain more genuinely human. Tennyson's description of Lancelot as "warm with a gracious parting from the Queen" seems to equate the two couples; yet as their adultery affirms the physical body which Pelleas has tried to deny in himself, so their generosity allows them to transcend Pelleas' sterile dichotomy of true and false.[24] Perhaps because his guilt craves exposure, Lancelot proves himself more magnanimous than Pelleas can be vengeful:

> Lancelot, with his heel upon the fallen,
> Rolling his eyes, a moment stood, then spake:
> "Rise, weakling; I am Lancelot; say thy say."
>
>   (ll. 568–70)

Guinevere, though unwitting, opens herself to the same slander: "Or hast thou other griefs? If I, the Queen, / May help them, loose thy tongue, and let me know." (ll. 587–88).

With the exception of these two figures, a story redolent of the nostalgic passion in the 1859 *Idylls* is here told by a narrative voice chastened and coarsened by the symbolic struggles of "The Holy Grail" and the "Coming." Whether we identify this voice as Arthur's, or Tennyson's, or that of some authorial presence fusing the two, we must admit that the characters, setting, and plot of the resulting idyll all combine to deny the reality of its own fictional present. Constantly challenged by the artificiality of the narrative surface, this reality takes refuge within individual metaphors and individual incidents.

Eliot's recognition of the indissoluble link between words and meaning in Tennyson is transformed here into a tyranny of vehicle over tenor. In all of Pelleas' fiery visions, both early and late, the reality of both perceiver and perceived are burned away by the intensity of the visions themselves. Characters win this intensity only in brief moments when the rules of their particular game grow uncertain. Pelleas wins it when Ettarre's language finally shatters his image of her:

> if ye love me not,
> I cannot bear to dream you so forsworn:
> I had liefer ye were worthy of my love,
> Than to be loved again of you—farewell.
>
> (ll. 291–94)

And as he reevaluates his love, Ettarre simultaneously reevaluates her rejection: "In him / A something . . . / Seemed my reproach" (ll. 301–3). But the narrative structure offers no scope for such perceptions, and they wither just as quickly as Pelleas' early association with natural vitality.

As the games played by these characters collapse on each other, so the final scene collapses into a more tangled net of ironies than those which concluded "Elaine." Pelleas charges in to destroy his betrayers, is permitted by both to speak, and then can only hiss out an admission of his own psychic impotence: "I have no sword" (l. 570). Although Lancelot and Guinevere will this exposure, they suddenly find themselves reprieved. Although reprieved, they become all the more certain of some "dolorous day to be."[25] With Arthur either absent or withdrawn to the symbolic fringes of the poem, these two figures embody both the source of Camelot's ruin and the one set of human values which makes it worth preserving. Even in their brief appearance, they shape a passionate, pathetic human drama against which all other losses in the poem must be measured.

"The Passing of Arthur"

As our original study of the "Morte" has established, Tennyson always saw Arthur's story as both very important and very vulnerable. Hence Sterling's criticism that "the miraculous legend of 'Excalibur' does not come very near to us" (*Poems*, II, 4) struck at Tennyson's tacit claim that in all its forms the story portrayed an ambiguous encounter with an equally ambiguous Other: the "Morte" was to have presented two individuals transcending loss and death; "The Epic" was to have presented the means by which modern culture could confront change; the projected Arthurian poem was to have presented a golden age continually passing and yet continually recreated in art.

Although the reviews challenged all these interdependent assumptions, the immediate acclaim of the 1859 *Idylls* must have bolstered Tennyson's shaky confidence that the original "Morte" had indeed captured something "miraculous." Yet if time had validated it as a conclusion to the Arthurian story, time had also drastically altered the nature of the story to be concluded.[26] When asked why he had not already linked the "Morte" and the *Idylls*, Tennyson countered, "I could hardly light upon a finer close than that ghost-like passing away of the King" at the end of "Guinevere."[27] His real problem, however, arose from the fact that the two endings had very little in common.

In the "Morte" Arthur is finitely, almost pathetically human; in "Guinevere" his speech remained so—yet as he renounced the Queen,

> The moony vapour rolling round the King,
> Who seemed the phantom of a giant in it,
> Enwound him fold by fold, and made him gray
> And grayer, till himself became as mist
> Before her, moving ghostlike to his doom.
>
> (ll. 597–601)

In the full moon of the "Morte," by contrast, he can see his desolate surroundings all too clearly. In "Guinevere" his past failures overwhelmed him; he told her that he had lost not just his followers but his authority, his code, his purpose, and in her his only link with the physical world. The doom to which he moved became irrelevant because he had already suffered it. In the "Morte" he has a goal, but he wins our conviction only through his own realization that the "Arthurian" realm has grown as distant from him is it is from us.

With the inclusion of the "Grail," the "Coming," and "Pelleas" in 1869, Arthur's relation to the "Morte" grew, if possible, more confusing. Reed argues (p. 110) that the 1869 frame of the "Passing" transfers the focus of the "Morte" from the death of "the old order" to that of each individual. We can account for this shift without recourse to allegory by recalling Arthur's newly defined role of mediator between poet and poem. This role in turn may mitigate the bleak finality of "Guinevere." If Arthur has acknowledged that both Guinevere and the Grail have blurred the categories of mediator and Other, if he has defined his order, his code, and his marriage as institutions doomed to fail, then their doom may no longer presuppose his own.

Yet Arthur's absence as a mediator within "Pelleas" brings Tennyson to reexamine the causes of this failure within the new frame of the "Passing." Here Arthur is made to discover that the manifestations of the Other opposing him have grown both very threatening and very blurred. In a manuscript speech, possibly from 1862, Modred borrows the rhetoric and reasons of a Shakespearean villain to rally his troops against Arthur.[28] But as early as "Guinevere" Modred was compared first to an innocuous green caterpillar and then to inanimate nature, "a little bitter pool about a stone / On the bare coast" (ll. 51–52). By the time of the "Coming," his treason is measured in terms of its cost to him: he "struck for the throne, and striking found his doom" (l. 324).[29]

We can trace Tennyson's ongoing exploration of Arthur's failure, but not from a manuscript. Perhaps because no one wanted to admit that Tennyson was cannibalizing his own poetry, both the *Memoir* and Emily's *Journal* are strangely quiet about the "Passing." We know only that both it and "Pelleas" appear in an early trial proof of the *Holy Grail* volume (2104), now in the Ashley Library of the British Museum. Fortunately this volume contains a relatively early stage of the "Passing"; all but one of the extant manuscript fragments, though cut up like those of the other 1869 idylls, clearly develop additions to the trial proof.

Absent from this proof is roughly a quarter of the frame in which Tennyson would enclose the old "Morte": Arthur's epistemological doubts (ll. 6–28),[30] Bedivere's pledge of loyalty after Gawain's dream (ll. 50–64), Arthur's pessimistic contrast between present gloom and past glory (ll. 65–78), Bedivere's recollection of Merlin's rhyme (ll. 441–45),[31] and finally Bedivere's recognition of the three queens and his intimation that Arthur was being received in the spiritual city (ll. 452–62). Lacking all these later additions, the Ashley proof of the idyll represents more than another layer in an already well-layered poem. It represents a pivotal stage in Tennyson's ongoing confrontation with King Arthur.

The one recently discovered manuscript which predates the Ashley proof identifies the Battle in the Mist as the locus of Arthur's failure as a mediator. The fragment suggests that Tennyson originally planned to move directly to the battle on lines 8off. from the opening five-line frame establishing Bedivere as narrator.[32] In any context this battle portrays what Buckler describes (p. 38) as "human potential on a collision course with totally dehumanized meaninglessness." But in the early drafts it also stands as a brilliant transition from the mists of "Guinevere" to the desolate clarity of the "Morte": the wind "blew / The mist aside, . . . and the pale King glanced across the field / Of battle, but no man was moving there" (ll. 124–27).

What Arthur sees, the now-complete domination of the human by the impersonal sea, forces him to admit confusion for the first time in the Ashley proof. Bedivere reconfirms his blindness to Arthur's dilemma by urging him to pretend that he can still confront a single human embodiment of the Other: "He that brought / The heathen back among us, yonder stands, / Modred, unharmed, the traitor of thine house" (ll. 151–53). Arthur denies Bedivere's description of Modred as his ultimate enemy ("My house has been my doom"), but then proceeds to act on Bedivere's advice: "One last act of kinghood shalt thou see / Yet, ere I pass" (ll. 163–64). Their mutual destruction merely encompasses this action within the mutual carnage of the Battle in the Mist.

Such non sequiturs, in turn, may have convinced Tennyson to add still more soliloquies and dialogues to later drafts of the "Passing." He had confronted an equally impersonal flux in the late-added sections 54–56 of *In Memoriam*. There he discovered he could, in fact had to confront it as a female personification. Here the added predawn musings allow Arthur to delimit another apparently impersonal Other in much the same way. They allow him, now as coauthor of his poem, to ask whether the approaching battle is not only his own responsibility but in some sense his own imaginative creation.

In the 1873 addition, Arthur laments that he has now lost God "in his ways with men" (l. 11). As a consequence, the "deathwhite mist" of the battle remains the same "haze, which ever since I saw / One lying in the dust at Almesbury, / Hath folded in the passes of the world" (ll. 76–78). And the confusion of the battle, where "friend slew friend not knowing whom he slew" (l. 101), now merely projects Arthur's own confusion about the identity of friend and foe: "The king who fights his people fights himself. . . . the stroke / That strikes them dead is as my death to me" (ll. 72–74).

In this last admission, I think, Arthur acknowledges that his end must somehow redefine his relation to both his realm and his poem. In so doing he reinterprets the 1833 "Morte" once again. It now becomes a test of whether he, as a failed mediator, can persuade some other mediator to transform his own death into a "passing." Within it, he can transform his "one last act of kinghood" from a futile attack upon Modred into a demand for some sign of obedience from Bedivere. Tennyson's new frame for the "Morte" has certainly reaffirmed Bedivere's loyalty; yet as Kincaid pointed out the obtuseness of his birth narrative, so Hair (p. 220–22) points out the obtuseness of his exhortation, "Arise, go forth, and conquer as of old" (l. 64). Kincaid may be too harsh in claiming that the *Idylls* must end in irony because Bedivere is too stupid to understand anything of Arthur's passing.[33] Yet the most obvious of Tennyson's "faint Homeric echoes," the repeated epithet "bold Sir Bedivere," does come to imply that very little else can be said of him.

Whereas in the "Morte" both characters only *appeared* as Other to their partners, here Bedivere's opaque obtuseness has turned him into a more frightening agent of the Other than Modred himself. When he denies Arthur's faith that he will receive some sign from "the Powers who walk the world," Bedivere now contributes to the combined evidence of the landscape, the flow of history, and Arthur's own sense of failure. In so doing, however, he also restructures this personal argument into a symbolic recapitulation of Arthur's whole reign. Thus when Arthur affirms his vision against all these forces, when he asserts himself here as he has failed to do earlier, he can then implicitly contradict his own admission that "authority forgets a dying king." By refusing to accept the "water lapping on the crag" until it has been transformed into the mediating Lady of the Lake, Arthur can win for himself the reprieve which eluded his realm in "The Holy Grail."[34]

To what extent, however, does Arthur's personal salvation mediate between Bedivere and the "strange faces, other minds" which he must now confront? Although Kincaid dismisses the whole idyll as the narrative of a "sputtering old man,"[35] Buckler reinterprets Bedivere, somewhat more kindly (p. 26), as "a loyal geriatric voice, sobered by the events but not disconsolate." In the Ashley proof, Bedivere learns some means of confronting the naturalistic Other which has confronted Arthur in the opening section of this same draft. He sees that the entropy which has destroyed the realm is itself only part of a larger seasonal cycle. He also realizes that the sea, "this great voice that shakes the world" (l. 139), is also "the great deep" which once gave birth to Arthur and has now taken him back.

In the final additions, however, Bedivere must come to terms with Arthur's human mission. He sees that the three appendages to Arthur's coronation have indeed taken on life to "help him at his need." He also hears "sounds, as if some fair city were one voice / Around a king returning from his wars" (ll. 460–61). The Ashley proof had left unchallenged Bedivere's faith that "after healing of his grievous wound / He comes again" (ll. 450–51); it had thus reinforced the conception of Arthur's passing which Tennyson had described as early as the 1832 "Palace of Art." In the final version, however, Bedivere is made to realize that Arthur's final home is not Camelot but his own equivalent of Galahad's spiritual city. Bedivere has now lost Arthur just as irrevocably as he had Excalibur.

What *is* left him we are told in the opening frame to the idyll:

> That story which the bold Sir Bedivere,
> First made and latest left of all the knights,
> Told, when the man was no more than a voice
> In the white winter of his age, to those
> With whom he dwelt, new faces, other minds.
>
> (ll. 1–5)

This passage, for me, refutes Kincaid's claims about the poem's nihilism. We may not know which specific facts about Arthur or his destiny Bedivere has learned—what he *has* learned is "that story."[36] He had first asked, "What record or what relic of my lord / Should be to aftertime, but empty breath" (ll. 266–67). Now he finds himself not just with Arthur's story but in Arthur's shoes, trying to mediate between the shattered sanctuary of Camelot and what he defined in the "Morte" as his own vision of the Other. Since he now tells the story to these "new" (no longer "strange") faces, he may have found faith in its mediating power. In that faith, according to Buckler (p. 36), he becomes "our symbolic surrogate."

This renewal of faith in mediation parallels Tennyson's own. Like the wounded Arthur, he affirmed his vision of some transcendent order in the 1833 "Morte," but as Bedivere hid Excalibur, so in 1842 he hid the poem within modern dress to diffuse the criticism of a hostile audience. Thirty-six years later he offers a more vulnerable revision of it to an audience very different but perhaps equally hostile. As Arthur came to trust his vision against all evidence, as Bedivere came to proclaim it to all hearers, so Tennyson here comes to reaffirm the universality of this, his own seminal vision of the Arthurian story.[37]

CHAPTER ELEVEN

The Last Idylls

Both "Gareth and Lynette" and "The Last Tournament" have their genesis well before the composition of the 1869 idylls. In 1859 Tennyson read the chapters in Malory "where Launcelot behaves so courteously & Sir Palamedes so uncourteously & where Arthur goes to see La Beale Isoude (with a view to a poem on Tristram and Isolt)."[1] And in 1861 he read the tale of Sir Gareth or Beaumains. The ten- to thirteen-year gap which elapsed before the actual composition of either poem can be explained partially by the more pressing problem of the Grail, but partially too by the intransigence of both of these stories.

The particular episode mentioned from the Tristram story seems curiously peripheral both to the main action and to any use Tennyson could possibly make of it. Within these chapters (X, 71–73 or perhaps 71–78), Sir Lancelot pardons Palamedes for slaying his horse because he has fought out of a blinding passion for Isolt and "wel I wote that loue is a grete maystresse" (X, 71). Isolt's beauty is such that even Arthur is driven to disguise himself and visit her. Tristram recognizes Arthur by his willingness to forsake the trappings of royalty, "for all knyztes maye lerne to be a knyghte of hym" (X, 73). Five chapters later, in an episode perhaps included within the section referred to, Arthur again visits Isolt and declares, "now I dar say ye are the fayrest that euer I sawe, & sir Tristram is as fayrr and as good a knyghte as ony that I knowe, therfor me beseemeth ye are wel besett to gyders" (X, 78).

All these episodes presumably attracted Tennyson because they show Lancelot and Arthur as uniformly gracious. Yet besides lacking any narrative structure, they war against the ethos of even the 1859 *Idylls*. Most obviously, Arthur can hardly offer aesthetic justification for the liaison of Tristram and Isolt when he is about to excoriate his own wife for similar behavior. Neither can he be celebrated for slipping out of the palace and stealing glances at a woman whom he acknowledges to be more beautiful than the wife Tennyson portrays as "fairest of all flesh on earth."

The story of Beaumains had greater unity and greater consonance with the 1859 idylls, but it still demanded more extensive alteration than Tennyson was willing to spend on it in 1861. He could not possibly salvage the efforts of Beaumains (Gareth) and Lady Lyonors to consummate their love before they could be decorously married. But even Beaumains' disguised (and unexplained) arrival at court is celebrated by all, including the narrator, as an inventive means of self-expression. The king finally proves his perspicacity by recognizing Gareth's uncalloused and hence aristocratic hands despite his peasant dress. Neither genetic nobility nor anarchic self-expression nor royal whimsy had any place within Tennyson's Camelot.

The recalcitrance of these stories may explain his delay in returning to them until after the publication of the 1869 idylls; to discover why he returned to them at all we need to speculate on what new gaps he perceived in his ad hoc epic. The "Passing" had examined Arthur's own fate, had secured him some hints of a continuing existence within whatever metaphysical reality surrounded the fictive reality of his realm; yet Arthur's pointedly solitary escape had left his role within this realm even more in doubt. In the 1869 idylls as a whole, this role had positioned him midway between mediator and authorial presence. In composing these two stories simultaneously, therefore, Tennyson set them as complementary responses to the paradox inherent in Arthur's dual allegiance. "Beaumains" is set early enough to show that Arthur, as an active mediator, can transfer his power to a court still open enough to receive it; "Tristram" is set late enough to show that Arthur, now too noble for a hopelessly debased court, has withdrawn into the authorial presence to become an implicit rebuke to the remaining characters. If neither finished idyll completely supports its thesis, Arthur's two roles may simply have proven inseparable for both him and his creator.

"Gareth and Lynette" and "The Last Tournament"

By 1869 Tennyson seems to have settled on reshaping "Beaumains" into a reply to "Pelleas," an idealistic young knight's encounter not with a jaded court but with an actively mediating Arthur. Tennyson may have conceived Gareth as "a pattern [of?] youth for his boys," as he characterized him when presenting the poem's opening to Emily on October 7, 1869.[2] Yet a draft of this same opening in Harvard Notebook 40 suggests that Gareth's idealism had to confront an authorial bitterness which "Pelleas" had not fully expressed. In fact Tennyson was engaged in a determined though ultimately

futile effort to link both the Gareth and Tristram stories with a subplot in-
volving Bellicent, Lamorack, Modred, and ultimately Arthur himself.

The sketch sends Gareth to Camelot to spy on Lancelot and Guinevere:
for Bellicent "had been long haunted by a passion for Sir Lamorack had
yielded herself to him & thus dishonoured her house. But now she said to
herself . . . if Guinevere have sinned the sin will be hers & and my shame
covered by her shame" (Pfordresher, pp. 127–28). Joan Hartman, in her fine
source study of the idyll, points out the unsuitability of these motives in a
character who has already been honored with the most supernatural account
of Arthur's origins in the "Coming";[3] yet Tennyson, as we shall see, had an
even more sordid future in store for her.

The prose draft immediately moves Gareth from this seamy home life to
the city of the "fairy king," built to the "music" of his superhuman ideals.[4]
This, Tennyson seems to realize, represents his first and last chance to dramatize Arthur's power as a mediator. Arthur presented his code to
Guinevere only after it had failed; within the "Coming" the knights, though
properly imprinted with "a momentary likeness of the King" (l. 270), had no
opportunity to act upon it; Pelleas adopted a parody of Arthur's code almost
by default; within the "Passing," the "first made and latest left of all the
knights" (l. 2) had to be coerced into obedience. Hence Tennyson's successive revisions within this draft, like those within the "Coming," grope toward
a portrait of Arthur which is neither subjective nor locked in hopeless struggle against some pervasive corruption. Gareth first sees Arthur when he is
"speaking to his knights and rendering thanks for such service as they had
done him in subduing the heathen" (Pfordresher, p. 133). Yet in the midst of
Gareth's "kitchen vassalage," Tennyson breaks off his prose draft and begins
to versify the beginning. Only then does he replace the reference to the
heathen wars with Mark's request to join the Round Table, with the widows'
requests for justice, and with Arthur's scheme to carve the deeds of his
knights on their shields.[5]

In these revisions, however, Tennyson lays himself open to Culler's dismissal of the whole idyll (p. 221) for its "Boy Scout character." Arthur does
indeed act less like a king than like a scoutmaster. In fact he may act worse
still. Ryals' seminal article sees him attempting throughout the *Idylls* to impose his will upon his followers,[6] yet because his attempts within earlier-
written idylls have either failed or appeared after the fact, this one offers him
his most dangerous opportunity to reassume the role of a divine or paternal
Other. It also offers Tennyson a revealing opportunity to explore the effects
of this willfulness. In particular he must show that Gareth's loyalty to the

now-militant king can fulfill him as both a knight and a man. When Tennyson finally composed the quest, he claimed to be baffled by the "snip-snap" of dialogue.[7] At this stage, however, he appears baffled by the difficulty of shaping any quest to effect these transformations within Gareth.

In breaking off all work on the idyll at this point, Tennyson may be questioning whether the recipients of Arthur's power could win the same autonomy won by other mediators. In fact he moves from a celebration of this charisma to a repudiation of it as "the wholesome madness of an hour"; near the end of this same notebook appears the germ of his Tristram project. Within the Gareth fragment, Modred's shield and Mark's gift may have been added to offer Arthur some token opposition; within the Tristram fragment, the Other reigns supreme. Here Dagonet, in front of Arthur's hall, observes the passing of Bellicent's sons (Gawain, Modred, and Gaheris) and of Lamorack: "his head was down and his heart darkend for his old love Queen Bellicent was dead" (Pfordresher, p. 869). When Tristram joins Dagonet, the dwarf pretends to praise them all for keeping "the vows of the king . . . for ye have all lain by Queens, so that no King knoweth his own son."

While no background can salvage this muddled gesture at irony, Notebook 40 and Malory together can suggest what Tennyson may have meant by it. While its similarity to the completed "Last Tournament" leads us to focus on Dagonet and Tristram, the fragment itself points back first to Bellicent's shame in the Gareth draft and then to Malory's account of Lamorak and Morgause (Lot's wife in Malory). The two families are already at odds, for Lamorak's father, King Pellinore, killed Lot, and then Lot's son Gawain killed him (II, 10). Lamorak nevertheless makes several public professions of his love for Morgause, and she reciprocates (IX, 13). When her sons learn of the affair, Gaheris surprises them in bed together and cuts off his mother's head (X, 24). Although the entire court is horrified, the brothers, undaunted, ambush Lamorak and "sir Mordred gaf hym his dethes wound, behynde hym at his bak, and alle to hewe hym" (X, 54, 58). In Malory, of course, this episode only exacerbates the family quarrel which will turn Arthur's own kin first against Lancelot and then against Arthur himself.

A genealogy of both families in an early notebook (H.Nbk 16) establishes that Tennyson knew Malory's account of the feud, and in this fragment the three brothers and Lamorack do seem to be returning from the murder of Bellicent. In Malory, however, Dagonet's statements, "ye have all lain by Queens" and "no King knoweth his own son," would have to apply to Arthur and the bastard son, Mordred, whom he had fathered on Morgause. Yet

Tennyson has been moving in the opposite direction. After the first draft of
"Guinevere" (T.Nbk 39), he deleted his reference to Modred as "nearest to
the king, his heir / And nephew" (Pfordresher, pp. 913–14). In 1869 he
made Arthur reject Modred as "no kin of mine." In that same year he expanded the Novice's reference to Arthur's sea birth with Bellicent's account
of the differences between her family and Arthur.

This background, together with the following canceled account of the Last
Tournament itself, shows that Dagonet's reference to queens and sons is one
more attempt to distance Arthur from Modred:

> And once the laces of a helmet burst
> And showed him like a vermin in its hole,
> Modred, a narrow face; & some young knight
> (So rife a tounguester tost about the court
> The name of Bellicent and Lamorack) said
> Look whether he have not tumbled his own son
> The happy sire!
>
> (Pfordresher, p. 878)[8]

Through this episode, the Dagonet fragment, and perhaps even the opening
sketch for "Gareth," Tennyson is trying to establish Lamorack as Modred's
father. Now that he has drawn Arthur back into the authorial presence, Tennyson is in effect abandoning the realm to Lamorack and his fellows as a
collective embodiment of the Other.

Malory's Lamorak, of course, does not sleep with Morgause until after her
children have grown; nor does he display qualities which might account for
Modred's "motiveless malignity." These problems, and that of preserving
Bellicent as a reliable witness, finally forced Tennyson to jettison the whole
Lamorack subplot. Lamorack himself, however, is simply reincarnated in
Tristram. As such he acts as a literal catalyst, a figure absent from the final
idyll but necessary for its production. The Other that Tennyson wanted to
confront here manifested itself in an amoral naturalism, and no character in
Malory manifested naturalism more blatantly than his Sir Lamorak.

In one of Malory's more grotesque episodes, Lamorak redirects to Mark's
court a magic horn from which only chaste women can drink without spilling
(VIII, 34). When Isolt and two hundred others fail the test, it is Tristram who
fights Lamorak to avenge this unknightly action (VIII, 38).[9] In another context Lamorak refuses to fight Lancelot over the relative merits of Guinevere
and Morgause, "For euery man thynketh his owne lady fayrest, and though I
prayse the lady, that I loue moost, ye shold not be wrothe" (IX, 14). These

words foreshadow both the advice Tennyson's Tristram offers to Lancelot, "Be happy in thy fair queen as I in mine" (l. 204), and his salute to those assembled at the tournament: "Fair damsels, each to him who worships each / Sole Queen of Beauty and of love" (ll. 207–8). Finally, though Tennyson probably drew the circumstances of Tristram's death from the one-sentence reference in Malory, he may well have drawn much of its emotional intensity from the beheading of Morgause and the subsequent ambush of Lamorak. These scenes give perhaps Malory's closest parallel to Tennyson's portrait of blind sexual passion manipulated and betrayed by inhuman cunning.

If we then ask why Tennyson transferred the traits of one character to another, several reasons suggest themselves: first, he had made, as we saw, at least a private commitment to a Tristram idyll; second, Tristram was a far more famous character than Lamorack; third, curiously enough, the romantic Tristram story later popularized by Bédier was not well known, and the Malory account that Tennyson used is a particularly shapeless succession of jousts and battles; fourth, as Rosenberg points out (p. 116), he had already borrowed Tristram's embassy and much of its attendant intensity for Lancelot and Guinevere; fifth and probably most important, he saw naturalism as a late, decadent, and dehumanizing world view, one which eroded human values and the resulting distinctions between individuals. Because both Lamorak and Tristram see love as subjective and arbitrary, as embodiments of the Other they offer little to choose between them.

Having established an antagonist too faceless to be either heroic or tragic, Tennyson had still to justify Arthur's withdrawal into the authorial presence. To show that Arthur is simply too noble to function within a naturalistic world, Tennyson reinterprets several of the King's actions in the "Gareth" draft, giving them ironic sequels in "The Last Tournament."[10] In the prose draft, we remember, Arthur thanks his knights for their support in the heathen wars; this same scene is pushed into irrelevance by Tristram's reverie of *his* first glimpse of Arthur:

> when first
> I rode from our rough Lyonnesse, and beheld
> That victor of the Pagan throned in hall . . .
> he seemed to me no man,
> But Michael trampling Satan; so I sware,
> Being amazed: but this went by—The vows—
> O ay—the wholesome madness of an hour.
>
> (ll. 658–60, 667–70)

This dismissal of Arthur's vows, in turn, fulfills the part of Merlin's prediction left unfulfilled by Gareth: "The King will swear thee to vows which it is a shame that a man should not swear & which yet no man can keep" (Pfordresher, p. 132).

Later in the "Gareth" draft, Lynette challenges the King to offer her a knight because "there be thieves & and bandits enow left to ruin a realm & everyone that has a tower is King for a league round, nor canst thou be verily & indeed King till these be driven as thou hast driven the heathen" (Pfordresher, p. 134). Arthur replies, "I rest not nor my knights & so they keep their vows but for a year the whole realm will be safe as the centre of this hall." Much as in the "Coming," Arthur's promises are fulfilled in letter but broken (like the King himself) in spirit. In "The Last Tournament," Arthur dismisses the Red Knight's challenge as the futile gesture of the forces of anarchy, forces which

> Make their last head like Satan in the North.
> My younger knights . . .
> Move with me toward their quelling, which achieved,
> The loneliest ways are safe from shore to shore.
>
> (ll. 98–99, 101–2)

And with the Red Knight's followers slaughtered and their tower fired, "all the ways were safe from shore to shore, / But in the heart of Arthur pain was lord" (ll. 484–85).[11]

A third, more general parallel between the Gareth and Tristram stories may measure the effect of Arthur's withdrawal upon the other characters. Notebook 40 failed to show how the idealistic Gareth could put Arthur's mediating power into action. In the jaded yet still idealistic Dagonet, however, Tennyson may have created an ironic sequel to Gareth himself. Tennyson had a right to be pleased with the originality of this creation,[12] for he could draw scant inspiration from Malory. There Dagonet is a stock fool whom Tristram once throws into a well in a fit of love-madness. In Tennyson, however, Dagonet could show that Arthur's vows had ennobled him in despite of blood, youth, innocence, physical strength, and beauty: "I wallowed, then I washed— / I have had my day and my philosophies— / And thank the Lord I am King Arthur's fool" (ll. 318–20).[13] The paradoxes within this nobility, however, suggest that the lack of Arthur's active mediation has denied his realm any more conventional heroism.

We are undoubtedly missing manuscripts of "The Last Tournament" between the prose fragment and the virtually complete draft held by the Berg Library. Even from this late draft, however, we can see that Tennyson's revisions were separating Arthur as moral norm from the ineffectual character within the idyll itself. In the Berg manuscript his first inklings of social disobedience were originally unmotivated. By prefacing them with Lancelot's suggestion that he and Arthur reverse roles, Tennyson transforms Arthur's "Is it then so well?" from an attack on Lancelot to an ironic rejection of the only piece of good advice he is offered in the entire poem.

In these same revisions, however, Tennyson works to show that the failure of Arthur's mediating power takes his fictional world down with him in a Celtic Götterdämmerung. Without this power, the remaining characters not only fail, but in failing fall lower than the mock-heroic Dagonet. To this end Tennyson weaves "The Last Tournament" into a tapestry of disquieting discoveries. Several characters begin by trying to effect some new escape from their world; all discover that they cannot survive without the very mediation they have long ago rejected. While exploiting the social anarchy of Malory's Tristram story, Tennyson exposes its ebullient spontaneity as a naive and hence doomed escape from the blind causality of a naturalistic cosmos.

If naturalism undercuts heroism, however, it also undercuts the villainy of these erstwhile agents of the Other.[14] In Tennyson's revisions, their discoveries grow increasingly poignant and increasingly similar. This similarity not only binds them together, it binds them to an equally deluded Arthur in a curious brotherhood of grief. The completed idyll thus comes to dramatize Arthur's admission in the "Passing" that "the king that fights his people fights himself."

Within the Berg manuscript, for example, Arthur's doomed campaign against the Red Knight originally appeared in its more logical narrative sequence between the arrival of the maimed churl and the tournament itself. By moving it into the sequence of Tristram's dream, Tennyson links Arthur's pathetic failure to reestablish moral order with Tristram's failure to escape Isolt by fleeing to her namesake.[15] The poet also intensifies this entrapment through deletion. In several canceled passages within the Berg manuscript, Tristram appeases Isolt by comparing their love to Arthur's ideals. When Tennyson eliminates even this via media between lust and fidelity, he shows Tristram to be driven by a fatal desire he can neither explain nor control.

From this perspective, an ostensibly tawdry story of adultery discovered and avenged becomes as pathetic a *Liebestod* as Matthew Arnold's.[16] For all his protestations to the contrary, Tristram is drawn back to his first love against his will and his better judgment. Both he and Isolt are obsessed with transience—incapable of believing in either an enduring love or an existence without it. Though she demands that he "swear to me thou wilt love me even when old, / Gray-haired, and past desire, and in despair" (ll. 647–48), Isolt admits that in his absence death seemed "sweeter than all memories of thee, / Deeper than any yearnings after thee" (ll. 581–82). Finally Tristram calls for drink as the only means to a commitment he fears to make while sober. Although his murder obviates the need for such self-deception, this last meeting is itself an unconscious suicide.[17] Like Arnold's lovers, Tennyson's seem to court death as preferable to any other conceivable future. In this yearning, they prefigure the Arthur of "Guinevere," whose own love has also grown into an obsession. His premonition of his wife's "ghostly footfall echoing on the stair" (l. 504) brings him to see life itself as something he cannot "greatly care to lose" (l. 492).

Other additions within the Berg manuscript show Tennyson enclosing Lancelot and Guinevere within a more complex temporal trap. When he parallels Lancelot's failure to control the joust with Guinevere's failure to control the ball, he superimposes on them earlier patterns from "Elaine" and "Guinevere." The lovers are again forced to suffer the consequences of their own code. Yet as we learn from the darkened window at the end of this idyll, the whole action fits within the opening flashback of "Guinevere," within the time when the Queen is haunted by guilty dreams and both are struggling to break off the affair. Rather than mediating almost against their wills, as in these earlier idylls, both join with Arthur in trying to preserve at least the hollow shell of Camelot. When both also join with him in defeat, Tennyson must acknowledge the parallel: in the "bosom" of Guinevere and the "heart" of Arthur, "pain was lord" (ll. 239, 435).

If we grant sufficient weight to this last metaphor, we can argue that here in "The Last Tournament," well before his return of Excalibur in the "Passing," Arthur has already renounced the kingship. In acknowledging the now-universal sovereignty of pain, he also acknowledges his bond, not just with his queen, but with all his former subjects. When all actions, obedient or rebellious, lead to a tissue of irony, the norms of authorial presence lapse into irrelevance and the three categories within Tennyson's model collapse into one. At the end of the idyll, when Dagonet and his music are reduced to a "sobbing" voice, he too binds himself with Arthur and both pairs of lovers in this increasingly inclusive fellowship. As Tristram produces the ruby carcanet, Isolt wishfully proclaims it "the collar of some Order, which our King / Hath newly founded, all for thee" (ll. 735–36). Tristram reinterprets it as his "last / Love-offering and peace-offering unto thee" (ll. 741–42). But with Mark's appearance, as if in response to the word "last," all who come in contact with the carcanet find themselves bound together in the new "Order" of suffering.

It can be no accident that the story of the carcanet, the tree, and the eagle-fostered child finds itself foreshadowed in Tennyson's subsequent revisions of "Gareth." Here, however, it appears as yet another mythic origin for Arthur, found now "on Caer-Eryri's highest . . . , / A naked babe" (ll. 490–91). This parallel, along with the reference to Arthur's harp by both Gareth and Dagonet, suggests that Tennyson was trying to read backwards from the end of his story to its beginning. Yet the same device which had undermined the "Coming" could not succeed in salvaging "Gareth" or reinstating Tennyson's model to its former integrity.

The completed Gareth idyll has never been considered a complete success. But if we recognize the complexity of the problems Tennyson faced within it, we may gain more respect for his solutions. To reaffirm the power of Arthur's mediation, Tennyson makes him less acquiescent than he appeared in Malory or even in Tennyson's own prose draft. Arthur now learns from Bellicent of Gareth's disguise, persuades him to let Lancelot in on the ruse, yields "half unwillingly" to the quest, and finally sends Lancelot after him for protection. Tennyson here has it both ways: while softening Arthur's apparently arbitrary choice, he relieves him of that delusion of control which "The Last Tournament" exposed so mercilessly.

Tristram described Arthur's vows as

> the wholesome madness of an hour—
> They served their use, their time; for every knight
> Believed himself a greater than himself,
> And every follower eyed him as a God.
>   ("Last Tournament," ll. 670–73)

When Tennyson finally came to compose Gareth's quest, he could not show Arthur's power lasting any longer than "an hour," but he could show it as something more than "madness." He could show the young knight gradually coming to mediate more effectively than Arthur ever did in his own person. By doing the deed, "for the deed's sake," Gareth not only restores the category of mediator, he forces Lynette to revise her until-now fixed categories of "knight" and "knave." Where she at first holds Malory's conception of nobility as an inherited trait, she is finally saddened to learn of Gareth's identity: "but now, if knight, / The marvel dies, and leaves me fooled and tricked" (ll. 1219–20).

This much power Tennyson dramatizes well, but—like Lancelot—more than this he cannot. After the vow of "utter faithfulness in love," Arthur had demanded "uttermost obedience to the King" (l. 544). And while this idyll refuses to acknowledge it, the *Idylls* as a whole reiterate the truth of the biblical maxim that no man can serve two masters. Lynette, forsaking pride and selfishness, can quite convincingly yield herself to love, but Arthur, as Ryals points out, has compelled Gareth and all his followers to yield up their wills to him. At the poem's close, we are not surprised that Gareth marries Lynette instead of Malory's Lyonors; we are surprised that he marries anyone at all.

Besides this lack of emotional depth, the idyll has been criticized by Hartman (pp. 254–56) and others for the confusion within its symbolic levels. The brothers are "fools" to imitate "the war of Time against the soul of man" (l. 1168), yet Gareth must experience their allegory as real: in fighting Evening Star, "he seemed as one / That all in later, sadder age begins / To war against ill uses of a life" (ll. 1100–1102). Tennyson, as we saw in the prose drafts, was hard put to create a world both idealistic enough to make mediation possible and realistic enough to make it meaningful. He has failed to find a viable Other in Bellicent's adultery, Merlin's irony, Mark's hypocritical request, the widow's hatred, Modred's blank shield, even Lynette's scorn. Now Tennyson is forced to provide a partially realistic Other for his partially realistic mediator. As he has gradually dissociated Arthur from the narrative level of his story, Tennyson here opens some personal space for one of Arthur's followers. All the characters in "The Last Tournament" strove to open similar spaces of their own—but with Arthur's help Gareth keeps his open longer. This idyll, like Arthur's realm, is "built to music" and remains equally insubstantial. Yet here, at least, the music is audible to the sympathetic reader and not to Arthur's fool alone.

"Balin and Balan"

To some it may seem symptomatic that Tennyson finished his work on Arthur with an idyll so parenthetical to the poem's structure that he described it (*Poems*, III, 375) as an introduction to "Vivien." In the context of the themes and characters we have been tracing, however, this idyll stands as the most complex because the most synthetic. Tennyson had portrayed

Arthur as an active mediator within "Gareth" and as a normative presence outside the world of "The Last Tournament." Here he returned to the midpoint of Arthur's joint odysseys through the poem and through Tennyson's model.[18] Tennyson wrote "Balin," I think, to show this midpoint as Arthur's synthesis of both his roles; yet given Arthur's inherent need to embody his power within some secondary mediator, Tennyson had to find a candidate who stood midway between Gareth and Tristram: midway between blind obedience and open rebellion, midway between the allegorical world which Gareth vanquishes and the naturalistic world which vanquishes Tristram, midway between an image of the Other as trivial and a decay so pervasive that its center cannot be identified.

To embody all these contraries within a coherent story and a believable character, Tennyson turned once again to Malory. Yet the real strengths of Malory's Balin did not match the particular needs of Tennyson; as a result this idyll required a fifteen-year genesis and perhaps a greater variety of manuscript drafts than any before it. For clarity we can divide the resulting compositional mosaic into three clearly defined stages: (1) from the source in Malory to the prose sketch entitled "The Dolorous Stroke"; (2) from that sketch to the first continuous verse draft (Huntington 1323); and (3) from that draft to the printed text.

Where Tennyson had to move Gareth from the middle of Malory to the beginning of the *Idylls*, here he has to move Balin from the beginning to the middle. Malory's Balin embodies the youth of Arthur's realm; he is violent, impulsive, implicitly lower class—and Arthur, like his creator, comes to celebrate each of these qualities. Balin, for example, beheads one of the Ladies of the Lake but works off his punishment with similar recklessness. In some ways he sets the stage for the more established Arthurian heroes, planting a sword in a stone so that Lancelot can withdraw it, and accidentally striking Pellam with the holy spear so that Galahad can cure him.[19] Although Malory's Balin is constantly surrounded by martial and sexual violence, very little of it originates with him. His principal virtue is his determination to move through all this bloodshed until it finally reaches him. His tragic combat with his brother is no fault of either, only the perversity of a fate which entraps even the most resolute of Malory's heroes.

As early as "The Dolorous Stroke," Tennyson relocates this outer fate within Balin himself.[20] That Balin's once-impetuous nature has paralyzed him is clear from the opening of this prose draft. He and his brother sit like stones beside a fountain, hoping that if they unhorse enough knights, Arthur will notice them. Tennyson may have borrowed this scene from the one in Malory where the dying Balan tells how he had been forced to remain on an island, challenging every knight who passed (I, 43).[21] Yet by moving Balin's final condition to an initial one, Tennyson may imply that *his* hero can never act, except against himself, while away from Arthur.[22]

Even in this role, however, Balin shows the blind idealism of Gareth and Dagonet,[23] mediators through whom Arthur manifested his power within these last-written idylls. Like Arthur (and like Lancelot), Balin will settle for no beloved save Guinevere. Even Balin's nameless rage echoes that which drives Arthur to cry out "I loathe thee" to his prostrate wife. By riding out in disguise to overthrow the brothers, Arthur is reliving through them the same violent world of the past to which Balin longs to return.

To exorcise the inner demon he shares with Arthur, Balin turns to the court and its current leader, Lancelot. In so doing he actually reverses the Malory account in which he legitimizes Lancelot's authority.[24] In fleeing to Pellam's court, Tennyson's Balin again reverses Malory's time scheme. Instead of preparing for Galahad's future miracles, Balin finds himself surrounded by an order whose meaning lies hidden from him in the past. The ambivalence Tennyson showed toward medieval Catholicism in the "Grail" now seems to verge on open incredulity. Hearing the churls' tales of bleeding spears and invisible knights, "Sir Balin doubted him whether he could believe aught that they told him of Sir Garlon or aught else."[25]

As in the "Grail," however, Tennyson could not convincingly debunk the miraculous while affirming his own intimations of the unseen. Just as Arthur lives through Balin, the introspective Balin lives within a world of symbols which draw him away from Arthur's mediation. The domain of an Other far more ominous than the three "fools" in "Gareth," Pellam's court incorporates both rank credulity and cynical skepticism. Balan may be properly skeptical of its religious fakery, but it remains equally skeptical of Balin's claims for the queen. Because he refuses to acknowledge either the power of this Other or his own vulnerability to it, Balin murders the scandalmongering Garlon and rides away with the sacred spear. In assuming the allegorical role he thought he had destroyed, he reinterprets and reenacts the Dolorous Stroke itself.

In Vivien Tennyson works an even more complex transformation. He ostensibly planned the idyll to introduce a character who in Malory's tale appears only long enough to lose her head. Since he has already separated Nimue (the original of Vivien) and the Lady of the Lake, he here allows the Lady to solemnize the brothers' deaths with her "high song." Vivien may owe something to the mysterious woman in Malory who urges the brothers to fight and then seems grief-stricken at their deaths. In "The Dolorous Stroke," however, she appears at Arthur's court just before "Merlin and Vivien" is to begin. Here she offers a second interpretation of the Dolorous Stroke. Her scandal becomes the blow which not only killed the two brothers but "first shook to its base the stately order of the Table Round."[26]

When Tennyson reshaped this prose sketch for the first complete verse draft in Huntington manuscript 1323, he made two parallel but ultimately conflicting sets of changes. On the one hand, to a degree unusual with the *Idylls*, he tightened both the formal consistency of his plot and the realism of his social setting. Now Balin identifies his brother as his more rational half, and Balan, in his parting speech, warns his brother to see Arthur's ideals and not his violent self as his true identity. Balin's reinstatement, now described as a "woodland welcome," tries to reconcile his natural intensity with the social grace of Lancelot and Guinevere.

By adding their overheard dialogue in the garden, however, Tennyson undercuts both the integrity of this society and the realism with which he has so far described it. In their rather stilted botanical debate, the lovers fail to achieve the same sympathy and intensity that they achieve elsewhere. Instead they are made to embody, once again at midpoint, the world of their poem. No longer Arthur's sanctuary but not yet the domain of Tristram's naturalistic Other, this world lies uniquely vulnerable to the particular Other which opposes it. To the precise degree that the lovers at its center seem to transcend all human depravity, they invite this depravity to find its own image mirrored within them.

If Balin here equates Arthur's power with the grace of his court, the mistake is natural. Although Arthur has strongly identified with Balin, Balin is given no guidelines for identifying with him beyond the cryptic warning that "the crown is but the shadow of the King" (l. 199). Thus when Balin flees the implications of the garden scene, he does not ride off like Balan on a quest of Arthur's; instead he begins taking literally his brother's advice to see his "moods . . . [as] outer fiends, / Who leap at thee to tear thee" (ll. 137–39). Balan may have sought to strengthen his brother's sense of self by distancing its darker side, but in redefining psychological space as the physical domain of the Other, he has cast Balin into its power. By abandoning Arthur, Balin does not win the autonomy of Tennyson's other mediators; he only exchanges one form of psychological enslavement for another.

In a parallel set of manuscript additions, Tennyson actually begins to support Balin's growing faith in the reality of the Other. Now the attacking Garlon appears to him as an almost preternatural "light in armour." Next, searching to replace the sword broken in killing Garlon, Balin now discovers the relic-filled chapel, an incident from Malory (I, 40) which Tennyson had rejected in "The Dolorous Stroke." Now too, seen through Balin's eyes, all of Pellam's "wonders" regain their credibility. From this same perspective, Vivien comes to personify an Other eager to enlist the help of this would-be mediator. Now named, she ends a much fuller account of the lovers' tryst with the suggestion that Balin join with her in blackmailing them:

> And I have set thee now on vantage-ground
> And our great Queen when knowing that thou knowest
> Will fear thee, and so honour thee the more.
>
> (Pfordresher, p. 493)[27]

Even in the Huntington manuscript Vivien began to regain some of the power she won in her own idyll; between this draft and the printed text she receives even more of Tennyson's attention. The first revisions actually grant her so much importance that Tennyson must finally detach them from the beginning and end of "Balin" and combine them into a new introduction for "Merlin and Vivien."[28] Yet even after composing a new exposition given by Arthur's ambassadors, the poet continued to brood on Vivien. As late as the fair copy of "Balin" pasted together for the printers, he gave her a pagan song drawn both from rejected passages for the "Grail" and from an 1833 lyric originally assigned to Lancelot. In 1856 Tennyson opened the *Idylls* with Vivien's operational self-definition; here he concludes them by letting her formulate the relativism which will lead to "The Last Tournament" and the collapse of roles within his own model: "The fire of Heaven is not the flame of Hell."

To keep the reader from condoning Vivien's corruption of Balin, Tennyson needed some objective measure of his hero's subjective deterioration. His response to this problem, Balan, was little more than a cipher in "The Dolorous Stroke." While the successive drafts explored Balin's inner world, they also developed Balan as a double for his brother and a surrogate for both Arthur and his creator. With the addition of his speech of advice, Balan becomes the inner voice of Balin's conscience. With the addition of his specific quest, on the other hand, he undertakes the official, public counterpart of Balin's nightmare journey. When he engages Balin at the end, therefore, Balan can assert Arthur's mediating power against the web of bigotry, allegory, and miracle which Balin has substituted for it.

Tennyson's conflicting goals for these final revisions engender conflicting versions of the idyll's conclusion. Within this internecine struggle, moreover, truth and falsehood are just as hard to distinguish as they were in "Vivien." Vivien—though she has fabricated the lovers' tryst—is actually right; Balan—though he believes himself right—is actually wrong: Guinevere is hardly "pure as our true Mother." The fact that Balin needs this fiction signals that he remains psychologically weak; the fact that Balan must proclaim it may signal that his creator remains unable to control all the implications of his story.

This double failure may be caused by the presence of a particularly threatening Other, scandal. Its appearance within virtually all of the idylls might be explained by Tennyson's lifelong crusade to protect his own privacy. His obsession with it in "Balin," however, may betray as much fascination as outrage. The roles within both story and model collapse once again as characters find themselves simultaneously perpetrators and victims of scandal. Many of them have something of value they wish to protect: Lancelot and Guinevere their love, Balin his idealization of them, Pellam his relics, Vivien her mask of sincerity, Garlon his dual identity, Arthur his illusion of a loyal kingdom. Yet many of these same characters are driven to "see through" some other person or institution whose integrity disconcerts them. Garlon may initially personify scandal; yet the purpose of Balan's quest is to expose Garlon's black magic as simple murder. Pellam's court cannot countenance either Arthur's marriage ethic or Guinevere's ethic of courtly love; yet Arthur's demand for tribute implicitly compromises Pellam's ascetic isolation. Even Arthur's disguised sortie against the two brothers suggests that he cannot tolerate their claim that they are "mightier than all / In Arthur's court" (ll. 31–32). Though poor Balin finally takes Garlon's place as the personification of scandal, he is actually less interested in exposing others than is anyone else in the idyll—including its author.

In fact the ultimate source of scandal in this story may rest within Tennyson himself. In the Grail idyll and the later *Queen Mary*, he felt driven to see through the claims and trappings of Catholicism. Throughout the *Idylls*, he has seen through the sexual hypocrisy of his royal lovers. He wrote "Balin" to explore a case of sexual transference which would have been taboo at the time of the "Morte." During the intervening fifty years, he worked to demystify Arthur's progress through his model. Finally, within what he must have seen as his last idyll, he takes one more furtive look into his own creation. By beginning and ending the body of his poem with Vivien, he may be acknowledging that like her he remains the voyeur of a fictional world he cannot yet fully appreciate.

CHAPTER TWELVE

Some Late Poems and "Merlin"

A. J. Carr (p. 63) sees Tennyson's entire career as essentially monolithic: "Because he did not really advance towards 'solutions,' . . . Tennyson's later poetry does not break from the pattern of his past. . . . With thorough integrity he could publish in his later books some poems written long before." Most of these poems are indeed retrospective, most of them reevaluations, however indirect, of Tennyson's earlier poetry. Yet these very reevaluations mount a complex and paradoxical challenge to Tennyson's model. On the one hand, Arthur's almost Blakean descent into the authorial presence seems to have foreshadowed the author's regressive need to assert himself by denying the autonomy of his characters, past as well as present. On the other hand, the model's static, mutually opposed tensions seem thrown out of balance by his radical need to move forward, to transcend space, time, and often life itself. As David Shaw sums up these changes (p. 251), "Tennyson is too old now to be patient, too old to play with masks."

More specifically, the model's operational definition of life as an aesthetically fulfilling conflict can no longer mediate two manifestations of the Other which now return with even greater immediacy. Tennyson has often confronted death, most notably in the death of Hallam, but there he could eventually win Hallam from Other to mediator; now Tennyson faces death not as a poet but as a decrepit old man. Similarly he has often confronted social change, most intensely in *Maud* and the *Idylls*, but now a change which he sees as regressive is pushing him, an old man with old ideas, into social irrelevance.

The three juxtaposed roles within our model have so far assured it of the two dimensions necessary to enclose fictional space. Yet as Tennyson here tries to narrow the range of possible Others, he also tries to collapse the model into a single dimension by collapsing its two remaining roles into one. In fact he makes it increasingly difficult for us even to speak of an authorial presence; that term, after all, implies some interaction with other roles in the

model, and such relativity is what Tennyson is here challenging. Those mediators who answer his own increasingly narrow needs he gathers unto himself much as he did the late Arthur. Those who do not he relegates to an
irrelevant past or castigates as unwitting agents of the Other. To distinguish
the two groups, he measures their relative success by requiring them to sum
up their struggle within some brilliant object or image.

If we examine the results of this strategy, we find that "Locksley Hall Sixty
Years After" and "The Ancient Sage" both employ a surrogate for the present poet to belabor a reincarnation of his past self. While the late classical
poems leave their mediators trapped within a sterile past, they appropriate
the mediation itself as a kind of talisman to help Tennyson face the future.
Demeter alone, by first reshaping and then renouncing her own world, is
allowed to posit a future one for her poet. He could not easily dismiss his
friends into some past irrelevance, but after FitzGerald died while Tennyson
was composing his dedication, he began using them much as he had Demeter, covertly inviting them to precede him in his journey toward death. Finally, "Merlin and the Gleam," by rewriting most of his past work and dis-
crediting most of his past mediators, attempts to fuse Tennyson, the
mediating Merlin, the gleaming power of his mediation, and the ultimate
Other of death.

In poems such as "The Ancient Sage" and "Locksley Hall Sixty
Years After," Tennyson employs a mediator so transparent as to make laugh-
able the universality he wants to claim for his often visionary perceptions.
When we encounter a seer "a thousand summers ere the time of Christ" (l.
1) attributing to *his* boyhood phrases like "the Passion of the Past," "lost and
gone," "far and far away"—or when we hear him describe how he descended
into a mystic trance by invoking "the word that is the symbol of myself"—
we begin to wonder idly whether there *were* any seers named Alfred in 1000
B.C.[1] Even more hypocritical, the Sage uses Tennyson's own visionary experiences to rebuke his hapless companion for the brooding melancholia which
actually spawned them. The ranting couplets of the young poet, on the other
hand, echo less Tennyson's own past than that of the old cynic in "The
Vision of Sin."[2]

The undeniably personal ranting within "Locksley Hall Sixty Years After"
is disconcertingly powerful when directed toward the present age and predictably didactic when directed toward the grandchild, but it is simply disconcerting when directed toward the speaker's past self. Faced with a society
which seems to be surrendering *all* human values, the aged speaker comes to

find a nostalgic appeal in the more easily personified Other of class oppression. Hence he resurrects the speaker of the original "Locksley Hall" specifically to make him recant, to make him acknowledge that his rival, the "clown" who was to drag Amy down in "the grossness of his nature," was really a fine fellow all along:

> Worthier soul was he than I am, sound and honest, rustic Squire,
> Kindly landlord, boon companion—youthful jealousy is a liar. . . .
> I that loathed, have come to love him. Love will conquer at the last.
>
> (ll. 239–40, 280)

In using the pretense of dramatic distance to attack the dramatic integrity of his past self, the present speaker grows perilously close to the Other whom he had once challenged.[3] Yet his past self, though powerless to preserve his beloved, remains so powerful a witness to her loss that we can almost hear a ghostly "Perish in thy self-contempt!"—a whisper directed no longer at some future Amy but at his own present reincarnation.

Classical Poems

The two Roman poets, Catullus and Virgil, win more integrity than Tennyson's personal surrogates, but as the surrogates are trapped within his revisions of his own past, so the poets are trapped within a long-dead age. In "Frater Ave atque Vale," for example, Tennyson graciously revives Catullus, but only on his own terms and for his own purposes. Catullus is remembered for his elegy on his dead brother and his celebration of his country house on the isthmus at Sirmio, now only a "Roman ruin where the purple flowers grow." He lives, in other words, as the voice of loss itself. Tennyson builds this loss into a paradox: he can celebrate "sweet Catullus's all-but-island" only because of the Roman's "paene insularum"; yet Catullus's own voice endures primarily because his "frater, ave atque vale" haunts the equally bereaved Tennyson through nine repetitions of the hollow "o" rhyme.[4]

Tennyson's casual reference to flowers here hints at a device which gradually comes to dominate the late poems. Within them, images of brightness and beauty (flowers, fire, precious stones, and metals) suggest Tennyson's shift in emphasis from the process of mediation to its results. These images, the results of an often wasting struggle against historical forces, become his measure of the success of the mediation itself. In some cases Tennyson, but not the mediator himself, wins some solace for all this waste in the lasting beauty of the object or its power as a microcosm of the struggle. In other cases the transience of the flower or the destructive potential of fire comes to suggest that both mediator and authorial presence must pass beyond such vain quests for aesthetic permanence.

Virtually all of these symbolic patterns, often in juxtaposition, shape "To Virgil" into Tennyson's evaluation of the worth and cost of such mediation. When Silenus is awarded such distillations of beauty, the award seems to come from nature's plenty: "Poet of the poet-satyr whom the laughing shepherd bound with flowers" (l. 8). Yet from a draft of the poem in Harvard Notebook 66, Shaw concludes ("Elegies," p. 3) that

> when Tennyson revises he consistently balances his first impressions of Virgil's opulence and ease with pictures of brooding and gloom . . . , subordinat[ing] the landscape painter, the celebrant of "balsam-bearing" trees, to the sage "majestic" in his "sadness" (l. 12). The poet who sees "Universal Nature" is no longer the authority quoted in council halls, as he was in the first version. Nor does he see "Universal Mind" in an exotic catalogue of "Sun and Moon and Star and Earth and Sea." Virgil now broods over "the doubtful doom of human kind" in the gravest line of the poem, and—significantly—the last stanza to be written.

While Tennyson's revision thus gives Virgil the mediator a graver dignity, it simultaneously undermines the value of his mediation. When Silenus' flower is troped as Virgil's poetry itself ("All the charm of all the Muses, often flowering in a lonely word"), the transient and "lonely" bloom appears a pathetically small reward for the imaginative effort which produced it. Virgil's "golden phrase," after all, sums up not only all the linguistic resources of Latin ("All the chosen coin of fancy") but also Hesiod and the whole tradition of Greek pastoral.

Whenever these summations appear more lasting, the Other which Virgil confronted appears more intractable and the confrontation itself more wasteful. As Shaw observes (p. 3), Virgil "alchemizes all his elements to gold," but if he becomes his own golden bough, he lights the way for generations of "kings and realms" moving inexorably to an existence as mere "shadows." If his *Aeneid* retains its brilliance, it lives by reflecting "Dido's pyre" and "Ilion's lofty temples robed in fire."[5]

Tennyson's justification of the episodic structure of his *Idylls*, "that a small vessel built on fine lines might float further down the stream of time than a big raft,"[6] here reaches its bleak but logical conclusion: Only words, only language itself can survive the ruin of "the Rome of slaves" and be transplanted on the "Northern Island sundered once from all the human race." Here, in a revision of Bloom's anxiety of influence, Tennyson takes the caricature of himself as only a coiner of phrases, applies it to his master, and then claims that no matter how grandiose the conflicts which constitute the poet's theme, these conflicts will engender such mutual destruction that phrases alone will remain.

In his last classical monologues and narratives, Tennyson combines a compulsion to control his mediators with a refusal to free them until they have distilled their conflicts into some quintessentially poetic form. The late revision of "Tiresias," as we saw, reduced the blind seer to a mouthpiece for Tennyson's attack upon a society mired in mutually destructive extremes, yet deaf to his "counsel that the tyranny of all / Led backward to the tyranny of one" (ll. 74–75). Tiresias gains his freedom only when he replaces all of Tennyson's frustrations with a flame of inspiration which perpetuates itself even as it is consumed, "on one far height in one far-shining fire" (l. 176).

The original "Oenone" narrated Paris's progressive failure as a mediator. With Tennyson's new emphasis upon results, however, the very appearance of male sexuality within "The Death of Oenone" leads directly to desolation. Alive, Paris now sounds to Oenone "thin as the batlike shrillings of the Dead / When driven to Hades" (ll. 21–22). Only in memory can she see him "climbing toward her with the golden fruit, . . . / Her husband in the flush of youth and dawn" (ll. 15, 17). As his apple, both a fruit and golden, was the distillation of discord, so *its* fruits are the physical and spiritual ruin she sees around her. Like Tiresias in his revised monologue, she finds herself firmly entrapped within the Other's domain:

>   the goodly view
> Was now one blank, and all the serpent vines
> Which on the touch of heavenly feet had risen,
> And gliding through the branches overbowered
> The naked Three, were withered long ago.
>
>   (ll. 3–7)

Originally, Oenone herself strove vainly but powerfully to preserve her sanctuary and her past against successive agents of the Other. Now, just as bereft of options as Tiresias, she can only choose between a present controlled by Paris's golden apple and both a past and a future controlled by the symbol she chose at the end of her earlier poem: "All earth and air seem only burning fire." The light of his funeral pyre has rekindled in her "the morning light of happy marriage," but by leaping upon it, she "mixt herself with *him* and past in fire" (l. 106). Ostensibly she may regain their physical union; in reality she gains the same transcendence desired by her creator, the perpetual possession of that evanescent element she could only perceive in "Oenone."

The more powerful, yet more warmly maternal mediator of "Demeter and Persephone" retrieves her daughter from the two most powerful beings in the cosmos, Jupiter and Dis, even though "Bright and Dark have sworn that [Persephone] . . . / Should be for ever and for evermore / The Bride of Darkness" (ll. 95, 98–99).[7] To Priscilla Johnston (pp. 76–77), Demeter "becomes the surrogate spirit of the poet himself, who pines amid a barren present and strives constantly to revive a lost vision—the seer whose imagination is so potent, so aggressive, and so persistent that it . . . forc[es] a vanished ideal back from the remote past." Yet as Johnston admits (pp. 78–79), "No amount of pretending can renew innocence or maintain eternal springtime"; Demeter must submit to "the facts of change, discontinuity, and death in Aidoneus' ultimate proprietorship."

Johnston feels that Tennyson has embodied his sense of a "blind repetition that only revolves around a central stasis" (p. 90) within the seasonal reenactment of Dis's rape; yet neither the classical story nor Tennyson's suggests that the actual rape will be repeated. Instead Tennyson's story in particular may imply that Demeter, Persephone, and the Brothers themselves are all pawns of the same impersonal forces which frustrated Tiresias and the speaker of "Locksley Hall Sixty Years After." The Brothers' attempt to "bury" Persephone permanently must fail because the forces of death and masculine sexuality which they embody make up only part of the natural cycle. Persephone must be returned for nine—but only nine—months, because the fertility she represents must die into winter before it can be reborn.

Like Ida, Enoch, and Arthur before her, Demeter is threatened even by the formal constraints of her poem. The form of the epyllion, as Hair notes (p. 54), may work to redefine the cosmic order in terms of human relationships. Yet the same equation may also be read backwards, trapping all the participants within a myth which constantly threatens to reassert its own origins in natural etiology. From the beginning, Demeter searches as much for teleology as for her daughter; she asks the waves, "Do ye make your moaning for my child?" (l. 64). Yet their denial of purpose, "We know not why we moan," is less frightening than her discovery that in her temples men are seeking answers from her, the fruitless questioner.

Even the success of her quest can be read as a capitulation to process. Lucretius strove to drain the spring of Venus's personality: "I meant not thee; I meant not her" (l. 85), but Demeter hopes to win back the "human-godlike" spirit of her daughter:

> a gleam as of the moon,
> When first she peers along the tremulous deep,
> Fled wavering o'er thy face. . . .
> > the Sun
> Burst form a swimming fleece of winter gray,
> And robed thee in his day from head to feet.
> > (ll. 13–15, 19–21)

Yet the very splendor of the passage, its fusion of natural and human waking, must make us ask whether the spring reawakens her or whether she re-awakens the spring. Which is the tenor and which the vehicle of this complex metaphorical pattern; or does the pattern, as Stange claims, simply dissolve Persephone and the spring into one another?[8]

In her vision of some redeeming future, Demeter follows Tennyson's other late mediators in distilling beauty from her suffering. Fusing flower with fruit, spring with autumn, her own numen with her daughter's, she promises her, "Thou . . . shalt ever send thy life along with mine / From buried grain through springing blade, and bless / Their garnered harvests also" (ll. 140, 143–45). But even here fertility suggests fire: "the dimly glimmering lawns," which Demeter hopes to "see no more," lead her instead to contemplate "all the hateful fires / Of torment" (ll. 149–50). As Shaw points out (pp. 253–54), "The prophetic certitude of 'see no more' is quietly discarded . . . until Demeter's prophecy of obliterating that world is all but forgotten."

Despite these qualifications, however, Demeter remains more complete and more compelling than these other classical figures—in part because her problems, goals, and powers match those of her creator almost point for point. From Oenone, one suspects, Tennyson needed primarily a spectacular death. In Tiresias he could project his own frustrations but no obvious means of relieving them. From Catullus he could extract exactly two lyrics because more might reveal that the Roman poet belonged less to him than to "little Swinburne." In Virgil he perceived almost too painfully the disparity between the costs and the rewards of imaginative achievement. But through Demeter Tennyson could recant his boyhood identification with Dis's sexual aggression by showing its results: "one black blur of earth" (l. 37) amid the fertility of spring. He could then show that even this aggression manifested a far more impersonal Other. Finally he could show that his mediator was powerful enough to redefine the parameters of her own fiction in order to deny the universality of this Other. However hedged, her apocalyptic vision remains better realized than any Tennyson could claim through his own powers or through those of less autonomous mediators.

Dedications

All these portraits of classical figures Tennyson prefaced with equally powerful, equally radical dedications. Though apparently limited by some real occasion, the poet seizes it to demand of his friends what he could not of his mythic or long-dead protagonists. His dedication of the newly revised "Tiresias" to FitzGerald actually lets us watch him working out the nature of these demands. While drafts of both sections of the frame exist, none is so revealing or so moving as the mistake which Tennyson allows to stand, the gracious verse letter to a living friend who, unbeknownst to its author, has already died.

This letter begins as unashamedly nostalgic, confident of its own ability to invoke and perpetuate a mediating power not fully embodied in either of them but enveloping their shared past. Tennyson recreates his flirtation with Fitzgerald's vegetarianism so vividly that Peter's dream of "the full sheet / Let down" becomes both sanction and inspiration for the imaginative energy of youth. Here too FitzGerald's translation of Omar grants him the power to revivify these proffered verses from Tennyson's not-quite-so-distant past,

> which you will take
> My Fitz, and welcome, as I know
> Less for its own than for the sake
> Of one recalling gracious times. . . .
> (ll. 50–53)

Yet in the closing frame occasioned by FitzGerald's sudden death, Tennyson must admit that

> The tolling of his funeral bell
> Broke on my Pagan Paradise,

<blockquote>
And mixt the dreams of classic times,
   And all the phantoms of the dream,
   With present grief. . . .
(ll. 63–67)
</blockquote>

Within this metaphorical "mix" of paradise, dream, and phantom, Tennyson can no longer separate the kinds of mediation claimed severally by his fictional creation, his past imaginative power, and his present invocation of it. He must acknowledge, however, that the implacable Other of death has challenged the reality of all these claims. Although he graciously compares the original dedication to friends' discovering that their host has departed, the metaphor cannot sustain the new weight he places upon it: "Gone into darkness . . . past in sleep, away / By night, into the deeper night!" (ll. 73–75). Here the "golden hours" of friendship, so spontaneously invoked in the opening frame, must now serve as metaphorical surety that the dark may itself prelude "a clearer day / Than our poor twilight dawn on earth" (ll. 76–77). It is only this hope which keeps Tennyson's flowers, "this wreath" laid "above his honored head," from withering into a metaphor for this small elegy itself.

This same hope, however, provides a pattern for all Tennyson's remaining dedications. Where the classical protagonists contemplated flowers, fire, or gold as compensation for past suffering, his friends, all of his own generation, must contemplate them as symbols of the death awaiting them all in the near future. If he cannot bear to see FitzGerald's death as passive surrender to "the deeper night," he must see FitzGerald himself as seeking out the same escape from life into transcendence which Tennyson has forced upon Oenone and Tiresias. And as his friend appropriates the role of adventurous mediator, he also serves as a model for the other friends whom Tennyson "favored" with similar dedications.

The dedication of "Demeter" to R. C. Jebb, for example, may seem a spontaneous celebration of flowering life. Here Jebb, having already resurrected Pindar, is asked to use his "classic smile" to bring Tennyson's myth to "blossom again on a colder isle." But here too Tennyson implies that life and blossom can emerge only from death: the wheat from an Egyptian mummy, Jebb's ode from "the Ghost of Pindar" in him, and even Tennyson's quintessential myth of rebirth from a literary death in its native Sicily.

The dedication of "The Death of Oenone" "To the Master of Balliol" hides a similar invitation within the apparent effortlessness of its art: its spontaneous fusion of four-beat iambic with a very classical blend of dactyls and spondees, its opportunistic syntax in which one clause seemingly begets another just as thought begets thought, its celebration of Benjamin Jowett as one who has recreated a long-dead past in scholarship as Tennyson has in poetry. After these gracious compliments, however, Jowett is asked to "lay [his] Plato for one minute down," and "hear my cataract's / Downward thunder in hollow and glen, / Till, led by dream and vague desire . . ." (ll. 15–17)—in reality it is Oenone who is being led down her mountain by the cataract, but the delayed subject implies that Jowett himself should be drawn by the rush of Tennyson's poetry toward some mysterious end in the hypnotic beauty of the "funeral pyre."

Tennyson's mythical and historical mediators garnered up these images of brightness; FitzGerald challenged their efficacy; his other friends were enticed by them toward the unknown. For his own journey toward death, Tennyson subordinates these mediators and their images to the journey itself. The paradox implicit within the title of "The Silent Voices," for example, works itself out in a conflict between unwanted and undiscovered mediation, between the call he does not want to hear, "toward the lowland ways behind me, / And the sunlight that is gone" (ll. 5–6), and the call he cannot hear, "forward to the starry track / Glimmering up the heights beyond me" (ll. 8–9). Perhaps because this celebration of death as an interstellar voyage must reject even ghostly mediators, Tennyson usually chooses to travel by boat.

Our very familiarity with this and the other metaphors in "Crossing the Bar" helps explain the poem's most insistent problem. Although the Pilot never appears during either the voyage or the poem, he may not actually be needed.[9] To understand how and why Tennyson has done most of his work for him, we need to follow up on David Sonstroem's observation that "the situation, the concerns, the images, and the key words of 'Crossing the Bar' all occur elsewhere in Tennyson." Besides the sea voyages of Ulysses, Arthur, the crew in "The Voyage," and Tennyson himself in *In Memoriam* 103, Sonstroem cites liminal scenes in several other poems.[10] Similarly the sunset of this lyric can be linked with poems of dreamlike isolation like "The Hesperides" and "The Lotos-Eaters." The evening star as both Hesper and Phosphor has adjudicated the rival claims of past and future in *In Memoriam* 121. As the Planet of Love, it has also inflamed the passionate speaker as he waits for Maud in her garden. The "call," as Ricks notes (*Poems*, III, 253n), harkens back to the "calling of the sea" which summoned Enoch to his last voyage. Even in the "moaning of the bar," as in the "moanings of the homeless sea" in *In Memoriam* 35, nature laments its own impersonality with a human voice.[11]

The personification implicit within many of these images may account for the gap between what Sonstroem calls (p. 55) their "note of irresolution" and the comparative tranquillity of "Crossing the Bar." Such retrospection, in fact, becomes a prerequisite for Tennyson's quest to see the Other of death as a new beginning. Where he appropriated the struggles of his late mediators in some artifact, here he combines all the conflicting roles within these earlier poems into a single tableau. As the autonomous early mediators fuse with the indefinable Others they confronted, the resulting images personalize both the sea and the death it tropes. Even the "moaning of the bar" transforms the dying anguish he hopes to avoid into a lament offered by death itself. Thus when he journeys "from out our bourne of Time and Place," Tennyson actually "turns again home" with the tide.[12]

"Merlin and the Gleam"

In "Crossing the Bar," the poet exercised his triumphant control over his creative past, his imaginative universe, even his own death. In "Merlin and the Gleam" he uses a fictional character for much the same purpose. Like the speakers of "The Ancient Sage" and "Locksley Hall Sixty Years After," Merlin transparently projects Tennyson's reevaluations of his own life and those of his earlier mediators. Yet where those two speakers reinterpreted only one episode or one character, Merlin virtually rewrites Tennyson's entire life and canon. As such he transforms an old man's frightened, narrow-minded grumblings into the proclamation of a new poetic manifesto.[13]

As Catherine Stevenson has shown ("Druids," pp. 14–23), Tennyson spoke through Merlin himself in his political poems of the 1850s and through similar bardic, prophetic figures all during his life. Furthermore, Merlin as mediator possesses his own secondary mediator in the Gleam. Hence he allows Tennyson to celebrate the individual creativity of the authorial self while shielding its transience within some transcendent power:

> *I* am Merlin,
> And *I* am dying,
> *I* am Merlin
> Who follow The Gleam.
>
> (ll. 7–10)

As a medieval magician Merlin can also go where the unaided poet cannot, can reenter fictional worlds long since closed to Tennyson, can reorder them within a pattern which gives appropriate shape and purpose to Tennyson's own life and career.

At the very beginning, for example, Tennyson-Merlin can award himself a disciple. The "young Mariner, . . . watching / The gray Magician / With eyes of wonder" (ll. 1, 4–6) certainly proves far more faithful than those Pre-Raphaelites who adulterated Tennyson's own poetic technique with "poisonous honey stolen from France." In the next stanza, Tennyson's earlier creation of Bleys as Merlin's master becomes a precedent for awarding himself a master as well. Critics' difficulties in identifying "the Wizard / Who found me at sunrise" (ll. 11–12) only reaffirm the difficulties we encountered in identifying clear sources for Tennyson's earlier poetry.

Rather than acknowledging or even misreading some poetic father figure, he seems to be appropriating patterns of development associated with widely divergent poetic schools. He opens by conflating the Romantic pattern variously formulated within Wordsworth's "Tintern Abbey," "Intimations Ode," "Peele Castle," and Keats's "House of Life" letter. This sequence—spontaneous nature worship, intruding social problems, and renewed response to natural magic—then cedes to a Virgilian sequence of apprenticeship, pastoral, and epic.[14] Then Merlin transposes the order of Tennyson's *Idylls* and *In Memoriam* within his own celebration and subsequent loss of Arthur. In so doing he shifts into a Miltonic extension of the Virgilian sequence, where implications of the epic must be explored through some transparently personal mediator like Samson. While this sequence proves equally unfaithful to these paradigms and to Tennyson's own life, it does offer his career a shape and direction that few others have found within it. With its progressive stages and public referents, the sequence also disguises his dependence on his model, on the endlessly repeated conflicts between projections of the self and imperfectly comprehended forces from without.

This progression, however, only grows clear when the disappearance of Arthur transforms Merlin's relation to his own mediator, the Gleam. This phenomenon, of course, belongs to the images of brightness which dominate these late poems. In fact its changing role within this poem parallels the different roles which Tennyson has assigned to all these images. As they determined the results and value of mediation, so during the early stanzas the Gleam manifests the beauty which Merlin has distilled from specific stages of life. Tennyson's placement of "Gleam" as the last word in each stanza identifies it as a kind of transcendent highlighter, affirming by its luminous presence Merlin's current choice of poetic subject. Both the variety and the sequence of its appearances, however, suggest that the Gleam is neither Tennyson's newly mastered art, nor the inspiration nearly snuffed out by critics, nor the magical spirit of place, nor the romance of pastoral life, nor even the ideals of "Arthur the blameless."

As it deserts one of these forms for the next, the Gleam gradually disengages itself from all of them, gradually transforms itself from an inanimate measure of mediation to a marginally personified mediator and, finally, to a reality transcending both personality and the model itself. Within the earlier stanzas, inversion hid the Gleam's syntactic control: "Floated The Gleam," "Flitted The Gleam," "Slided The Gleam," "Rested The Gleam." Now it assumes its dominant position as grammatical subject: "The Gleam, that had waned to a wintry glimmer / . . . Fell on the Shadow" (ll. 83, 92). Or "whenever / In passing it glanced upon / Hamlet or city, / . . . The Mortal hillock, / Would break into blossom" (ll. 102–4, 107–8).

At this point the poet's focus also shifts from some "local habitation" of the Gleam to the Gleam itself, its shining indefinable except by negation: "Not of the sunlight, / Not of the moonlight, / Not of the starlight!" (ll. 120–22). The Gleam now comes to represent for Merlin what flowers, fire, and gold were meant to represent for the subjects of the dedications: a call to move through all these stages, to move through life itself. Whether Merlin boards the young Mariner's boat or literally "die[s] rejoicing" on shore, the Gleam has now so collapsed its metaphorical vehicle that such an embarkation becomes a metaphor for death, while death itself, as in "Crossing the Bar," can best be imaged as an eternal quest for the transcendent. In so doing, it has also collapsed the roles within Tennyson's model—authorial presence, mediator, and Other—within an unknowable reality which subsumes them all.

In reshaping Tennyson's career as the gradual acceptance of this quest, "Merlin" has certainly played fast and loose with his own biography; we must now ask how faithful it has been to the plots, characters, and settings of his individual poems. His model, as we have seen, takes the imaginative landscape of any poem as a given within which the entire drama of mediation can be played out. Like many of his other late poems, however, "Merlin" takes each landscape as a necessarily incomplete stage within a quest to escape landscape altogether. Hence it tacitly ranks Tennyson's mediators according to their participation in the quest itself, identifying with those who complete it, delimiting and subverting those who stubbornly insist on dallying in any one spot. A surprising number of the mediators do experience a gleam-like vision which is initially associated, like Merlin's, with some person or object. Those who pass beyond this transient association are validated; those who commit themselves to it are dismissed retroactively as unwitting agents of an idol turned Other.

The most completely validated journey, as we might expect, is that of Tennyson himself in *In Memoriam*. He anticipates, not just Merlin's loss of Arthur, but virtually the whole of his journey: a "golden vapour" surrounds the lark in his boyhood visions (canceled section before 22); a "light" of fancy surrounds his early interchanges with Hallam (23); in memories of Hallam, Tennyson sees "the god within him light his face" (87); Tennyson begs for vision as a "finer light in light" (91); in a final apotheosis the physical Hallam dissolves into the Gleam itself: "Thou standest in the rising sun, / And in the setting thou art fair" (130).

Among fictional mediators, the one closest to this Merlin is Arthur—not Arthur as the object of Merlin's loss but Arthur as a fellow quester. The late Tennyson has shown few scruples about appropriating his own mediators; yet this poem reinterprets Arthur's appropriation of the Gleam as the cause of his political and spiritual downfall. Arthur's origins, youth, and early realm are resplendent in gleams: the "shining people" on the ship which brings him; the sea creatures, "each with a beacon star upon his head / And a wild sea-light about his feet"; the "lightnings and great thunders over him" during his first battle; and finally the sun in three colored streams pouring "down from the casement" over him at his coronation.

In a significant conflation of stanzas 6 and 7, however, Arthur's self-identification with the Gleam becomes a signal for his subjects to seek their own gleams elsewhere. First Lancelot and Guinevere find it in each other. He sees her in the bower with "the morning on her face," and she later reaffirms her choice of him over Arthur because "the low sun makes the colour." Then others begin to worship the gleam in the couple. Watching Lancelot, Balin feels like a lame boy trapped in a dark valley, watching another climb near to the "sun-flushed" mountain peak. Elaine places Lancelot's shield "where morning's earliest ray / Might strike it, and awake her with the gleam." While the Grail, as we saw, consistently parodied Arthur's spiritual authority, it leads Galahad—as the Gleam will Merlin—out to the sea in search of some new life. Only when Arthur renounces his throne can he pass on his barge into the sunrise; only then can he follow Merlin in following his gleam beyond loss, beyond the destruction of his society toward some kind of personal transcendence.

"Merlin" can validate the *Idylls* because the idylls allow their principal characters to accept, adopt, and discard a series of contingent mediators. Through this process many of them learn that nothing short of Merlin's full voyage, nothing short of transcendence, can offer them freedom. Among Tennyson's other poems, "Merlin" also validates those naysayers who refuse to identify their gleams with any single person or object. Since they grow out of the same loss which produced the "Morte," Tennyson's other questers— Ulysses, Tithonus, Tiresias—all share a compressed version of Arthur's own passing. Even the jilted speakers of *The Lover's Tale*, "Locksley Hall," and "Edwin Morris" are seconded when they refuse to equate their gleams with any of Merlin's early subjects: tradition, social conformity, wish fulfillment, or domesticity.

If "Merlin" implicitly encourages these mediators, however, it rejects most of the others. Those who commit themselves to any *one* of Merlin's stages are consigned to death or, even worse, to stagnation. In some cases this judgment matches the commonly accepted one: when the youth in "The Vision of Sin" finds his gleam and his melody in the "sleet of diamond-drift and pearly hail" which accompanies the bacchanal, he comes to personify this cynical world. "Merlin"'s reinterpretation of "The Lotos-Eaters," while more critical than the one offered in chapter 3, is also generally accepted: the seer's vision of the Gleam in the distance appears to the Mariners as only "the dark-blue sky, / Vaulted o'er the dark-blue sea" (ll. 84–85). To this darkness they oppose the "wavering lights and shadows" of "a land / In which it seemed always afternoon" (ll. 2–4). They even hope to imitate the Lucretian gods in "their golden houses, girdled with the gleaming world" (l. 158). Yet unless dragged off by their leader, they will stagnate in the fantasy land of Merlin's stanza 4.

The poem also relegates to this stage another group we have seen as sympathetic mediators, Tennyson's high-born maidens. Some of these build their gleam into a sanctuary like the Hesperides, watched over by the "silver eye" of Father Hesper, or like the Palace of Art, "golden-railed, / Burn[ing] like a fringe of fire" (ll. 47–48). Others—Oenone, the Marianas, the Lady of Shalott, and Fatima—try in vain to move from this stage in Merlin's quest to a new sanctuary of pastoral fulfillment. These fail, according to the paradigm in "Merlin," because they embody their gleam in some beloved object:

Paris, "white-breasted like a star / Fronting the dawn"; or Lancelot, a "bearded meteor, trailing light"; or Fatima's celestial lover, "that from thy noonday height / Shudderest when I strain my sight." But what "Merlin" interprets as a stultifying idolatry we interpreted as mediation; their idolatry embodies the Other within a figure who can no longer threaten the sanctuary of the authorial presence.

"Merlin," in other words, supports Tennyson's mediators better in their rebellions than in their affirmations. His quest parallels Ida's flight from social repression and from fairy-tale stereotypes. But even though she also rejects "the splendors of the hills," she finally sinks into the stultifying domesticity he passes through in stanza 5. Despite the Prince's final smoke-enshrouded vision of some "statelier Eden," "Merlin" abandons her and her poem to the idolatrous worship of some pastoral gleam.

The speaker in *Maud* follows Tennyson's other spurned lovers through the early stages of Merlin's journey: from his gleaming early memories of Maud, "the moon-faced darling of all"; to his present scorn of the "dark old" Hall, "gilt by the touch of a millionaire"; and then to the phantasmagoric world of Maud's "passionless, pale, cold face, star-sweet on a gloom profound." Maud's return of his love reinterprets this fantasy world of stanza 4 as one bathed in the rosy glow of her face. This love then promises him the domestic fulfillment of stanza 5, bathed now in the newly softened splendors of the stars. At this point he reverses the Arthurian stages of Merlin's sequence, first losing the gleam with his loss of Maud and then rediscovering it in "the blood-red blossom of war with a heart of fire." "Merlin" thus leaves the speaker with Arthur in stanza 6, fixated upon a martial militancy only one stage beyond Ida's pastoral dead end.

To me "Merlin" fails as a touchstone for Tennyson's earlier poetry because Tennyson has failed to remember a paradox implicit in his choice of Merlin as surrogate. As Stevenson interprets this paradox ("Druids," pp. 17–22), Merlin's bardic vision remains vulnerable to sensual corruption because it looks inward and hence away from social responsibility. In fact the early manuscripts for "Vivien" suggest that as Merlin never really existed apart from her, so his imaginative power remained bound up with her sexuality.[15] While Tennyson gradually rehabilitated him in the later-written idylls, he linked Merlin's present quest with his original seduction on the basis of an extremely dubious etymological connection. He thought that "Nimue" was related to the Welsh word for "a female who appears and disappears," apt symbol for his "higher poetic imagination."[16]

While the Gleam thus shares both the origin and function of Goethe's *Ewig-Weibliche*, Tennyson has here stripped it of all feminine, to say nothing of erotic, associations. Where he reduced sexual love to violence, darkness and death within "Demeter," here he banishes it altogether. The only women Merlin encounters are the "innocent maidens" he includes on his pastoral checklist. Hence Tennyson not only passes over Rosa Baring and Emily Sellwood within his own life, he also passes over what is arguably his most important poetic subject.

This omission forces him to reinterpret most of his love poems as negative exempla, traps which the poet must avoid in his pursuit of the transcendent. Their mediators, in turn, become mere scapegoats, whose idolatrous loves and sad ends should point the poet an appropriate warning. Because "Merlin" reinforces the popular stereotype of Victorian prudery, Tennyson's earlier poems have often been so read. So to read them, however, ignores the host of mediators who have molded their own fictive worlds on their own values.

Within this internecine power struggle, the collective authority of Tennyson's other works ultimately overpowers this one. As Tennyson's earlier characters deny Merlin's attempt to reinterpret them, so Tennyson the creative poet asserts his independence from Tennyson the revisionist critic. When his mediators reaffirm the integrity of his much-beleaguered model and reassume their original roles within it, they actually force the later Tennyson to assume the role of hostile god figure from his own earliest poems. In so doing, however, they merely distinguish this poem's speaker from Tennyson and its course from the course of his life. In effect, these earlier characters award to Merlin the character the same autonomy from authorial intervention which they have won for themselves.

Introduction

1. James R. Kincaid, *Tennyson's Major Poems: The Comic and Ironic Patterns* (New Haven: Yale University Press, 1975), p. 73. All parenthetical references to Kincaid are to this book.

2. Daniel Albright offers a different version of this discrepancy: "In his series of dramatic monologues he tried to approximate a description of his own nameless self by adding up a long sequence of names, as if every new term . . . offered a fuller allusion to that unspeakable being Alfred Tennyson." *Tennyson: The Muses' Tug-of-War* (Charlottesville: University Press of Virginia, 1986), p. 82. All parenthetical references to Albright are to this book. What Albright takes as linguistic approximations of an unknowable center, I take as dramatic creations to protect a very vulnerable one.

3. W. H. Auden, introduction to *A Selection from the Poems of Alfred, Lord Tennyson* (Garden City, N.Y.: Doubleday, 1944), pp. xvii–xix. On the frozen landscape of "The Day-Dream," Albright comments, "This nostalgia for the unhatched egg, for speechless self-involvement, is strong in Tennyson's work" (p. 191).

4. Barbara Johnson, "Nothing Fails Like Success," *SCE Reports*, 8 (1980), 14.

5. Priscilla Johnston, "Tennyson's Demeter and Persephone Theme: Memory and the 'Good Solid' Past," *Texas Studies in Literature and Language*, 20 (1978), 71.

6. See W. D. Paden, *Tennyson in Egypt: A Study of the Imagery in His Earlier Work* (Lawrence: University of Kansas Press, 1942), pp. 28–30. Herbert F. Tucker, "Tennyson and the Measure of Doom," *PMLA*, 98 (1983), 8–20, or *Tennyson and the Doom of Romanticism* (Cambridge: Harvard University Press, 1988), pp. 12–30. Clyde de L. Ryals, "The 'Fatal Woman' Symbol in Tennyson," *PMLA*, 74 (1959), 438–43. Gerhard Joseph, *Tennysonian Love: The Strange Diagonal* (Minneapolis: University of Minnesota Press, 1969), pp. 129–45. Unless otherwise indicated, all parenthetical references to Paden, Tucker, and Joseph are to these books.

7. Many of my initial perceptions may have grown from an unconscious memory of Patricia M. Ball's seminal article on mediation, "Tennyson and the Romantics," *Victorian Poetry*, 1 (1963), 7–16.

8. We possess the most interesting drafts for these poems, in part because they have more valuable and hence better-preserved manuscripts. The longer poems in particular were also the most difficult for Tennyson to carry around in his head. Yet I have come to believe that these same poems cost Tennyson more, and that this cost is reflected in the drafts themselves. In tracing these compositional stages, I have had to rely largely on internal evidence. Apart from stories of long walks, port, tobacco, and

after-dinner sequestering, we have little first-hand evidence of Tennyson's creative processes. We have instead to deal with a poet who ripped out manuscript sheets to clean his pipe and an early editor, Thomas Wise, who cut up several manuscripts to make them go farther and who forged trial proofs when he could not find real ones. Consequently I have had to draw my conclusions with no manuscript evidence for some poems, fair copies for others, preliminary jottings for others, and a full range of drafts for still others. My conclusions, moreover, rest on what must remain conjectures: that Tennyson actually wrote the drafts in the order suggested by their position in the notebooks, that each draft reproduces faithfully his current conception of his poem, that he saved the more refractory sections for last, that fragmentary patterns within existing drafts demand and hence presuppose completion within later ones—in short that the poems did in some sense write themselves.

9. They also employ the French term, *style indirect libre*. "It is as if the speaker, while insisting upon that third-person pronoun which constantly reminds us that the "she" [or "he"] and the uncharacterized and unlabelled "I" are two different consciousnesses, nonetheless allows himself to be nearly camouflaged, chameleon-like, by the mind he observes." John D. Boyd and Anne Williams, "Tennyson's 'Mariana' and 'Lyric Perspective,'" *Studies in English Literature: 1500–1900*, 23 (1983), 583.

10. Throughout my investigation, model and manuscript study have shaped one another: the model suggested where to look among the manuscripts and the manuscripts suggested modifications within the model. I would argue further that apart from some very general ordering of drafts, most studies of compositional process remain equally tenuous, if only because any attempt to trace a sequence within an author's notebooks presupposes *some* a priori criteria. This uncertainty, however, is no reason why such conclusions should not be presented, supported, questioned, and modified. As John Maynard has pointed out, the Higher Criticism of the last century engendered violent controversy, and textual study today has an equally radical potential for mediating between traditional notions of a fixed author and text and contemporary efforts to fragment the author and take unbridled liberties with the text. Remarks delivered as a respondent in the section "Revision among Victorian Writers: Motivations and Modes," MLA convention, New York, 29 December 1986.

11. Jonathan Culler, *On Deconstruction: Theory and Criticism after Structuralism* (Ithaca: Cornell University Press, 1982), p. 110.

12. Both Lacan in psychology and Derrida in philosophy exploit what Jonathan Culler describes as "a self-reference that ultimately brings out the inability of any discourse to account for itself" (p. 201). Hence proponents of deconstruction claim that any reading which claims fidelity to a text not only supplements what is lacking within it but itself assumes some ultimately self-contradictory metaphysic. Marxist exposures of the implicit ideologies within writer and reader also expose interpretive objectivity as thrall to bourgeois humanism. Indeed, I have come to admit that I have been in part finding what I was looking for, that criteria such as novelty and explicability have been shaping my choice of thesis, that I have been protected by my subjectivity from other, incompatible approaches to Tennyson. Yet I have also come to believe that my spatial metaphor gains credibility, if not "reality," through its cumulative ability to produce persuasive, mutually supportive interpretations of Tennyson's

major poetry. After trying numerous models which did not "fit," I retain some confidence that this one does.

13. Girard's actual model is vastly different from mine. He sees most romantic fiction as driven not only by desire, but by a mediated desire. This mediation undermines the hero's claims that his beloved object is unique and that his love is, *sui generis*, a liberation from cultural norms and forces. René Girard, *Deceit, Desire, and the Novel: Self and Other in Literary Structure*, trans. Yvonne Freccero (Baltimore: Johns Hopkins University Press, 1965), pp. 2–3.

14. It remains difficult, nevertheless, to privilege apparently peripheral characters, to grant them an autonomy beyond context, and yet to deny the humanistic values underlying traditional conceptions of character and autonomy. To quote Jonathan Culler: "Since this move to another level of investigation may result in interpretations that treat the work as an allegory of Marxist, psychoanalytic, feminist, or deconstructive concerns, it may not always be easy to distinguish from the thematic criticism it aims to transcend" (p. 208).

15. Morton Kaplan and Robert Kloss, *The Unspoken Motive: A Guide to Psychoanalytic Literary Criticism* (New York: Free Press, 1973), pp. 4, 7.

16. Meredith Anne Skura, *The Literary Use of the Psychoanalytic Process* (New Haven: Yale University Press, 1981), p. 55–56. See also her claim that such a psychological reading would "relate . . . structure and conflicts to a drama within some human mind—a mind located ambiguously between the people mentioned in the text and the speaker himself" (p. 32). She points out further that even Lacan's treatment of "The Purloined Letter" and Hartman's treatment of *The Ancient Mariner* constitute covert character analyses (pp. 30–31).

17. Baruch Hochman, *Character in Literature* (Ithaca: Cornell University Press, 1985), p. 68.

18. This unpredictability approaches what Vincent B. Leitch calls a joyous Nietzschean freeplay: "Interpretation imposes structures to delimit and arrest *play*. . . . Nevertheless, *play* precedes the operations of structuration. . . . Before the alternative of presence or absence and prior to the possibility of center or structure, *play* operates." *Deconstructive Criticism: An Advanced Introduction* (New York: Columbia University Press, 1983), pp. 36–37.

19. Roland Barthes, *Tel Quel*, pp. 142–43; quoted in Leitch, p. 106. Leitch gives other, even pithier formulations: "The author may visit the text only as a guest" (p. 107) and "The author is a name" (p. 177).

20. Jonathan Culler defines intention deconstructively as "not something prior to the text that determines its meaning but . . . an important organizing structure identified in readings that distinguish an explicit line of argumentation from its subversive other" (p. 218). Yet how do we know here which of the two structures is intentional and which subversive of it? As critic after critic resurrects intention in order to dismember it anew, the author comes to resemble one of the heroes in Valhalla, killed off during the day only to be resurrected every evening to fight again on the morrow.

21. While I hope to show that he succeeds, and succeeds consistently, by embodying intent within a separate presence, I realize that for Derrida presence remains as problematic a concept as intent. The presence I am here affirming, however, is itself

rendered problematic by the spatial model within which it is placed. In the very affirmation of its presence, it must define (and so delimit) itself against an Other which not only threatens its existence but denies its self-ascribed plenitude.

22. As we consider individual poems in the sequence of their composition, moreover, we discover that a given outcome in one seems almost to predetermine a very different outcome in the next. The model, in other words, maintains its autonomy by alternating among its possible permutations.

23. The model proposed by Linda K. Hughes claims that Tennyson controlled his turbulent inner world through a formal structure which gave it dramatic credibility: he "could release one aspect of his divided mentality [what Hughes calls the *Ding an Mich*] at a time, then juxtapose the results, as in his paired monologues. . . . He could even participate in what he most desired yet feared (through the sympathetic identification used to flesh out first-person utterance) yet protect himself from his source of fear by conquering and encapsulating it through poetic form." *The Manyfaced Glass: Tennyson's Dramatic Monologues* (Athens: Ohio University Press, 1987), p. 23. While this model is both powerful and elegant, to me it works better for nineteenth- and twentieth-century poetry as a whole than for Tennyson in particular. It posits a ratio—inner is to outer as content is to form—which fails to acknowledge T. S. Eliot's famous remark that "Tennyson's surface, his technical accomplishment, is intimate with his depths." "In Memoriam," *Essays Ancient and Modern* (London: Faber and Faber, 1936), pp. 186–203; cited in *Critical Essays on the Poetry of Tennyson*, ed. John Killham (London: Routledge and Kegan Paul, 1960), p. 215. See also Alan Sinfield's more radical formulation: "Rather than closing the gap between sign and referent, Tennyson creates, as it were, a plenitude of the sign." *Alfred Tennyson* (Oxford: Basil Blackwell, 1986), pp. 86–91.

24. Hallam Tennyson, *Alfred Lord Tennyson: A Memoir by His Son* (London: Macmillan, 1897), II, 225. Hereafter cited as *Memoir*.

25. Letter to Clough, 12 February 1853. If we may believe Hallam's claim (II, 225) that Arnold "told [Tennyson's comment] about himself gleefully all over London," we may see just how flattered he was to be still considered a poet.

26. Despite fine source studies like Lourie's, despite Bloom's claims that Tennyson ultimately failed to surpass the high Romanticism embodied for him in Hallam, I will argue that his achievement remained his own principally because his model remained his own. I do not doubt that modifications of it would show comparable scenarios dramatizing the works of other ostensibly lyric poets. Yet I do doubt that other poets would define the particular qualities of the Other so resolutely as other, would grant to their mediating characters such consistent yet such grudging independence, would work to subvert the lyric as vehicle of desire by granting such fullness to the authorial presence. Finally I doubt that any poet but Tennyson would give such bafflingly complex expression to his own intentions. Margaret Lourie, "Below the Thunders of the Upper Deep: Tennyson as Romantic Revisionist," *Studies in Romanticism*, 18 (1979), 3–27. Harold Bloom, *The Ringers in the Tower* (Chicago: University of Chicago Press, 1971), pp. 145–54.

27. See Elizabeth Wright, *Psychoanalytic Criticism: Theory in Practice* (London: Methuen, 1984), pp. 9–11.

28. Ernest Jones, "The Theory of Symbolism" (1916), in *Papers on Psychoanalysis*, 5th ed. (Boston: Beacon, 1961), p. 97.

29. Leo Bersani, *A Future for Astyanax: Character and Desire in Literature* (Boston: Little Brown, 1976), p. 6.

30. Skura offers a Freudian topography closer to this one: "Where Freud seems to have pictured a heroic ego barely holding up the dam on the banks of the id, Shakespeare has his cities and encampments surrounded by Turks and oceans and witch-infested heaths. Again and again we see the boundaries of ordinary rational life breaking down, and with them the boundaries of the ordinary rational self" (p. 35). In some cases, to be sure, the position of the Other may be more central and its nature less foreign than Tennyson wants to admit. He may actually be projecting into it qualities which he does not want to acknowledge as his own.

31. Lionel Stevenson, "The 'High-Born Maiden' Symbol in Tennyson," *PMLA*, 63 (1948), 234–43.

32. Gerhard Joseph, "Tennyson's Three Women: The Thought within the Image," *Victorian Poetry*, 19 (1981), 8–13.

33. See Jacqueline Rose, introduction to *Feminine Sexuality: Jacques Lacan and the école freudienne* (New York: Norton, 1982), pp. 30–31, 45. Sinfield (pp. 67–69, 98–100) describes Lacan's relevance to Tennyson primarily in terms of loss.

34. In current feminist theory the Other is the woman's self, decentered from its rightful position by social and psychological forces which deny its claims to autonomy. In the context of this study, however, the Other frequently becomes an aspect of these same social forces, attempting to oust the authorial presence from its central position in order to control and enlarge some spatial domain of its own. In explaining Foucault's notion of the *archive*, a culture's cache of unchallenged rules and practices, Leitch notes that "to us the *archive* appears as 'Other'—as difference" (p. 147).

35. *The Poems of Tennyson*, ed. Christopher Ricks, 2d ed., 3 vols. (Berkeley: University of California Press, 1987). Hereafter cited parenthetically as *Poems*. Unless otherwise indicated, all quotations from Tennyson's printed poems are taken from this edition. Ricks's modernization of spelling and punctuation will have no bearing upon this study.

36. See Hanna Segal's description: "The memory of the good situation, where the infant's ego contained the whole loved object and the realization that it has been lost through his own attacks gives rise to an intense feeling of loss and guilt, and to the wish to restore and recreate the lost loved object outside and within the ego. This wish to restore and recreate is the basis of later sublimation and creativity." "Psychoanalytical Approach to Aesthetics," quoted in Reuben Fine, *A History of Psychoanalysis* (New York: Columbia University Press, 1979), p. 272. Fine also analyzes another possible formulation of Tennyson's aesthetic strategy, Ernst Kris's work on regression in the service of the ego (pp. 274–75, 303–5).

37. The fact that this story was probably fabricated only testifies to its continuing hold on our imagination.

38. Steven C. Dillon, "Milton and Tennyson's 'Guinevere,'" *ELH*, 54 (1987), 153. Dillon supports this paradox (pp. 132–33) with telling Miltonic parallels: When Lancelot pulls the spying Modred from his lair and drops him to the ground, "Lan-

celot suddenly and astonishingly becomes Christ: '[Satan] the Almighty Power /
Hurl'd headlong flaming from th'Ethereal Sky.' . . . The passage is finally more con-
vincing . . . than any of the Christlike figures later bequeathed to Arthur." Yet be-
cause Modred "is spying, after all, on the adulterous lovers Lancelot and Guinevere,
. . . Lancelot is ultimately also a Satan figure, and . . . even more responsible than
Modred for laying waste to Camelot."

1. The Adolescent Poems

1. Carol Christ, *The Finer Optic: The Aesthetic of Particularity in Victorian Poetry*
(New Haven: Yale University Press, 1975), p. 12. All parenthetical references to
Christ are to this book. Albright's version of the disease presents slightly different
symptoms: "Preoccupation with one's feelings leads to a smeared . . . state of being,
in which the line of demarcation between oneself and one's environment grows faint.
Nature bulges . . . while the men within it grow oddly depleted" (p. 25). Hallam,
privy to Tennyson's earlier poetry, sees in this morbid individuality the difference, not
between Romantic and Victorian poetry, but between nineteenth-century and Elizabethan *Zeitgeists*: "Hence the melancholy, which so evidently characterizes the spirit
of modern poetry; hence that return of the mind upon itself, and the habit of seeking
relief in idiosyncrasies rather than community of interest. In the old times the poetic
impulse went along with the general impulse of the nation; in these, it is a reaction
against it, a check acting for conservation against a propulsion towards change." Unsigned review, *Englishman's Magazine* (August 1831), i, 616–28; cited in *Tennyson: The
Critical Heritage*, ed. John D. Jump (London: Routledge and Kegan Paul, 1967), p. 41.

2. The appearance of Tucker's *Tennyson and the Doom of Romanticism* a few months
before this study went to press allowed me to cite it thoroughly but prevented me
from making use of his consistently powerful readings in formulating my own. I have
retained frequent references to his articles, in part because they offer fuller analyses
of Tennyson's individual characters. In one of these, Tucker argues that "the tech-
nically musical perfection of [Tennyson's] craft is associated with a power that isolates
and anaesthetizes the self." "Strange Comfort: A Reading of Tennyson's Unpublished Juvenilia," *Victorian Poetry*, 21 (1983), 24.

3. Letter to Benjamin Bailey, 22 November 1817, quoted in *Letters of John Keats*,
ed. Robert Gittings (London: Oxford University Press, 1970), p. 37.

4. Tennyson's early problems in integrating imaginative identification and formal
control are well analyzed by Hughes, *Glass*, pp. 30, 40–44.

5. Though far more intuitive, far less self-consciously mythopoeic, his response
almost foreshadows that of Rilke when confronted with *his* intimation of supernatural
presences: "Who if I cried out would hear me from out the angelic orders? / And
even if one should take me suddenly to his heart, I would expire from his stronger
existence" (*Duino Elegies*, I, 1–2).

6. Although Tucker sees Tennyson's approach as more direct than I do, he accurately points out the potential solipsism inherent in any identification with such an
outer power: "the community addressed by Tennyson's earliest poetry approaches the
integer one, whether its 'oneness' is conceived as the solitude of his detached voice or

as the universality of sentient being in the grip of doom. There is no more emotional compromise or mediation in such poetry than there is middle distance in the landscapes it describes" ("Strange Comfort," p. 24).

7. A. Dwight Culler, *The Poetry of Tennyson* (New Haven: Yale University Press, 1977), p. 17. Unless otherwise indicated, all parenthetical references to Culler are to this book.

8. See, however, Paul Turner's suggestion that Tennyson stopped to avoid confronting a family conflict: "The translation stops just before the text of an angry message to the god of heaven, containing a complaint that might almost have been addressed by Dr Tennyson to his brother Charles at Bayons Manor." *Tennyson* (London: Routledge and Kegan Paul, 1976), p. 35.

9. *Memoir*, I, 15. While Paden (pp. 73–75) attributes this threat to sexual guilt, most of his examples come from Tennyson's later adolescence. In slightly different form this analysis appeared in my article, "Spatial and Temporal Vision in Early Tennyson," *Victorian Poetry*, 11 (1973), 323–29. A much fuller one has since appeared in Tucker's "Strange Comfort," pp. 9–14, and in his book. There (pp. 33–34) he notes that while these poems "ostensibly concern devils and gods, heaven and hell, and the battle of good against evil, they are remarkably amoral performances, explosions of a precocious verbal gift that may be most precocious in its cool exploration of the sources of its peculiar power."

10. This is one of the few poems in Tennyson which contains two opposing manifestations of the Other. Balanced against one another, however, they seem almost two halves of some larger force. For other serpents in Tennyson see Paden, *Egypt*, pp. 45–50, 136; and Joseph, *Love*, pp. 35–37.

11. Aidan Day, "The Spirit of Fable: Arthur Hallam and Romantic Values in Tennyson's 'Timbuctoo,'" *Tennyson Research Bulletin*, 4, no. 2 (1983), 64. Tucker argues (p. 46) that Tennyson is following Keats in that "the tendency toward transcendence . . . met in him a countermovement toward the body and earth."

12. Carl Robinson Sonn argues that "the experiences like those described in 'Armageddon,' 'Timbuctoo,' and 'The Mystic,' . . . represent less a communion with God than an intensification of individuality." "Poetic Vision and Religious Certitude in Tennyson's Earlier Poetry," *Modern Philology*, 57 (1959), 91. Or again (p. 87), "his intimations of God, like his intimations of infinite vision, are intimations of personal omnipotence." For Tucker, however ("Strange Comfort," p. 21), "as elsewhere in Tennyson's juvenilia, . . . events are mysteriously impelled through persons who are passive agents more than creative actors." And in a broader context, "recognitions of . . . the deep music of doom . . . demanded nothing less than the extinction of what he regarded as the human personality" ("Measure of Doom," p. 14). Although Albright prefers the term "sublime" (pp. 3–12 passim), he too sees the state as threatening personality. Tennyson's most detailed account (*Memoir*, I, 320) actually shapes both individuality and its surrender into prerequisites for the trances themselves: "out of the intensity of the consciousness of individuality, the individuality itself seemed to dissolve and fade away into boundless being, and this not a confused state, but the clearest of the clearest . . . the loss of personality (if it were so) seeming no extinction but the only true life. . . . But in a moment, when I come back to my normal state of 'sanity,' I am ready to fight for *mein liebes Ich*, and hold that it will last

for aeons of aeons." (According to David Staines, Hallam actually took this description from his father's letter to an American philosopher and mystic, Benjamin Paul Blood. "Tennyson's Mysticism: A Personal Testimony," *Notes and Queries*, 222 [n.s. 24], [1977], 404–5.) The early visions contain both these states; more significant, however, they contain a further prerequisite: just before succumbing to self-worship, Tennyson acknowledges that he is "a part of the Unchangeable, / A scintillation of Eternal Mind" (II, 46–47). Paradoxically, to reaffirm this "personal omnipotence," he needs to posit another source for such power.

13. See Ricks, *Poems*, I, 93n, 314, 514n; also Paden, *Egypt*, pp. 76–84.

14. Tucker finds in this "ontological throb . . . the poet's deep need to find in the rhythmic evidence of his own heartbeat a means of sympathetic contact with a power beyond anything he could see" ("Strange Comfort," p. 22).

15. This version still appears only in the notes to Ricks's *Poems*. Descriptions of it also appear in his article in *TLS* (21 August 1969), p. 921, and in Day's "Spirit of Fable," pp. 68–69. This passage became lines 132–37 of "Timbuctoo."

16. Simple geography also forces the transfer of the vision to the south from its eastern site in part 8 of the Trinity "Armageddon." For the historical context of Tennyson's fears about "keen Discovery," see Hallman B. Bryant, "The African Genesis of Tennyson's 'Timbuctoo,'" *Tennyson Research Bulletin*, 5, no. 5 (1981), 200–201.

17. W. David Shaw, *Tennyson's Style* (Ithaca: Cornell University Press, 1976), p. 52. Unless otherwise indicated, all parenthetical references to Shaw are to this book. For Tucker the "mythmaking faculty . . . now receives the homage Tennyson earlier paid to the intuitive mind alone. . . . He enters . . . into a lifetime contract with that great benefactor of imagination, the sense of the cultural past" (pp. 53–54).

18. *Ringers in the Tower*, pp. 145–54.

19. Quoted in Sylva Norman, *The Flight of the Skylark: The Development of Shelley's Reputation* (Norman: University of Oklahoma Press, 1954), p. 98.

20. Tucker, however, claims that Tennyson "seems to have been moved especially by turns of phrase that emphasize the sense of aftermath we find in his own writing" (p. 26).

21. Tucker (p. 63) finds a different, "distinctly poetic potential that this clearing operation holds forth. . . . Whatever the cutting edge of 'keen *Discovery*' may pare away from fable has never really been fable's to begin with."

22. Harvard Notebook 1 (H.Nbk 1) and Trinity Notebook 19 (T.Nbk 19). For the dating of each see *Poems*, I, 13–15. I have used Ricks's abbreviations throughout except for manuscripts of *In Memoriam*, *Maud*, and the *Idylls*, where the treatments of Shatto, Shaw, and Pfordresher are far more detailed.

23. Culler notes (p. 9) that Tennyson "has made this [the magical power of the word] into a major theme in his own play."

24. Even though I make frequent use of a text's order and position within a manuscript, I have finally decided against including folio numbers. This is not primarily a manuscript study but a critical study using manuscript evidence. Such numbers, in any case, could mean nothing to readers without access to the manuscripts or photocopies of them. Readers with such access can quickly find the relevant folios and check my interpretations for themselves.

25. W. D. Paden, "MT.1352: Jacques de Vitry, The Mensa Philosophica, Hödeken, and Tennyson," *Journal of American Folklore*, 58 (1945), 45.

26. Joseph points out (p. 124) that the "worm is within Amoret herself; she is both flower and worm."

2. The 1830 Volume and *The Lover's Tale*

1. Although not published even in a trial run until 1832, the poem exists in manuscript drafts dating, according to Ricks (*Poems*, I, 327), well back into the 1820s.

2. Clyde de L. Ryals, *Theme and Symbol in Tennyson's Poems to 1850* (Philadelphia: University of Pennsylvania Press, 1964), p. 38.

3. See also Paden's references (pp. 65–70) to thrones in Tennyson's earlier poetry.

4. Christopher Ricks reverses the roles but not the nexus when he puts Tennyson inside the mind of the Kraken: the poem's "depth of feeling comes from Tennyson's pained fascination with the thought of a life which somehow is no life at all." *Tennyson* (New York: Macmillan, 1972), p. 44. Hereafter cited parenthetically as *Tennyson*. For Robert Preyer, "all we know is that below the historical surface of events (or below the level of ordinary consciousness) lurk mindless forces capable of exploding to the surface in a burst of irrational frenzy." "Tennyson as an Oracular Poet," *Modern Philology*, 55 (1958), 240–41. Preyer's reading, though published in 1958, seems in retrospect almost deconstructive in its disjunction of image, emotion, and author: "Though our attention is continuously being directed toward a succession of images, our emotion is not about them. . . . We are left, not with the central inert image of the Kraken, but rather with . . . what . . . we may call 'oceanic feelings.' . . . The poem aspires to utter itself. It must avoid . . . indications of an informing authorial mind."

5. James Donald Welsh offers an extended analysis of these lines in both spatial and temporal dimensions. "Tennyson's Landscapes of Time and a Reading of 'The Kraken,'" *Victorian Poetry*, 14 (1976), 201.

6. Critics have become so entranced by the beautiful stanza on the bulbul that they tend to structure the poem around it. Timothy Peltason's extended reading, for example, argues that "the bulbul does seem truly central, occupying 'middle night' and the seventh of fourteen stanzas, and performing the crucial imaginative feat of mingling the contraries." "The Embowered Self: 'Mariana' and 'Recollections of the Arabian Nights,'" *Victorian Poetry*, 21 (1983), 337. Yet even here the transcendent claims of the nightingale's song are bathetically deflated by the temporal and spatial context of the refrain: "Apart from place, withholding time, / But flattering the golden prime / Of good Haroun Alraschid." Peltason does claim later (p. 338) that "bulbul and sultan are alike the great artificers of the realm," but Tucker counters (p. 84) that the "power that commands 'the darkness of the world' cannot quite be identical with the power wielded by good Haroun Alrashid." For him, "the voyeuristic quest of the boy's dream vision reaches its goal when he beholds an object of desire that is also a mirror of his satisfied self. A merrily narcissistic eros greets its own image" (pp. 84–85).

7. Peltason's extended analysis of this poem also points out that "the human and natural scene are related only through simile and through the excited simile-making

power of the poet's imagination." "Tennyson, Nature, and Romantic Nature Poetry," *Philological Quarterly*, 63 (1984), 88. Peltason claims that the disparate details in the whole scene are held together only by the swan's song. Tucker (p. 91) argues that "Tennyson's thronging nature reproduces in a minor key the joyful tumult immured in the simile."

8. Herbert F. Tucker, "Tennyson's Narrative of Desire: *The Lover's Tale*," *Victorian Newsletter*, no. 62 (Fall 1982), 22.

9. For Sunderland's reply see Robert Bernard Martin, *Tennyson: The Unquiet Heart* (New York: Oxford University Press, 1980), p. 98. All parenthetical references to Martin are to this book.

10. This progression is also analyzed by Hughes, *Glass*, pp. 51–55.

11. *Complete Poems*, ed. Jack Stillinger (Cambridge: Belknap Press, 1982), p. 372. All quotations from Keats are from this edition.

12. Peltason notes "the absence of any single perceiving figure who could compose of these details an integrated scene." He takes her weeping as "a part of that spreading sameness of mood through which Mariana converts every stimulus to the same response. . . . The poem is carefully staged to distinguish Mariana's perceptions from the narrator's . . . [who] is both everywhere in his poem and nowhere in particular in it" ("The Embowered Self," pp. 342–48). Boyd and Williams replace this split between figure and poet with the extension of *erlebte Rede* which we examined in the Introduction. The poet's participation, however, only emphasizes Mariana's psychological decline as her "field of perception is narrowed to scenes within the bedroom and the house. And even those perceptions . . . become interior in yet another sense, as the sights and sounds become noticeably distorted and exaggerated. . . . The speaker's field begins by encompassing an area that extends well beyond Mariana's, but then gradually narrows its circumference until, in the last two stanzas, the invisible speaker's vision and Mariana's (and the reader's) are very nearly one" (pp. 587–88).

13. Although Peltason rejects it, he does consider the possibility "that her own diseased perceptions may be creating her surroundings in a dangerous literalization of the poet's activity" ("The Embowered Self," p. 343). Shaw also defines Mariana's creativity (p. 79) as the power to "make even absent things more real than immediate impressions."

14. Tennyson did not call the speaker Julian and his beloved Camilla until the revision and extension of the poem in 1870. Consequently I have left him nameless and have used her 1832 name, Cadrilla.

15. Ricks notes (*Poems*, I, 326) that the text is actually dated 1833.

16. According to *Poems*, I, 327, Aidan Day argues that "*H.Nbk 8* (watermarked 1825, and containing poems 1828–30) is apparently fragmentary but can be reconstructed . . . to yield a complete 111-line version of Part i."

17. Albright (p. 63) parallels this relationship with that of Balin and Balan: "Both suggest narcissistic involution, a world collapsed into a deathly embrace."

18. Betty Miller, "Tennyson and the Sinful Queen," *Twentieth Century*, 158 (October, 1955), 362–63.

19. Clarice Short, "Tennyson and 'The Lover's Tale,'" *PMLA*, 82 (1967), 83. Tennyson, as Short observes, implicitly acknowledged the power of these visions by

exempting them from the wholesale revisions to which he subjected the rest of the poem.

20. Tucker also argues ("Strange Comfort," p. 28) "that by 1832 the poet was working his way towards a fuller understanding of such matters than Paden allows."

21. Johnston claims (p. 75) that Lionel here "as master of ceremonies becomes a kind of King of Death." This interpretation turns Cadrilla into Proserpine and the speaker into a male Demeter.

22. Tucker ("Lover's Tale," p. 28) interprets the detachment in the first vision as a "sour grapes consolation" that her love was not worth winning and in the second as a fear that his love would be fatal to her.

23. While Boccaccio's hero nurses an unrequited passion for a woman already married to another, Tennyson's hero and heroine, as orphaned first cousins, share a strong but initially undefined affection from birth. When Boccaccio's heroine dies in pregnancy, the hero decides to gain in her death what she had refused to grant him in life. He secretly visits her tomb, kisses her yet warm lips, and then, touching her breast, feels the faint beating of her heart. He carries her to his mother's house, where she is fully revived, is brought to bed of a healthy son, and finally (at a dinner full of much pomp) is magnanimously returned to her surprised and delighted husband. Within the 1832 poem, as we saw, even the visions contain only hints of Cadrilla's death.

24. Harvard Notebook 8, second and first stubs recto before f. 30*. The asterisk indicates that Tennyson was using the notebook upside down. Hence these folios would appear to him on the verso, and ripping off their outer edges would leave the last half of the lines quoted above. My transcription of the first fragment differs only slightly from Short's. Ricks notes that "A. Day . . . adduces other anticipations of the sequel" (*Poems*, I, 327).

25. Fragment ixB, *Poems*, III, 610. Short (p. 79) also prints a truncated version of this passage. All these fragments, coming from Harvard Notebook 8, presumably predate the long, unadopted concluding passage (*Poems*, III, 580–83) from Trinity Notebook 18.

26. This reading is meant to supplement, not supersede, Culler's emphasis on the speaker's opening meditation, a frame within which the remainder of the extant poem forms one long flashback. Culler sees the speaker bringing this past to life and reality only "in the very process . . . of re-experiencing his narrative even as he narrates it. . . . The real subject of the poem is not the things that happened to him in the past but the things that happen to him now, as he relives the past" (p. 36). As Ricks's second edition of *Poems* makes clear, this frame was even longer in Trinity Notebook 18 than in the 1832 version.

3. The 1832 Volume

1. For an example of this reading see Paull F. Baum, *Tennyson Sixty Years After* (Chapel Hill: University of North Carolina Press, 1948), pp. 85–86. Though dated 1833, the volume actually appeared in December of 1832. See Martin, p. 160.

2. Tucker (p. 131) sees such strategies as impediments to the poet's frequently

impeded quest for engagement and relationship: "If my account of the 1832 *Poems* is accurate, life to the Hesperides was death to him, and he should have sought routes of escape from the static perfection of their seductively inhibited chant." Such readings seem to me distorted by a correlation Tucker assumes between aesthetic and psychological norms.

3. Tucker (p. 121) sees this function as the culmination of a gradual process: "what began as a 'pleasure-house' has at length become a fortress."

4. Tennyson's own note to the 1832 volume, *Poems*, I, 450.

5. F. E. L. Priestley, *Language and Structure in Tennyson's Poetry* (London: Deutsch, 1973), p. 40. Unless otherwise indicated, all parenthetical references to Priestley are to this book.

6. J. W. Croker savaged this stanza for what he saw as its grotesque inconsistency. Unsigned review, *Quarterly Review*, xlix (April 1833), 81–96; in Jump, *Critical Heritage*, p. 79.

7. William Cadbury, "Tennyson's 'Palace of Art' and the Rhetoric of Structures," *Criticism*, 7 (1965), 30–31.

8. The 1832 version differs slightly. See *Poems*, I, 441n.

9. James R. Kincaid, "Tennyson's Mariner's and Spenser's Despair: The Argument of 'The Lotos-Eaters,'" *Papers on Language and Literature*, 5 (1969), 281.

10. Douglas Bush, *Mythology and the Romantic Tradition in English Poetry* (Cambridge: Harvard University Press, 1937), p. 207. All parenthetical references to Bush are to this book.

11. Alan Grob, "Tennyson's 'The Lotos-Eaters': Two Versions of Art," *Modern Philology*, 62 (1964), 127. For him (p. 125) the earlier version intimates that "the perfected image of art . . . alone can introduce a note of permanence and order into a world composed of otherwise fleeting sensation." Linda Hughes feels that the forceful rhythms of the original last stanza, complementing the seductive imagery of earlier stanzas, approximate the continuity of human response which the reader's judgment demands. "The Reader as Mariner: Tennyson's 'The Lotos-Eaters,'" *English Language Notes*, 16 (1979), 304–8.

12. For example, see Shaw, *Style*, p. 68; Priestley, *Language*, p. 59; Ryals, *Theme and Symbol*, p. 98.

13. Harvard Notebook 3. Since this manuscript breaks off in the middle of a page, we for once do not have to consider the possibility of missing sheets.

14. Robert Pattison describes the idyll form as making cosmic flux "knowable," but to me the Mariners are after something more permanent than knowledge. *Tennyson and Tradition* (Cambridge: Harvard University Press, 1979), p. 63. All parenthetical references to Pattison are to this book.

15. Ernest Fontana, "Virginal Hysteria in Tennyson's 'The Hesperides,'" *Concerning Poetry*, 8, no. 2 (Fall 1975), 17.

16. For a detailed analysis of their tree's complex relation to both the Tree of Life and the Tree of Knowledge, see Aidan Day, "Voices in a Dream: The Language of Skepticism in Tennyson's 'The Hesperides,'" *Victorian Newsletter*, no. 62 (Fall 1982), 15–16.

17. Christine Gallant, "Tennyson's Use of the Nature Goddess in 'The Hes-

perides,' 'Tithonus,' and 'Demeter and Persephone,'" *Victorian Poetry*, 14 (1976), 157–58.

18. Harold Bloom, *Poetry and Repression: Revisionism from Blake to Stevens* (New Haven: Yale University Press, 1976), p. 156.

19. According to Kerry McSweeney, the whole poem "is only a single moment endlessly prolonged." *Tennyson and Swinburne as Romantic Naturalists* (Toronto: University of Toronto Press, 1981), p. 46. Unless otherwise indicated, all parenthetical references to McSweeney are to this book.

20. Matthew Rowlinson, "The Skipping Muse: Repetition and Difference in Two Early Poems of Tennyson," *Victorian Poetry*, 22 (1984), 354–61. I am less convinced by his interpretations of the language as autoerotic and of the poem itself as "a masturbatory fantasy." While this landscape, like many of Tennyson's, holds ample free-floating eroticism, Rowlinson simply needs too many defensive displacements to support his scenario.

21. See, for example, Day (p. 19): "Issuing from a region for which there are effectively no literal spatial equivalents the voices of the Garden are . . . essentially enclosed with the space of Hanno's own consciousness."

22. Tucker, *Doom*, p. 127. He continues by suggesting how the Sisters' incantation generates itself from its own patterns of sound and rhythm.

23. Fontana (p. 19) sees Tennyson imitating Hanno by charting new psychological territory. But Rowlinson argues (pp. 358–61) that in distancing the garden from Hanno, Tennyson was disguising his debt to Keats's "To Autumn" by claiming a temporal anteriority.

24. Day's reading baptizes one made originally by James D. Merriman. "The Poet as Heroic Thief: Tennyson's 'The Hesperides' Reexamined," *Victorian Newsletter*, no. 35 (Spring 1969), 5.

25. Paden, *Egypt*, pp. 39, 132n.

26. For the date of composition see *Poems*, I, 630.

27. Tucker, *Doom*, p. 150; Hughes, *Glass*, p. 65. Tucker and Hughes are the first to challenge traditional readings which speak condescendingly about Tennyson's sexual indirection and then dismiss this poem as derivative or even tasteless. Yet even Tucker decries "its stridency of tone and formal shakiness" (p. 145) and assures us that Fatima is striving for "a consummate mutuality whereby she and her deified lover will possess each other and stand in each other's place" (p. 152). For me, an encounter between the sun and a mediator with the cosmic, amoral sexuality of an Amoret seems an odd context for the norms of twentieth-century interpersonal relations.

28. Comparing the 1842 Mariana to her 1830 counterpart Tucker concludes (p. 139) that "palpability of detail increases in proportion to the poet's imaginative distance from the character through whom he speaks."

29. Although her wish for a "night . . . that knows not morn" certainly includes death, I cannot see it as nihilistic. In a world where light is a "furnace," darkness itself assumes a transcendence.

30. While two recent articles have carefully analyzed the extant manuscripts of the poem, they indirectly support our continued use of the 1832 and 1842 texts of these poems as representative early and late stages within Tennyson's composing process.

See Philip Gaskell, *From Writer to Reader* (London: Oxford University Press, 1978), pp. 118–41; and Aidan Day, "Two Unrecorded Stages in the Revision of Tennyson's 'Oenone' for *Poems*, 1842," *Library*, 6th series, 2 (1980), 315–25.

31. For Rowlinson (p. 353), this judgment remains crassly artificial: "desire is [here] not naturally attached to its object but constituted as a written sign, referring only to other signs, and available for arbitrary exchange. . . . Fairness becomes a quality constituted as possession of the apple bearing the inscription 'For the most fair.'"

32. Joseph points out (pp. 144–45) that all the goddesses' offers would have proven equally disastrous for Oenone.

33. Because he sees all these attempts at "self-embowering" as psychologically regressive, Tucker is less concerned that Oenone's attempt fails than that it might succeed.

34. For Shaw (p. 82), "her circling syntax is necessary as a psychological defense, a stay against confusion." In fact its very artificiality mitigates against the distinction which Rowlinson makes (p. 353) between her evocation of nature and the reduction of desire to arbitrary commodity in Paris's judgment.

35. Tucker compares her to "Samson in her determination to take others with her" (p. 169).

36. Epistle 5, "Oenone to Paris." For a different series of contrasts between Tennyson's Oenone and Ovid's, see Paul Turner, "Some Ancient Light on Tennyson's *Oenone*," *JEGP*, 61 (1962), 66–70.

37. To quote Shaw (p. 63), Tennyson "never allows the Lady to assume an individualized form."

38. McSweeney (pp. 38–67) analyzes these transitional times in many of Tennyson's early poems, but not in this one.

39. Ann C. Colley, "The Quest for the 'Nameless' in Tennyson's 'The Lady of Shalott,'" *Victorian Poetry*, 23 (1985), 370–71.

40. See Edgar F. Shannon's analysis of this figure as a synthesis of his world. "Poetry as Vision: Sight and Insight in 'The Lady of Shalott,'" *Victorian Poetry*, 19 (1981), 213–14. Tucker (p. 112) is more cynical: "Lancelot is no presence, but pure representation: a man of mirrors, a signifier as hollow as the song he sings." For the poem as a proof text for postmodern criticism, see Gerhard Joseph, "Victorian Weaving: The Alienation of Work into Text in 'The Lady of Shalott,'" *Victorian Newsletter*, no. 71 (Spring 1987), 7–10.

41. Shannon (p. 216–22) sees her moving into spiritual transcendence, Colley (pp. 372–76) into a figurative integrity denied to the rest of her world, and Lona Mosk Packer into a fuller participation in life. "Sun and Shadow: The Nature of Experience in Tennyson's 'The Lady of Shalott,'" *Victorian Newsletter*, no. 25 (Spring 1964), 7–8. Colley argues that by naming her boat she is inscribing herself upon her landscape, but her 1832 attempt to dictate her reception with a written parchment drew Mill's well-earned rebuke (*Poems*, I, 395n).

42. Flavia M. Alaya, "Tennyson's 'The Lady of Shalott': The Triumph of Art," *Victorian Poetry*, 8 (1970), 286–87. Tucker (p. 114) finds in the journey her recognition that she has entrapped herself "in the vicious circle of a desire for illusions of her

own making." Her curse thus recapitulates that of the speaker in *The Lover's Tale*: "she has given her heart to an image nothing in the wide world can rival."

43. Colley argues (pp. 377–78) that Tennyson finds himself on the bank with Lancelot and the reader, uncomfortably conscious of the figurative inadequacy of his world, yet unwilling to commit himself to death and "the Nameless" with his heroine. For a useful summary of different responses to the epitaph, see Shannon, "Poetry," p. 222.

44. For the connection of forests in Tennyson with the unconscious, see Paden, *Egypt*, pp. 61–62.

45. Kincaid, by contrast, argues (p. 25) that the Christian references to organs and cathedrals ironically undermine her rationalizations.

46. Tennyson was fond of quoting these lines. See Tucker, *Doom*, pp. 26–27 passim.

47. Ricks (*Tennyson*, pp. 96–97) includes virtually the whole poem within this failure.

4. The 1842 Volume

1. *Theme and Symbol*, p. 161.

2. Herbert F. Tucker, "From Monomania to Monologue: 'St. Simeon Stylites' and the Rise of the Victorian Dramatic Monologue," *Victorian Poetry*, 22 (1984), 133.

3. *Theme and Symbol*, p. 143.

4. Martin Dodsworth claims that Tennyson cast "Simeon" as a dramatic monologue because he was uncomfortable in his mockery. "Patterns of Morbidity Represented in Tennyson's Poetry," in *The Major Victorian Poets: Reconsiderations*, ed. Isobel Armstrong (Lincoln: University of Nebraska Press, 1969), pp. 16–17. James R. Kincaid traces Simeon's religious terror to the celebration of pain which Camus finds at the center of the Christian mythos. "Rhetorical Irony, the Dramatic Monologue, and Tennyson's *Poems* (1842)," *Philological Quarterly*, 53 (1974), 234–35.

5. Ricks, *Poems*, I, 598n, 602n. Dorothy Mermin attributes the increasingly sympathetic image of Simeon in these added passages to a switch of sources from Hone's *Every-Day Book* to Gibbon. *The Audience in the Poem* (New Brunswick: Rutgers University Press, 1983), pp. 22–23.

6. As Ricks notes (*Poems*, I, 586n), both the Heath Manuscript and a virtual copy of it in another hand (Harvard Lpr 254) break off with a single stanza added after line 309. The Harvard manuscript, in particular, has a definitive double line drawn after this stanza.

7. Ricks, *Poems*, I, 570. In his *Tennyson* (p. 103) Ricks questions "whether Kemble thought that the suicidal voice or the soul was 'floored.'"

8. Arthur J. Carr, "Tennyson as a Modern Poet," in Killham, *Critical Essays on the Poetry of Tennyson*, pp. 51–54.

9. See Tucker (p. 178): "Hallam's death must have portended for Tennyson, if not the death of poetry, then the death of the poetry of confrontation and social responsibility."

10. "On a Mourner," though not in the *In Memoriam* stanza, appears in manuscript with those lyrics. I am also omitting unpublished poems such as "Youth" and "Hark! The Dogs Howl."

11. See Priestley, *Language*, pp. 52–55 and Shaw, *Style*, pp. 259–60.

12. Thomas J. Assad analyzes the circular movement, both spatial and psychological, from the nearby sea, to the boy, to the ships, and back. "Tennyson's 'Break, Break, Break,'" *Tulane Studies in English*, 12 (1963) 74.

13. For Shaw (p. 260), "the poignant life of 'a day that is dead' (l. 15) hovers just beyond language."

14. According to Ryals (*Theme and Symbol*, p. 105), Tennyson "is projecting himself into the 'object,' the sea . . . so completely . . . that the object is allowed to generate its own laws." For a cogent summary of the sea's various roles, see H. Sopher, "The 'Puzzling Plainness' of 'Break, Break, Break': Its Deep and Surface Structure," *Victorian Poetry*, 19 (1981), 93.

15. Though he may underemphasize Tennyson's formal originality, Pattison offers (pp. 156–57n) a concise and carefully researched history of the genre.

16. For Tucker, Tennyson is here "running the contextualizing devices of his newly discovered genre in reverse. . . . All three are in quest of a hidden yet imaginable god abiding apart from nature and history. In forecasting meetings with this power they explicitly discount contingency, decontextualize themselves" ("Monomania," pp. 136–37; see also *Doom*, p. 192). For me their discovery of context seems both more vivid and ultimately more impressive than their quest to escape it in some further encounter.

17. Trinity Notebook 15. For a fuller account of the compositional process, see my article "Three Stages of Tennyson's 'Tiresias,'" *JEGP*, 75 (1976), 154–67.

18. Tucker (p. 194) extrapolates from this indeterminacy that the passage may have been more lyric than dramatic.

19. See Culler, *Poetry*, p. 89. Tucker argues that in using Menoeceus as such a mediator, Tiresias is still seeing him as an extension of self: the prophet remains one "for whom context is no obstacle but rather a convenience" (p. 198).

20. For Tucker (p. 221), Ulysses figures experience as an arch, "not in order to bridge the split between self and context, but in order to hurl the two yet further apart." To me, the arch constitutes less Ulysses' context than his escape from it. By "hurling," Tucker implies not mere opposition but a Romantic transcendence: "Saving the self as spirit requires spending the self as historically constituted psyche" (p. 227).

21. Linda K. Hughes, "Dramatis and Private Personae: 'Ulysses' Revisited," *Victorian Poetry*, 17 (1979), 201–2.

22. Following Ryals, Arthur D. Ward uses the fact that Odysseus' mariners have all been killed off in Homer to argue that Ulysses' tunnel vision has here loosened his hold on reality. "'Ulysses' and 'Tithonus': Tunnel Vision and Idle Tears," *Victorian Poetry*, 12 (1974), 311–19. It remains difficult for me to imagine him talking to thin air.

23. Georg Roppen, "'Ulysses' and Tennyson's Sea-quest," *English Studies*, 40 (1959), 85.

24. For an extended analysis of the poem's sexual themes, see Michael E. Greene,

"Tennyson's 'Gray Shadow Once a Man': Erotic Imagery and Dramatic Structure in 'Tithonus,'" *Victorian Poetry*, 18 (1980), 293–300.

25. E. D. H. Johnson, *The Alien Vision of Victorian Poetry: Sources of the Poetic Imagination in Tennyson, Browning, and Arnold* (Princeton: Princeton University Press, 1952), p. 123.

26. W. David Shaw, "Tennyson's 'Tithonus' and the Problem of Mortality," *Philological Quarterly*, 52 (1973), 275–79.

27. Whether Coelus has been reduced to this condition or was never anything more is not clear from context, but he does offer (ll. 311–18) some Tithonus-like recollections of erotic excitement at Hyperion's conception.

28. See Shaw, "Tennyson's 'Tithonus,'" p. 279.

29. Compare Tucker (p. 250): "The beating of the horses' hooves joins Aurora's 'bosom beating with a heart renewed,' to own the very pulse of the machine in which all are caught." Gallant also claims (p. 158) that Eos is a chthonic goddess and hence cyclical.

30. While the bases for it seem deliberately buried within the smug opening soliloquy, the "much-enduring man" whom Tennyson knew from Homer had often triumphed over the same inscrutable, potentially hostile powers which inhabited Tennyson's early poetry.

31. This gap may underlie the one which W. W. Robson observed between Ulysses' rousing message and the poem's elegiac tone. "The Dilemma of Tennyson," in Killham's *Critical Essays*, pp. 156–58. Tucker reinterprets such questions about the speaker's fate: "What the [final paragraph] actually bring[s] to pass, as a psychological and linguistic event, is the effacement of the speaking subject, the replacement of 'Ulysses' as a man's name by 'Ulysses' as a text" (p. 230). "The voice beyond Ulysses' bespeaks . . . an unidentified multitude corresponding to the 'we' that is about to assume the poem, disband the self, and dissipate the self's old anxieties as to time, place, and destination" (p. 238).

32. See Ward, "Tunnel," pp. 314–16; Kincaid, *Major*, pp. 43–45; and Charles Altieri, "Arnold and Tennyson: The Plight of Victorian Lyricism as Context of Modernism," *Criticism*, 20 (1978), 294.

33. Arthur Simpson, Jr., "Aurora as Artist: A Reinterpretation of Tennyson's *Tithonus*," *Philological Quarterly*, 51 (1972), 915.

34. Linda K. Hughes, "From 'Tithon' to 'Tithonus': Tennyson as Mourner and Monologist," *Philological Quarterly*, 58 (1979), 85–87.

35. Culler points out (p. 102) the poem's ambivalent focus although he considers Bedivere the more central character because of his being closer to Tennyson's own plight.

36. Tucker (p. 320) notes that in both poem and frame Tennyson is "conceiving his theme in perennial recession from the present, and then making that recession his theme."

37. Marcia Culver, "The Death and Birth of an Epic: Tennyson's 'Morte d'Arthur,'" *Victorian Poetry*, 20 (1982), 55. Her efforts to ascertain Tennyson's emotional condition are weakened by the absence of the last folio of this draft and by the fact that Tennyson could hardly have intended to end the work before getting Arthur safely launched.

38. Walter Nash, "Tennyson: 'The Epic' and 'The Old "Morte,"'" *Cambridge Quarterly*, 6 (1975), 349. Some of Nash's parallels were noted earlier in J. S. Lawry, "Tennyson's 'The Epic': A Gesture of Recovered Faith," *Modern Language Notes*, 74 (1959), 400–403. Culler (p. 108) sees the frame's value as a setting for the lapidary art of the "Morte" itself.

39. Joseph Sendry, "*In Memoriam*: The Minor Manuscripts," *Harvard Library Bulletin*, 27 (1979), 45–48.

40. To show Tennyson's covert identification with his heroine, Culler identifies Tom with "the type of the critic" (p. 111), supporting his point with a canceled passage from the Trinity manuscript.

41. *Theme and Symbol*, pp. 147–48.

42. J. W. Mackail, "Theocritus and the Idyl," in *Lectures on Greek Poetry* (London: Longmans Green, 1911), pp. 212–17, 233–34. See also Pattison, pp. 15–29, and H. M. McLuhan, "Tennyson and the Romantic Epic," in Killham's *Critical Essays*, pp. 86–95.

43. By seeing Tennyson's idylls as inclusive rather than disrupted, Tucker sets them up as foils to his lyrics: "The [lyric] was a lifelong and often submerged quest for communion with an unresponsive yet indubitable destiny, a quest that proceeded according to the now imperative, now listless mood of the spirit; the [idyll] was a professional program executed in the writer's workshop and delivered on schedule for publication" (p. 278). "The Tennysonian idyll intends a reader who seeks impressions and consumes effects." Even the blast and echoing "flap" which end "The Golden Year" are "designed to render . . . unflappable music for a worried class on the make" (p. 276). This shift from Romantic celebration to Marxist subversion renders the celebration itself suspect by confining it to poems in which the setting is ancient enough or fuzzy enough to be exempt from social implications. The stance thus opens itself to Jerome McGann's formulation of a fundamental Romantic fallacy: "The idea that poetry, or even consciousness, can set one free of the ruins of history and culture is the grand illusion of every Romantic poet." *The Romantic Ideology* (Chicago: University of Chicago Press, 1983), p. 91.

44. June Steffensen Hagen, "Tennyson's Revisions of the Last Stanza of 'Audley Court,'" *Costerus*, 4 (1975), 39–49.

45. Both Pattison (p. 77) and Donald S. Hair analyze the parallels between these two stories. *Domestic and Heroic in Tennyson's Poetry* (Toronto: University of Toronto Press, 1981), p. 84. All parenthetical references to Hair are to this book.

46. Michael Timko, "The Central Wish: Human Passion and Cosmic Love in Tennyson's Idyls," *Victorian Poetry*, 16 (1978), 11–15.

47. Trinity Notebook 26 makes the entire scene mock-heroic, mentioning a ring split by the two lovers but controlled by an evil personification of the king's nouveau riche station. Vestiges of this tone remain in the speaker's reference to his indictment for trespassing as "a mystic token from the king" (l. 132).

48. June Steffensen Hagen, "The 'Crescent Promise' of 'Locksley Hall': A Crisis in Poetic Creativity," *Victorian Poetry*, 11 (1973), 170.

49. F. E. L. Priestley, "Locksley Hall Revisited," *Queens Quarterly*, 81 (1974), 519.

50. Though I think Priestley's the single best analysis of the poem, I cannot accept

his description of it (p. 512) as a "relatively light-hearted dramatic study of a jilted adolescent." While right in emphasizing Tennyson's dramatic distance from his speaker, Priestley may underestimate the tenuousness of this distance and the effort it cost Tennyson to gain it.

5. *In Memoriam*

1. Timothy Peltason, *Reading "In Memoriam"* (Princeton: Princeton University Press, 1985), pp. 17–18.

2. T. S. Eliot, *"In Memoriam,"* in *Essays Ancient and Modern* (London: Faber and Faber, 1936), pp. 186–203; cited in the Norton Critical Edition of *In Memoriam*, ed. Robert H. Ross (New York: Norton, 1973), p. 176. His namesake, George Eliot, noted much earlier that "the deepest significance of the poem is the sanctification of human love as a religion." *Westminster Review*, October 1855. Quoted in Peltason, *Reading*, p. 15. Needless to say, the two critics put very different values on their very similar perceptions.

3. *In Memoriam* (Oxford: Clarendon Press, 1982). I have followed their very sensible use of arabic numbers for the individual sections. All parenthetical references to Shatto and Shaw are to this book. Except as noted, source citations to *In Memoriam* are to section and line.

4. Joseph Sendry, *"In Memoriam*: The Minor Manuscripts," *Harvard Library Bulletin*, 27 (1979), 36–64. All parenthetical references to Sendry are to this article.

5. Such hypotheses must remain only that. Shatto and Shaw, with admirable caution, warn that their collation of all known manuscripts cannot possibly comprise even most of those Tennyson actually used. They cite the large number of sections which appear for the first time in the Trinity Butcher's Book in what certainly looks like fair copy form. Granting this point, however, I would argue that what we *do* have can support at least some probable conclusions, both because the manuscripts space themselves so conveniently along Tennyson's seventeen-year ordeal and because the Trinity and Lincoln Butcher's Books themselves offer some tantalizing clues about their use.

6. In a different context, Peter Hinchcliffe discusses the refusal of the final sections to reach closure. "Elegy and Epithalamium in *In Memoriam*," *University of Toronto Quarterly*, 52 (1983), 255–62.

7. J. C. C. Mays, *"In Memoriam*: An Aspect of Form," *University of Toronto Quarterly*, 35 (1965), 29–35. See also Shaw, *Style*, p. 139.

8. Peltason (p. 5) sees this rhyme scheme working to very different ends, or rather to no end at all: "The short sections of the poem, . . . each stanza closed in upon itself by rhyme, present to the reader discrete fragments of experience, momentary and present apprehensions." The enveloping *abba* rhyme is also deftly analyzed in Ricks's *Tennyson* (pp. 227–29).

9. Shatto and Shaw, *In Memoriam*, p. 52.

10. The Huntington manuscript, HM 1321, exists now as a probably incomplete set of loose sheets, two of which contain *In Memoriam* lyrics. Harvard Loosepaper

101 consists of a formerly sewn gathering of ten folios with sixteen sections in Emily Sellwood's hand. For a full description of either manuscript the reader should consult both Sendry (pp. 49–51, 62–64) and Shatto and Shaw (pp. 11, 306–7, 311–12).

11. I assume that both manuscripts precede the Trinity Butcher's Book because the Huntington and probably the Sellwood readings are further from the printed text, and because if Emily were copying the selections into the loosepaper directly from the butcher's book, her ordering would probably not differ as much as it does from the one found there.

12. Andrew Fichter, "Ode and Elegy: Idea and Form in Tennyson's Early Poetry," *ELH*, 40 (1973), 413. See also James Kilroy, "The Chiastic Structure of *In Memoriam, A.H.H.*," *Philological Quarterly*, 56 (1977), 358–73; and Peltason (p. 6): "Many individual lyrics subvert or challenge the process by which they are assimilated."

13. These and other passages, which will begin to appear with increasing frequency, should persuade us to modify E. D. H. Johnson's claim that *In Memoriam* portrays Tennyson's gradually successful quest to regain his own imaginative powers. "*In Memoriam*: The Way of a Poet," *Victorian Studies*, 2 (1958), 139–48; cited in the Norton Critical Edition of *In Memoriam*, ed. Ross, pp. 227–28.

14. Harry Puckett, "The Subjunctive Imagination in *In Memoriam*," *Victorian Poetry*, 12 (1974), 101–2.

15. They are sections 34, 36, and 48. Of these sections 34 and 36 appear together with 33 both here and in the Sellwood Notebook, while section 48 appears with 46 both here and in the Huntington notebook. Thus Tennyson may have regarded both those groups as so tightly knit that he did not think it necessary to leave the customary space between their members. Sections 33, 34, and 36, for example, appear in the same dark ink on recto and verso of folio 15 while 35 appears in lighter ink, presumably as a later addition.

16. These are, in order of appearance, "The path by which I walkt alone," sections 38, 13, 43, and 71.

17. The earlier pages were actually ripped out and have surfaced only as loosepapers now owned by Harvard and by individual collectors. The stubs between the opening section (still appearing only as a four-line motto) and section 38 presumably contain folios which Shatto and Shaw have identified (pp. 12–13) as loosepapers in various collections. These loosepapers themselves contain all the extant early-written sections we know about except section 17, which may well have been lost. From the annotation on the folio containing section 18, Sendry argues persuasively (pp. 52, 63) that these sections were still in the butcher's book when Spedding perused it on 9 November 1840. The ordering in the earlier-written Purdy sheet from the Huntington notebook (sections 9, 1, 17, 18, 21) and in L.MS both suggest that these folios may have originally appeared close to their final order in a sequence something like: 1 (ll. 1–4), 3, 9, 17, 18, 19, "The paths by which I walked alone," 22, and 21.

18. Shatto and Shaw do offer (pp. 12–14) a careful description of the poem as it appears in this manuscript, "the poem Tennyson might have published in, say, 1843."

19. The beginning of this process is rendered conjectural by the dispersed state of the manuscript.

20. Henry Kozicki, "'Meaning' in Tennyson's *In Memoriam*," *Studies in English Literature: 1500–1900*, 17 (1977), 675–88.

21. Clyde de L. Ryals, "The 'Heavenly Friend': The New Mythos of *In Memoriam*," *Personalist*, 43 (1962), 393–94.

22. Ryals argues (pp. 400–401) that within the poem Christ stands as the symbol for such a human love.

23. The stanza containing this phrase originally followed line 4 of section 22. While Shatto and Shaw feel (p. 184) that it was composed within section 23 and then provisionally moved, Sendry more convincingly argues (p. 54) that section 23 may have been written around it.

24. James Kissane, *Alfred Tennyson* (New York: Twayne, 1970), pp. 77–78.

25. John Dixon Hunt analyzes sleep and dream in the poem as a means of exploring the unconscious. "The Symbolist Vision of *In Memoriam*," *Victorian Poetry*, 8 (1970), 189.

26. A stanza added to the earlier version of this section sets it firmly within his years with Hallam.

27. Jonathan Bishop argues that the dreams themselves open him to the discovery of rhythm and vitality in nature: "The Unity of *In Memoriam*," *Victorian Newsletter*, no. 21 (Spring 1962), 10.

28. The missing folio could not have held the ninety-odd lines which appear in the later L.MS. Yet the first surviving line, "So hold I commerce with the dead," implies a fuller version than that in the early Trinity notebook. We might assume as a rough maximum that the lost text included the thirty-two lines of that version up to line 76 and then, newly added, the fourteen lines of Hallam's speech to which Tennyson responds.

29. In their detailed analysis of these last folios (pp. 13–14), Shatto and Shaw see Tennyson's attempts to conclude this manuscript as more controlled than I do.

30. Dolores R. Rosenblum, "The Act of Writing *In Memoriam*," *Victorian Poetry*, 18 (1980), 120.

31. Quoted in Shatto and Shaw, *In Memoriam*, p. 12.

32. As I mentioned in the Introduction, Tennyson's apparent use of his own voice within his confessional poems makes it hard for us to identify an authorial presence distinguished from the author by its role *within* the poem. These early, though late-written, efforts at introspection offer the clearest evidence of such a role, but even here it has been fragmented into a landscape much like the one within Tennyson's model. For a different analysis of Tennyson's fixated, repetitive absorption in his own grief, see Bishop, pp. 9–10.

33. For Hughes, it is the yew which "is given the power of action, not the poet—the yew grasps at the tombstones, nets empty skulls, coils around bones" (*Glass*, p. 146).

34. See Shatto and Shaw, *In Memoriam*, pp. 13–14.

35. Kozicki attributes these visions ("Meaning," p. 685) to Tennyson's reading of Carlyle's *French Revolution*.

36. A. C. Bradley makes this point as early as his *A Commentary on "In Memoriam"* (London: Macmillan, 1901), p. 42.

37. Richard J. Dunn claims that section 95 plays off against one another the destructive alternatives of the "imposition of a paralytic memory" and "total submission" to an unknown universe. "Vision and Revision: *In Memoriam* XCV," *Victorian Poetry*, 18 (1980), 145–46. I am suggesting that a similar epistemological strategy may constitute a prerequisite to this section.

38. W. David Shaw, "The Transcendentalist Problem in Tennyson's Poetry of Debate," *Philological Quarterly*, 46 (1967), 92. For the power of Tennyson's Romantic imagination to valorize itself see J. L. Kendall, "A Neglected Theme in Tennyson's *In Memoriam*," *Modern Language Notes*, 76 (1961), 416.

39. Lawrence Kramer, for example, feels that Tennyson here breaks down the delicate balance of section 95 by affirming Hallam's presence without sufficient qualification and thus risks "losing himself in a world of his own making." "The 'Intimations' Ode and Victorian Romanticism," *Victorian Poetry*, 18 (1980), 326.

6. *The Princess*

1. Curiously, Ralph Wilson Rader criticizes *Maud* principally for what he sees as its *lack* of control, a feature which for him separates it from the best of the Tennyson canon. *Tennyson's Maud: The Biographical Genesis* (Berkeley: University of California Press, 1963), p. 120. All parenthetical references to Rader are to this book.

2. John Killham, *Tennyson and The Princess: Reflections of an Age* (London: Athlone, 1958), pp. 188–90. All parenthetical references to Killham are to this book. Ryals, *Theme and Symbol*, pp. 172–78.

3. Ryals, *Theme and Symbol*, pp. 172–73. Joseph, *Love*, pp. 89–90.

4. While Tucker readily admits (p. 351) that "the extended poems of Tennyson's middle years are not the idyllic shutouts they seem from a distance," he insists on Tennyson's "idyllic strategies being always strategies of containment." James Harrison describes the same strategy in more neutral terms: "He is able to put forward with conviction opposing and relatively extreme points of view without necessarily becoming identified with either." "The Role of Anachronism in *The Princess*," *English Studies in Canada*, 1 (1975), 314.

5. Eileen Tess Johnston, "'This were a medley': Tennyson's *The Princess*," *ELH*, 51 (1984), 563, 569. Albright (p. 217) also sees the form as too expansive to be repressive: "The fable is . . . a whale that has eaten seven Jonahs and much of England, and yet this skin of myth is thin enough that one can feel under it knots and contusions, tangled veins, broken bones, human suffering."

6. See Killham, *Princess*, p. 276. On the mixture of different worlds within the poem, Valerie Pitt comments, "The *mores* of the fairy tale and the *moeurs* of the Victorian elite jostle one another in surprising confusion, and yet the final effect is not inharmonious." *Tennyson Laureate* (London: Barrie and Rockliff, 1962), p. 30.

7. This challenge was issued by James Spedding in his review of Tennyson's *Poems* of 1842, *Edinburgh Review*, 77 (1843), 391. Cited in Baum, *Tennyson Sixty Years After*, p. 39.

8. I agree with Harrison (p. 314) that "each [character] can speak with the kind of directness and candour possible within the comparable restrictions of the dramatic

monologue," but I am less persuaded by his further claim that "in a sense the characters do not reach or impinge on one another." In fact they simply do not care whether they impinge on one another or not.

9. The particular threat she poses may account for the authorial hostility which Ricks sees as another of the poem's evasions: "By contrast Tennyson's best work is strikingly free from any recourse to villainy as a problem-dissolver whether in literature or in life" (*Tennyson*, p. 194).

10. At one point she *is* more deliberately critical. As the three men "muffled like the Fates," observe the student's after-dinner pastimes, "often came / Melissa hitting all we saw with shafts / Of gentle satire, kin to charity" (II, 443–45).

11. For extended discussions of the paired and tripled characters surrounding the two leads, see Eileen Johnston, "Medley," pp. 551–52, and Gerhard Joseph, "Tennyson's Three Women," pp. 8–13.

12. Catherine Barnes Stevenson sees Cyril as symbolic of the hostile forces approaching Ida. "Tennyson's 'Mutability Canto': Time, Memory, and Art in *The Princess*," *Victorian Poetry*, 13 (1975), 28.

13. A number of other manuscripts between the Harvard one and this one exist in the University Library at Cambridge. Unfortunately someone has conflated them into a single palimpsest which effectively blocks any attempt to establish a compositional ordering among them. Charles Tennyson draws some general conclusions from the manuscripts in "Tennyson Papers. IV. The Making of *The Princess*," *Cornhill Magazine*, 153 (1936), 672–80.

14. For an expanded version of this section, see my "Character and Structure in Tennyson's *The Princess*," *Studies in English Literature*, 14 (Autumn 1974), 563–73. Since then Albright (pp. 242–46) has analyzed the statue imagery in roughly similar ways.

15. Henry Kozicki sees Ida's goal as an escape from the past into the future. "The 'Medieval Ideal' in Tennyson's 'The Princess,'" *Criticism*, 17 (1975), 123–24.

16. Albright (p. 224) reverses the relation we have been tracing between Ida and her story: "All [metaphorical] forms of natural delight are the natural manner of expression in a fable; the Princess is struggling to freeze herself out of the fabulous action, grow sober and self-contained."

17. For this parallel, see Ryals, *Theme and Symbol*, pp. 172–73.

18. For an analysis of what Tennyson found inadequate in Ida's conception of science, see G. Glen Wickens, "The Two Sides of Early Victorian Science and the Unity of 'The Princess,'" *Victorian Studies*, 23 (1980), 386–87.

19. This imagery has been similarly analyzed by Jerome Hamilton Buckley, *Tennyson: The Growth of a Poet* (Cambridge: Harvard University Press, 1961), p. 102.

20. The situations are not quite parallel: the Priestess is appealing to her idol in the face of an attack from without, not transforming the Other itself into an idol. Albright compares Ida "to the Soul in 'The Palace of Art' and to the Lady of Shalott, great rigid superb women who have sequestered themselves in impermeable fantasy—the Princess's chief henchwoman is Psyche, the Soul" (p. 228).

21. Eileen Johnston elaborates upon this passage as a critique of Romantic imaginative self-sufficiency. "Medley," pp. 564–65.

22. A number of critics have noted the interpenetration of the Prince and Ten-

nyson as joint narrators. See Joseph (p. 89) and Winston Collins, "The Princess: The Education of the Prince," *Victorian Poetry*, 11 (1973), 292.

23. See in particular Terry Eagleton, "Tennyson: Politics and Sexuality in 'The Princess' and 'In Memoriam,'" *1848: The Sociology of Literature*, ed. Francis Barker et al. (Essex: University of Essex, 1978), pp. 98 passim. As we have seen, Tucker's equally Marxist reading identifies the passive inclusiveness of idyll less with the Prince than with the whole poem.

24. Critics have offered many different descriptions for this "signature": Ryals (*Theme and Symbol*, p. 186) complains of self-indulgent blocks of description. Ricks admits (*Tennyson*, pp. 196–98) that the poem's protected hothouse atmosphere permits passages in which metaphoric and syntactic ambiguities allow the poet to escape the confines of natural law. Kozicki ("Medieval Ideal," p. 130) sees the poem itself as an idyll, overgrowing the structure Tennyson had mastered in the English idylls of 1842.

25. S. E. Dawson's early analysis of this image is famous, perhaps by now infamous: "Everywhere are busts, and statues, and lutes, and such like *bric-a-brac* aids to knowledge. . . . Instinctively the male reader shrinks through this part of the poem, fearful of upsetting something." *Study of the Princess*, 2d ed. (Montreal, 1884); cited in the edition of William J. Rolfe (Boston: Houghton Mifflin, 1897), p. 155n. All parenthetical references to Rolfe are to this book.

26. Even when the Prince's sexual identity is revealed and he himself pursued by the female proctors, "secret laughter tickled all [his] soul." Catherine Barnes Stevenson argues that in this passage the poem is self-consciously mocking the extravagant failures of its own imaginative vision. "The Aesthetic Function of the 'Weird Seizures' in *The Princess*," *Victorian Newsletter*, no. 45 (Spring 1974), 24. But the passage may also manifest the Prince's discovery of one more incongruity available within *his* own broadly idyllic vision. Eagleton (p. 102) reinterprets such humor in Freudian terms as an embarrassed displacement of a sexually threatening situation.

27. These have been interpreted as the hero's withdrawal either from life and action or only from what is false within Ida and her scheme. They have also been seen as the author's mistaken afterthought, as a projection of his own epilepsy, as an extension of his visionary powers, as a foray into mesmerism, as doubts aroused by his apparent loss of Emily, as doubts about the poem itself. For a useful synthesis of some of these interpretations, see Stevenson, "Aesthetic Function," pp. 22–25.

28. Anita B. Draper observes that Tennyson emphasized the "awfulness" of Ida within the same set of 1851 revisions in which he added the Prince's seizures. "The Artistic Contribution of the 'Weird Seizures' to *The Princess*," *Victorian Poetry*, 17 (1979), 182–83.

29. Eagleton (pp. 97–103), revising Ricks's interpretation of the poem as a tissue of escapes, sees even this dilemma as Tennyson's attempt to distance both the male aggression of the older generation and the female sexuality of Ida by turning the Prince into a helpless child and Ida into a nurturing mother. Joseph, however, quotes Frye's assertion that "New Comedy unfolds from what may be described as a comic Oedipal situation. Its main theme is the successful effort of a young man to outwit an opponent and possess the girl of his choice. The opponent is usually the father."

"The Argument of Comedy," *English Institute Essays* (New York, 1948), p. 58; cited in *Tennysonian Love*, pp. 88–89.

30. Collins (p. 292) argues that the "I" of the Prince and the narrator tend to merge. In this particular context, their demands on Ida seem to me quite different.

31. Bayard Taylor, in Rolfe, p. 184n. For the archetypal implications of this change, see E. T. Johnston, "Medley," p. 554.

32. Leo Spitzer finds in "Tears, Idle Tears" a gradually more specific invocation of 'Death-in-Life' as a 'Sondergott,' a pagan deity of the underworld who acts much like the Other by frustrating all the speaker's desires. "'Tears, Idle Tears' Again," *Hopkins Review*, 5 (1952), 71–72. See also Gerhard Joseph, "Tennyson's Death in Life in Lyric and Myth: 'Tears, Idle Tears' and 'Demeter and Persephone,'" *Victorian Newsletter*, no. 34 (Fall 1968), 13–15.

33. See Ricks (*Tennyson*, pp. 200–204) and Shaw (pp. 126–27) for perceptive interpretations of the carefully blurred sexual roles in this lyric.

34. Compare Tucker (p. 375): "Ida ends her reading in the accents of a mourning dove, and what she mourns is both the proleptic loss of her virgin sufficiency and her hold on an independent, critical stance toward the culture that possesses her." Fully as sympathetic toward Ida as Kincaid, Tucker also sees her as ultimately contained by the idyllic form. These songs seem to offer her an escape from the idyllic into the lyric, but here the lyrics which offered Tennyson's earlier speakers a Romantic transcendence of context "seduce" her not just into love but into "the conventional women's roles that circumstances have forced upon her after all" (p. 367). Yet to read the songs with their deliberately exotic settings as simple metaphors for Victorian domesticity is to dismiss without trial the Prince's later claim that the couple have won the power to "type" some new form of relationship.

35. Ryals describes this ending as reversing that of "The Lady of Shalott"; it is the curse that is broken, not the character. *Theme and Symbol*, p. 192.

36. It is ironic that the above lines have their origin in the Heath MS (*Poems*, I, 331; II, 296) as part of the opening frame of *The Lover's Tale*. There the intimations of transcendence are constrained within an increasingly claustrophobic context. Kincaid, in fact (p. 78), argues cogently that the discontinuities of the conclusion betray a discomforting awareness that Ida's heroic will has not been allowed full play within her story.

7. *Maud*

1. Philip Drew, "Tennyson and the Dramatic Monologue: A Study of 'Maud,'" *Writers and Their Backgrounds: Tennyson*, ed. D. J. Palmer (Athens: Ohio University Press, 1973), p. 138.

2. Roy P. Basler, "Tennyson the Psychologist," *South Atlantic Quarterly*, 43 (1944), 144–45. James Waltar, "Tennyson's Patrimony from 'The Outcast' to 'Maud,'" *Texas Studies in Literature and Language*, 11 (1969), 745. Jonathan Wordsworth, "'What is it, that has been done?': The Central Problem of *Maud*," *Essays in Criticism*, 24 (1974), 358, 362. All parenthetical references to Jonathan Wordsworth are to this article.

3. Other analyses are almost equally reductive. Jonas Spatz sees the speaker's un-controlled hostility to his world's laissez-faire capitalism as an unconscious desire to participate in any acceptable form of aggression. "Love and Death in Tennyson's *Maud*," *Texas Studies in Literature and Language*, 16 (1974), 505–6. Kincaid (pp. 113, 118) interprets this hostility as directed against the very complexity necessary for any balanced social vision. For him the speaker's relationship with Maud is doomed by his refusal to accept a woman who can love both him and her brother. Marilyn Kurata claims that this love comes not from Maud herself but from his own compulsive need to turn wish into reality. "'A Juggle Born of the Brain': A New Reading of *Maud*," *Victorian Poetry*, 21 (1983), 369–76. There is a hint of determinism even in Ricks's observation (*Tennyson*, pp. 251, 256) that the speaker belongs to a uniquely Tennysonian world where any attempt at union—of partners in marriage, of members of a family, of families themselves—leads to conflict, to separation, and ultimately to death.

4. Quoted in Edgar F. Shannon, Jr., "The Critical Reception of Tennyson's 'Maud,'" *PMLA*, 48 (1953), 400.

5. It was written within the same notebook with the earliest draft of "Ulysses" (Harvard Notebook 16) and then copied into the Heath Manuscript in a draft dated "1833."

6. George O. Marshall, Jr., "Tennyson's 'Oh! That 'Twere Possible': A Link Between *In Memoriam* and *Maud*," *PMLA*, 78 (1963), 228–29. Many of the *In Memoriam* sections he cites are also included within the Heath Manuscript. Because Ricks's *Poems* reproduces the 1837 revision of the lyric in *The Tribute*, I have cited Marshall's transcription of the Heath drafts.

7. Rader, *Maud*, p. 51.

8. This temporal reversal can be complicated still further: even though the urban wasteland imprisons this speaker as well within the domain of a specifically modern Other, nevertheless "the shouts, the leagues of lights, / And the roaring of the wheels," can define by negation Tennyson's demands for some psychological land-scape of the future.

9. Actually this draft precedes "Locksley Hall" by some five or six years.

10. This version introduces the celestial "sister" of the Phantom, a figure which Tennyson will reintroduce in part 3 of *Maud* even though he will reject most of these newly added stanzas. I have been arguing that the Phantom of the Heath drafts had already defined this "sister" by negation.

11. See Susan Shatto, *Tennyson's "Maud": A Definitive Edition* (Norman: University of Oklahoma Press, 1986), p. 201. Charles Tennyson's evidence for dating this section from the 1830s may be secondhand and sixty years after the fact, but some admittedly slim evidence in the poem's principal manuscript, Trinity Notebook 36, suggests that some much earlier shell lyric consisted only of stanzas 1–4 (Shatto suggests 1–3) with another word substituted for "Breton" in the last line. If written after Hallam's death, the lyric might have shown Tennyson groping for just such a concrete object as the shell to keep from losing his sanity.

12. That it seems fitting to *Maud* and foreign to the earlier poem may not be due wholly to our own associations. There love is usually described as a descent, a relaxa-tion: "Come down O maid from yonder mountain height," "Let the great water take

me to the main," "So slip into my bosom and be lost in me." But in "Go not, happy day" both the passionate, blushing red and the violence with which the passion is flung centrifugally around the globe signal a redefinition of erotic love. Certainly Tennyson did not have a coherent story worked out to drop the lyric into, but the fact that he read it to Palgrave in 1853 (*Poems*, II, 552n) suggests a renewed interest in the romantic quest of "O that 'twere possible" and in the "roseate" lyrics to Rosa Baring.

13. Susan Shatto, "The Textual Genesis of *Maud*," presented at the session "Processes of Revision among Victorian Writers," MLA convention, Chicago, 29 December 1985.

14. In her talk Shatto claimed that while every one of the secondary characters in the poem has a very negative biographical model, Maud herself remains largely a locus for Tennyson's own desires. I will argue, however, that Tennyson came to see the speaker, Maud, and her family as ever more closely intertwined.

15. With some impressive detective work (pp. 18–19), Shatto has identified the first of these sections (I, i) from some loose sheets at the Huntington, the twentieth (III, vi) from Harvard Notebook 30, and at least the existence of the seventeenth (afterwards replaced by II, iii) from a later remark by Tennyson to Knowles.

16. Shatto (p. 19) dates it through Emily's *Journal* as 1 February 1855.

17. A. Dwight Culler, "Monodrama and the Dramatic Monologue," *PMLA*, 90 (1975), 366–85.

18. *Language and Structure*, pp. 107–14.

19. Albright (p. 154) claims that Tennyson's identification of the poem as a monodrama "is little more than a plea that the reader pretend that an anthology of poems, positing a great variety of speakers, is in fact a single poem with a single speaker." Ricks suggests (*Tennyson*, p. 249) that the speaker divides his different selves between sections, and Priestley (p. 110) that he internalizes his conflicts; in fact he may actually argue the conflicts out between his various selves within a given section. Denying the speeches any deliberative force, Tucker argues (p. 413) that "*Maud* thus situates its hero reactively. . . . His speech . . . [is] a product of his social environment. As we read we learn to ask not what he will do next, but what will have happened to him in the interim."

20. James Killham, "Tennyson's *Maud*—The Function of the Imagery," in Killham's *Critical Essays*, p. 226.

21. Chris R. Vanden Bossche, "Realism Versus Romance: The War of Cultural Codes in Tennyson's *Maud*," *Victorian Poetry*, 24 (1986), 78. Bossche notes that the scene "is primal only in the sense of a retrospective projection, an imaginary attempt to assign origins, not an initial encounter with reality." A somewhat less graphic account of the scene appears in Frank R. Giordano, Jr., "The 'Red-Ribbed Hollow,' Suicide, and Part III in 'Maud,'" *Notes and Queries*, 24 (1977), 402–4.

22. Ricks argues (*Tennyson*, p. 250) that all other characters only pulsate into phantoms for the diseased eye of the narrator, but I am here less interested in the health of his vision than in the use he makes of it.

23. Robert E. Lougy, "The Sounds and Silence of Madness: Language as Theme in Tennyson's *Maud*," *Victorian Poetry*, 22 (1984), 412. He follows this parallel with a more extended one to Graves's White Goddess.

24. See Shaw, *Style*, pp. 174–75.

25. This dissociation of voice from speaker is noted by Ian Kennedy, "The Crisis of Language in Tennyson's *Maud*," *Texas Studies in Literature and Language*, 19 (1977), 167. For Kennedy, however, it belies a psychological weakness, a falling away from Maud's own "human" language, not a potential source of imaginative power.

26. Kurata, "Juggle," p. 372. Her argument, strong here, seems to me to weaken when she must explain away (pp. 374–75) all the evidence of Maud's love and commitment to him which the speaker offers near the end of part 1.

27. Jonathan Wordsworth even argues (pp. 356–62) that the speaker's nearly incoherent description of the duel betrays his guilt and vicarious self-punishment for the defloration of Maud. Unfortunately the article fails to make clear whether he has actually made love to Maud, thinks he has, or only wants to. John Holloway, while insisting that demanding clinical proof "would be a crude way of dealing with the evidence," nevertheless draws a bold connection between the wood of the love scenes and the hollow behind it where his father and Maud's brother die: "The poem implicitly states . . . that there is no separating the wonderful life-fulfilling and life-restoring powers of such love from its power for destruction, chaos and death." *The Proud Knowledge: Poetry, Insight and the Self, 1620–1920* (London: Routledge and Kegan Paul, 1977), pp. 204–05.

28. Kurata also notes "the speaker's ability to subordinate reality to a desired delusion" (p. 374), but she would not grant that this language of desire can become in some sense performative.

29. For Tucker (pp. 410–29), the speaker has always been driven by a hunger for commercial prosperity and for Maud as a symbol of and means to it. While Tucker cites economic metaphors throughout the poem, his reading seems to deny a priori any change in their use and meaning or any change within the speaker.

30. J. L. Kendall, "Gem Imagery in Tennyson's *Maud*," *Victorian Poetry*, 17 (1979), 391–92.

31. Pauline Fletcher, *Gardens and Grim Ravines: The Language of Landscape in Victorian Poetry* (Princeton: Princeton University Press, 1983), p. 54.

32. As A. S. Byatt implies, the inevitably tragic outcome to this section may actually permit Tennyson to explore what love could accomplish when freed from the restriction of happily ever after. "The Lyric Structure of Tennyson's *Maud*," in *The Major Victorian Poets: Reconsiderations*, ed. Isobel Armstrong (Lincoln: University of Nebraska Press, 1969), pp. 81, 89. This final celebration of what might have been chooses a metaphorical construct so far removed from the one in which the speaker has trapped himself that it is largely destroyed along with his love. It becomes again available to the speaker only in the haunting memories of "O that 'twere possible." Here the speaker's longings for *his* past merge with Tennyson's return to the personal longings embedded in the lyric seed of the present poem. The speaker here establishes himself as a fellow poet in more than Kennedy's sense of the term (pp. 166–73) as one concerned with language. The speaker has here preserved in words both what he could not preserve in life and what Tennyson could not otherwise find in either realm.

33. Dorothy Mermin, "Tennyson's *Maud*: A Thematic Analysis," *Texas Studies in Literature and Language*, 15 (1973), 275. Lougy claims (pp. 414–15) that "Maud exists in silence, defined by a world in which she is variously seen as daughter, sister,

and potential wife, submerged wholly within those primarily male-oriented sexual and social structures around her. . . . Once she is removed from the public realm, she must necessarily become without a voice." Kincaid adds (pp. 113, 128–30) that the speaker has ignored the militant spirit of her song; he has violated her family loyalty; he has allowed her no voice in choosing her often grotesque metaphorical clothing.

34. While Lougy offers a persuasive reading of this scene in particular, I cannot agree with the thesis he borrows from Foucault (p. 408) that madness is "the very annihilation of the work of art, the point where it becomes impossible and where it must fall silent." Tennyson's reference to his work as "a little Hamlet" places the poem within a long tradition of works exploiting the literary potential of madness. As I argued earlier in this chapter, the speaker's madness validates artistic claims which Tennyson could make in no other way.

35. Its departure, "I saw the dreary phantom arise and fly / Far into the North, and battle, and seas of death" (III, 36–37), echoes the departure of the obscuring cloud within "Armageddon": "In one dense, dry, interminable mass / Sailing far North-ward . . . full it was of living things, / Strange shapings and anomalies of Hell" (IV, 7–8, 11–12). In both cases a celestial mediator drives off some manifestation of the Other.

36. James R. Bennett argues that by referring to Maud's brother as "the Sultan" within the page proofs, Tennyson was also dissociating himself from the other princi-pal in the conflict. "The Historical Abuse of Literature: Tennyson's *Maud: A Mono-drama* and the Crimean War," *English Studies*, 62 (1981), 40–41.

8. The 1859 *Idylls of the King*

1. We might assume that he would begin by immersing himself in the world of his hero, and indeed Hallam (*Memoir*, II, 125) refers to his reading in medieval sources, traveling to Wales and Cornwall, and talking with other Arthurian experts. In the 1940s, however, Gordon Haight discovered that Tennyson had probably never read the actual French source for his first idyll in the *Vulgate Merlin* but only the English summary of it in the notes to Southey's 1817 edition of Malory. "Tennyson's Merlin," *Studies in Philology*, 44 (1947), 551–53. Even more incriminating, George Meinhold found all the relevant passages on Merlin reproduced from Southey in Lady Charlotte Guest's *Mabinogion* translations of 1838, a source from which Tennyson drew his second-written idyll, "Enid." "The *Idylls of the King* and the *Mabinogion*," *Tennyson Research Bulletin*, 1, no. 3 (1969), 61–62. Within the more general debate on Tennyson's Arthurian scholarship, Hugh Wilson takes the earlier critic Tom Peete Cross to task for believing that Tennyson did serious research into King Arthur's Celtic origins. He also takes Tennyson to task for relying on popular histories and the introductions to contemporary editions of medieval works. "Tennyson: Unscholarly Arthurian," *Victorian Newsletter*, no. 32 (Fall 1967), 5–11.

2. Catherine Barnes Stevenson, "Druids, Bards, and Tennyson's Merlin," *Vic-torian Newsletter*, no. 57 (Spring 1980), 14–23. These figures in turn overlap with those whom Paden (pp. 73–94) calls warriors of God.

3. Sir Thomas Malory, *The Byrth, Lyf, and Actes of Kyng Arthur*, ed. Robert Southey,

Esq. (London: Longman, 1817). For consistency I have quoted from this edition throughout. By this time Tennyson was using a variety of Malory editions, almost all of them using the standard Caxton divisions into books and chapters.

4. For a brief account of Harvard Notebooks 30 and 31 and the Loosepapers 152 and 153, see *A Variorum Edition of Tennyson's "Idylls of the King,"* ed. John Pfordresher (New York: Columbia University Press, 1973) p. 24. All parenthetical references to Pfordresher are to this edition.

5. Hugh Wilson charges (p. 11) that the poet's lack of scholarly vigor led him to distort his material for his own subjective purposes. This charge, of course, assumes that an objective reality is there to distort, and since even Tennyson acknowledged that as an historical figure, Arthur could be no more impressive than a British warlord fighting a rearguard skirmish against the Saxon advance (*Memoir*, II, 126), fidelity to his sources could only have meant reproducing the equally subjective intention of some late-medieval author.

6. I have referred to the first four idylls by their 1859 titles because these are both shorter and more accurate in their focus on the female leads. After some hesitation I decided it would be too confusing to use "Nimue," the name given to Vivien and her idyll in the manuscripts and early proofs.

7. See Pfordresher, *Variorum*, pp. 24 and 521, ll. 236–37.

8. Ryals ("Fatal Woman," p. 443) traces an extensive lineage of "fatal women" in early Tennyson, though for him Vivien settles into the stereotype of an obsession Tennyson has finally put behind him. Joseph, however, argues (p. 120) that "she appears in Tennyson's later poetry with increasing rather than diminishing frequency and intensity, either as fatal woman or as fatal classical goddess." Betty Miller (pp. 357–63) also sees her as still very threatening. Comparing Merlin's "letting his wisdom go" in sexual surrender with a remarkably similar passage in *Samson Agonistes*, she argues that from the time he read Milton as an impressionable adolescent, Tennyson saw such surrender as the greatest possible threat to male identity. She claims that while Malory attracted Tennyson chiefly as a celebration of male bonding, the poet's moralistic attack on Malory's heroines belied a dormant fear of them. Elliot L. Gilbert sees Arthur as instigating a feminine, nonpatrilineal reign, though to secure it he attempts in vain to domesticate the sexual instinct itself. "The Female King: Tennyson's Arthurian Apocalypse," *PMLA*, 98 (1983), 868–74.

9. For the social relevance of Merlin's ideals, see in particular Stevenson, "Druids," pp. 17–19.

10. David Staines, *Tennyson's Camelot: The "Idylls of the King" and Its Medieval Sources* (Waterloo, Ontario: Wilfred Laurier University Press, 1982), pp. 29–30. All parenthetical references to Staines are to this book.

11. See J. M. Gray, "Two Transcendental Ladies of Tennyson's *Idylls*: The Lady of the Lake and Vivien," *Tennyson Research Bulletin*, 1, no. 4 (Nov. 1970), 104–5. Adrienne Munich has argued that Tennyson here subverts the traditional epic identification of the forging of armor with sexual fecundity, giving the first role to the "lonely" Lady of the Lake and the second to the promiscuous but equally sterile Vivien. "Gender and Authority in *Idylls of the King*," talk presented at the MLA convention, Chicago, 29 December 1985.

12. For Vivien as both the fallen Eve and, even more sinister, the tempting Satan

from *Paradise Lost*, see Thomas Adler, "The Uses of Knowledge in Tennyson's *Merlin and Vivien*," *Texas Studies in Literature and Language*, 11 (1970), 1397–1400.

13. Fred Kaplan, "Woven Paces and Waving Hands: Tennyson's Merlin as Fallen Artist," *Victorian Poetry*, 7 (1969), 286–89.

14. Tennyson may have drawn this incident from the highly speculative Richard John King, whose *Fairy Mythology of Tintagel* Tennyson once borrowed. King describes Broceliande as the abode of Arthur, where "his voice answered to the responses of the twelve peers . . . and the notes of their shadowy horns could be heard on calm nights reechoing through the wood, while the spectre heroes . . . hunt[ed] the phantom stag." *Two Lectures Read before the Essay Society of Exeter College, Oxford* (Oxford, 1840), p. 83. The borrowed book is mentioned in *The Life and Letters of R. S. Hawker*, ed. C. E. Byles (London, 1905), p. 194. In the even more suspect *Barzaz-Breiz* of Theodore de la Villemarqué, Merlin and his companions stop while hunting by an oak and a well. *Barzaz-Breiz: Chants Populaires de la Bretagne* (Paris, 1846), pp. 124–25. Matthew Arnold was content to borrow his Tristram story from Villemarqué. See Kenneth Allott, *The Poems of Matthew Arnold* (New York: Barnes and Noble, 1965), pp. 194–96. Tennyson, however, seems to have had inklings that the Frenchman's claims of arcane bardic origins for the major Arthurian stories would ultimately prove groundless. He remarked to the far more authoritative Celticist Renan (*Memoir*, II, 232) that Villemarqué was more a poet than a scholar. He nevertheless relies on such sources to let his Merlin transform the Breton woods into a setting, even a source for Camelot itself. For more parallels between Merlin and Celtic mythology, see Stevenson, "Druids," pp. 15–20.

15. *The Devil and the Lady*, "Sense and Conscience," and "A Dream of Fair Women" are some striking examples.

16. To support this connection, she points out that "the 'Siege perilous' with its 'scroll of letters in a tongue no man can read' resembles in its inscrutability and potential hazardousness the magician's book . . . , which is written in a language no man can read (even Merlin can decipher only the marginalia)."

17. Hugh Wilson (pp. 8–11) uses a passage on Geraint's jealousy (ll. 101–15) as proof text for his claim that Tennyson responded to his sources subjectively. Indeed Tennyson captures little of his medieval Welsh source, but it is doubtful that any modern author could. Morris, the one nineteenth-century poet who tried to recapture such medieval moral anarchy, fell into a self-conscious aestheticism just as alien to the vitality of his sources as Tennyson's moralizing.

18. John Philip Eggers, "The Weeding of the Garden: Tennyson's Geraint Idylls and *The Mabinogion*," *Victorian Poetry*, 4 (1966), 46–47. Eggers argues (p. 45) that this tale in *The Mabinogion* "is visible through a Celtic twilight darkly if at all." To me the Welsh tale, though very different from its probable source in Chrétien, consistently reflects a naive delight in physical experience.

19. Paul Zietlow, "Psychological Exploration in *Idylls of the King*: The Case of Geraint and Enid," *Studies in English Literature: 1500–1900*, 24 (1984), 737.

20. Arthur Wayne Glowka, "Tennyson's Tailoring of Source in the Geraint Idylls," *Victorian Poetry*, 19 (1981), 302–7.

21. See Zietlow, "Psychological," p. 733.

22. John D. Rosenberg, *The Fall of Camelot: A Study of Tennyson's "Idylls of the King"*

(Cambridge: Harvard University Press, 1973), p. 75. All parenthetical references to Rosenberg are to this book.

23. See Staines, *Camelot*, pp. 5–9. His discussion also includes some more fragmentary sketches from the Harvard Notebook 16.

24. For another interpretation of this parallel, see Stevenson, "Druids," pp. 18–19.

25. *Memoir*, I, 419. These specific lines are not contained in *Lady Tennyson's Journal*, ed. James O. Hoge (Charlotte: University of Virginia Press, 1981), p. 95. The publication of this journal has only complicated questions of Tennyson's biography and the composition of the *Idylls* in particular. While Hallam Tennyson *seems* to have interpolated comments which give this process more coherence than it may have had, according to Hoge ("Editorial Method") he did have access to earlier drafts of the *Journal*, which he subsequently destroyed.

26. *Theme and Symbol*, pp. 135–36.

27. Gilbert finds these visions (pp. 868–71) full of an ahistorical, archetypally female power. He admits, however, that they are characteristic of the early stages of Romanticism.

28. See Stanley Fish, *Surprised by Sin: The Reader in Paradise Lost* (London: Macmillan, 1967), pp. 1–22 passim.

29. Hugh Wilson, "The Evolution of Tennyson's Purposes in the Building of the *Idylls of the King*," Diss. Wisconsin 1965, pp. 210.

30. Russell M. Goldfarb, *Sexual Repression and Victorian Literature* (Lewisburg: Bucknell University Press, 1970), pp. 87–88. See also Catherine Barnes Stevenson, "How It Struck a Contemporary: Tennyson's 'Lancelot and Elaine' and Pre-Raphaelite Art," *Victorian Newsletter*, no. 60 (Fall 1981), 13.

31. Stevenson (p. 13) compares Elaine's progress to that of a Pre-Raphaelite artist as she moves from fantasy to "actualizing a truly symbolic vision." For Stevenson, however, this vision is directed not toward winning Lancelot but toward arranging her own funeral barge.

32. Even more demeaning, in the prose continuation of this poem he is shamed by the purity of his illegitimate son, Galahad. See Staines, *Camelot*, pp. 12–14.

33. *Idylls of the King*, Eversley Edition, 9 vols. (London: Macmillan, 1907–08), 5, 487n.

34. Noting this passivity, John Philip Eggers characterizes Lancelot's sadness as "Virgilian." *King Arthur's Laureate: A Study of Tennyson's "Idylls of the King"* (New York: New York University Press, 1971), p. 90.

35. In Malory Arthur can go along with Lancelot's deception and can preside over Elaine's final self-revelation because he makes no claim to control such events.

36. *Memoir*, II, 124–25. This irony, in turn, leads us to find another one in the "murmurs," "Lo, thou likewise shalt be King" (l. 55). The Virginia manuscript description of the original fratricide, "for each [?] was mad to have his brother's bride" (Pfordresher, p. 604), ties their conflict with Lancelot's longing for Guinevere and deepens the "likewise" to suggest even here that Arthur's kingship will come to an equally disastrous end.

37. Although more impressed than Guinevere, Albright comes to agree with her: "The only power Arthur requires is vision; and he is the human sublime. Therefore

he cannot be the true subject of Tennyson's poem; he . . . threatens to render trivial all the things surrounding him" (p. 65). "The lower strata of personages are in continual danger of falling out of the high meaningfulness of King . . . Allegory down into common characterhood. It is as if Arthur's relation to his knights were that of white light to the various bands of color in the rainbow; each is a faulty . . . expression of some aspect of his piercing integrity" (p. 68).

38. For Lancelot's paradoxical role as both Satan and Christ, see Dillon, "Milton," pp. 129–53.

39. On Elaine's self-dramatization, see also Albright, *Muses' Tug-of-War*, pp. 34–35.

40. Dillon's summary (p. 152) also notes "Tennyson's peculiar form of dialectical irony, perceptible as either a quiet satanism (these days we might say gnosticism) or as a Virgilian poetics of loss, neither of which allow choice without ambivalence."

9. Longer Poems of the 1860s

1. P. G. Scott, *Tennyson's "Enoch Arden": A Victorian Best Seller* (Lincoln, U. K.: Tennyson Research Centre, 1970), p. 23. All parenthetical references to Scott are to this monograph.

2. Maurice Montabrut, "Tennyson, le Dit et le Non-Dit dans *Enoch Arden* (1864) ou le Sens d'une Nostalgie," *Caliban*, 13 (1976), 70.

3. For example, Scott, *Enoch*, p. 23.

4. Kissane, *Alfred Tennyson*, pp. 92–93.

5. Scott (p. 35n) questions Nicolson's report of this incident.

6. Woolner's story, in fact, ascribes the decision less to economics than to the fact that "he began to grow anxious and somewhat desponding." Amy Woolner, *Thomas Woolner, R.A.: Sculptor and Poet: His Life in Letters* (1917; rpt. New York: AMS Press, 1971), p. 208.

7. Henry Kozicki parallels the careers of Enoch and Ulysses. *Tennyson and Clio: History in the Major Poems* (Baltimore: Johns Hopkins University Press, 1979), p. 152–54. Unless otherwise indicated, all parenthetical references to Kozicki are to this book.

8. Ricks, *Tennyson*, p. 280.

9. Kozicki (p. 151n) compares Enoch to Crusoe.

10. Kozicki (p. 153) sees Enoch's realization as one of "selflesshood." I would instead draw a distinction between self-perception and self-expression.

11. This gap forces us to reexamine the debate over the poem's appropriation of religion. Ruskin (quoted in Ricks, *Tennyson*, p. 280) saw it as an indirect but telling attack on Providence, with the "Good Spirit becoming a Lying one." Scott (pp. 19–20) sees all the religious references as mere evocations of the cultural setting. From our new perspective, each of these interpretations has value: Enoch does indeed undergo a religious purgation as a means to a new religious insight, but that insight is so threatening to conventional religious values that he must disguise it within that very terminology. Instead of the insight, he finally reveals himself: "His head is low, and no man cares for him. / I think that I have not three days more to live; / I am the

man" (ll. 846–48). This revelation clearly echoes that of Jesus, but only in the sense that both figures appear to a world unable and unwilling to accept them.

12. See Ricks (*Tennyson*, pp. 278–80) for this and similar parallels, including that of Dr. Tennyson's unwanted return from Paris, where he had gone to dry out in 1825.

13. As Ricks makes clear in both his edition (II, 658) and his biography (pp. 282–84), the thwarted lovers, tyrannical father, hypocritical greed, and self-destructive pride within the poem all have obvious biographical referents and appear with compulsive regularity in the Tennyson canon.

14. As victims of male dominance, Edith, Burleigh's peasant wife, and Enid are implicitly compared to trapped animals.

15. See Priestley, *Language*, pp. 98–99.

16. Philip Drew, "'Aylmer's Field': A Problem for Critics," *The Listener*, 71 (2 April 1964), 556.

17. For a detailed description of this manuscript, see Edgar F. Shannon, Jr., "The Publication of Tennyson's 'Lucretius,'" *Studies in Bibliography*, 34 (1981), 155–57, 174.

18. For the historical resonance of this metaphor, see Kozicki, *Clio*, pp. 162–63.

19. Joseph argues (pp. 140–41) that Lucretius hopes to turn Venus herself into Tranquillity.

20. Numerous parallels have already been drawn between "Lucretius" and the *Idylls*. Ward Hellstrom compares Lucretius' rejection of his wife to Arthur's blindness to the passionate nature of Guinevere. *On the Poems of Tennyson* (Gainesville: University of Florida Press, 1972), p. 144. Kozicki (p. 161) compares the sexuality of Lucretius' visions to that surrounding Vivien. Kozicki also sees the sword Pelleas lays "athwart the throats" of the sleeping lovers as prefigured in Lucretius' sword falling before the breasts of Helen.

10. The 1869 Idylls

1. Her prayers certainly echoed those of Tennyson's friend and fellow Arthurian R. S. Hawker in his *The Quest of the Sangraal* (Exeter, 1864). For an account of Hawker and his curious poem see Staines (p. 67) and Eggers (pp. 233–34).

2. *Memoir*, I, 456–57.

3. McSweeney suggests the troubling nature of these visions (p. 117) when he places this whole set of idylls within the central Romantic quest tradition.

4. Clyde de L. Ryals sees Percivale's visions as retracing the stages of Tennyson's life and Lancelot's visions as recreating some of those celebrated in *In Memoriam*. *From the Great Deep: Essays on "Idylls of the King"* (Athens: Ohio University Press, 1967), pp. 172–75.

5. *Ibid.*, p. 166.

6. My conception of Percivale's role approaches Katharyn Crabbe's conception of the whole idyll as a fantasy, holding open the possibility of different levels of reality. "The Function of Fantasy in Tennyson's 'The Holy Grail,'" *Cithara*, 17, no. 2 (May 1978), 52–61. Percivale is seen less as narrative voice than as tragic protagonist in

David Staines, "Tennyson's 'The Holy Grail': The Tragedy of Percivale," *Modern Language Review*, 69 (1974), 747–53.

7. William E. Buckler comments on the "bumptious superiority" of Galahad in this encounter. *Man and His Myths: Tennyson's "Idylls of the King" in Critical Context* (New York: New York University Press, 1984), p. 56.

8. Charles Tennyson, "Some MSS. of the 'Idylls of the King' and a Note on Tennyson as a Narrative Poet," in *Six Tennyson Essays* (London: Cassel, 1954), p. 162.

9. In commissioning a winged statue of himself, Arthur is asking for *some* kind of cosmic reprisal.

10. M. W. MacCallum, *Tennyson's Idylls of the King and Arthurian Story from the XVIth Century* (New York: Macmillan, 1894), pp. 392–94.

11. See William R. Brashear, "Tennyson's Tragic Vitalism: *Idylls of the King*," *Victorian Poetry*, 6 (1968), 44–45.

12. Staines, *Tennyson's Camelot*, p. 78.

13. James Martin Gray, *Man and Myth in Victorian England: Tennyson's "The Coming of Arthur"* (Lincoln, U.K.: Tennyson Research Centre, 1969), p. 3.

14. The Stark manuscript gives this speech to Leodogran's chamberlain.

15. A recently discovered manuscript draft of this passage is analyzed by Christopher Ricks, "The Lincoln Ms. from 'The Coming of Arthur,'" *Tennyson Research Bulletin*, 2, no. 3 (1974), 68–72.

16. Collectively these parallels imply a conclusion even more troubling than Shaw's claim that all commands and covenants imply their downfall. "The Idealist's Dilemma in *Idylls of the King*," *Victorian Poetry*, 5 (1967), 49. For P. G. Scott (p. 23), Tennyson included the ironies within *Enoch Arden* to give the audience a *frisson* of recognition on second reading. Virtually all the manuscript additions to the "Coming," and consequently all Arthur's actions within it, feed even more parasitically on their ironic sequels.

17. Although each has explained it differently, a number of critics have defined Arthur as existing at least partially outside both his story and his poem. In particular see Brashear, "Tragic Vitalism," pp. 29–32; Shaw, "Idealist's Dilemma," pp. 44–49; Ryals, *From the Great Deep*, pp. 73–77, 87–92; Kozicki, *Clio*, pp. 118–27, 148; and Margaret Homans, "Tennyson and the Spaces of Life," *ELH*, 46 (1979), 693–709.

18. David Staines, "The Prose Drafts of Tennyson's *Idylls of the King*," *Harvard Library Bulletin*, 22 (1974), 292.

19. Hallam Tennyson, *Materials for a Life of A.T. Collected for My Children*, 4 vols. (privately printed, no date), 2, 220. Again Emily's *Journal* (p. 137) lacks the quoted phrase.

20. Several critics interpret the entire idyll as an ironic foil for some other. See McSweeney, *Tennyson*, p. 107; and John R. Reed, *Perception and Design in Tennyson's "Idylls of the King"* (Athens: Ohio University Press, 1969), p. 101. All parenthetical references to Reed are to this book.

21. "Contemporary," pp. 13–15.

22. As Reed has noted (p. 109), her love proves as futile as did his love for her—he has fallen into bitter cynicism just as she has awakened from it.

23. Robert Browning, Letter to Isa Blagden, 19 January 1870, in *Dearest Isa*, ed. Edward McAleer (Austin: University of Texas Press, 1951), p. 328.

24. See Rosenberg, *Fall*, pp. 108–9.

25. See Reed, *Perception*, p. 108.

26. The status of the "Morte" as a conclusion must of course be qualified by its description in "The Epic" as "the eleventh" of "some twelve books."

27. *Memoir*, II, 126.

28. Pfordresher (p. 67) thinks the hand is not Tennyson's, but Kozicki (p. 113) sees the whole passage "in Tennyson's fine 'early' hand (such as that in his Cambridge notebooks)," and Ricks (*Poems*, III, 602) supports this attribution. Another hand has added "1862" on the page.

29. Perhaps because this doom and Modred along with it had grown so impersonal, in the British Museum proof Tennyson decided to preface the Battle in the Mist with Arthur's own realization that he was warring against nature itself. His dream of Gawain, drastically revised from the one included in manuscript drafts of the original "Morte," has been dismissed as yet another stage in Tennyson's debasement of this figure, but in context the dream seems to dismiss Arthur's conflicts with mere men, just as the inarticulate cries into which Gawain's words fade seem to dismiss the preternatural support which began to fail Arthur with the advent of the Grail: "Doth all that haunts the waste and wild / Mourn, knowing it will go along with me?" (ll. 47–49).

30. These were not to be added until 1873.

31. This appeared here after what would come to be the end of the poem.

32. John Pfordresher, "Yet Another Idylls Manuscript," *Tennyson Research Bulletin*, 2, no. 5 (1976), 203–4.

33. James R. Kincaid, "Tennyson's Ironic Camelot: Arthur Breathes His Last," *Philological Quarterly*, 56 (1977), 243–45.

34. Reed notes (p. 110) that in 1869 Tennyson reinterprets Arthur's death as Everyman's.

35. "Tennyson's Ironic Camelot," p. 244. Hair (pp. 132–34) sees it more sympathetically as a romance narrative of Bedivere's successful quest for wisdom.

36. Homans sees Arthur, after being engulfed by his own creation, being transformed into narrative by Bedivere. "Spaces of Life," p. 706.

37. Tucker (pp. 317–43) sees the original "Morte," particularly the transmission of Excalibur and the translation of Arthur, as a set of "intratextual emblem[s]" for epic as a genre: "The Poet's need of a myth to write, and the public's need of a myth to live by, conspired to produce Victorian epics whose values center in the making, breaking, and dissemination of myth itself" (p. 322).

11. The Last Idylls

1. *Journal*, p. 135. Again the parenthetical purpose appears only in Hallam's *Materials*, II, 218.

2. *Journal*, p. 297.

3. Joan Hartman, "The Manuscripts of Tennyson's 'Gareth and Lynette,'" *Harvard Library Bulletin*, 13 (1959), 247. All parenthetical references to Hartman are to this article.

4. The University of Texas collection holds the earliest version of Gareth's arrival at court, one which initially omits Merlin's riddles but preserves some of Malory's more problematical details: Gareth feigning hunger by leaning on the shoulders of his companions and later demanding three boons, the first being only meat and drink for a year. Tennyson obviously had to feel his way to an awareness of which details fit his king and his poem.

5. Tennyson probably omitted the reference to the wars because it could not allow sufficient time for Bellicent's younger son to come of age. In so doing Tennyson may indirectly support Culler's claim (pp. 219–21) that this action occurs later than usually supposed.

6. Clyde de L. Ryals, "The Moral Paradox of the Hero in *Idylls of the King*," *ELH*, 30 (1963), 53–69. Reprinted in *From the Great Deep*, pp. 69–93.

7. *Memoir*, II, 113–14. While Pfordresher (pp. 45–47) is more cautious about the compositional sequence, the *Journal* entry (p. 297) and the appearance of Notebook 40 together suggest that Tennyson's dissatisfaction with the progress of "Gareth" made him turn to the Tristram story at this point.

8. While in sequence within the manuscript, in Pfordresher these lines have to be pieced together from alternate readings after lines 163 and 166.

9. Malory's Tristram shares some of this naturalism; Arthur makes him one of the Round Table, "for of alle maner of huntynge thou berest the pryce, and of alle mesures of blowynge thou arte the begynnynge" (X, 6); these same skills in Tennyson become Isolt's reproach: "O hunter, and O blower of the horn, / Harper, and thou hast been a rover too" (ll. 540–41).

10. Critics, particularly Eggers (pp. 166–70), have traced numerous parallels between the completed idylls.

11. In another ironic parallel, already established by J. M. Gray, Tennyson's Red Knight owes many of his traits to the Knight of the Red Lawns, whom Gareth defeats in Malory. "The Red Knight in Tennyson's 'The Last Tournament' and Malory," *Notes and Queries*, 222 (n.s. 24, no. 4), (1977), 407.

12. *Idylls of the King*, Eversley Edition, 5, 500.

13. Staines (pp. 100–101) sees Dagonet modeled on the fool in *Lear*.

14. For a sympathetic, if not heroic, portrait of Tristram as a spokesman for naturalism, see McSweeney (pp. 108–13).

15. As Rosenberg has noted (pp. 135–36), this move also blends dream and reality.

16. Catherine R. Harland offers a useful summary of the critical debate on Tristram's nature and role in the *Idylls*. "The Modernity of Tennyson's Tristram," *Studies in English Literature: 1500–1900*, 22 (1982), 647–48.

17. This interpretation may explain what Harland sees (p. 656) as Tristram's failure to harp his Eurydice "up from her private underworld."

18. Buckler points out (p. 141) that the three "new idylls form of themselves an inner poetic ring, the beginning, middle, and end of a 'little *Idylls of the King*.'"

19. Douglas Wayne Cooper, "Tennyson's *Idylls*: A Mythography of the Self," Diss. Missouri 1966, p. 85.

20. Pfordresher (p. 55) considers this sketch in Knowles's handwriting "little more than a curiosity which played no organic part in the composition of the poem." For an argument that it does play an important part in that process, see my article, "The

Stages in Tennyson's Composition of 'Balin and Balan,'" *Huntington Library Quarterly*, 38 (1975), 248–49n.

21. J. M. Gray argues that Tennyson borrowed this incident from the brothers' joint defeat of King Rience (I, 31). "Fact, Form, and Fiction in Tennyson's *Balin and Balan*," *Renaissance and Modern Studies*, 12 (1968), 94.

22. Before the sketch opens, Arthur has exiled him for slaying a thrall, while for his corresponding crime in Malory Arthur has imprisoned him in his dungeon (I, 27).

23. See R. B. Wilkenfeld, "Tennyson's Camelot: Kingdom of Folly," *UTQ*, 37 (1968), 282–87.

24. Where Tennyson's Balin requests Guinevere's crown upon his shield to exorcise his own obviously sexual aggressions, Malory's hero receives a sword with which he leaves the court, wins glory, and atones for beheading the Lady of the Lake (I, 28–34).

25. *Memoir*, II, 137.

26. *Ibid.*, 141.

27. Huntington manuscript 1323 concludes here—perhaps because the verse is impinging on earlier-written material, but perhaps because Tennyson has not decided on the direction and mission of his female villain—toward Mark, as in "The Dolorous Stroke," or instead from him and toward Camelot.

28. In an introductory prose sketch Vivien, a femme fatale of Mark's court, bets him that she can corrupt the Round Table—even bring back a curl from Arthur's beard. At Camelot she falls before the queen, claims that she is fleeing both Mark and Tristram, presents her with Balin's hair, and recounts the brothers' deaths. Like Merlin in Malory she eulogizes them, but here she perverts Balin's final discovery into a celebration of Guinevere as "stainless wife & perfect Queen / Heaven's white Earth-angel" (Pfordresher, p. 507). His dying request, according to Vivien, was that the queen grant her shelter. Tennyson concluded the episode with the burial of the two brothers, Guinevere's lapsed intention of testing Vivien further, and her hawking expedition with Lancelot.

12. Some Late Poems and "Merlin"

1. Tennyson freely admitted the personal references. See Ricks, *Poems*, III, 138–45.

2. Sharon Mayer Libera reports that Tennyson's scientist friend John Tyndall defended the young poet's position against the attacks of his aged mentor. "John Tyndall and Tennyson's 'Lucretius,'" *Victorian Newsletter*, no. 45 (Spring 1974), 19–22.

3. For a more sympathetic picture of this speaker, see Priestley, "Locksley Hall Revisited," pp. 521–32.

4. For a somewhat different analysis of this nexus of place, inspiration, and loss, see W. David Shaw, "Tennyson's Late Elegies," *Victorian Poetry*, 12 (1974), 2. For a fuller account of Tennyson's debt to Catullus, see Elizabeth A. Francis, "Late Poems," in *Tennyson: A Collection of Critical Essays*, ed. E. A. Francis (Englewood Cliffs: Prentice Hall, 1980), pp. 189–91.

5. Shaw does conclude (p. 4) that "Tennyson's praise is all put in negative terms."

6. Charles Tennyson, *Alfred Tennyson*, p. 218.

7. Joseph (p. 159) sees Demeter as neither the high-born victim, nor the fatal goddess, but the earth mother, one who empathizes with human desires because she shares them and suffers for them.

8. "Tennyson's Mythology," p. 142.

9. Francis Golffing ascribes a similar function to the God of the later cosmic poems: "It is fascinating to watch how theology creeps into the poetry whenever there is an empty place on Tennyson's conceptual map." "Tennyson's Last Phase: The Poet as Seer," *Southern Review*, 2, (1966), 264–85; quoted in *Tennyson's Poetry*, ed. Robert W. Hill, Jr. (New York: Norton, 1971), p. 654.

10. David Sonstroem, "'Crossing the Bar' as Last Word," *Victorian Poetry*, 8 (1970), 55. Although Sonstroem thinks this section contains the strongest parallels to "Crossing the Bar," the later lyric "transforms the private vision of *In Memoriam* CIII into a public one: one poet's dream is translated into Christian mythos; one man's Hallam becomes every man's Pilot, easily associated with Christ." Sonstroem also offers a convenient checklist of criticism on this much-discussed poem through the late 1960s. Shaw points out that while "Ulysses still places heroic adventures between himself and death, Tennyson finally accepts and celebrates his 'end'" ("Elegies," p. 10).

11. Sonstroem (p. 57) also points out this parallel.

12. See Ricks, *Tennyson*, p. 314, and Francis, "Late Poems," p. 209.

13. As such "Merlin" can be instructively compared to the much earlier lyric "Youth," particularly as analyzed by Ryals in *Theme and Symbol*, pp. 109–12. Both use a beckoning voice or gleam to reevaluate the poet's career in the context of some ongoing quest. In "Youth," however, the quest is actually open-ended; in "Merlin" it only claims to be.

14. While he refers to the last two of these stages in "To Virgil," he ignores the sequence itself.

15. See Kaplan, "Woven Paces," pp. 292–94.

16. Haight, "Tennyson's Merlin," pp. 557–60.

Virtually every page contains references to mediation, to the model which this study posits, and to its component figures: authorial presence, Other, and mediator. References to individual characters have been included with the poems in which they appear. Italic page numbers indicate detailed discussion of individual poems. Because of their reappearance throughout Tennyson's canon, Arthur, Guinevere, Lancelot, and Merlin have been given separate listings.

Alienation: in Tennyson, 10, 39, 45; in his characters, 27, 31, 44, 50, 76, 131, 133, 169, 192, 289

Anachronism, 118, 131, 278

Anarchy, xxiii, 60, 116, 125, 144, 200. *See also* Psychomachia

Arabian Nights, The, 23, 123, 265

Arnold, Matthew, xix, 230, 231

Art: in Tennyson, 39, 54, 56, 58, 59, 98, 100, 103, 116, 124, 147, 162, 248, 252, 268, 274, 285; in his characters, 40, 42, 47, 51, 54, 56, 124, 129, 270, 288

Arthur, xii, xiii, xxiv, 3, 42, 59, 65, 74, 76–79, 84, 94, 103, 117, 149, 155, 157–187, 192–194, 198, 202–241, 245, 249, 251–255, 262, 263, 271–273, 285–294

Artists, xiii, xv, xviii, xx, xxii, 39, 44, 80, 81, 161, 199, 200, 210, 214, 273, 287, 288. *See also* Character types

Asceticism, 161, 162

Authorial control, xi, xiv, xviii, xxiv, 116, 118, 132, 174, 185, 240, 241, 256, 259, 278, 279

Authorial identification, 40, 41, 44, 47, 50, 52, 74, 75, 77, 80, 81, 119, 123, 128, 132, 135–138, 141, 152, 160,

168, 173, 175, 178, 183, 185, 196–198, 205, 207, 210, 212, 216, 220, 224, 238, 241, 245, 246, 250, 260, 262, 266, 285

Autonomy, xiv, xviii, xxiv, 3, 30, 69, 197, 208, 242, 244, 247, 254, 266. *See also* Psychomachia

Balzac, Honoré de, xxiv

Baring, Rosa, 87–89, 137, 139, 140, 158, 195, 256, 283

Blake, William, xxiv, 178, 201, 240. *See also* Romanticism

Boccaccio, Giovanni, 36, 267

Brontë, Charlotte, 197

Browning, Robert, xv, 62, 79, 128, 215, 273, 291

Byron, George Gordon, Lord, 3, 24, 32, 33, 187, 193, 207. *See also* Romanticism

Camelot, xxiv, 55, 56, 76, 77, 157–160, 164, 170, 171, 175, 178–180, 203, 217, 221–225, 231, 262, 286–288, 291, 292, 294. *See also* Court

Catullus, 242, 246, 294

Character types. *See* Artists; Enthroned figures; Fatal goddesses; Fatal

Character types (*continued*)
  women; Father figures; High-born
  maidens; Infernal powers; Male aggressors; Old men; Senex figures
Chaucer, Geoffrey, 56, 57, 87
Childhood, xxii, 32, 57, 135, 142, 175,
  176, 187, 204, 205, 210, 215, 261,
  265, 267
Children, xi, xvi, xx, xxi, 32, 42, 47, 48,
  67, 82, 90, 122, 146, 150, 160, 172,
  173, 184, 190, 191, 195, 197, 215,
  227, 232, 246, 280, 291
Chrétien de Troyes, 287
Class: lower, xxiii, 60, 81, 85, 117, 234;
  middle, xvii, 41, 81, 140, 148, 189,
  258, 284; upper, 80, 82, 85–87, 139,
  141, 151, 173
Closure, 62, 84, 86, 94–97, 106, 107,
  110, 113, 133, 275. *See also* Framing
  devices; Genre
Coleridge, Samuel Taylor, 6, 9, 25, 171,
  194, 195, 259. *See also* Romanticism
Compositional process, xv, xviii, 137,
  188, 201, 258, 272. *See also* Drafts;
  Manuscripts; Revision
Conflation, xvii, 20, 29, 32, 42, 60, 184,
  198, 205, 217, 231, 237, 238, 240,
  251–253, 266. *See also* Psychomachia
Confrontation: in Tennyson, xiv, xix,
  xxi, xxiii, 3, 19, 20, 24, 39, 59–61,
  66, 74, 77, 86, 93–95, 98, 100, 101,
  103, 109, 110, 112, 115, 116, 140,
  143, 155, 177–180, 185, 189, 202,
  205, 218–220, 224, 227, 240, 242,
  243, 263, 271; in his characters, 3,
  17, 23, 27, 29, 30, 35, 37, 48, 54, 61,
  64, 68–70, 72, 78, 79, 84–89, 91,
  119, 140, 142, 145, 151, 155, 158,
  165, 167, 171, 180, 186, 193, 196,
  204, 212, 220, 221, 243, 250, 272.
  See also Psychomachia
Court, xxiv, 84, 125, 126, 129, 130,
  157, 160, 164, 166–171, 174, 177,
  180, 181, 184, 187, 190, 191, 203,
  204, 211, 224, 226, 227, 231, 235,

  236, 238, 274, 293, 294. *See also*
  Camelot
Croker, J. W., 40, 41, 268
Cycles, 44, 50, 55, 65, 86, 100, 101,
  103, 105, 111, 107, 187, 188, 211,
  221, 245

Darwin, Charles, 119
Death: in Tennyson, xxiv, 30, 35, 54,
  57, 59, 64, 66, 70, 71, 79, 99, 108,
  111, 112, 155, 183, 218, 240, 241,
  246–252, 256, 268, 271, 281, 282,
  292, 295; in his characters, 21, 29–
  31, 35, 37, 42, 44, 49, 53, 54, 57–59,
  63, 64, 66, 69, 70, 73, 88, 126, 131,
  140, 145, 151–156, 164, 170, 174,
  176, 180, 186, 187, 190–198, 211,
  220, 228, 231, 235, 236, 244, 245,
  254, 267, 269, 271, 284. *See also*
  Hallam: death of
Defoe, Daniel, 193
Derrida, Jacques, xv, xvi, 258, 259
Desertion, 49, 57–59, 76, 99, 111, 252.
  See also Psychomachia
Devil, 2, 3, 5, 7, 11–15, 17, 20–22, 25,
  27, 32, 43, 61–63, 67, 76, 85, 162,
  175, 263, 287. *See also* Infernal
  powers; Satan
Distance: in Tennyson, xviii, 2–4, 17,
  23, 24, 39, 47, 50, 67, 73, 79, 88, 91,
  98, 102, 107, 124, 139, 162, 175,
  196, 198, 205, 227, 242, 263, 269,
  275, 280; in his characters, 8, 11, 31,
  34, 53, 68, 72, 73, 77, 130, 145, 204,
  254. *See also* Psychomachia
Doom of God, xix, 2, 35, 137, 152,
  154, 191, 198, 204, 218, 236. *See also*
  Psychomachia
Dostoevsky, Fyodor, 191
Drafts, xiv, xxii, 5–7, 11–17, 25, 31, 34,
  36, 37, 44, 61, 69, 73, 75, 78, 84, 86,
  90, 99, 102, 103, 106, 107, 119, 123,
  124, 129, 137–140, 157, 159–164,
  167, 168, 172, 173, 175, 179, 182–
  185, 196, 204, 205, 209–213, 219,

221, 224–237, 243, 247, 257, 258, 265, 273, 274, 282, 288, 291, 292. *See also* Compositional process; Manuscripts; Revision

Dream, xiii, xviii, 1, 2, 8, 10, 11, 13, 25, 35–37, 47, 50, 56, 57, 59, 72, 79, 81, 89, 102–104, 108, 109, 111, 116, 125, 130, 131, 140, 144, 147, 149, 154, 156, 171, 172, 177, 181, 184, 192, 201, 202, 209–213, 217, 219, 230, 231, 238, 247–249, 257, 265, 268, 277, 287, 292, 293, 295

1830 volume, xviii, xxii, 5, *19–31*, 39, 45, 48, 53, 57, 60, 63, 79, 80, 88, 91, 92, 93, 100, 101, 108, 111, 141, 142, 150, 177, 199, 204, 208, 269, 282

1832 volume, xii, xviii, xxii, 5, 28, 31, 32, 34–36, 38, *39–59*, 60–61, 63, 64, 71, 80, 85, 100, 103, 111, 116, 117, 122, 124, 133, 141, 173, 185, 192, 221, 265–270

1842 volume, xxiii, 5, 40, 41, 43, 44, 48, 50, 52, 55, 59, *60–92*, 93, 98, 137, 155, 179, 222, 269–271, 278, 280

Eliot, T. S., 93, 113, 197, 216, 260, 275

English idylls, 80, 83, 91, 136, 280. *See also* Idyll; Genre

Enthroned figures, 20, 22, 23, 30, 45, 265. *See also* Character types

Entrapment: in Tennyson, 26, 37, 51, 80, 81, 111, 176, 178, 200, 201, 205, 230, 241, 242, 256; in his characters, 15, 26, 30, 34, 37, 59, 67, 69, 70, 73, 80, 82, 83, 124, 126–128, 131, 150, 170, 183, 196, 198, 200, 205, 231, 234, 241, 242, 244, 245, 253, 270, 284, 290. *See also* Isolation; Psychomachia

Entropy, 21–23, 109, 110, 120, 221. *See also* Flux

Erlebte Rede, xiv, 197, 258, 266. *See also* Genre

Escape: in Tennyson, xxiii, xxiv, 39, 45,

60, 68, 73–75, 79, 98, 100, 101, 110, 115, 117, 136, 138, 155, 189, 195, 210, 248, 252, 268, 280; in his characters, xiv, xxiii, 34, 42, 45, 51, 59, 62, 68–75, 78, 89, 99, 116–118, 125, 128, 130, 131, 133, 144, 153, 155, 168, 170, 171, 177, 183, 192, 194, 205, 211, 224, 230, 272, 279, 281

Fairy tale, 40, 117, 123, 133, 161, 188, 278. *See also* Closure; Framing devices; Genre

Fatal goddesses, xiii, 70, 72, 115, 116, 125, 199–201, 286, 295. *See also* Character types; Venus

Fatal women, xiii, 83, 115, 125, 157, 158, 160, 161, 164, 173, 175, 199, 176, 257, 286, 294. *See also* Character types

Father figures, 2, 57, 172, 189, 195, 225, 251. *See also* Character types

Fire, 4, 26, 30, 41, 49, 54, 61, 128, 154, 172, 209, 214, 237, 242–246, 248, 249, 252, 254, 255

FitzGerald, Edward, 163, 241, 247–249

Flowers, 12, 13, 15, 29, 31, 87, 145, 148, 151, 154, 176, 196, 236, 242, 243, 246, 248, 252, 265

Flux: in Tennyson, xiii, 2, 13, 20, 21, 25, 60, 63, 77, 80, 81, 110, 205, 220, 268; in his characters, xiii, 2, 16, 17, 28, 30, 31, 34, 35, 40, 55, 63, 76, 78, 120, 128, 189, 190, 194, 195, 199–201, 221, 245. *See also* Entropy

Fragmentation, xii, xvii, xx, 26, 31, 42, 43, 67, 74, 108, 110, 144, 145, 152, 154, 159, 199, 258, 277. *See also* Psychomachia

Framing devices, 9, 10, 79, 116, 124, 133, 177, 183, 185, 190, 209, 224, 231. *See also* Closure; Genre

Freud, Sigmund, xix, xx, 57, 135, 215, 261, 280. *See also* Unconscious

Frustration, xi, 15, 17, 21, 28, 48, 64, 71, 84, 90, 93, 99, 103, 244–246

Fulfillment, xv, xxi, 16, 17, 44–46, 49,
    70, 71, 86, 91, 102, 106, 131, 132,
    137, 138, 145, 149, 161, 195, 197,
    226, 254, 255
Future, 8, 44, 70, 80, 89–91, 109, 114,
    129, 131, 137, 138, 162, 166, 173,
    174, 192, 198, 209, 225, 231, 235,
    241, 242, 244, 246, 248, 249, 261,
    279, 282. *See also* Past; Time

Gardens, 31, 46, 47, 117, 137, 139,
    140, 142, 145, 148–151, 214, 236,
    249, 257, 269, 287
Genre, 48, 79, 80, 86, 117, 119, 122,
    124, 128, 132, 142, 159, 171, 196,
    197, 202, 244, 245, 247, 251, 260,
    280, 283. *See also* Closure; Fairy tale;
    Framing devices; Monologue; Narra-
    tive
God figures, 2, 3, 6, 8, 10, 11, 22, 23,
    46, 49, 58, 60, 69, 80, 81, 83, 88, 89,
    98, 110, 204, 225, 245, 263, 269,
    272. *See also* Character types
Goethe, Johann Wolfgang von, 34, 101,
    173, 256
Gray, Thomas, 193
Guest, Lady Charlotte, 285
Guilt, xix, 2, 5, 6, 17, 28, 35, 41, 83,
    109, 137, 152, 172, 174, 177, 178,
    186, 191–194, 216, 231, 261, 263,
    284
Guinevere, xiii, 15, 157, 159, 160, 166,
    168–187, 198–200, 203, 208, 210–
    219, 225, 227, 228, 231, 235, 236,
    238, 253, 261, 262, 288, 290, 294

Hallam, Arthur Henry, xvii, xviii, xxii,
    xxiii, 9, 10, 59, 60, 65–71, 73, 76, 80,
    88, 91, 93, 94, 96, 97, 99–105, 108–
    115, 121, 137–140, 144, 158, 171,
    175, 177, 182, 183, 192, 193, 200,
    212, 240, 253, 260, 262–264, 271,
    277, 278, 282, 295; death of, xviii,
    xxii, 60, 65–68, 71, 73, 76, 80, 93,

    100, 103, 115, 137–140, 158, 171,
    175, 200, 240, 271, 282
Hardy, Thomas, 194
Hawker, R. S., 290
Heath Manuscript, 137, 271, 282
Heraclitus, 21, 25
Hesiod, 243
High-born maidens, xii, xiii, xx, 81, 85,
    115, 173, 176, 177, 180, 182, 254,
    261, 295. *See also* Character types
Hypocrisy, 84, 121, 150, 160, 166, 171,
    180, 191, 192, 202, 233, 238, 241,
    290

Idealism, xxii, 24–26, 163, 224, 235
Idolatry, 11, 30, 46, 48, 126, 127, 187,
    204, 253, 255
Idyll, 80, 83, 84, 91, 129, 133, 136,
    198, 274, 278, 280. *See also* English
    idylls; Genre; *Idylls of the King*
Imagination: in Tennyson, xiii, xix, xxi,
    1–3, 10, 24, 39, 41, 56, 63, 66, 75,
    89, 94, 98, 100–103, 109, 111–114,
    138, 140, 165, 244, 247, 248, 255,
    264, 266, 276, 278, 279; in his char-
    acters, xiii, 7, 10–13, 15, 30, 37, 39,
    40, 44, 63, 89, 91, 128, 129, 131,
    133, 143, 146, 149–152, 161, 165,
    200, 245, 255, 284. *See also* Romanti-
    cism
Infernal powers, 3–5, 11, 13, 16, 18,
    20, 22, 196, 245, 247, 281. *See also*
    Character types
Introspection, 57, 199, 235, 262, 277
Isolation: in Tennyson, xxii, 19, 24, 80,
    108, 249, 262; in his characters, 31,
    42, 55, 80, 115, 130, 238. *See also*
    Entrapment; Withdrawal

Jung, Carl, xx

Keats, John, 1, 9, 29, 58, 71, 72, 78, 84,
    145, 161, 193, 251, 262, 263, 266,
    269. *See also* Romanticism

Keightley, Thomas, 175
Kemble, John, 27, 65, 123, 162, 174,
  271
King, Richard John, 287

Lacan, Jacques, xx, 258, 259, 261
Lancelot, xxiv, 54–56, 93, 116, 157,
  159, 160, 162, 171–187, 204–207,
  210, 211, 213–217, 223, 225–238,
  253, 255, 261, 262, 270, 271, 288–
  290, 294
Landscape, xv, xx, 6, 22, 29, 31, 32, 34,
  35, 39, 40, 42, 44, 45, 48, 49, 52, 55,
  56, 59, 60, 63, 71, 76, 77, 79, 82–86,
  88, 93, 108, 112, 117, 129, 138, 142,
  143, 151, 163, 170, 193, 205, 221,
  243, 252, 257, 265, 269, 270, 277,
  282, 284, 287. *See also* Psychomachia
Lévi-Strauss, Claude, xvi
Lincoln Butcher's Book, 98, 99, 106–
  111, 276, 277
Loss: in Tennyson, xii, xxii, 35, 60, 74–
  76, 79, 80, 88, 91, 93, 94, 98–104,
  106–109, 114, 137–139, 152, 171,
  182, 242, 251, 253, 261, 280, 289,
  294; in his characters, 15, 35, 53, 54,
  60, 72, 80, 90, 152, 172, 194, 217,
  242, 253–255, 281. *See also* Death;
  Hallam: death of
Love: in Tennyson, xxiii, 23, 26–28, 32,
  71, 136–141, 158, 181, 182, 195,
  196, 249, 256, 259, 274, 275, 277,
  284; in his characters, xviii, xxiii, 15,
  16, 26–28, 30, 32–35, 49, 53, 58, 73,
  83, 86, 87, 89–91, 123, 131–133,
  135, 136, 139, 141, 142, 144, 146,
  149–151, 155, 169, 173, 176– 182,
  184–187, 196, 197, 204, 205, 210,
  211, 214, 215, 217, 224, 226, 228,
  230–233, 256, 267, 269, 281–284,
  291
Lucretius, xxiv, 45, 52, 189, 198–204,
  246, 254, 290, 294
Lyell, Sir Charles, 119

Mabinogion, 166, 167, 285, 287
Mackail, J. W., 84, 128, 274
Magic, 16, 38, 47, 58, 71, 146, 161,
  180, 181, 203, 210, 211, 227, 237,
  238, 251, 252, 287
Male aggressors, 46, 48, 52, 80, 82,
  111, 115, 116, 121, 122, 124, 126,
  127, 130, 133, 152, 244, 280. *See also*
  Character types
Malory, Sir Thomas, 76, 78, 157, 160,
  171, 174, 177, 179–181, 184, 186,
  187, 205, 206, 213, 223, 226–230,
  232–237, 285, 286, 288, 293, 294
Manuscripts, xiv, xxiii, 4, 6, 11–15, 31,
  36, 44, 68, 69, 74, 78, 94–106, 109,
  124, 137, 139, 157–168, 171–175,
  179–188, 196–201, 204–206, 209,
  212, 218, 219, 230, 231, 234, 236,
  237, 255, 257, 258, 264, 265, 268,
  269, 271–277, 282, 286, 288–294.
  See also Compositional process;
  Drafts; Heath Manuscript; Lincoln
  Butcher's Book; Revision; Trinity
  Butcher's Book
Marxism, xvii, 258, 259, 274, 280. *See
  also* Class
Mask of age, xix, 2, 17, 67, 75, 155,
  162, 194. *See also* Psychomachia
Merlin, xxiv, 5, 16, 75, 157–166, 170,
  172, 174, 193, 203, 207, 209–211,
  219, 229, 233, 236, 237, 240, 241,
  250–256, 285, 286, 287, 293–
  295
Milton, John, xxiv, 2, 6, 7, 9, 12, 42,
  149, 161, 178, 187, 206, 251, 261,
  286, 289
Monologue, xii, xxii, 3, 60, 67, 68, 70,
  76–79, 114, 142, 172, 204, 244, 257,
  260, 271, 281, 283. *See also* Genre
Morris, William, 287. *See also* Pre-
  Raphaelites
Myth, 6, 8, 43–47, 54, 65, 78, 84, 101–
  103, 114–117, 125, 127, 143, 151,
  160, 184, 192, 200, 210, 211, 245,

Myth (*continued*)
248, 249, 255, 262, 268, 278, 281, 287, 291, 295

Narcissism, xx, xxi, 32, 50, 265, 266. *See also* Psychological perspectives
Narrative, xii, xvi, xxii, 5, 19, 32, 37, 40, 46, 50, 53, 54, 60, 76–79, 87, 107, 115, 117, 120, 122, 128, 131, 133, 141, 155, 159, 163, 180, 187, 188, 196, 197, 202–204, 209, 212, 216, 217, 220–223, 230, 233, 244, 266, 267, 290–292. *See also* Genre
Naturalism, 207, 208, 221, 227, 228, 230, 234, 236, 293
Negative capability, xv. *See also* Keats; Romanticism
Nihilism, xii, xxiii, 88, 195, 222, 269

Object-relations, xx. *See also* Psychological perspectives
Obsession: in Tennyson, xv, xvii, xxiv, 1, 74, 93, 102, 111, 135, 158, 167, 189, 193, 196, 238, 244, 286, 290; in his characters, 73, 74, 120, 132, 135, 140, 146, 151, 166, 168, 170, 199, 282
Old men, 59, 67, 137, 164, 194, 231. *See also* Character types; Senex figures
Ovid, 54, 270

Paralysis, xxii, 32, 67, 100, 133, 159, 172, 182, 193, 194, 234. *See also* Stasis
Passivity: in Tennyson, 27, 57, 63, 68, 86, 100, 108, 115, 167, 210, 263, 280; in his characters, 15, 27, 31, 44, 49, 50, 57, 63, 68, 78, 86, 128, 154, 166, 167, 180, 182, 191, 288
Past: in Tennyson, xix, xxiii, xxiv, 9, 59, 60, 64, 65, 74, 81, 88, 89, 91, 94, 99–102, 109, 114, 137, 138, 183, 203, 210, 211, 240–242, 245, 247–

250, 264, 284; in his characters, 8, 17, 32, 44, 64, 65, 67–70, 72, 74, 76, 77, 88, 89, 129, 131, 140, 145, 162, 163, 173, 175, 176, 192, 194, 195, 209–211, 218, 219, 235, 241, 242, 244, 267, 279. *See also* Future; Time
Pastoral, 84, 101, 129, 137, 205, 243, 251–256. *See also* Genre
Personification, xi, xiii, xxiii, 10, 11, 15, 22–28, 39, 49, 52, 54, 66, 78, 81, 93, 94, 100, 110, 130–133, 136, 151, 158, 165, 174, 194, 201, 214, 215, 220, 237, 238, 242, 250, 252, 254, 274, 284. *See also* Psychomachia
Pirandello, Luigi, xxiv
Poems by Two Brothers, xix, 3, 14, 23, 24, 26, 152
Pope, Alexander, 2
Pre-Raphaelites, 1, 214, 251, 288. *See also* Morris; Swinburne
Projection: in Tennyson, xii, xvi, xx, 2, 3, 7, 19, 24–31, 39, 40, 47, 50, 52, 53, 63, 67, 69, 70, 93, 94, 97, 100, 105, 112, 116, 138, 141, 182, 208, 250, 251, 261, 272, 280; in his characters, xiv, 7, 13, 16, 25, 27, 29, 30, 47, 89, 90, 116, 133, 136, 143, 147, 152, 153, 175, 192, 208, 220, 250, 283. *See also* Psychomachia
Psychological perspectives: in Tennyson, xvi, xvii, xix–xxii, 1–3, 20, 24, 59, 73, 81, 135, 141, 152, 162, 258, 259; in his characters, 24, 32–35, 144, 236, 284. *See also* Freud; Lacan; Object-relations; Narcissism; Obsession; Regression; Unconscious
Psychomachia, xi, xiv, 5, 63. *See also* Anarchy; Autonomy; Conflation; Confrontation; Desertion; Distance; Doom of God; Entrapment; Escape; Fragmentation; Landscape; Mask of age; Personification; Projection; Sanctuary; Space; Stasis; Transcendence; Withdrawal

Quests, xv, 26, 31, 32, 43, 52, 70, 73,
74, 77, 89, 99–102, 107, 113, 133,
139, 140, 155, 166–169, 174, 181,
192, 193, 204–207, 209, 226, 232,
236–238, 243, 246, 248–250, 252–
255, 265, 268, 270, 272, 274, 276,
283, 290, 292, 295

Rawnsley, Sophie, 139, 140
Regression, xxi, 215, 261. *See also* Psychological perspectives
Relativism, 64, 65, 147, 179, 208, 237
Renan, Ernest, 287
Retrospection, 87, 88, 176, 177, 200,
240, 250, 256, 267, 283
Revision, xiv, xvii, xxiii, 5, 7–9, 11, 14–
17, 21, 24, 31, 34, 36, 37, 40, 44, 47,
52, 55, 59, 61, 65, 68–70, 73–75, 80,
94, 96, 99, 124, 141, 155, 159, 164,
175, 179, 183–186, 198, 200, 212,
222, 225, 230, 232, 237, 238, 242,
243, 244, 258, 266–270, 274–276,
278, 280, 282, 283, 293. *See also*
Compositional process; Drafts;
Manuscripts
Rilke, Rainer Maria, 262
Romanticism, xvi, 1–3, 7, 9, 10, 12, 32,
71, 88, 104, 136, 147, 195, 251, 257,
260, 262, 263, 266, 268, 269, 272,
274, 278, 279, 281, 288, 290. *See also*
Blake; Byron; Coleridge; Keats;
Shelley; Wordsworth

Sanctuary, xii, xiii, xxii, 3, 8, 24, 27, 37,
42, 44–48, 51–58, 76, 77, 84, 89–
91, 103, 108–110, 116, 118, 124,
127, 133, 141–143, 160, 163, 169,
170, 176, 177, 187, 189, 190–193,
196, 199, 210, 212, 214, 222, 236,
244, 254, 255. *See also* Psychomachia
Satan, 6, 7, 11, 12, 27, 161, 165, 187,
228, 229, 262, 286, 289. *See also* Devil; Infernal powers
Saussure, Ferdinand de, xv

Savary, Claude-Etienne, 2, 48
Sea, 13, 16, 22, 25, 30, 33, 38, 47, 63,
67, 74, 76, 78, 145, 155, 172, 193,
206, 207, 213, 214, 219, 221, 227,
243, 249, 250, 253, 254, 272
Seduction, 122, 157, 159, 163, 164,
189, 255, 268, 281
Self: in Tennyson, xii, xx, xxi, 1, 4, 6,
24, 39, 48, 64, 67, 72, 73, 86, 93, 98,
108, 109, 112, 207, 241, 242, 250,
251, 257, 261, 262, 265; in his characters, 32, 58, 64, 69, 73, 76, 173,
190, 199, 205, 207, 210, 236, 250,
272, 273
Senex figures, 15, 17, 61. *See also* Character types; Old men
Sexuality: in Tennyson, xi, xiii, xviii–xxi,
xxiii, 2, 4, 5, 21, 26, 28, 32, 33, 35,
50, 57, 59, 71, 158, 159, 162, 163,
165, 166, 168, 170, 175, 176, 182,
189, 193, 195, 199, 238, 247, 255,
256, 263, 269, 280, 281, 286, 288; in
his characters, xxiii, 5, 12, 14–17, 28,
30, 32, 49, 50, 52, 57, 58, 81–83, 88,
90, 91, 120, 121, 127–132, 144, 151,
152, 154, 160, 163, 167, 168, 173,
176, 180, 183, 186, 200, 201, 206,
213–215, 225–228, 244, 245, 272,
280, 284–286, 290, 294; eroticism,
22, 50–52, 55, 73, 84, 131, 132, 141,
151, 170, 191, 200, 256, 265, 269,
273, 283
Shakespeare, William, 13, 42, 145, 161,
261, 293
Shelley, Percy Bysshe, 1, 9, 29, 264. *See
also* Romanticism
Skepticism, 25, 106, 203, 205, 235, 268
Snakes, 6, 7, 26, 47, 263
Southey, Robert, 157, 159, 285
Space: in Tennyson, xiv, xv, xvii, xxi,
xxiv, 1, 3, 6, 9, 18, 20, 24, 37, 63, 64,
80, 93, 97, 104, 105, 109, 117, 159,
168, 240, 258, 260, 261, 263, 272; in
his characters, xiii, xxiv, 3, 9, 23, 31,

Space (*continued*)
    40, 45, 46, 55, 63, 64, 73, 84, 88, 90,
    148, 149, 233, 236, 265, 269. *See also*
    Psychomachia
Spedding, James, 163
Spenser, Edmund, 43, 161, 268
Stasis, xix, 6, 8, 54, 72, 117, 126, 132,
    133, 161, 240, 255, 268. *See also* Pa-
    ralysis; Psychomachia
Sterling, John, 136, 217
Stevens, Wallace, 29
Storm, 15, 16, 30, 62, 87, 127, 163,
    206, 207
Sun, 21, 25, 33, 48, 49, 52, 71, 72, 111,
    119, 125, 151, 177, 184, 199, 211,
    214, 215, 243, 246, 253, 269, 270
Swift, Jonathan, 193
Swinburne, Algernon Charles, 202,
    246, 269. *See also* Pre-Raphaelites

Teleology, 201, 245
Tennyson, Alfred, Lord: family of, xix,
    2, 5, 28, 47, 58, 87, 95, 97, 101, 103,
    109, 115, 182, 195, 198, 210, 242,
    263, 282, 290. *See also* Alienation;
    Art; Authorial control; Authorial
    identification; Confrontation; Death;
    Distance; Doom of God; En-
    trapment; Escape; Flux; Imagination;
    Isolation; Loss; Love; Mask of age;
    Obsession; Passivity; Past; Projection;
    Psychological perspectives; Psycho-
    machia; Retrospection; Self; Sex-
    uality; Space; Time. Individual
    poems are listed at the end of the in-
    dex.
Tennyson, Emily Sellwood, 88, 97, 115,
    139, 140, 158, 172, 204, 219, 224,
    256, 276, 280, 283, 288, 291
Tennyson, Hallam, xxiv, 123, 181, 260,
    263, 285, 288, 291, 292
Theocritus, 84, 161, 274
Time: in Tennyson, 9, 10, 20, 23, 64,
    86, 97, 102–104, 109, 114, 115, 117,
    190, 198, 218, 240, 243, 250, 262,
    273; in his characters, 42, 43, 45, 53,
    63, 69, 89, 90, 125, 146, 148, 233,
    273
Transcendence, 45, 64, 95, 99, 125,
    222, 245, 248, 250, 252, 254, 256,
    263, 265, 269, 270, 272, 281. *See also*
    Psychomachia
Trinity Butcher's Book, 94, 96, 98–101,
    104–112, 275, 276

Unconscious, xviii, xix, 66, 74, 83, 127,
    152, 154, 160, 170, 191, 202, 231,
    257, 265, 271, 277, 282. *See also*
    Freud; Psychological perspectives

Venus, xxiii, 132, 189, 199, 200, 246,
    290. *See also* Fatal goddesses
Villemarqué, Theodore de la, 287
Virgil, 242, 243, 246, 251, 289, 295

West, 6, 39, 149, 211
Withdrawal, 23–27, 110, 148, 213, 228,
    229, 234, 280. *See also* Isolation; Psy-
    chomachia
Woolner, Thomas, 179, 189, 195, 289
Wordsworth, William, 94, 135, 251,
    281, 284. *See also* Romanticism

Yeats, William Butler, 47, 164

Poems

"All Things Will Die," 21
"Ancient Sage, The," 75, *241, 250*
"Armageddon," 2, 3, 5, *6–8,* 9–12, 22–
    24, 27, 38, 47, 48, *61–64,* 89, 129,
    193, 208, 279, 285
"Audley Court," *84–85*

Aylmer's Field, xxiii, 189, 190, *195–198*, 199, 202, 203, 206, 215, 290

"Babylon," 23
"Balin and Balan," 164, *233–239*, 253, 266, 294; "The Dolorous Stroke," *234–236*, 237, 294
"Break, Break, Break," 67, 76, 93, 272

"Character, A," *26*
"Chorus," 20
"Coach of Death, The," *5–6*, 8, 175
"Come Down, O Maid," *133*
"Coming of Arthur, The," xxiv, 206, 208, *209–212*, 216, 218, 219, 225, 232, 253
"Crossing the Bar," 75, *249–250*, 252, 295

"Death of Oenone, The," *244–245*, 246, 248
"Demeter and Persephone," 3, 241, *245–247*, 248, 256, 267
"Deserted House, The," *23*
Devil and the Lady, The, 2, 3, 5, *11–18*, 20, 21, 25, 27, 32, 34, 38, 57, 61, 63, 67, 70, 76, 93, 115, 128, 161, 162, 175, 193, 287
"Dream of Fair Women, A," xiii, 40, *56–59*, 89, 116, 287
"Druid's Prophecies, The," 23
"Dying Swan, The," *23–24*

"Edwin Morris," *86–88*, 90, 141, 173, 181, 254
Enoch Arden, xii, xxiii, *189–195*, 196, 198, 199, 202, 203, 205, 215, 245, 249, 289, 291
"Epic, The," *79*, 171, 217, 292

"Fall of Jerusalem, The," 23
"Fatima," *48–50*, 254, 269
"Frater Ave atque Vale," *242*

"Gardener's Daughter, The," 86
"Gareth and Lynette," *223–226*, 228, 229, *232–233*, 234, 235, 293
"Geraint and Enid," *165–171*, 177–180, 190, 193, 202, 285, 287
"Godiva," *81–82*, 88
"Golden Year, The," 89, 274
"Guinevere," xiii, *171–178*, 193, 235, 253

"Hail Briton," 80
"Hero to Leander," *30*, 53
"Hesperides, The," xiii, *45–48*, 48, 53, 73, 108, 116, 119, 124, 192, 249, 254, 268
"Holy Grail, The," 165, *203–208*, 209, 218, 235, 237, 238, 253
"How and the Why, The," *21*

"I Dare Not Seek My Father's Halls," 2
"Idealist, The," *25*
Idylls of the King: allegory, 174; 1859 *Idylls*, xxiii, 5, *157–188*, 189, 193, 195, 199, 203, 204, 216, 217, 223, 224; 1869 *Idylls*, 5, *203–222*, 219, 223, 224; last *Idylls*, *223–239*; play scenario, 171, 174, 180, 184, 185; prose fragment, 171, 174, 230; *The True and the False*, 159, 178, 203, 209, 216. *See also* individual idylls
In Memoriam, xvii, xxiii, 5, 9, 30, 66, 67, 79, 80, 91–92, *93–114*, 120, 121, 137, 138, 140, 141, 143, 144, 152, 154, 155, 171, 173, 177, 182, 183, 188, 190, 192, 193, 199, 200, 201, 205, 208, 212, 220, 249–251, 253, 260, 264, 272, 274–278, 280, 282, 290, 295
"Isabel," *28*
"I Wander in Darkness and Sorrow," 2

"Kraken, The," *22–23*, 26, 265

"Lady Clara Vere de Vere," *81*
"Lady of Shalott, The," *54–56*, 58, 72,
   116, 124, 159, 179–181, 214, 254,
   270, 271, 279, 281
"Lancelot and Elaine," *178–188*, 203,
   208, 213, 217, 231, 253, 288
"Last Tournament, The," 223, 224,
   226–232, 233–235, 237
"Lilian," *28*
"Locksley Hall," 88, *89–91*, 136, 141,
   155, 173, 181, 201, 242, 254, 275,
   282
"Locksley Hall Sixty Years After," 75,
   241–242, 245, 250
"Lord of Burleigh, The," 81, *82–83*,
   170, 176
"Lotos-Eaters, The," *43–45*, 46, 52,
   53, 73, 116, 195, 268
"Love," 23, *26*, 27
"Love and Duty," 88
"Love Thou Thy Land," *80–81*
Lover's Tale, The, xxii, 5, 19, *31–38*, 39,
   40, 50, 51, 55–57, 59, 70, 86, 90, 93,
   115, 128, 136, 138, 189, 193, 215,
   254, 266, 271, 281; "The Golden
   Supper," 36
"Lucretius," 189, *198–202*, 203, 204,
   246, 290

"Mariana," *30–31*, 37, 39, 48, 51, 59,
   73, 116, 124, 142, 147, 197, 254,
   266
"Mariana in the South," *50–51*, 269
"Marriage of Geraint, The," *165–171*,
   213
Maud, xii, xviii, xxiii, 5, 28, 66, 67, *135–
   156*, 158, 169, 170, 173, 178, 180–
   182, 189, 190, 193, 201, 202, 214,
   215, 240, 249, 255, 264, 278, 281–
   285
"Merlin and the Gleam," xxiv, 75, 161,
   241, *250–256*
"Merlin and Vivien," *157–165*, 167,
   168, 177, 200, 203, 236–238, 255,
   286, 290

"Mermaid, The," *22*
"Miller's Daughter, The," 48
"Morte d'Arthur," *76–79*, 91, 94, 103,
   117, 155, 158, 161, 167, 171, 183,
   192, 203, 206, 209, 217–222, 238,
   254, 273, 274, 292
"Mystic, The," 8, 23, 27, 263

"Nothing Will Die," 21
"Now Sleeps the Crimson Petal," *132–
   133*

"O that 'twere possible," 79, *137–139*,
   141, 154, 205, 283, 284
"Oenone," *51–54*, 70, 72, 73, 93, 116,
   160, 244, 245, 254, 270
"Oriana," *28*

"Palace of Art, The," *40–43*, 64, 77,
   83, 116, 124, 126, 147, 160, 169,
   171, 177, 254
"Pallid Thunder-Stricken Sigh for
   Gain, The," 22, *26*
"Passing of Arthur, The," xxiv, 212,
   217–222, 224, 230, 231, 254, 292
"Pelleas and Ettarre," 28, *212–217*,
   218, 290
"Perdidi Diem," 23
"Persia," 23
"Poet's Mind, The," *26–27*, 57, 63, 88
Princess, The, xi, xxi, xxiii, 5, 28, 92,
   115–134, 136, 139, 141, 146, 154,
   158, 167, 169, 177, 178, 182, 188,
   190, 193, 202, 245, 278–280

Queen Mary, 238

"Rape of Proserpine," 2, *3–4*, 5
"Recollections of the Arabian Nights,"
   23, 265

"St. Simeon Stylites," xxii, 59, *60–62*,
   63, 67, 172, 204, 271
"Semele," 48
"Silent Voices, The," *249*

"Sir Launcelot and Queen Guinevere,"
  173–174
"Spirit haunts the year's last hours, A"
  (Song), *29*, 39, 45
"Supposed Confessions," *27*

"Timbuctoo," *8–11*, 12, 17, 22–24, 34,
  43, 46, 126, 138, 204, 205, 208
"Tiresias," 67, *68–69*, 75, 76, 155, 244,
  246, 247, 254, 272
"Tithon," *70–73*, 74, 75
"Tithonus," 67, 72, *74–75*, 76, 83, 94,
  101, 115, 128, 155, 192, 254, 273
"To a Clear-Headed Friend," *27*
"To E. FitzGerald," *247–248*
"To J.M.K.," *27*
"To Professor Jebb," *248*

"To the Master of Balliol," *248–249*
"To Virgil," *243–244*, 294
"Two Voices, The," xxii, 59, 60, *63–65*,
  97

"Ulysses," 67–68, *69–70*, *73–74*, 75,
  76, 94, 101, 155, 192, 204, 249, 254,
  272, 282, 295

"Vision, The," 204
"Vision of Sin, The," *88–89*, 205, 241,
  254

"Walking to the Mail," 83, *85–86*

"Οἱ ῥέοντες," *25*